尾田栄一郎

I believe that language is difficult to hand down, and that's why we have both ancient language and modern language. In one diary from the Heian Era (794—1185 AD), there is an entry, "The young people these days do not know how to speak well." I find it interesting that these lamentations are passed down from era to era... And so when I grow old, I intend to make some complaints of my own.

Volume 42 gettin' jiggy wit it! Yeaaahhh!

-Eiichiro Oda, 2006

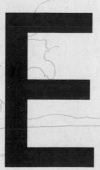

Eiichiro Oda began his manga career at the age of 17, when his one-shot cowboy manga **Wanted!** won second place in the coveted Tezuka manga awards. Oda went on to work as an assistant to some of the biggest manga artists in the industry, including Nobuhiro Watsuki, before winning the Hop Step Award for new artists. His pirate adventure **One Piece**, which debuted in **Weekly Shonen Jump** in 1997, quickly became one of the most popular manga in Japan.

ONE PIECE VOL. 42
WATER SEVEN PART 11

SHONEN JUMP Manga Edition

STORY AND ART BY EIICHIRO ODA

English Adaptation/Jason Thompson
Translation/JN Productions
Touch-up Art & Lettering/Elena Diaz
Design/Fawn Lau
Supervising Editor/Yuki Murashige
Editor/Alexis Kirsch

Printed in the U.S.A.

Published by VIZ Media, LLC
P.O. Box 77010
San Francisco, CA 94107

10 9 8 7 6 5 4
First printing, April 2010
Fourth printing, April 2013

www.viz.com

THE WORLD'S
MOST POPULAR MANGA
SHONEN JUMP
www.shonenjump.com

SHONEN JUMP MANGA

ONE PIECE

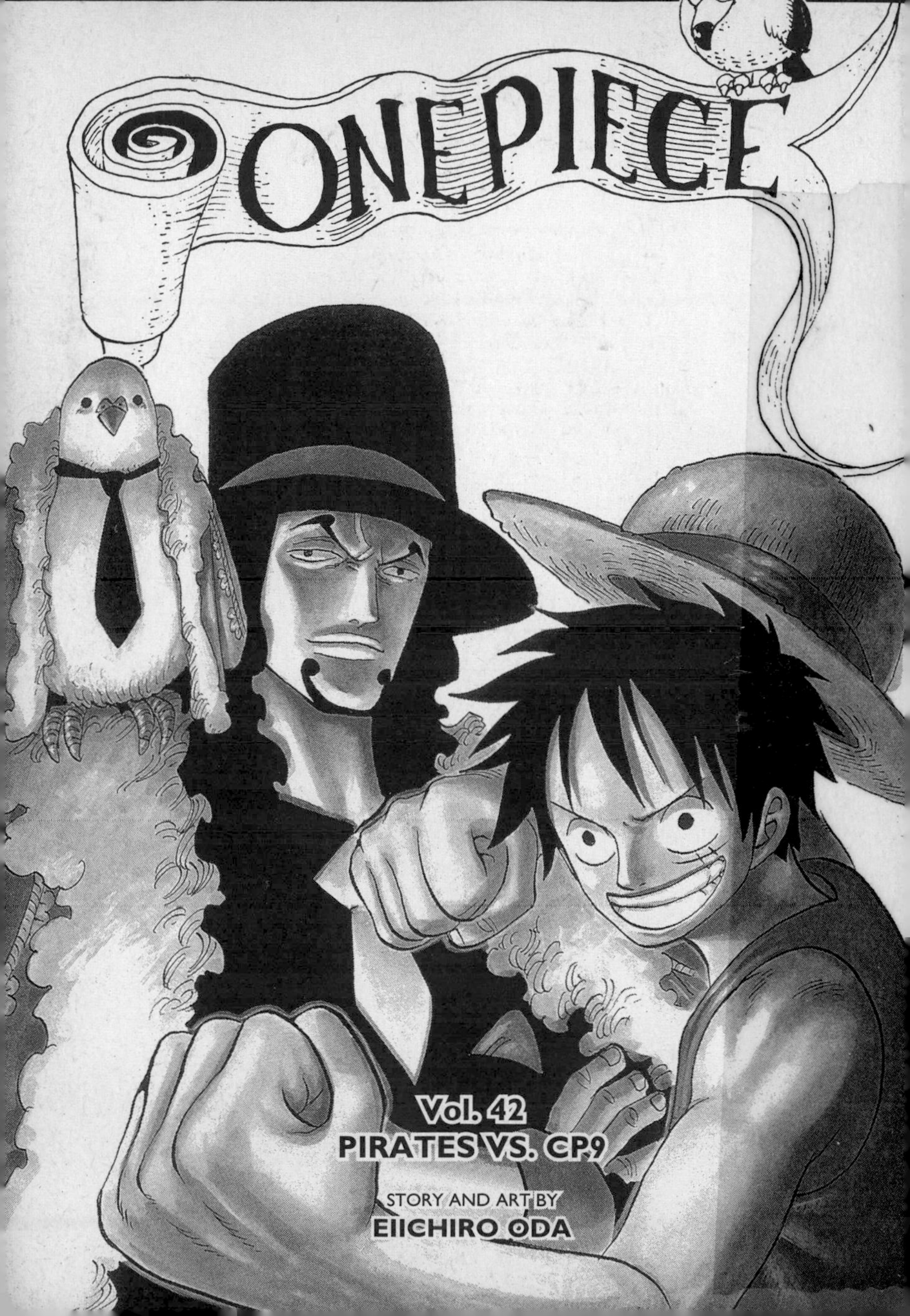

Vol. 42
PIRATES VS. CP9

STORY AND ART BY
EIICHIRO ODA

Cipher Pol No. 9

An undercover intelligence agency under the direct supervision of the World Government. They have been granted the right to kill uncooperative citizens.

Director
Spandam

Rob Lucci & Hattori

Kaku

Jabra

Blueno

Kumadori

Fukurô

Kalifa

Formerly the beautiful secretary of Tom's Workers. Now station-master of Shift Station.

Kokoro

The Straw Hats

Boundlessly optimistic and able to stretch like rubber, he is determined to become King of the Pirates.

Monkey D. Luffy

A former bounty hunter and master of the "three-sword" style. He aspires to be the world's greatest swordsman.

Roronoa Zolo

A thief who specializes in robbing pirates. Nami hates pirates, but Luffy convinced her to be his navigator.

Nami

The bighearted cook (and ladies' man) whose dream is to find the legendary sea, the "All Blue."

Sanji

A blue-nosed man-reindeer and the ship's doctor.

Tony Tony Chopper

A mysterious woman in search of the Ponegliff on which true history is recorded.

Nico Robin

Usopp's "good friend," a superhero who's come to save Luffy and company… or at least that's what he says.

Sniper King

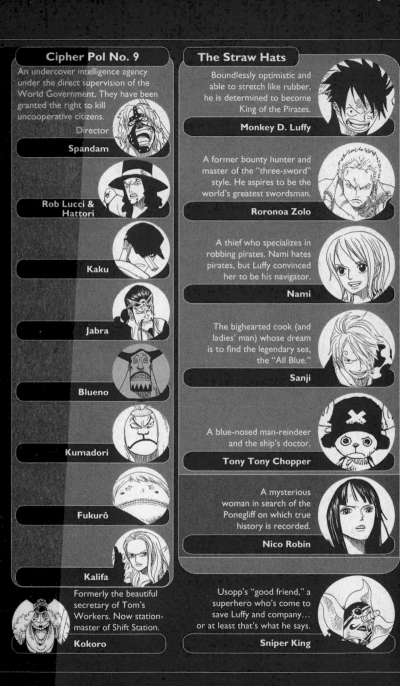

THE STORY OF ONE PIECE

Volume 42

Monkey D. Luffy started out as just a kid with a dream—to become the greatest pirate in history! Stirred by the tales of pirate "Red-Haired" Shanks, Luffy vowed to become a pirate himself. That was before the enchanted Devil Fruit gave Luffy the power to stretch like rubber, at the cost of being unable to swim—a serious handicap for an aspiring sea dog. Undeterred, Luffy set out to sea and recruited some crewmates—master swordsman Zolo; treasure-hunting thief Nami; lying sharpshooter Usopp; the high-kicking chef Sanji; Chopper, the walkin' talkin' reindeer doctor; and the mysterious archaeologist Robin.

After many adventures, Luffy and his crew traveled to Water Seven. Their goal: to find a shipwright to join their crew and also to get a new ship to replace the damaged *Merry Go*. Usopp is angry at the decision to find a new ship and leaves the crew. Then suddenly, Robin leaves the crew as well! It turns out that Robin is a double agent, working against her will for the secret government organization Cipher Pol No. 9!

CP9's mission is to recover the blueprints for the ancient super-weapon "Pluton." CP9 captures the shipwright Franky, who possesses the blueprints, and Robin, the only living person capable of deciphering the ancient writings. With Franky and Robin in tow, CP9 sets out for the government's special judicial island, Enies Lobby. Luffy and his crew go after them and succeed in freeing Franky, but not Robin, who despite aiding the government is condemned to be sent to the maximum-security prison Impel Down.

The crew defeats Blueno and confronts Robin, who reveals her tragic past. When she was a child, the government annihilated her homeland, her friends and her mother, all casualties of a deadly naval artillery barrage known as a Buster Call. For 20 years she lived a lonely, difficult life, until she met Luffy and his gang. To show their solidarity with Robin, Luffy and his friends declare war against the World Government by burning their flag! Riding a runaway train, they crash into the Tower of Law and prepare to rescue their friend!

The Franky Family

Professional ship dismantlers, they moonlight as bounty hunters.

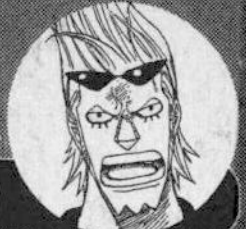

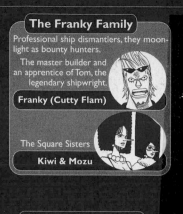

The master builder and an apprentice of Tom, the legendary shipwright.

Franky (Cutty Flam)

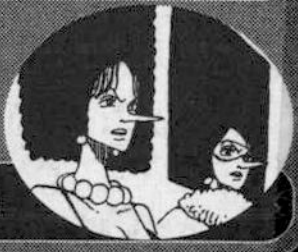

The Square Sisters

Kiwi & Mozu

Galley-La Company

A top shipbuilding company. They are purveyors to the World Government.

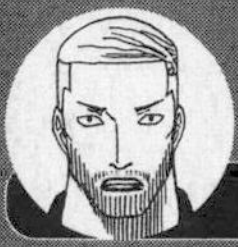

Mayor of Water Seven and president of Galley-La Company. Also one of Tom's apprentices.

Iceberg

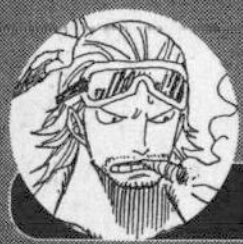

Rigging and Mast Foreman

Paulie

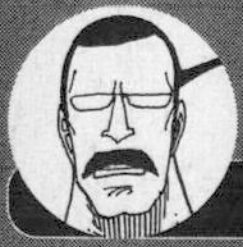

Pitch, Blacksmithing and Block-and-Tackle Foreman

Peepley Lulu

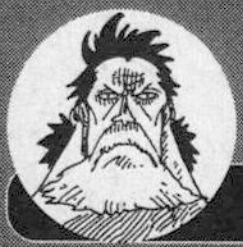

Cabinetry, Caulking and Flag-Making Foreman

Tilestone

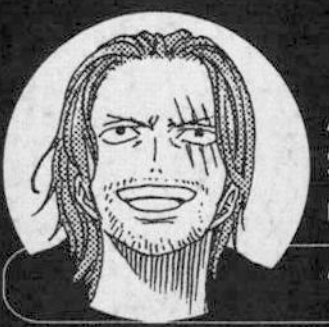

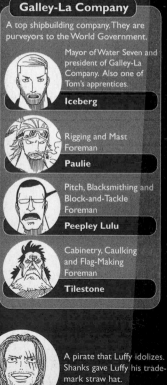

A pirate that Luffy idolizes. Shanks gave Luffy his trademark straw hat.

"Red-Haired" Shanks

Vol. 42
Pirates vs. CP9

CONTENTS

Chapter 400:
THE KEY TO FREEDOM

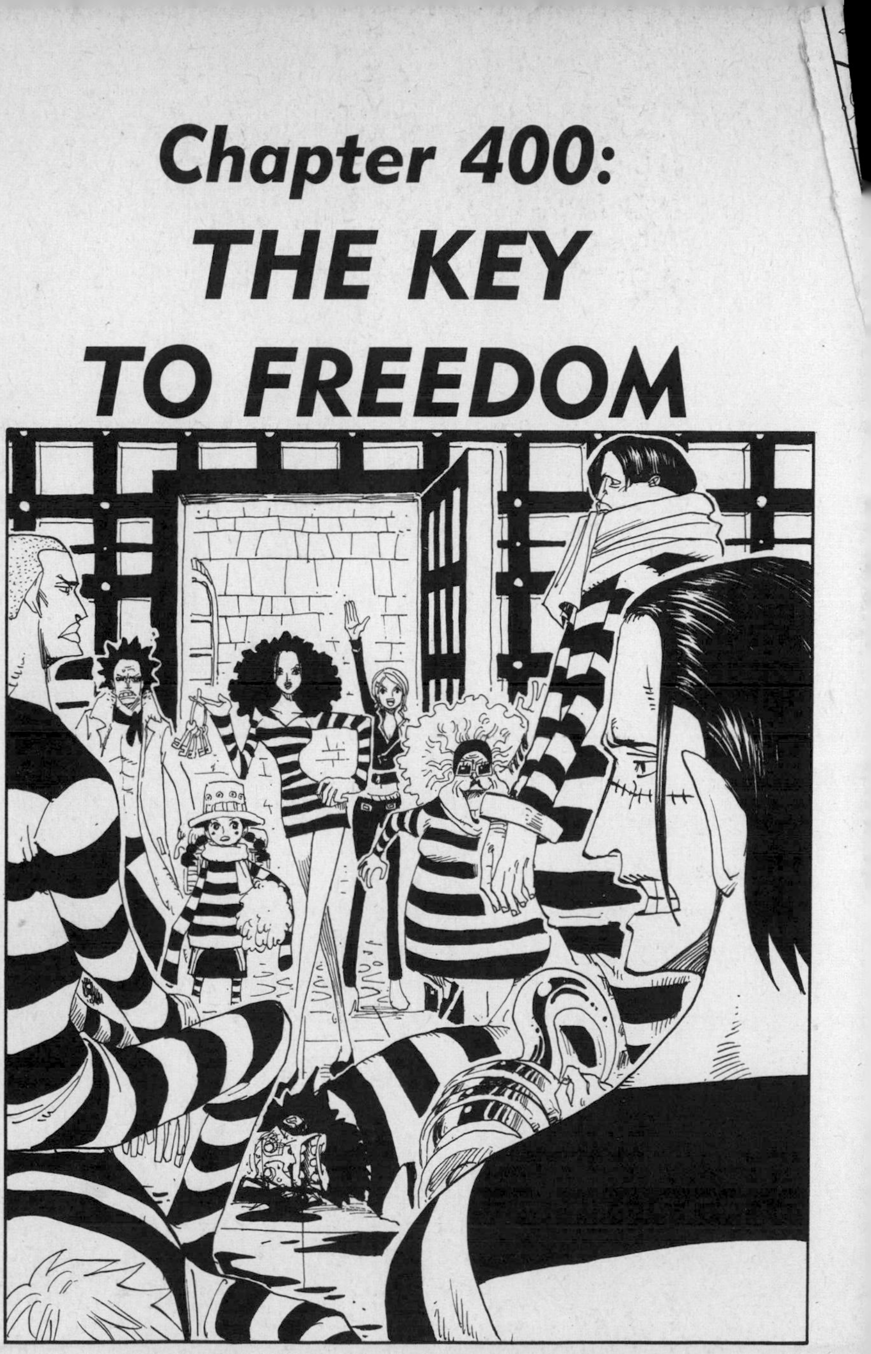

MS. GOLDEN WEEK'S PLAN, A BAROQUE REUNION, VOL. 32: "LET'S REUNITE!"

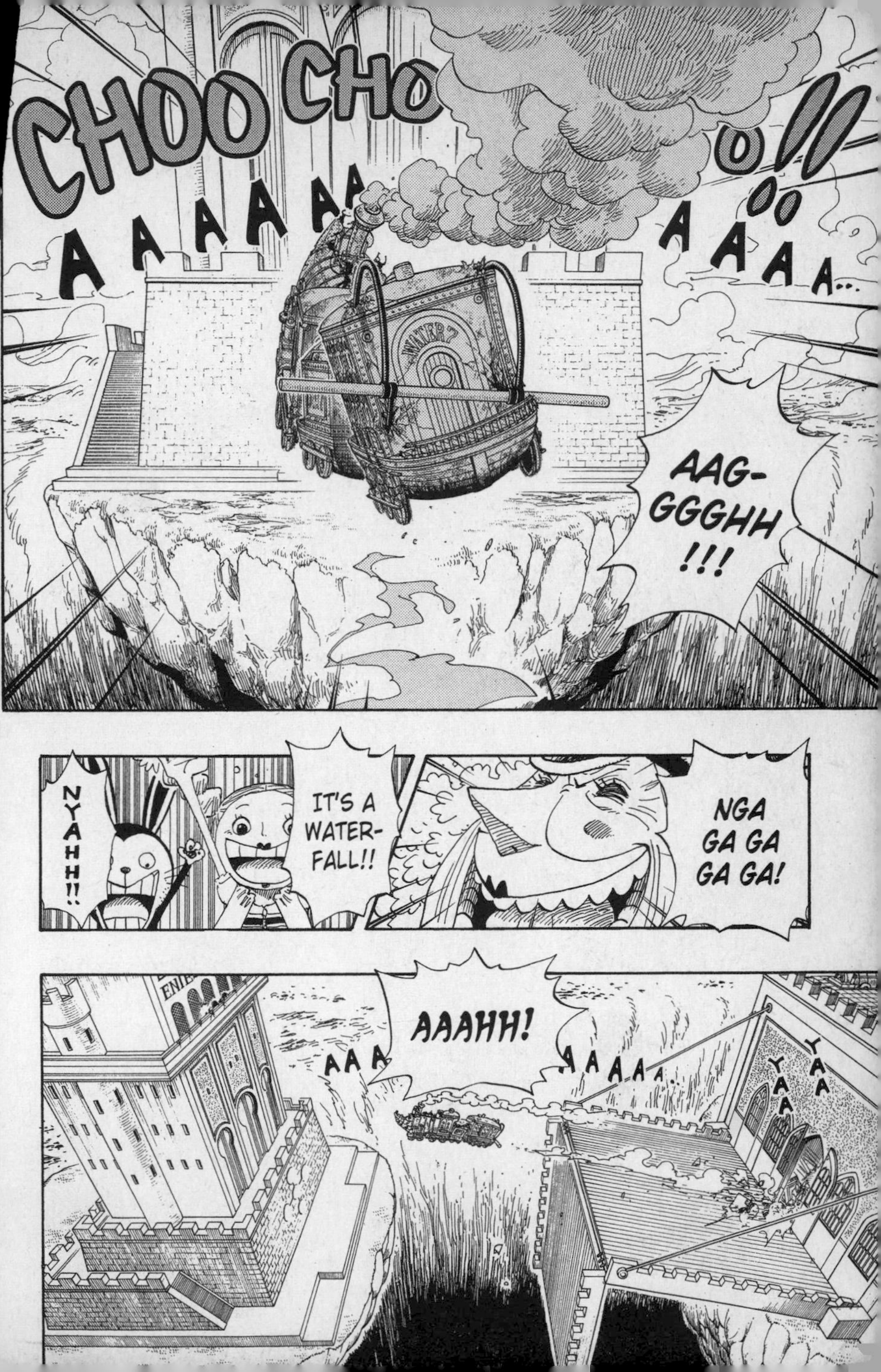

CHOO CHOO!!
AAAAAA
AAAA...
AAG-GGGHH!!!
NGA GA GA GA GA!
IT'S A WATER-FALL!!
NYAHH!!
AAAHH!
AAA
AAAAA...
YAA YAA

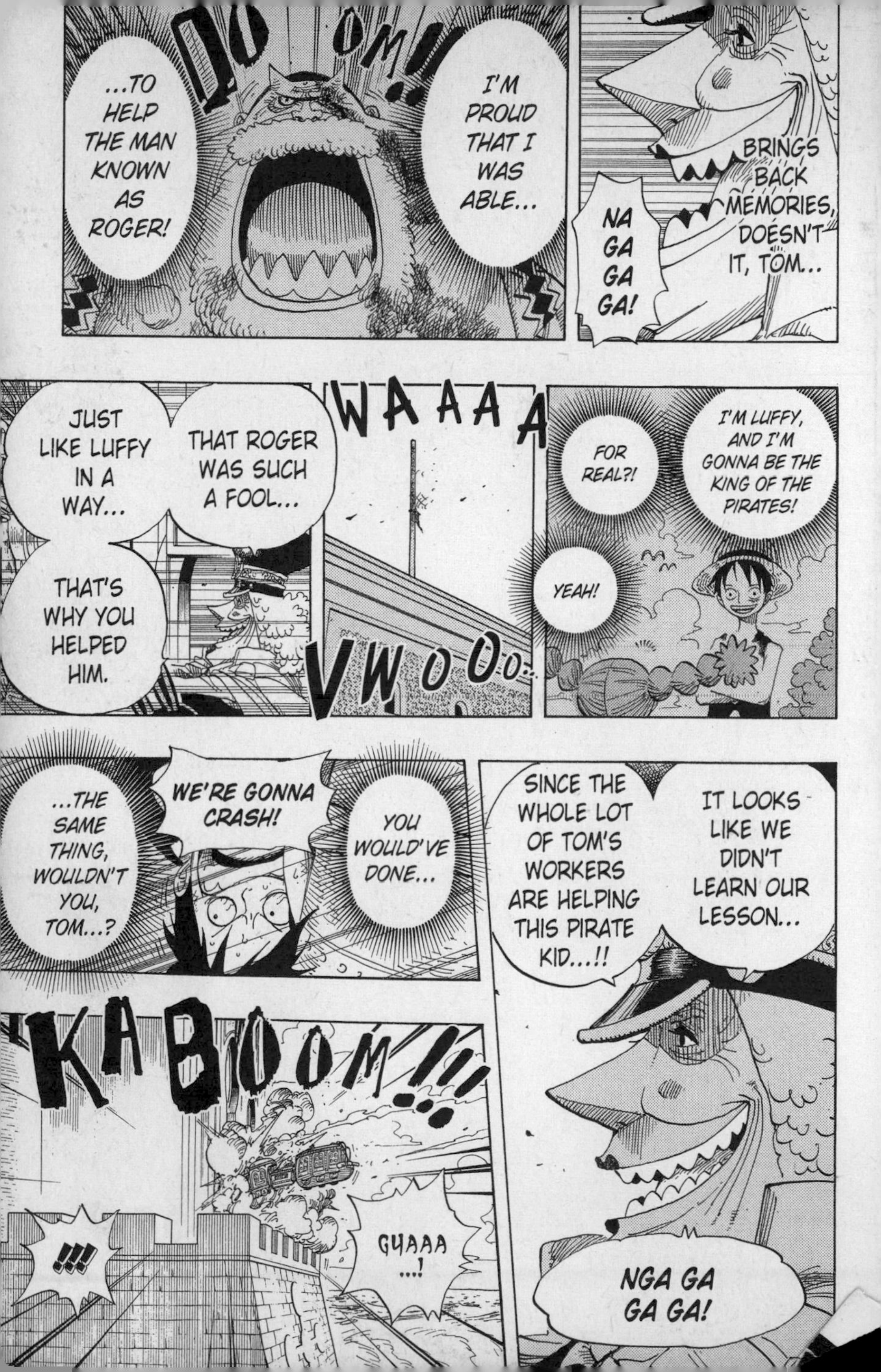
BRINGS BACK MEMORIES, DOESN'T IT, TOM...
NA GA GA GA!
DOOM!!
I'M PROUD THAT I WAS ABLE...
...TO HELP THE MAN KNOWN AS ROGER!
I'M LUFFY, AND I'M GONNA BE THE KING OF THE PIRATES!
FOR REAL?!
YEAH!
WAAAA
VWOOOO...
THAT ROGER WAS SUCH A FOOL...
JUST LIKE LUFFY IN A WAY...
THAT'S WHY YOU HELPED HIM.
IT LOOKS LIKE WE DIDN'T LEARN OUR LESSON...
SINCE THE WHOLE LOT OF TOM'S WORKERS ARE HELPING THIS PIRATE KID...!!
NGA GA GA GA!
YOU WOULD'VE DONE...
WE'RE GONNA CRASH!
...THE SAME THING, WOULDN'T YOU, TOM...?
KABOOM!!!
GYAAA...!
!!!

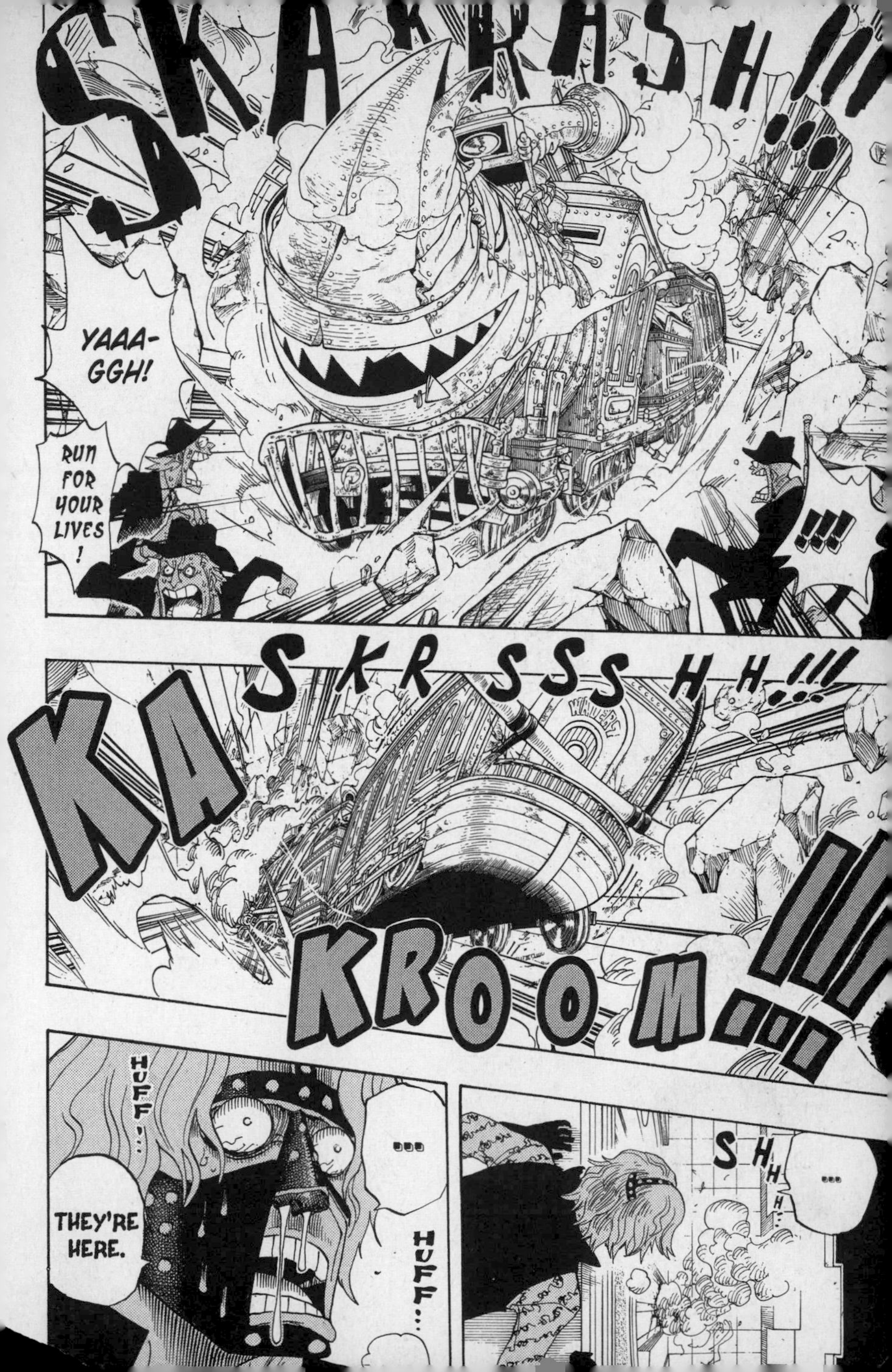
SKAKRASH!!
!!!
YAAA-GGH!
RUN FOR YOUR LIVES!
SKRSSSHH!!!
KA
KROOM!!!
SHHH...
...
HUFF...
...
THEY'RE HERE.
HUFF HUFF...

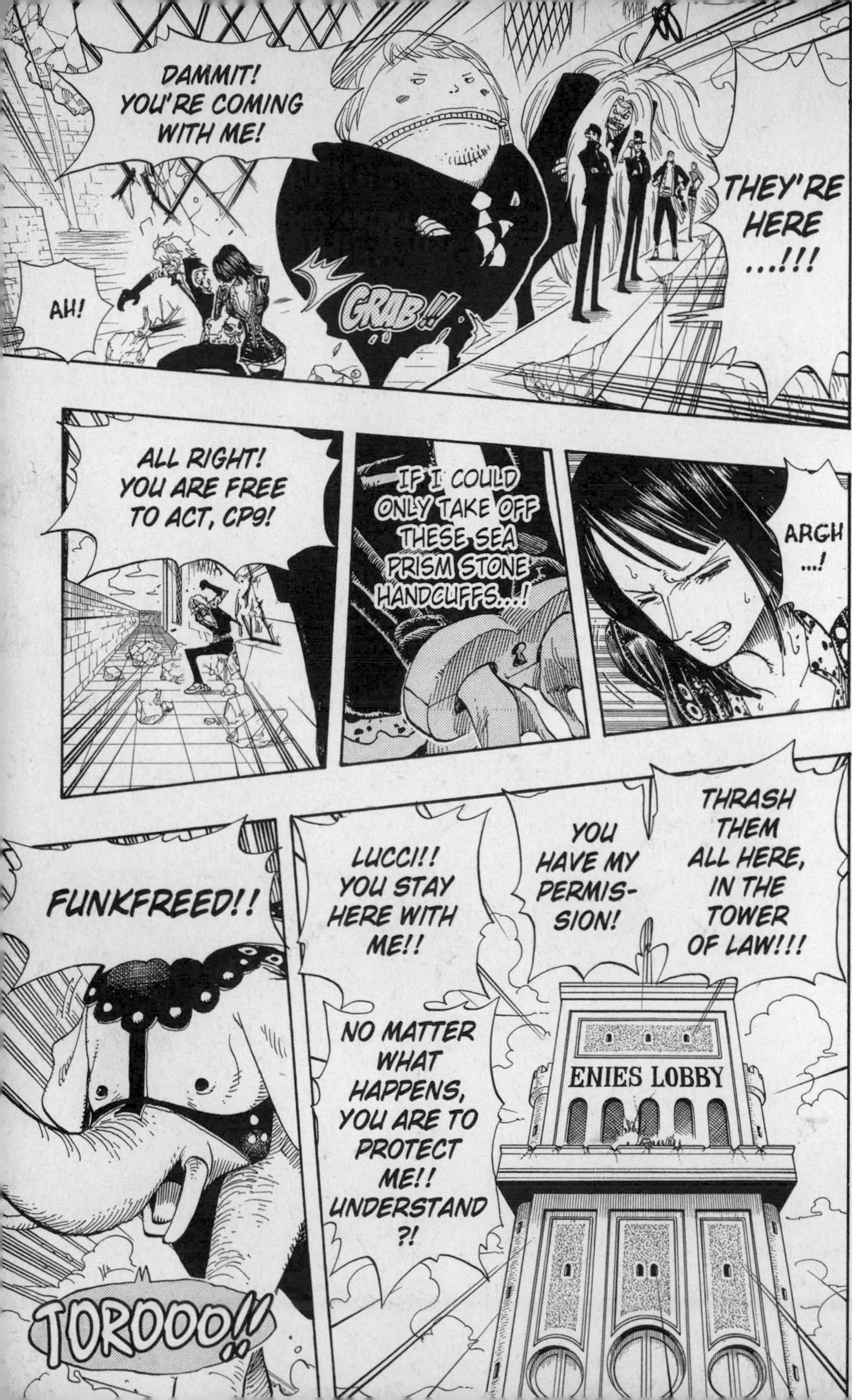
THEY'RE HERE ...!!!
DAMMIT! YOU'RE COMING WITH ME!
GRAB!!
AH!
ARGH ...!
IF I COULD ONLY TAKE OFF THESE SEA PRISM STONE HANDCUFFS...!
ALL RIGHT! YOU ARE FREE TO ACT, CP9!
THRASH THEM ALL HERE, IN THE TOWER OF LAW!!!
YOU HAVE MY PERMIS-SION!
ENIES LOBBY
LUCCI!! YOU STAY HERE WITH ME!!
NO MATTER WHAT HAPPENS, YOU ARE TO PROTECT ME!! UNDERSTAND ?!
FUNKFREED!!
TOROOO!!

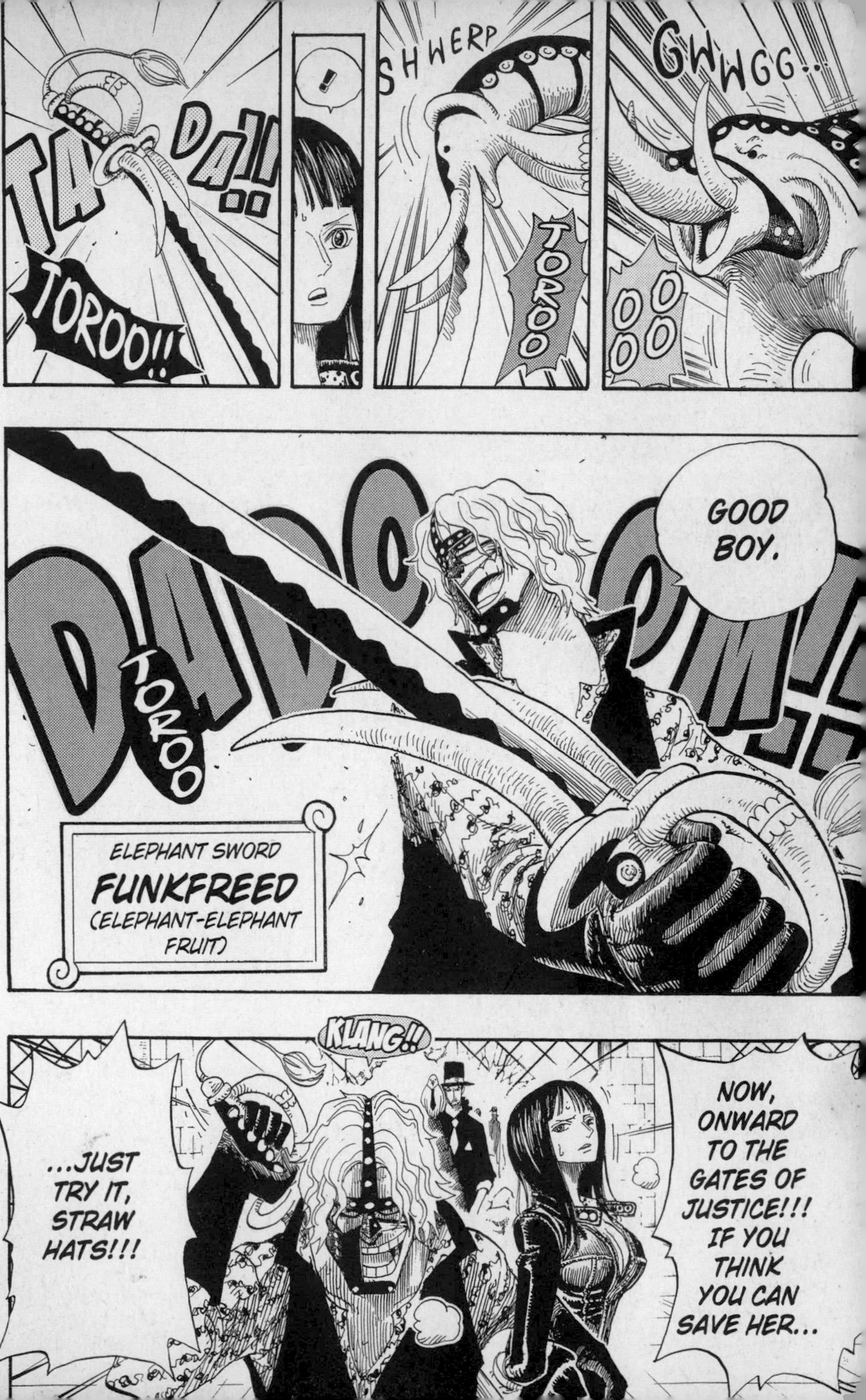
GWWGG..
OOOOOO
SHWERP
TOROO
!
TA DA!!..
TOROO!!
GOOD BOY.
TOROO
ELEPHANT SWORD
FUNKFREED
(ELEPHANT-ELEPHANT FRUIT)
KLANG!!
NOW, ONWARD TO THE GATES OF JUSTICE!!! IF YOU THINK YOU CAN SAVE HER...
...JUST TRY IT, STRAW HATS!!!

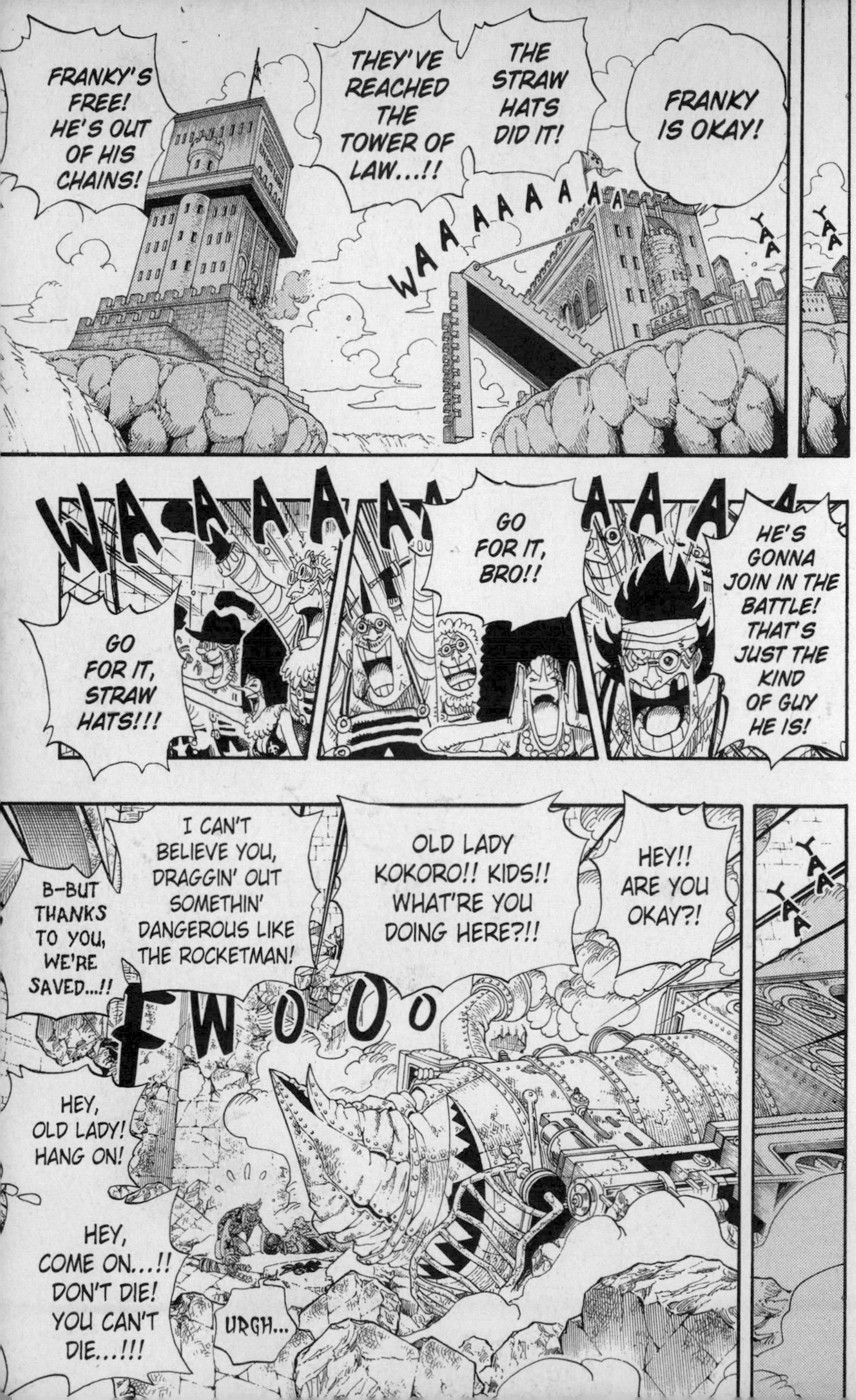
FRANKY IS OKAY!
THE STRAW HATS DID IT!
THEY'VE REACHED THE TOWER OF LAW...!!
FRANKY'S FREE! HE'S OUT OF HIS CHAINS!
YAA
YAA
WAAAAAAAA
HE'S GONNA JOIN IN THE BATTLE! THAT'S JUST THE KIND OF GUY HE IS!
WAAAAAAAA
GO FOR IT, BRO!!
GO FOR IT, STRAW HATS!!!
YAA
YAA
HEY!! ARE YOU OKAY?!
OLD LADY KOKORO!! KIDS!! WHAT'RE YOU DOING HERE?!!
I CAN'T BELIEVE YOU, DRAGGIN' OUT SOMETHIN' DANGEROUS LIKE THE ROCKETMAN!
B-BUT THANKS TO YOU, WE'RE SAVED...!!
FWOOO
HEY, OLD LADY! HANG ON!
HEY, COME ON...!! DON'T DIE! YOU CAN'T DIE...!!!
URGH...

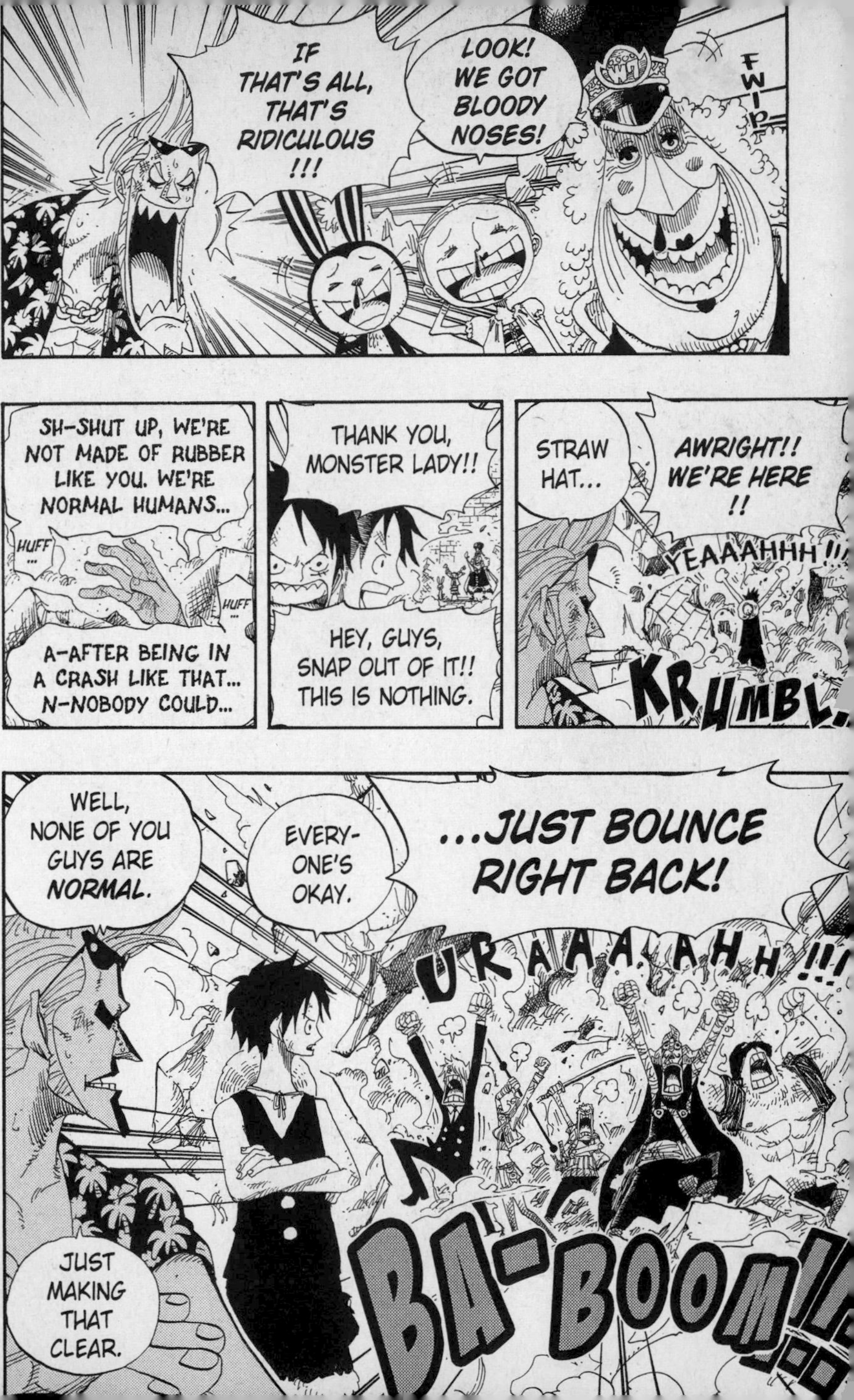
FWIP
LOOK! WE GOT BLOODY NOSES!
IF THAT'S ALL, THAT'S RIDICULOUS !!!
AWRIGHT!! WE'RE HERE !!
STRAW HAT...
YEAAAHHH!!!
KRUMBL...
THANK YOU, MONSTER LADY!!
HEY, GUYS, SNAP OUT OF IT!! THIS IS NOTHING.
SH-SHUT UP, WE'RE NOT MADE OF RUBBER LIKE YOU. WE'RE NORMAL HUMANS...
HUFF...
HUFF...
A-AFTER BEING IN A CRASH LIKE THAT... N-NOBODY COULD...
...JUST BOUNCE RIGHT BACK!
EVERY-ONE'S OKAY.
WELL, NONE OF YOU GUYS ARE NORMAL.
URAAAAAHH!!!
BA-BOOM!!
JUST MAKING THAT CLEAR.

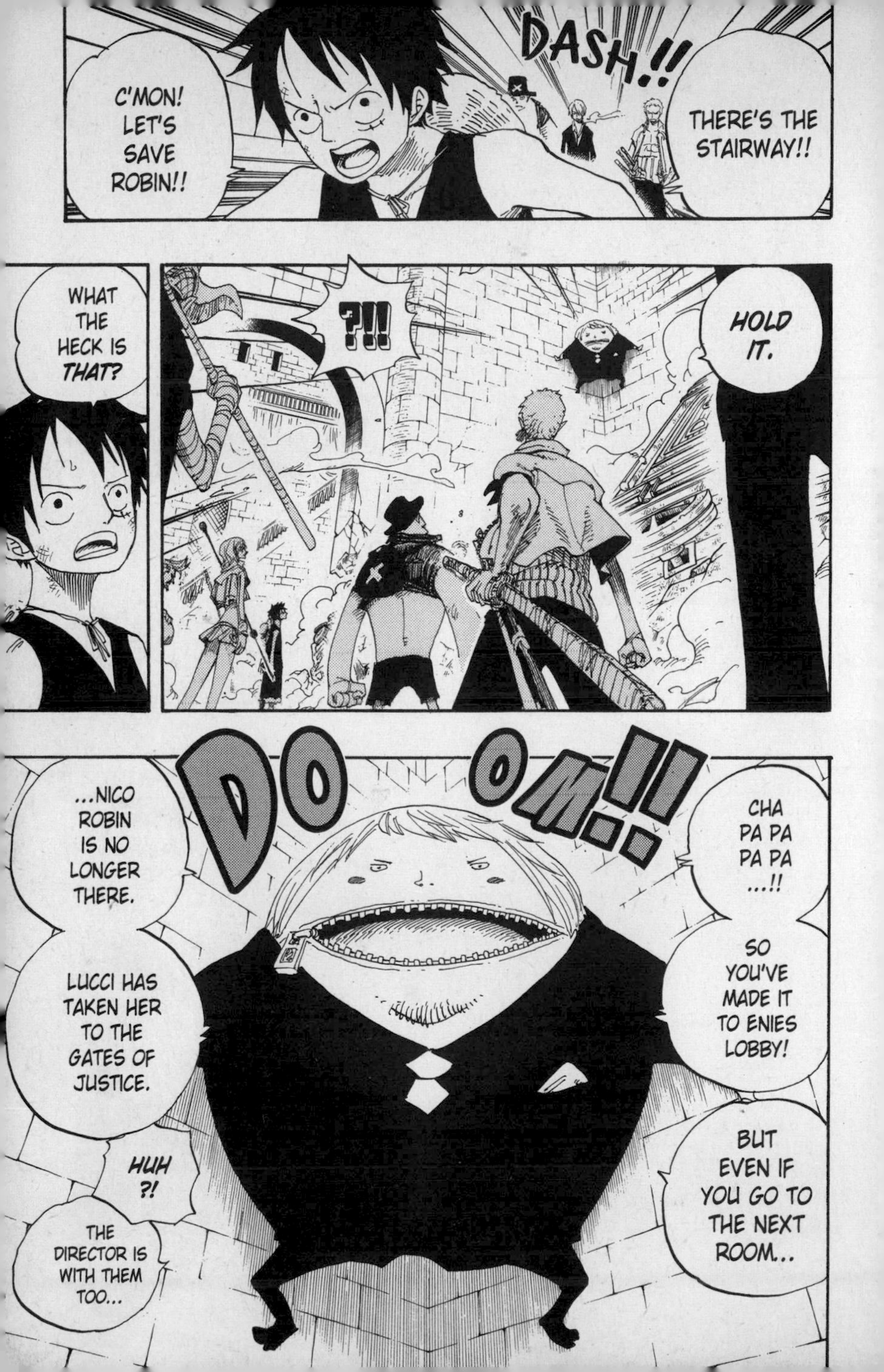
THERE'S THE STAIRWAY!!
DASH!!
C'MON! LET'S SAVE ROBIN!!
HOLD IT.
?!!
WHAT THE HECK IS THAT?
DOOM!!
CHA PA PA PA PA...!!
SO YOU'VE MADE IT TO ENIES LOBBY!
BUT EVEN IF YOU GO TO THE NEXT ROOM...
...NICO ROBIN IS NO LONGER THERE.
LUCCI HAS TAKEN HER TO THE GATES OF JUSTICE.
HUH?!
THE DIRECTOR IS WITH THEM TOO...

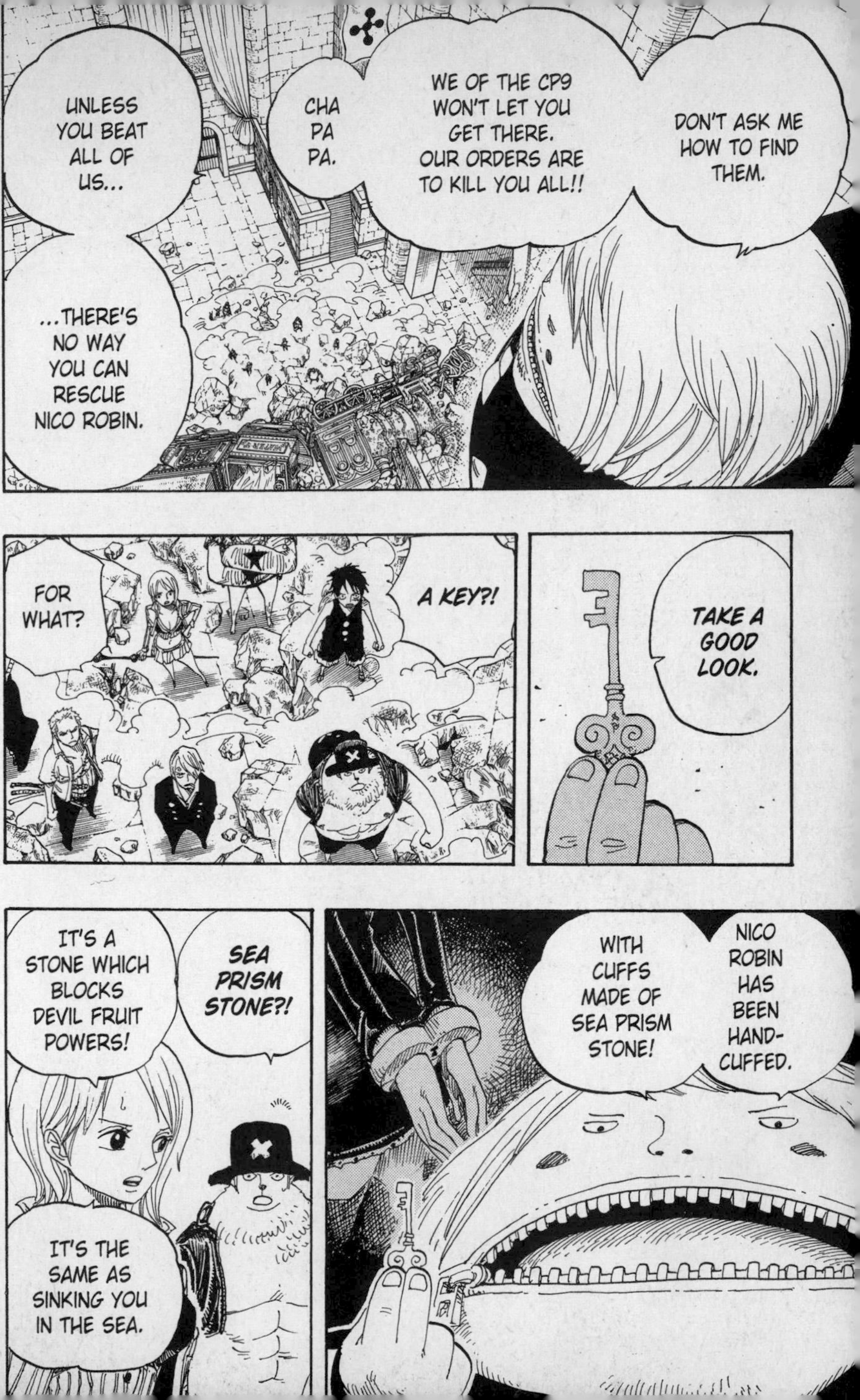
DON'T ASK ME HOW TO FIND THEM.
WE OF THE CP9 WON'T LET YOU GET THERE. OUR ORDERS ARE TO KILL YOU ALL!!
CHA PA PA.
UNLESS YOU BEAT ALL OF US...
...THERE'S NO WAY YOU CAN RESCUE NICO ROBIN.
TAKE A GOOD LOOK.
A KEY?!
FOR WHAT?
NICO ROBIN HAS BEEN HAND-CUFFED.
WITH CUFFS MADE OF SEA PRISM STONE!
SEA PRISM STONE?!
IT'S A STONE WHICH BLOCKS DEVIL FRUIT POWERS!
IT'S THE SAME AS SINKING YOU IN THE SEA.

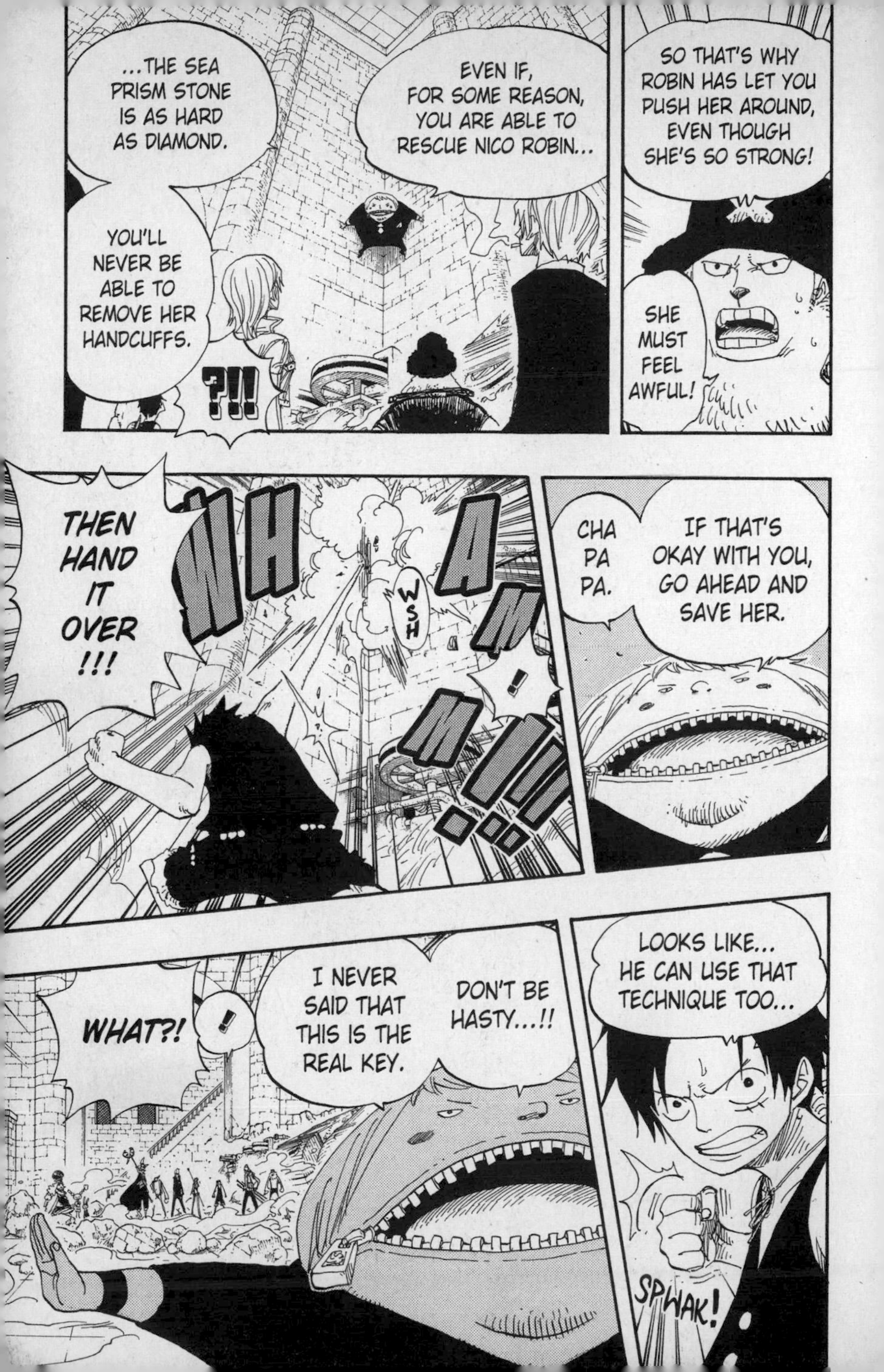
SO THAT'S WHY ROBIN HAS LET YOU PUSH HER AROUND, EVEN THOUGH SHE'S SO STRONG!
SHE MUST FEEL AWFUL!
EVEN IF, FOR SOME REASON, YOU ARE ABLE TO RESCUE NICO ROBIN...
...THE SEA PRISM STONE IS AS HARD AS DIAMOND.
YOU'LL NEVER BE ABLE TO REMOVE HER HANDCUFFS.
?!!
CHA PA PA.
IF THAT'S OKAY WITH YOU, GO AHEAD AND SAVE HER.
WHAM!!
WSH
!
THEN HAND IT OVER!!!
LOOKS LIKE... HE CAN USE THAT TECHNIQUE TOO...
SPWAK!
DON'T BE HASTY...!!
I NEVER SAID THAT THIS IS THE REAL KEY.
!
WHAT?!

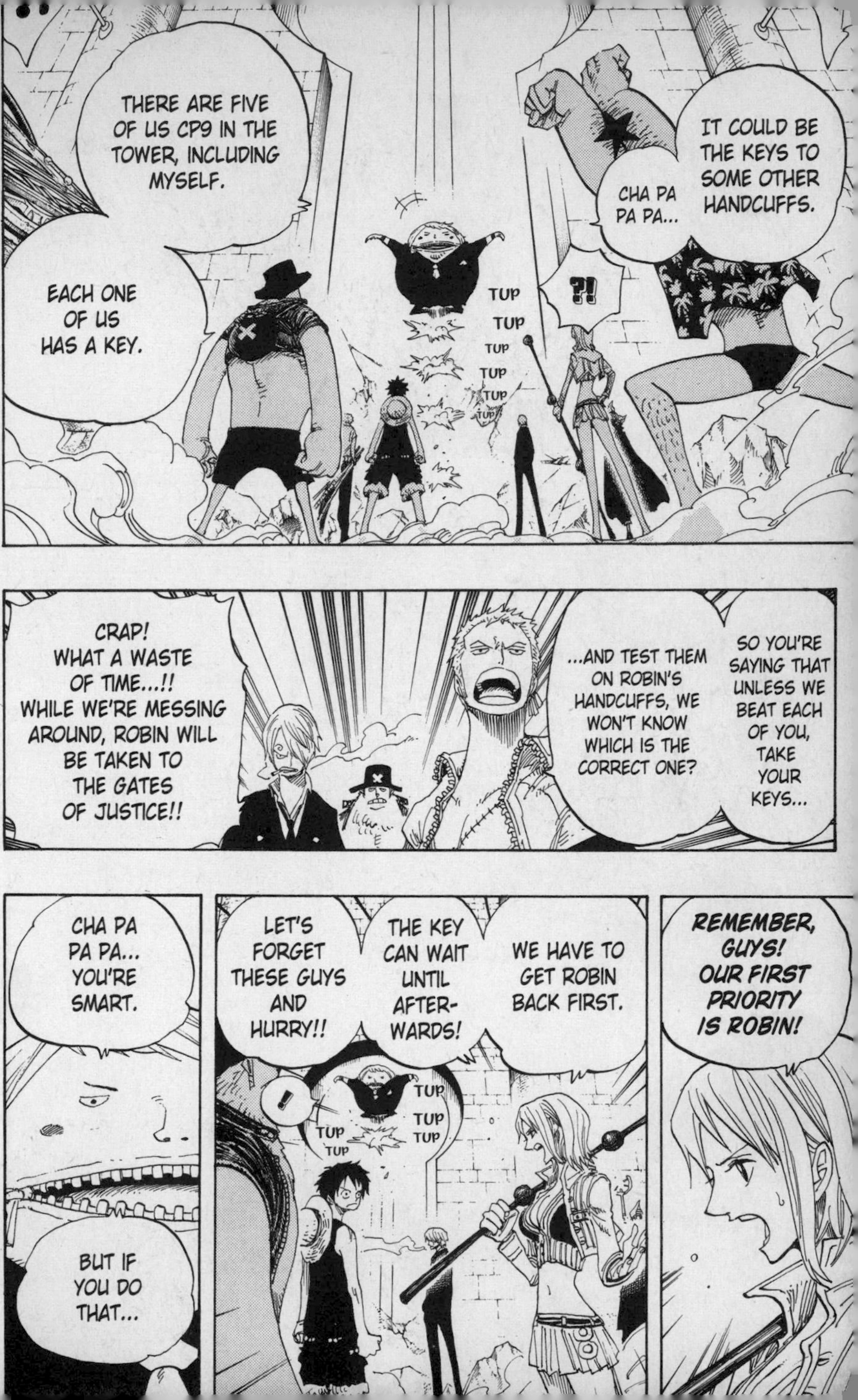
IT COULD BE THE KEYS TO SOME OTHER HANDCUFFS.
CHA PA PA PA...
?!
TUP TUP TUP TUP TUP TUP
THERE ARE FIVE OF US CP9 IN THE TOWER, INCLUDING MYSELF.
EACH ONE OF US HAS A KEY.
SO YOU'RE SAYING THAT UNLESS WE BEAT EACH OF YOU, TAKE YOUR KEYS...
...AND TEST THEM ON ROBIN'S HANDCUFFS, WE WON'T KNOW WHICH IS THE CORRECT ONE?
CRAP! WHAT A WASTE OF TIME...!! WHILE WE'RE MESSING AROUND, ROBIN WILL BE TAKEN TO THE GATES OF JUSTICE!!
REMEMBER, GUYS! OUR FIRST PRIORITY IS ROBIN!
WE HAVE TO GET ROBIN BACK FIRST.
THE KEY CAN WAIT UNTIL AFTER-WARDS!
LET'S FORGET THESE GUYS AND HURRY!!
TUP TUP TUP
!
TUP TUP
CHA PA PA PA... YOU'RE SMART.
BUT IF YOU DO THAT...

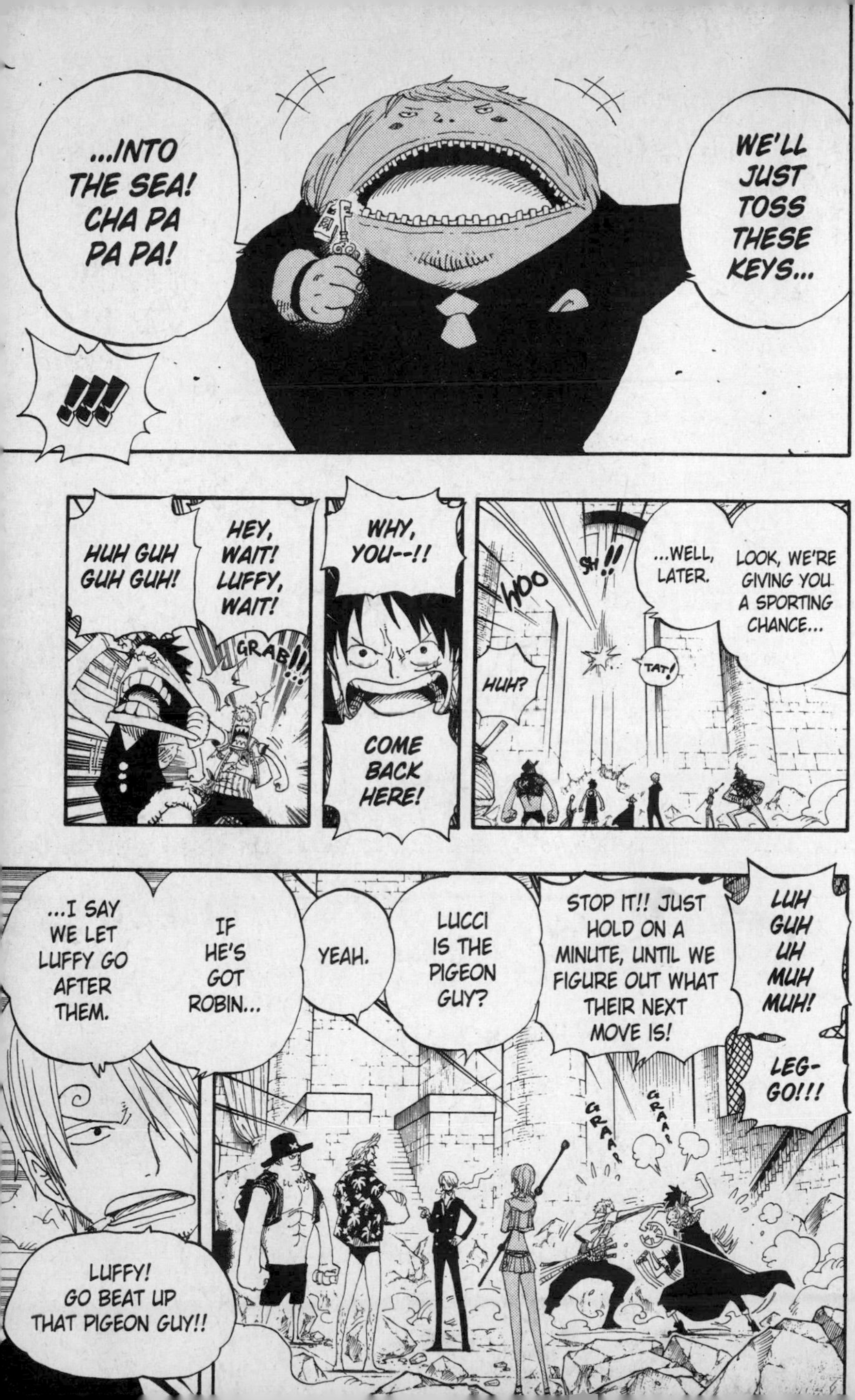
WE'LL JUST TOSS THESE KEYS...
...INTO THE SEA! CHA PA PA PA!
!!!
LOOK, WE'RE GIVING YOU A SPORTING CHANCE...
...WELL, LATER.
SH!!
WOO
TAT!
HUH?
WHY, YOU--!!
COME BACK HERE!
HEY, WAIT! LUFFY, WAIT!
HUH GUH GUH GUH!
GRAB!!!
LUH GUH UH MUH MUH!
LEG-GO!!!
STOP IT!! JUST HOLD ON A MINUTE, UNTIL WE FIGURE OUT WHAT THEIR NEXT MOVE IS!
GRAAR
GRAAR
LUCCI IS THE PIGEON GUY?
YEAH.
IF HE'S GOT ROBIN...
...I SAY WE LET LUFFY GO AFTER THEM.
LUFFY! GO BEAT UP THAT PIGEON GUY!!

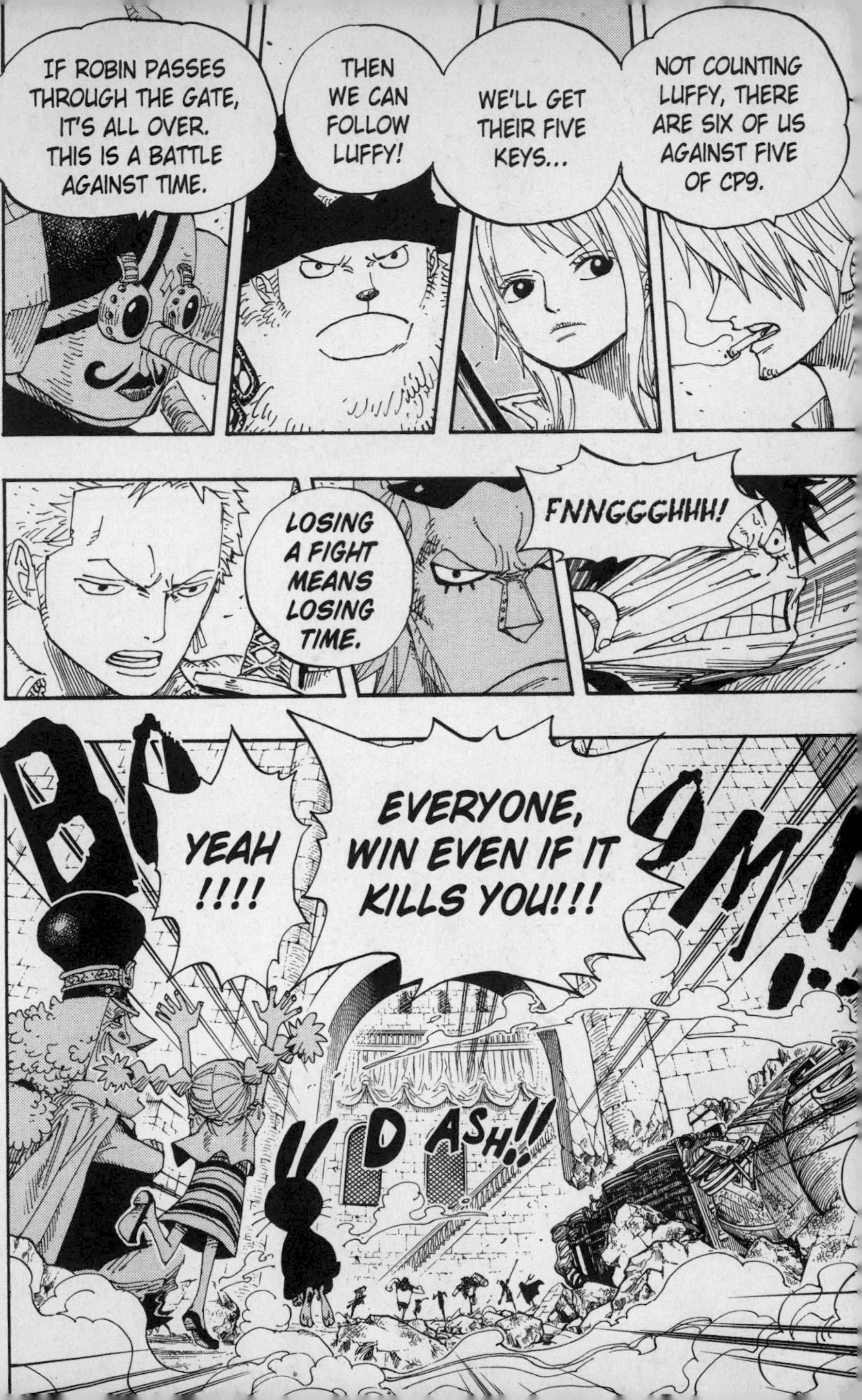

NOT COUNTING LUFFY, THERE ARE SIX OF US AGAINST FIVE OF CP9.
WE'LL GET THEIR FIVE KEYS...
THEN WE CAN FOLLOW LUFFY!
IF ROBIN PASSES THROUGH THE GATE, IT'S ALL OVER. THIS IS A BATTLE AGAINST TIME.
FNNGGGHHH!
LOSING A FIGHT MEANS LOSING TIME.
EVERYONE, WIN EVEN IF IT KILLS YOU!!!
YEAH !!!!
DASH!!

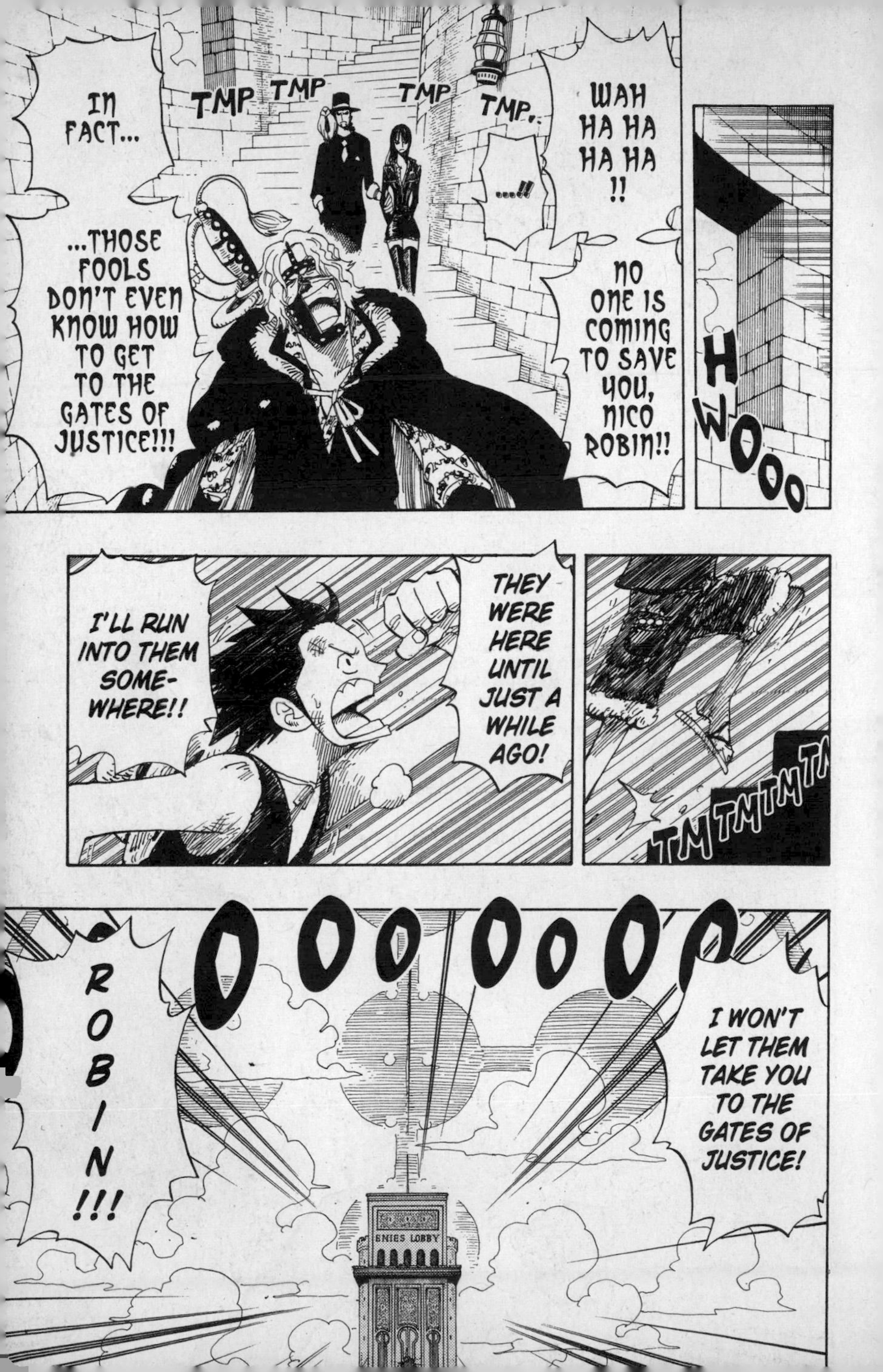
HWOOO
WAH HA HA HA!!
TMP TMP TMP TMP..
...!!
NO ONE IS COMING TO SAVE YOU, NICO ROBIN!!
IN FACT...
...THOSE FOOLS DON'T EVEN KNOW HOW TO GET TO THE GATES OF JUSTICE!!!
TM TMTMTMTM
THEY WERE HERE UNTIL JUST A WHILE AGO!
I'LL RUN INTO THEM SOME-WHERE!!
OOOOOOP
I WON'T LET THEM TAKE YOU TO THE GATES OF JUSTICE!
ROBIN!!!
ENIES LOBBY

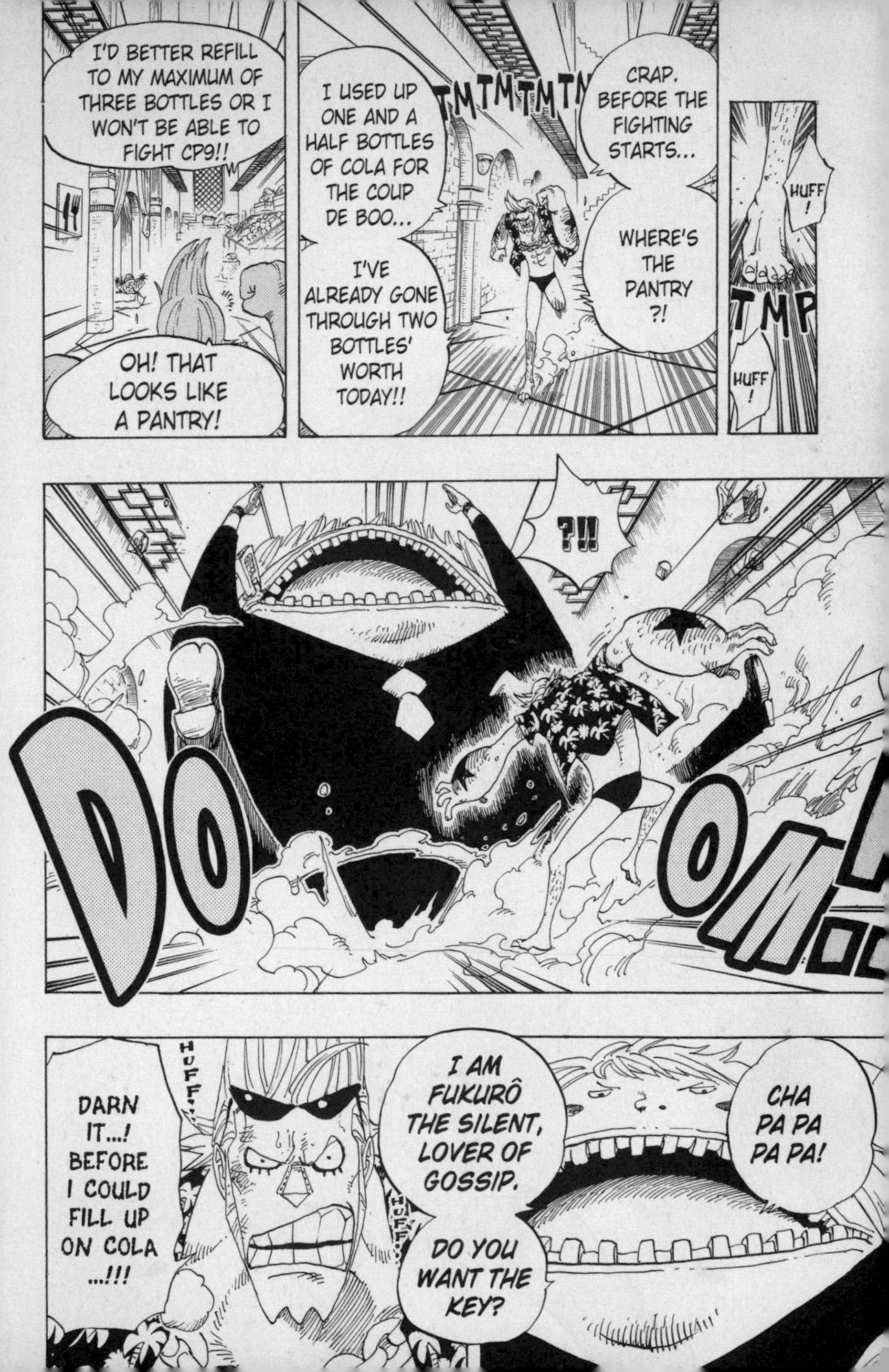
HUFF!
TMP
HUFF!
CRAP. BEFORE THE FIGHTING STARTS...
WHERE'S THE PANTRY?!
TMTMTMTM
I USED UP ONE AND A HALF BOTTLES OF COLA FOR THE COUP DE BOO...
I'VE ALREADY GONE THROUGH TWO BOTTLES' WORTH TODAY!!
I'D BETTER REFILL TO MY MAXIMUM OF THREE BOTTLES OR I WON'T BE ABLE TO FIGHT CP9!!
OH! THAT LOOKS LIKE A PANTRY!
?!!
DOOM
CHA PA PA PA PA!
I AM FUKURÔ THE SILENT, LOVER OF GOSSIP.
DO YOU WANT THE KEY?
HUFF...
HUFF...
DARN IT...! BEFORE I COULD FILL UP ON COLA ...!!!

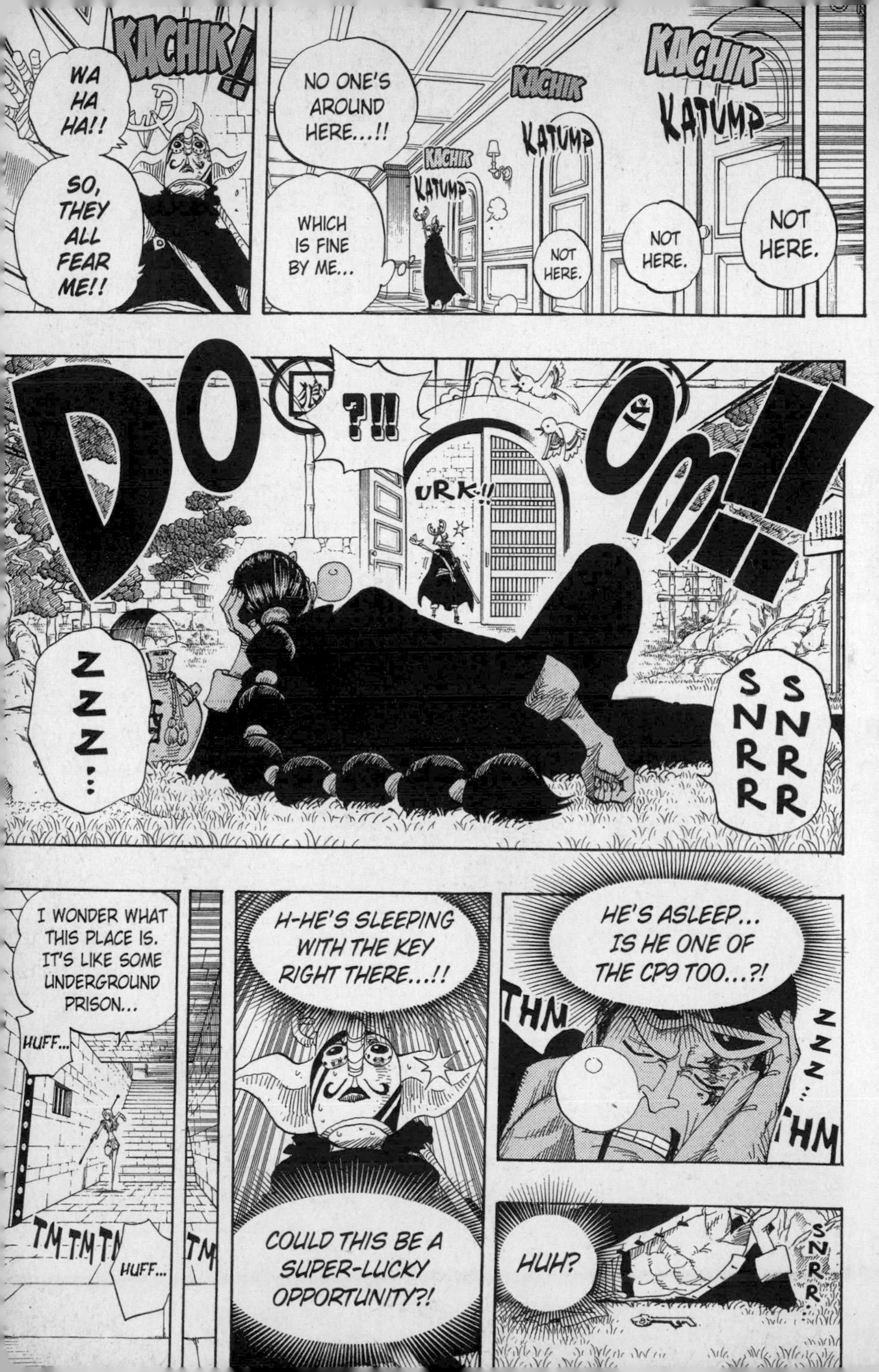
KACHIK
KATUMP
NOT HERE.
NOT HERE.
KACHIK
KATUMP
NOT HERE.
NO ONE'S AROUND HERE...!!
KACHIK
KATUMP
WHICH IS FINE BY ME...
KACHIK!!
WA HA HA!!
SO, THEY ALL FEAR ME!!
DOOM!!
SNRR SNRR
?!!
URK!!
ZZZ...
HE'S ASLEEP... IS HE ONE OF THE CP9 TOO...?!
ZZZ...
THM
THM
SNRR
HUH?
H-HE'S SLEEPING WITH THE KEY RIGHT THERE...!!
COULD THIS BE A SUPER-LUCKY OPPORTUNITY?!
TM
I WONDER WHAT THIS PLACE IS. IT'S LIKE SOME UNDERGROUND PRISON...
HUFF...
TM TM TM
HUFF...

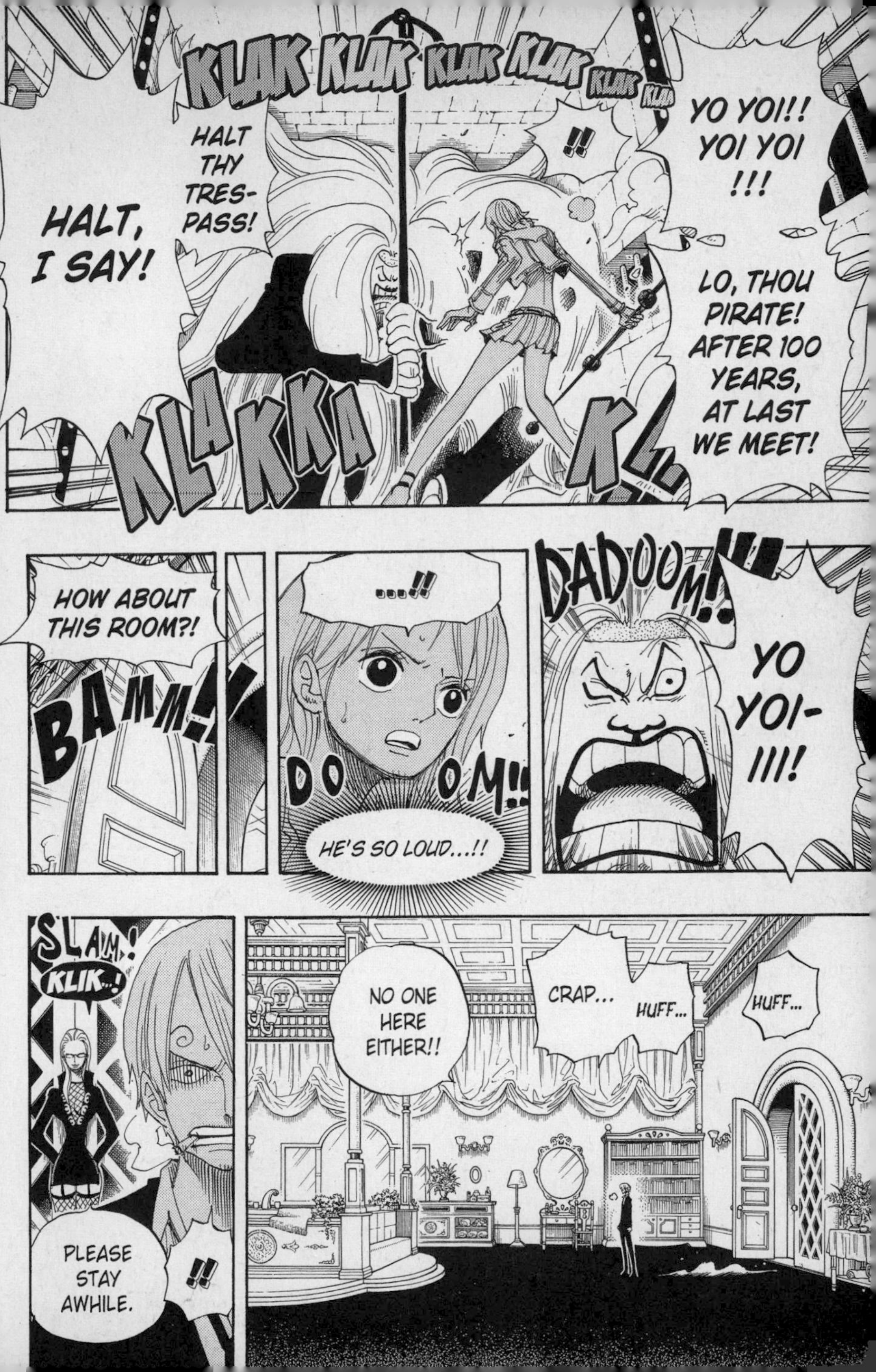
KLAK KLAK KLAK KLAK KLAK KLA
YO YOI!! YOI YOI !!!
!!
LO, THOU PIRATE! AFTER 100 YEARS, AT LAST WE MEET!
HALT THY TRES-PASS!
HALT, I SAY!
KL...
KLAKKA
DADOOM!!
YO YOI-III!
...!!
DOOM!!
HE'S SO LOUD...!!
HOW ABOUT THIS ROOM?!
BAMM!!
HUFF...
HUFF...
CRAP...
NO ONE HERE EITHER!!
SLAM!
KLIK...!
!!
PLEASE STAY AWHILE.

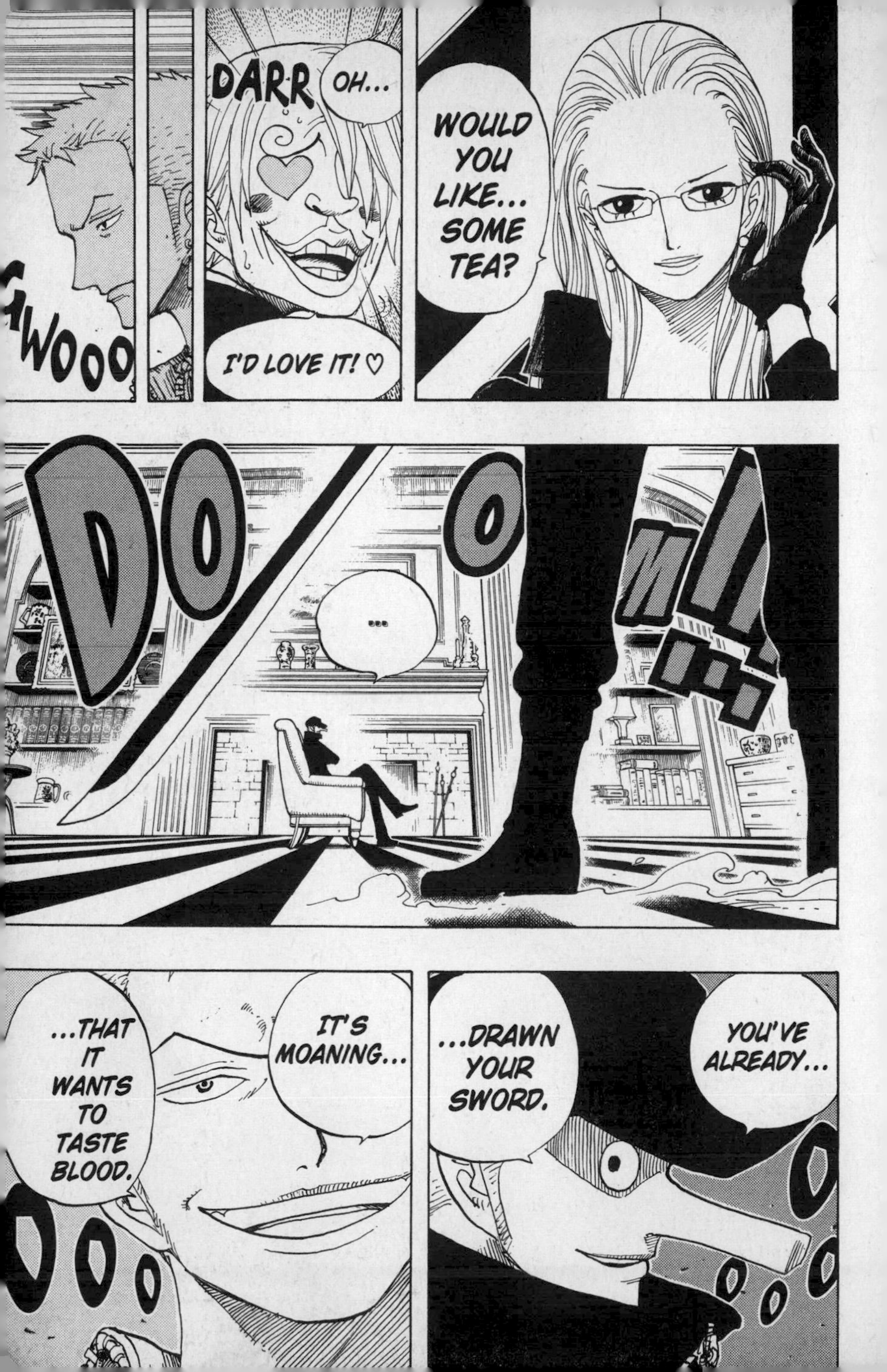
WOULD YOU LIKE... SOME TEA?
DARR
OH...
I'D LOVE IT! ♡
WOOO
DOOM
...
YOU'VE ALREADY...
...DRAWN YOUR SWORD.
IT'S MOANING...
...THAT IT WANTS TO TASTE BLOOD.

Pirates vs. CP9

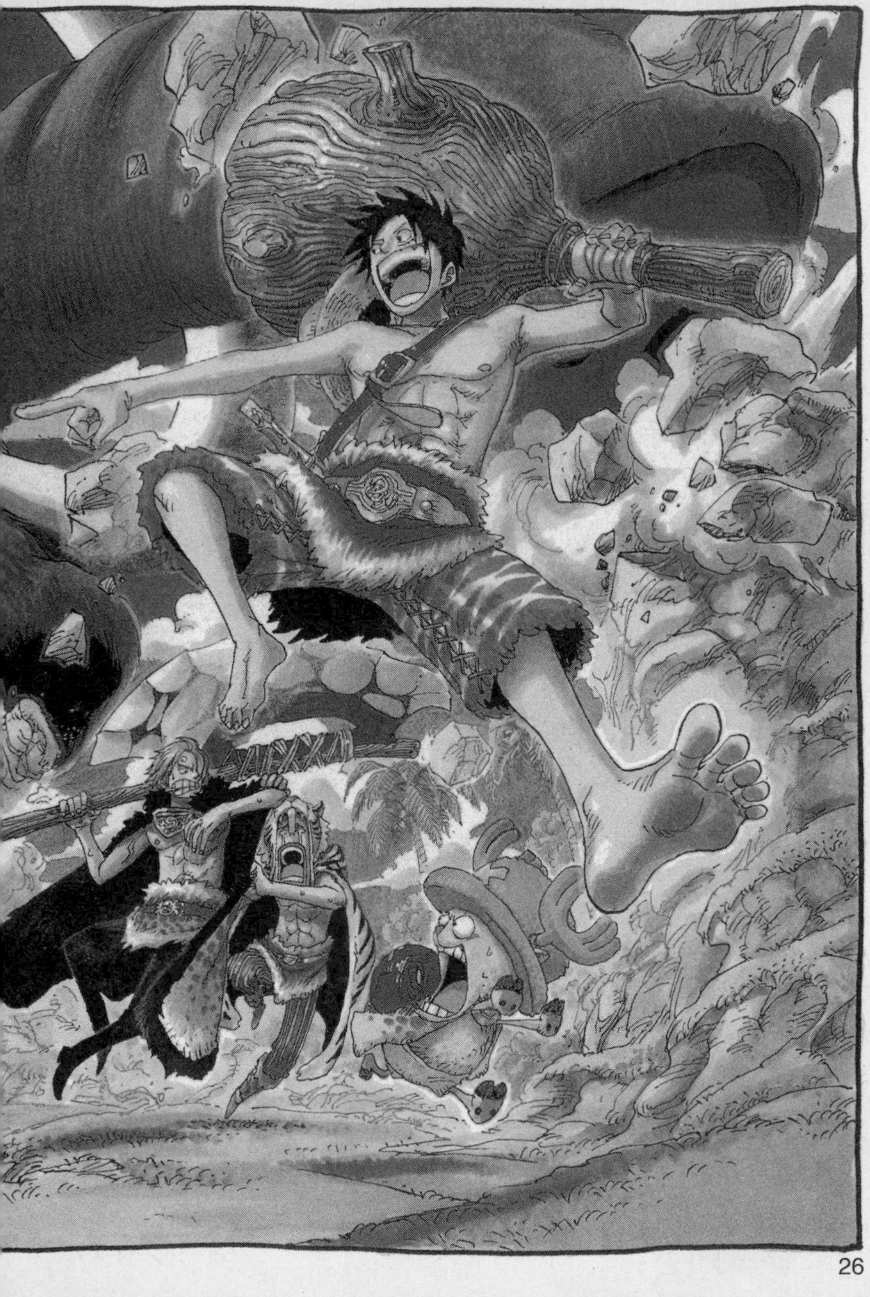

Chapter 401:

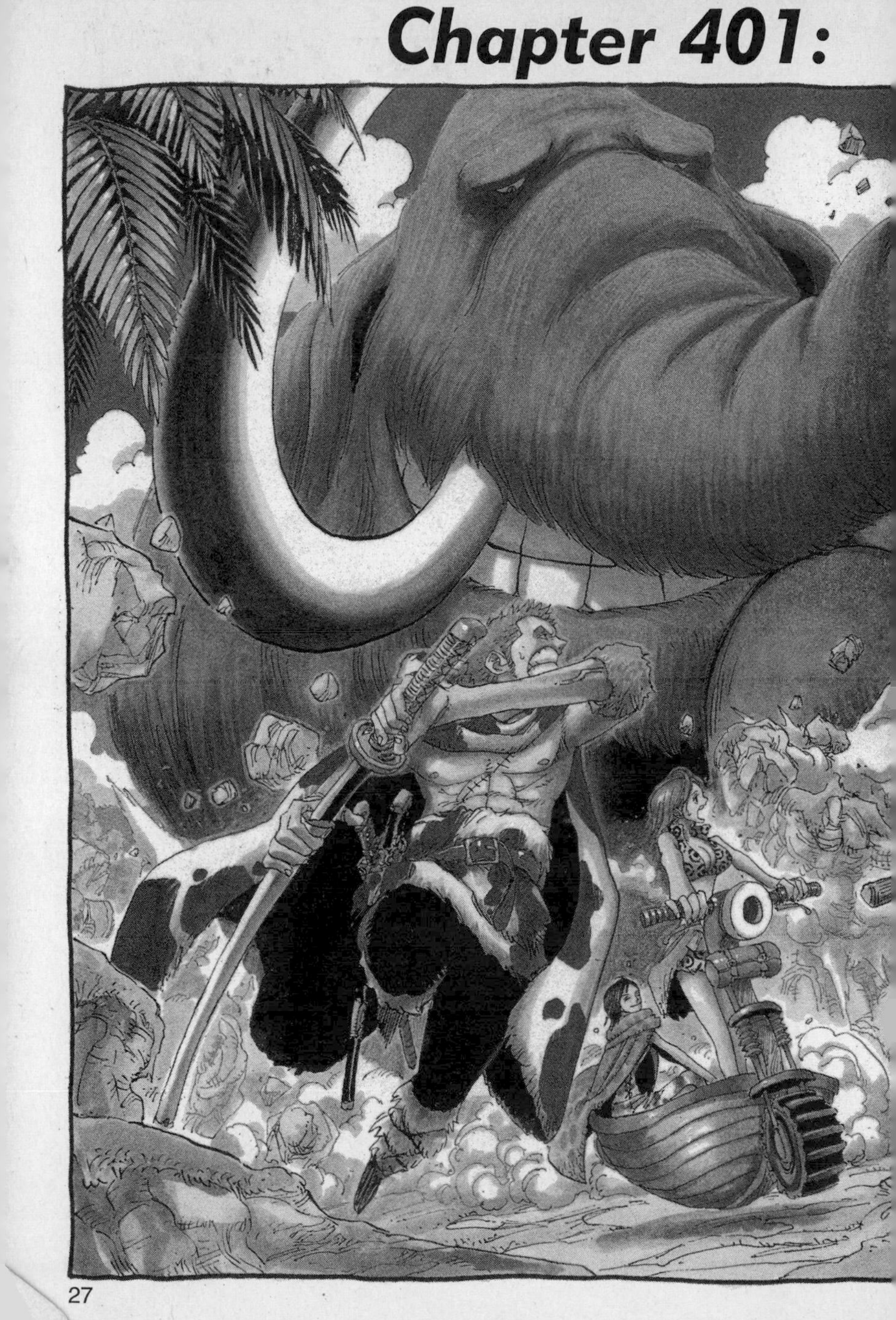

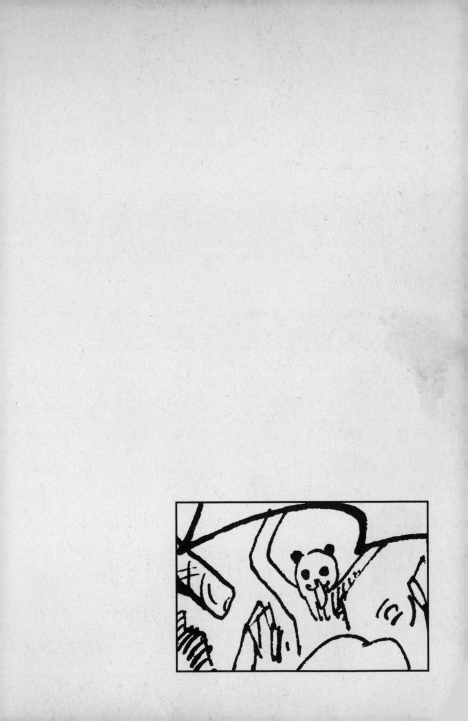

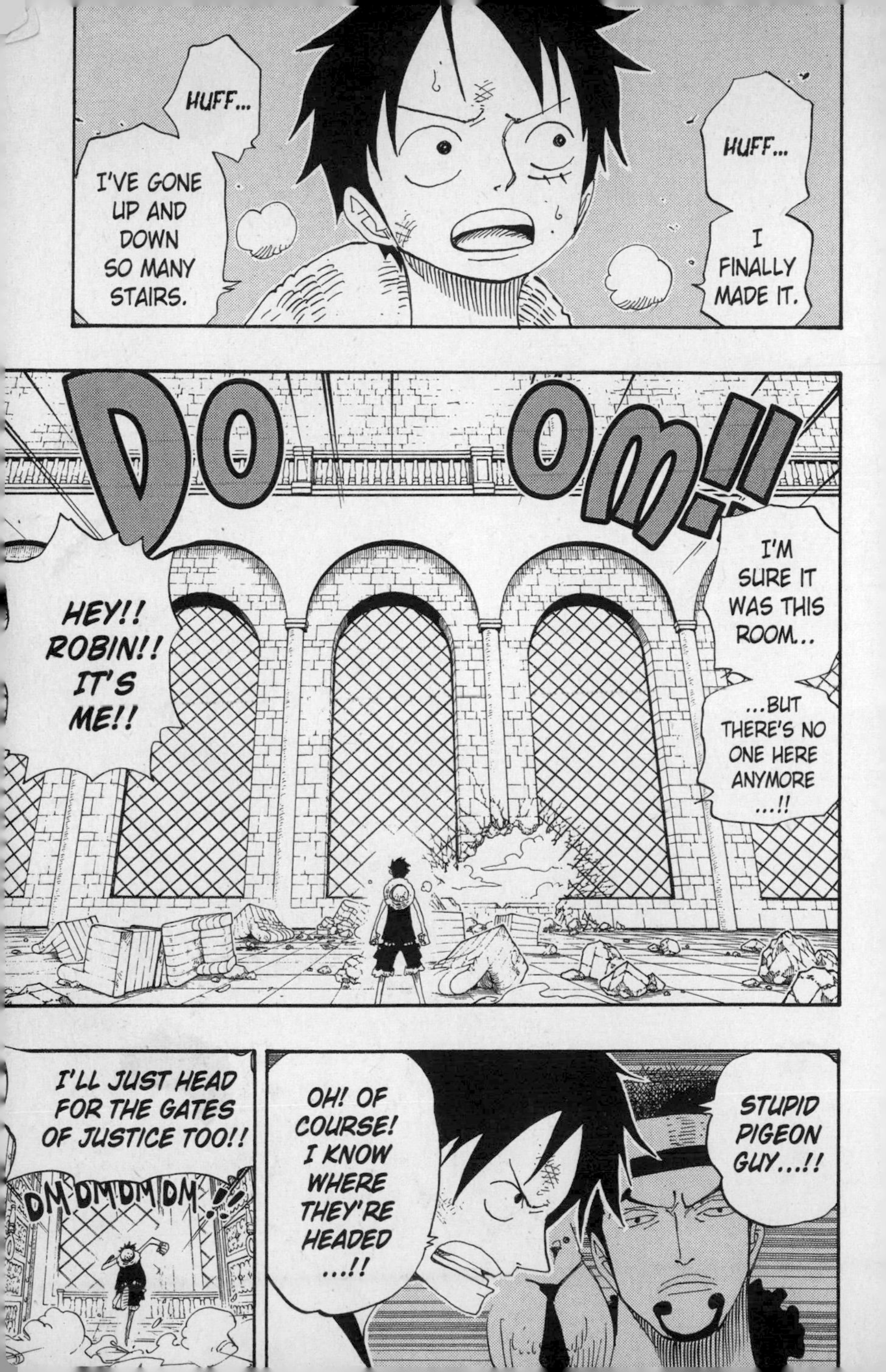
HUFF... I FINALLY MADE IT.
HUFF... I'VE GONE UP AND DOWN SO MANY STAIRS.
DO ÖM!!
I'M SURE IT WAS THIS ROOM...
HEY!! ROBIN!! IT'S ME!!
...BUT THERE'S NO ONE HERE ANYMORE ...!!
STUPID PIGEON GUY...!!
OH! OF COURSE! I KNOW WHERE THEY'RE HEADED ...!!
I'LL JUST HEAD FOR THE GATES OF JUSTICE TOO!!
DM DM DM DM!!

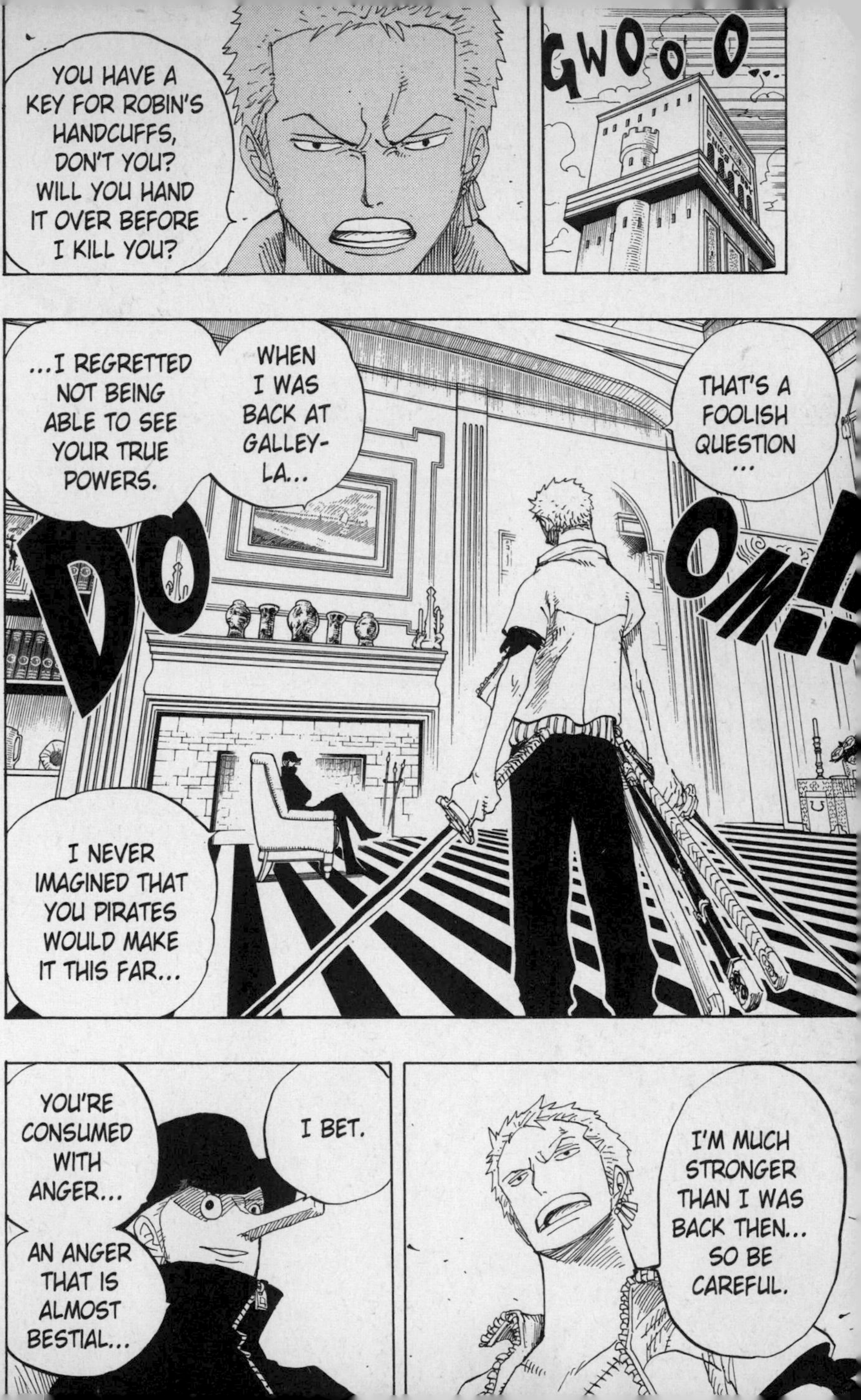
GWOOOO
YOU HAVE A KEY FOR ROBIN'S HANDCUFFS, DON'T YOU? WILL YOU HAND IT OVER BEFORE I KILL YOU?
THAT'S A FOOLISH QUESTION ...
DOOM!!
WHEN I WAS BACK AT GALLEY-LA...
...I REGRETTED NOT BEING ABLE TO SEE YOUR TRUE POWERS.
I NEVER IMAGINED THAT YOU PIRATES WOULD MAKE IT THIS FAR...
I'M MUCH STRONGER THAN I WAS BACK THEN... SO BE CAREFUL.
I BET.
YOU'RE CONSUMED WITH ANGER...
AN ANGER THAT IS ALMOST BESTIAL...

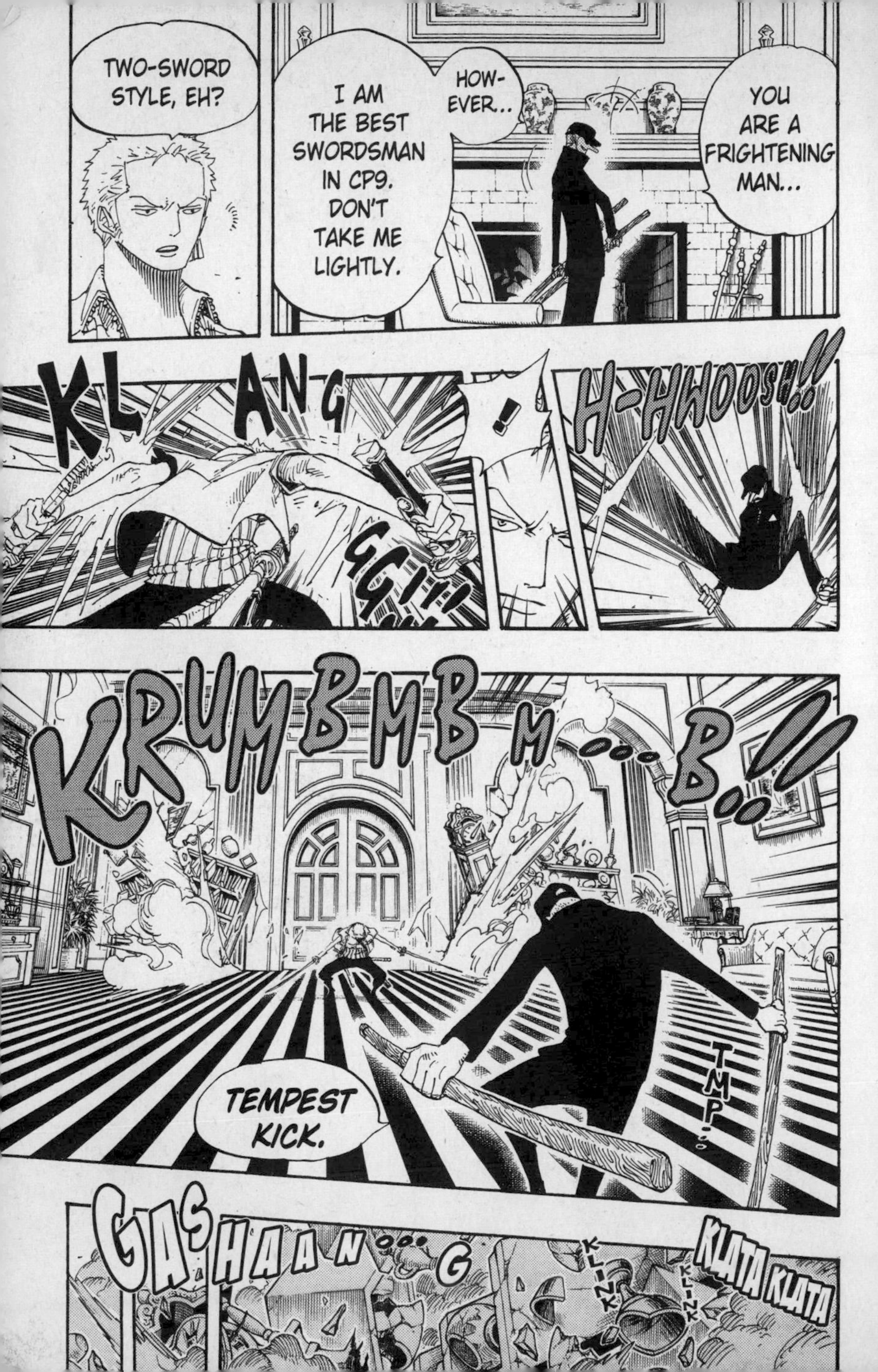
YOU ARE A FRIGHTENING MAN...
HOW-EVER...
I AM THE BEST SWORDSMAN IN CP9. DON'T TAKE ME LIGHTLY.
TWO-SWORD STYLE, EH?
H-HWOOSH!!
!
KLANG
GGI!!
KRUMBMB M...B..!!
TMP..
TEMPEST KICK.
KLATA KLATA
KLINK
KLINK
GASHAAN...G

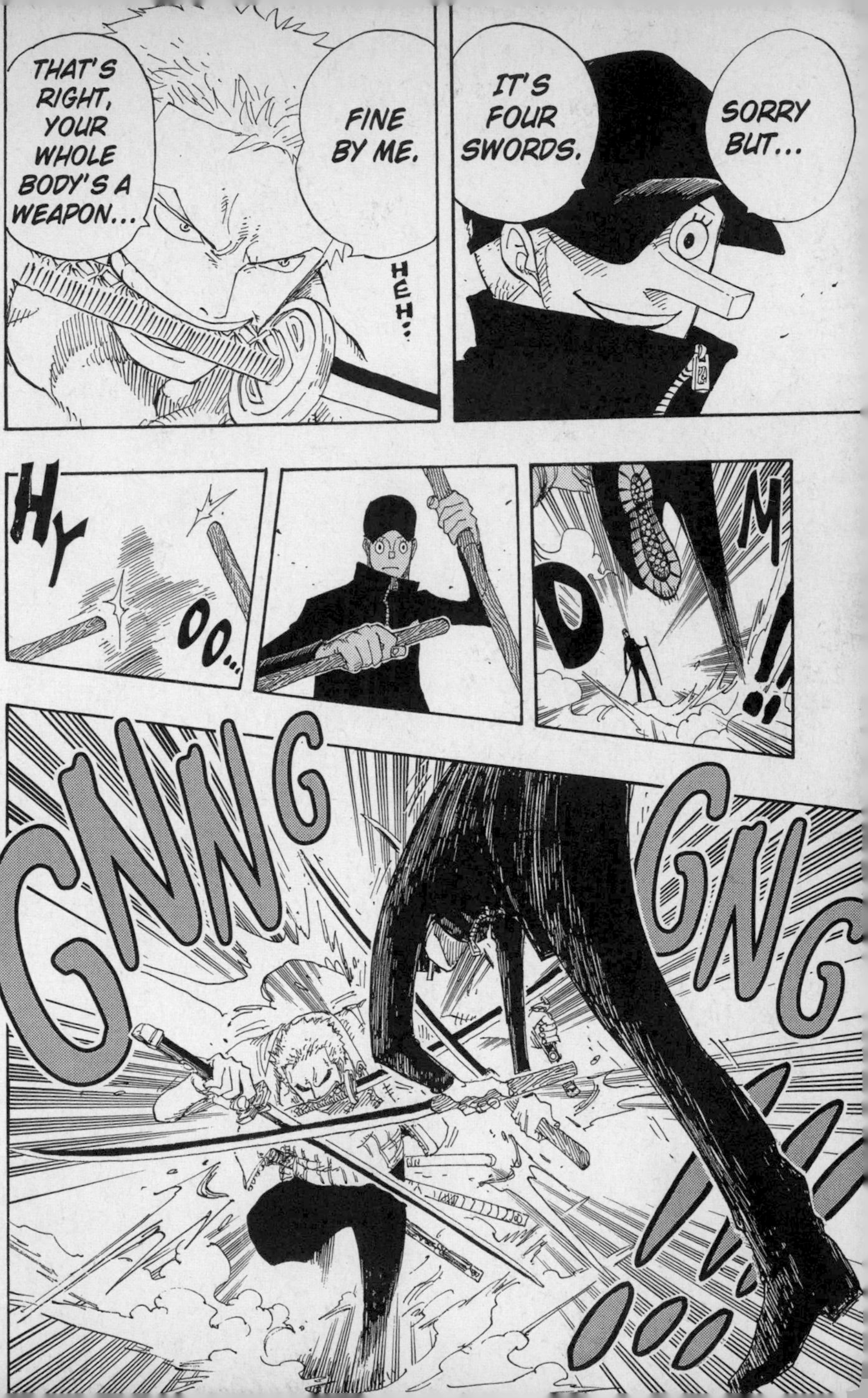
SORRY BUT...
IT'S FOUR SWORDS.
FINE BY ME.
HEH...
THAT'S RIGHT, YOUR WHOLE BODY'S A WEAPON...
DOM!!
HYOO...
GNG......
GNNG

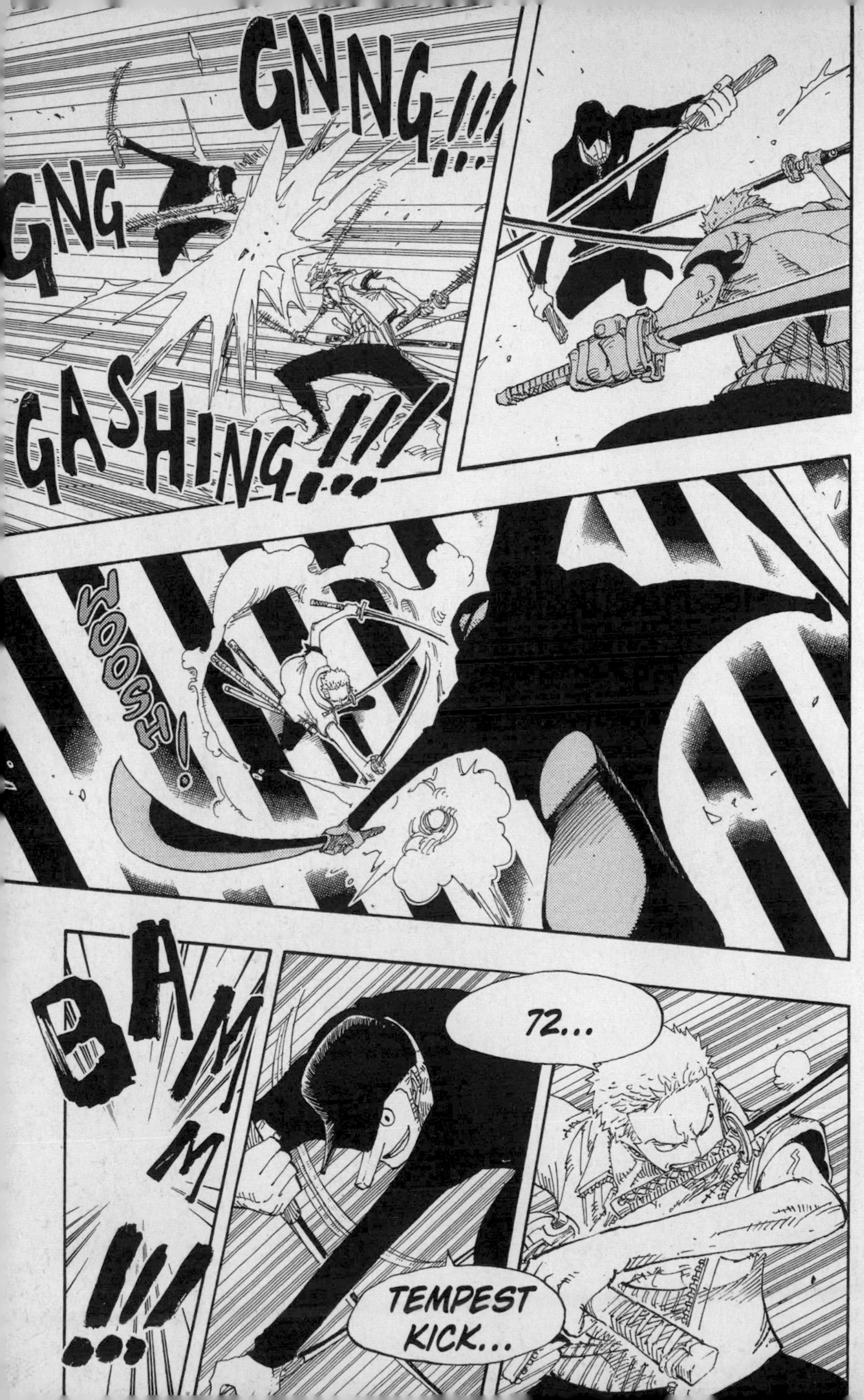
GNG
GNNG!!!
GASHING!!!
WOOSH!
72...
TEMPEST KICK...
BAMM!!!

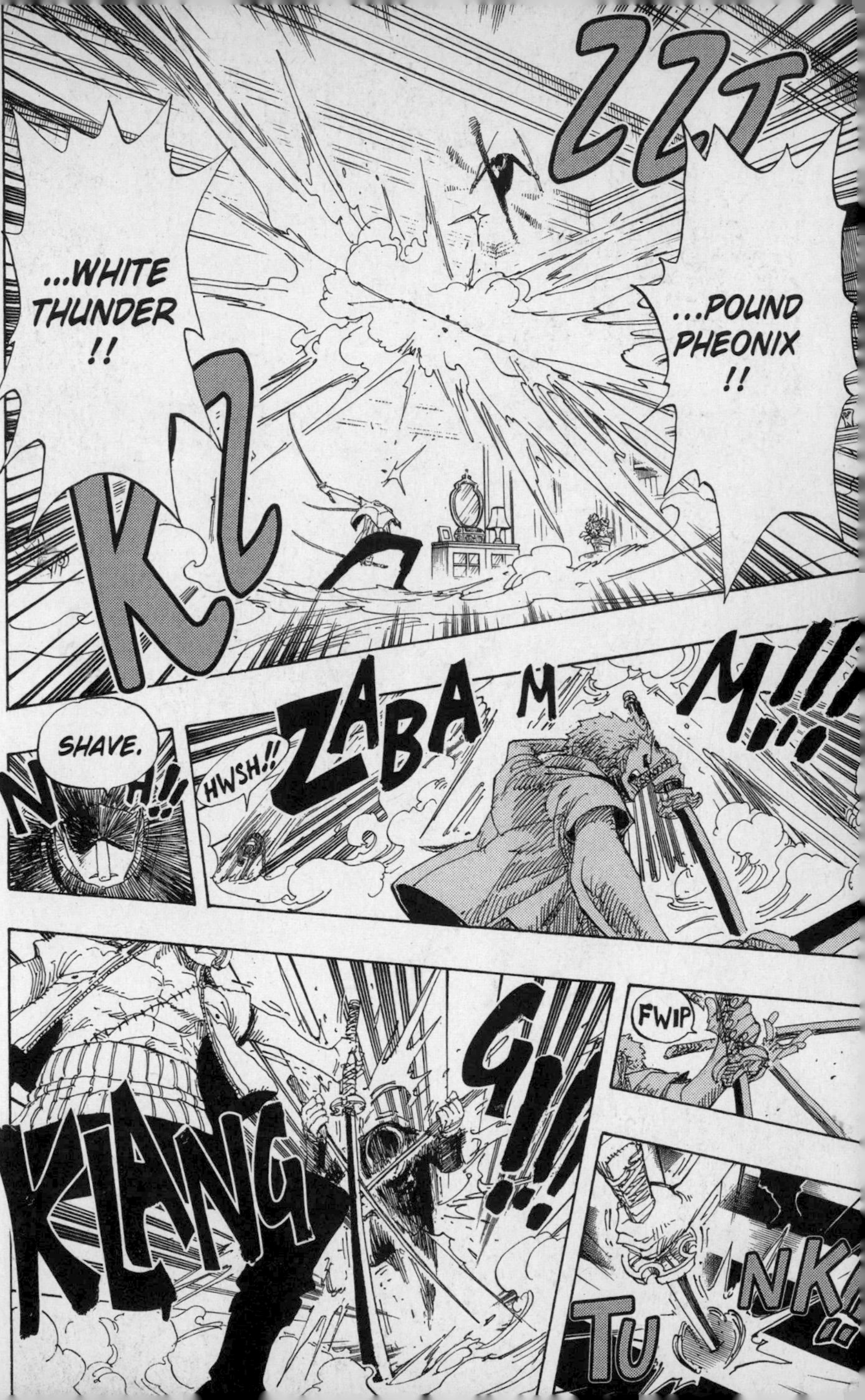
ZZZT
...POUND PHEONIX !!
...WHITE THUNDER !!
KZ
ZABAMM!!!
HWSH!!
SHAVE.
FWIP
TUNK
G!!!
KLANG

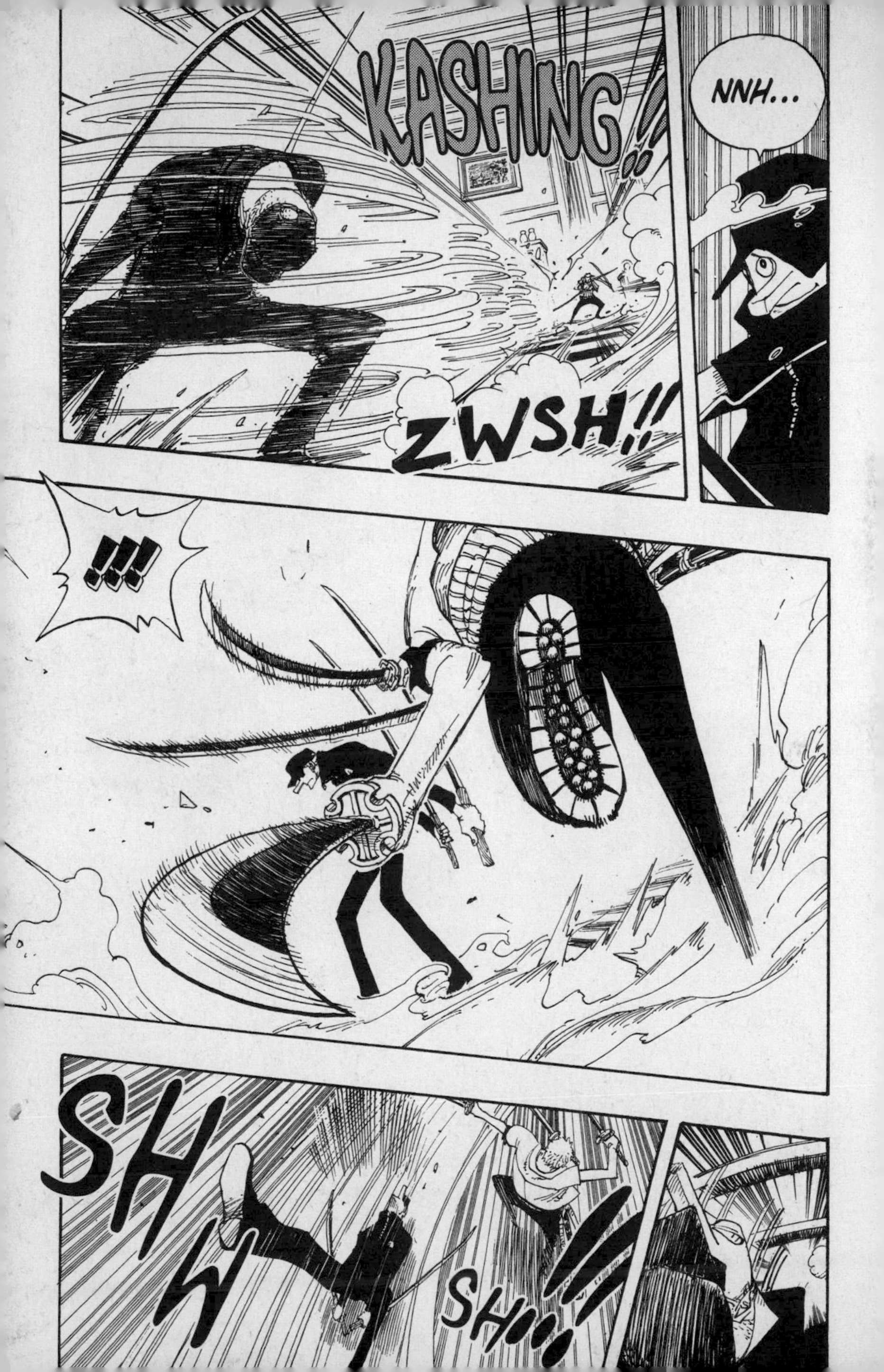
NNH...
KASHING!!
ZWSH!!
!!!
SH
SH!!

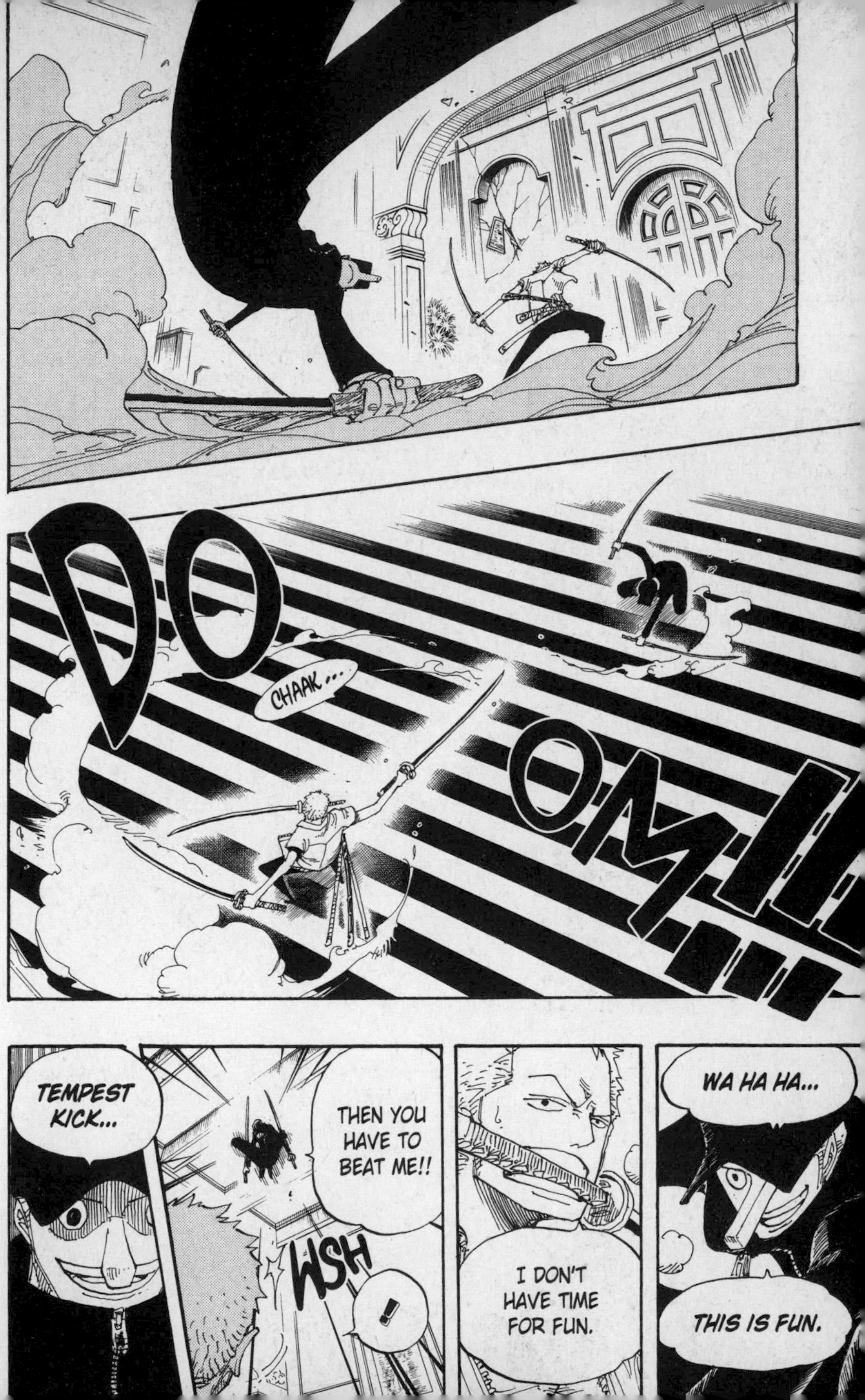
DOOM!!
CHAAK...
WA HA HA...
THIS IS FUN.
I DON'T HAVE TIME FOR FUN.
THEN YOU HAVE TO BEAT ME!!
WSH
!
TEMPEST KICK...

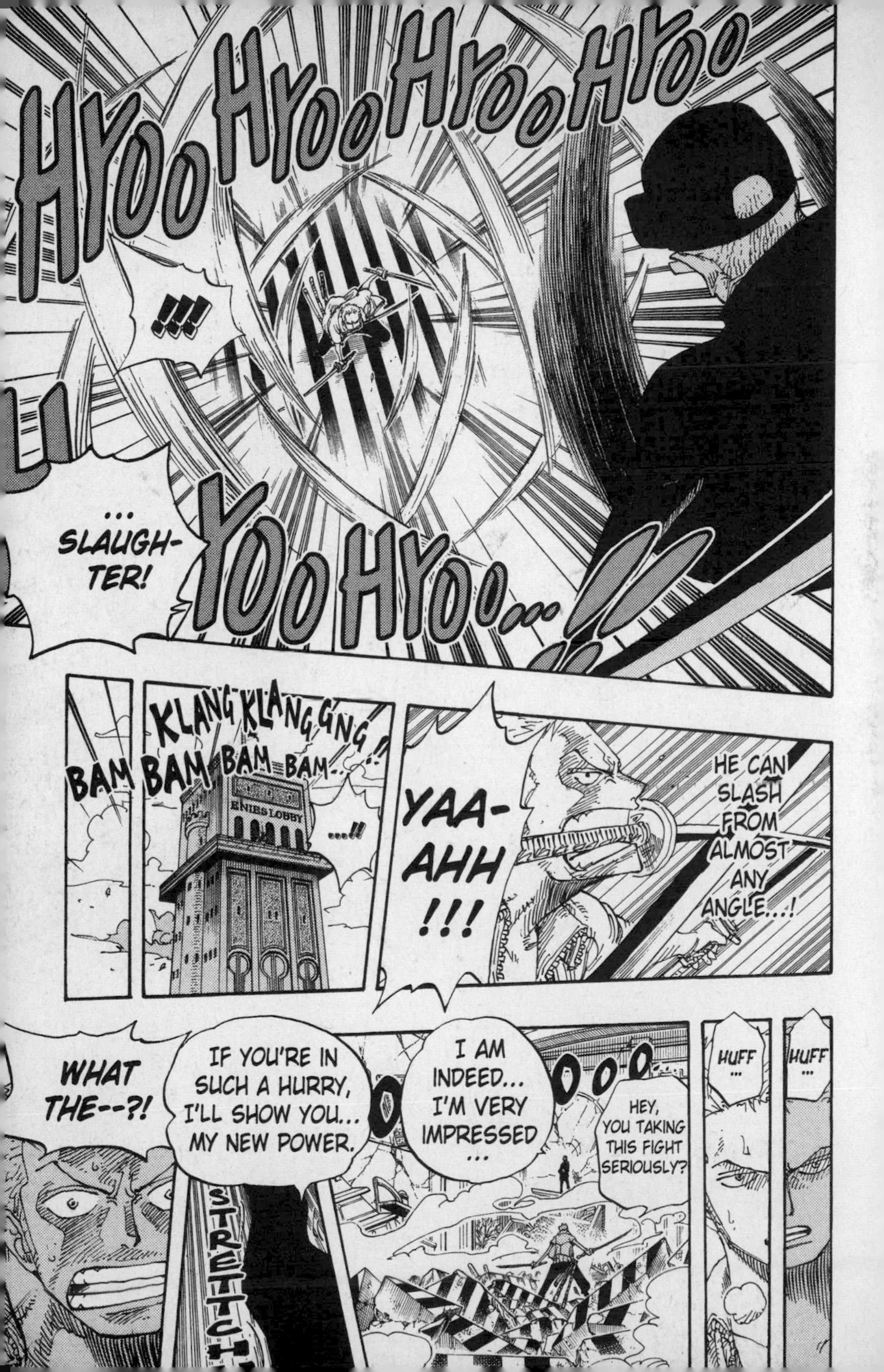
HYOO HYOO HYOO HYOO
!!!!
YOO HYOO...!!
... SLAUGHTER!
HE CAN SLASH FROM ALMOST ANY ANGLE...!
YAA-AHH!!!
KLANG KLANG GNG GNG!!
BAM BAM BAM BAM...!!
...!!
HUFF ...
HUFF ...
HEY, YOU TAKING THIS FIGHT SERIOUSLY?
I AM INDEED... I'M VERY IMPRESSED...
OOOO
IF YOU'RE IN SUCH A HURRY, I'LL SHOW YOU... MY NEW POWER.
STRETTCH
WHAT THE--?!

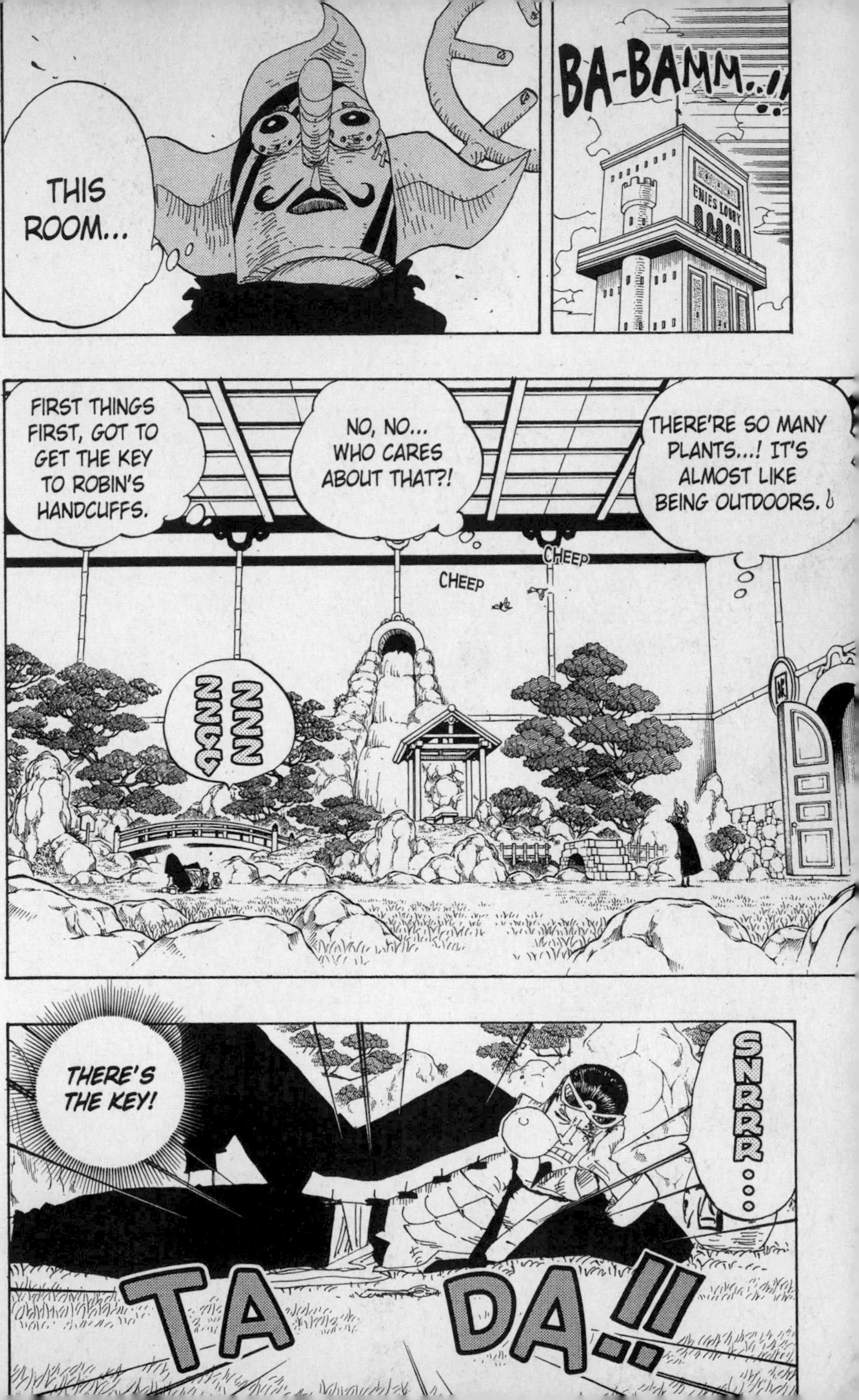
BA-BAMM..!!
ENIES LOBBY
THIS ROOM...
THERE'RE SO MANY PLANTS...! IT'S ALMOST LIKE BEING OUTDOORS.
NO, NO... WHO CARES ABOUT THAT?!
FIRST THINGS FIRST, GOT TO GET THE KEY TO ROBIN'S HANDCUFFS.
CHEEP
CHEEP
ZZZ ZZZG
SNRRR...
THERE'S THE KEY!
TA DA..!!

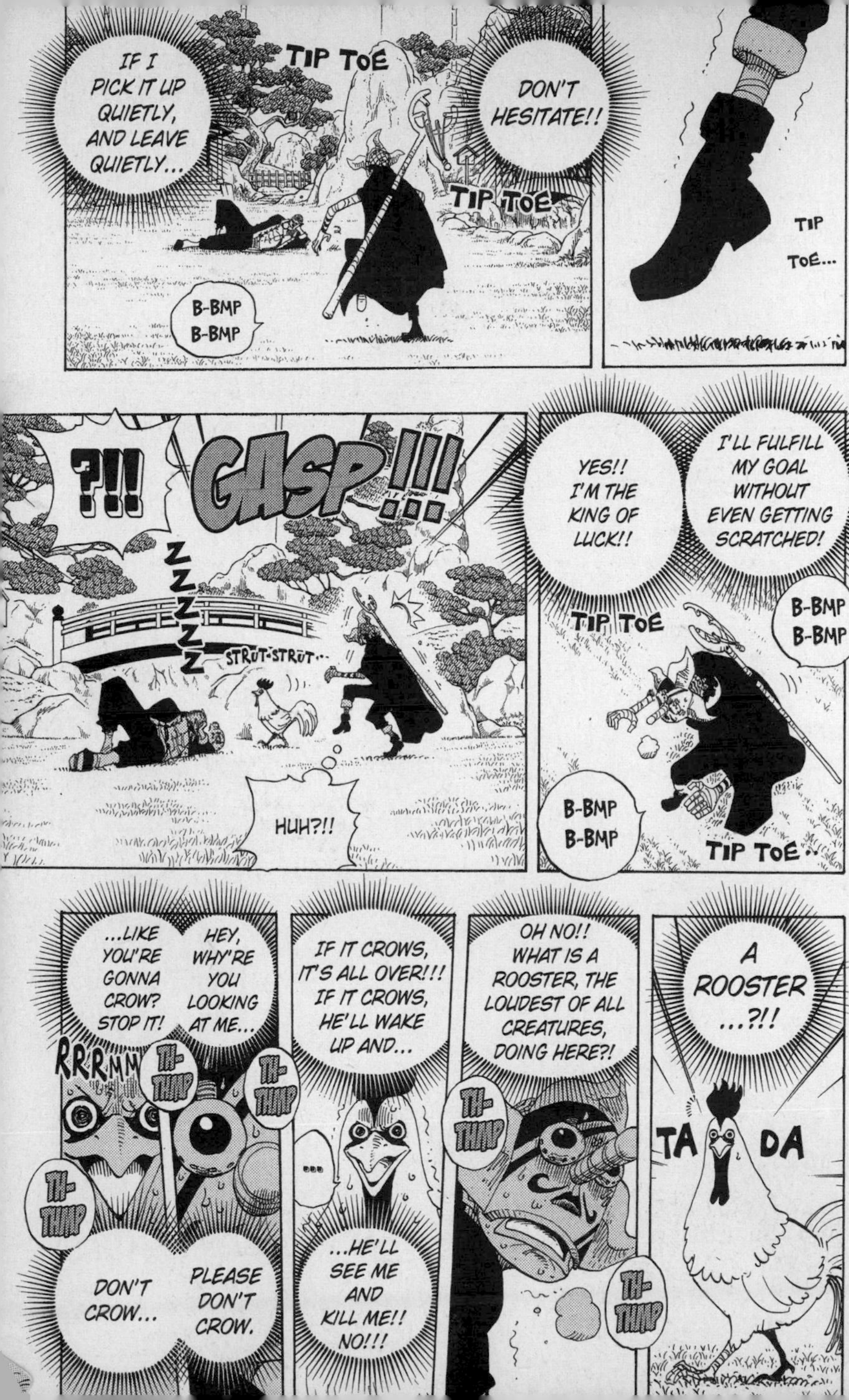
TIP
TOE...
DON'T HESITATE!!
TIP TOE
IF I PICK IT UP QUIETLY, AND LEAVE QUIETLY...
TIP TOE
B-BMP B-BMP
I'LL FULFILL MY GOAL WITHOUT EVEN GETTING SCRATCHED!
YES!! I'M THE KING OF LUCK!!
B-BMP B-BMP
TIP TOE
B-BMP B-BMP
TIP TOE..
GASP!!!
?!!
ZZZZZ
STRUT-STRUT..
HUH?!!
A ROOSTER ...?!!
TA DA
OH NO!! WHAT IS A ROOSTER, THE LOUDEST OF ALL CREATURES, DOING HERE?!
TH-THMP
TH-THMP
IF IT CROWS, IT'S ALL OVER!!! IF IT CROWS, HE'LL WAKE UP AND...
TH-THMP
...
...HE'LL SEE ME AND KILL ME!! NO!!!
HEY, WHY'RE YOU LOOKING AT ME...
...LIKE YOU'RE GONNA CROW? STOP IT!
TH-THMP
RRRMM
TH-THMP
TH-THMP
PLEASE DON'T CROW.
DON'T CROW...

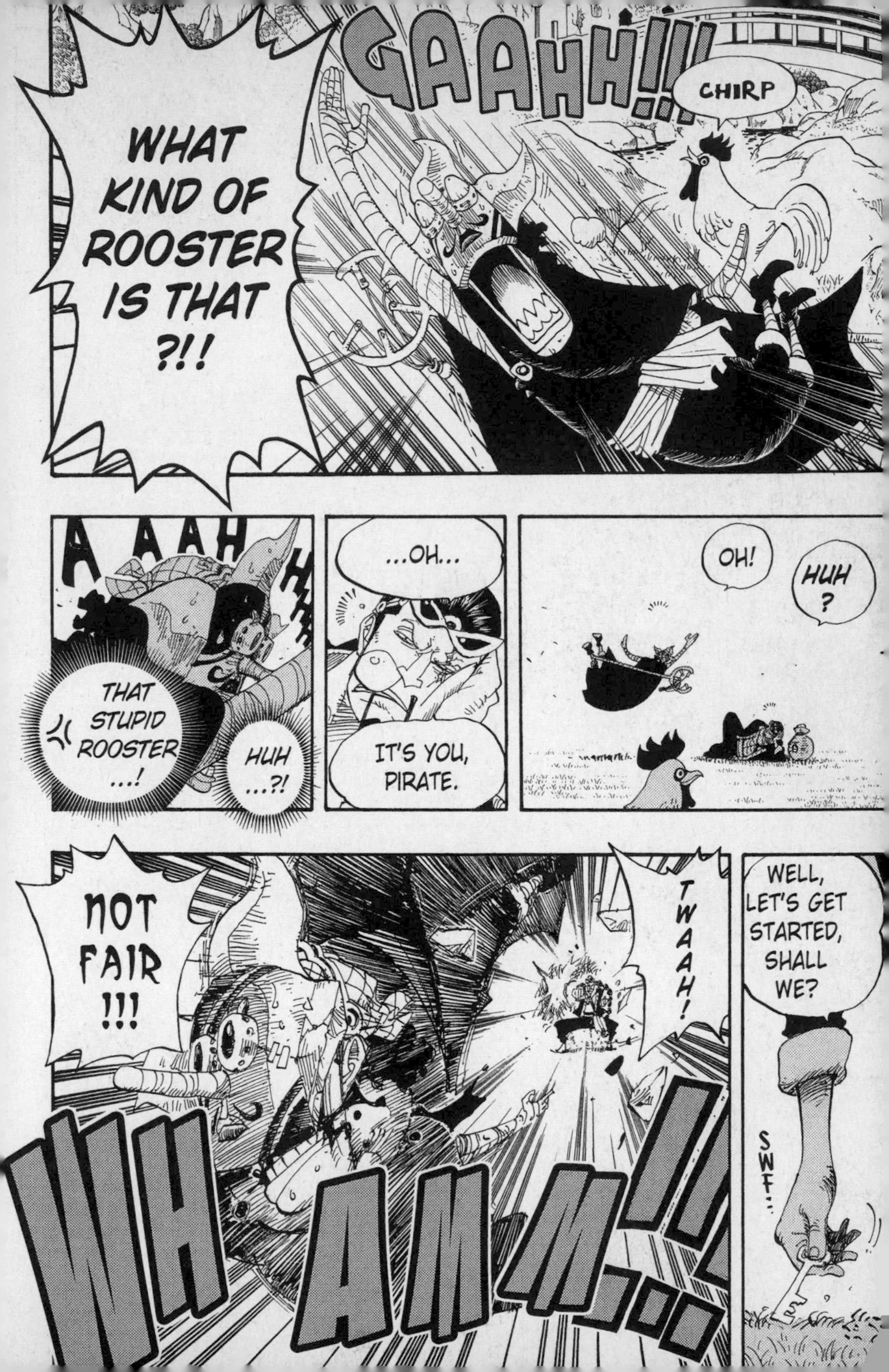
CHIRP
GAAHH!!!
WHAT KIND OF ROOSTER IS THAT ?!!
HUH ?
OH!
...OH...
IT'S YOU, PIRATE.
AAAHH
THAT STUPID ROOSTER ...!
HUH ...?!
WELL, LET'S GET STARTED, SHALL WE?
SWF...
TWAAH!
NOT FAIR !!!
WHAM...!!

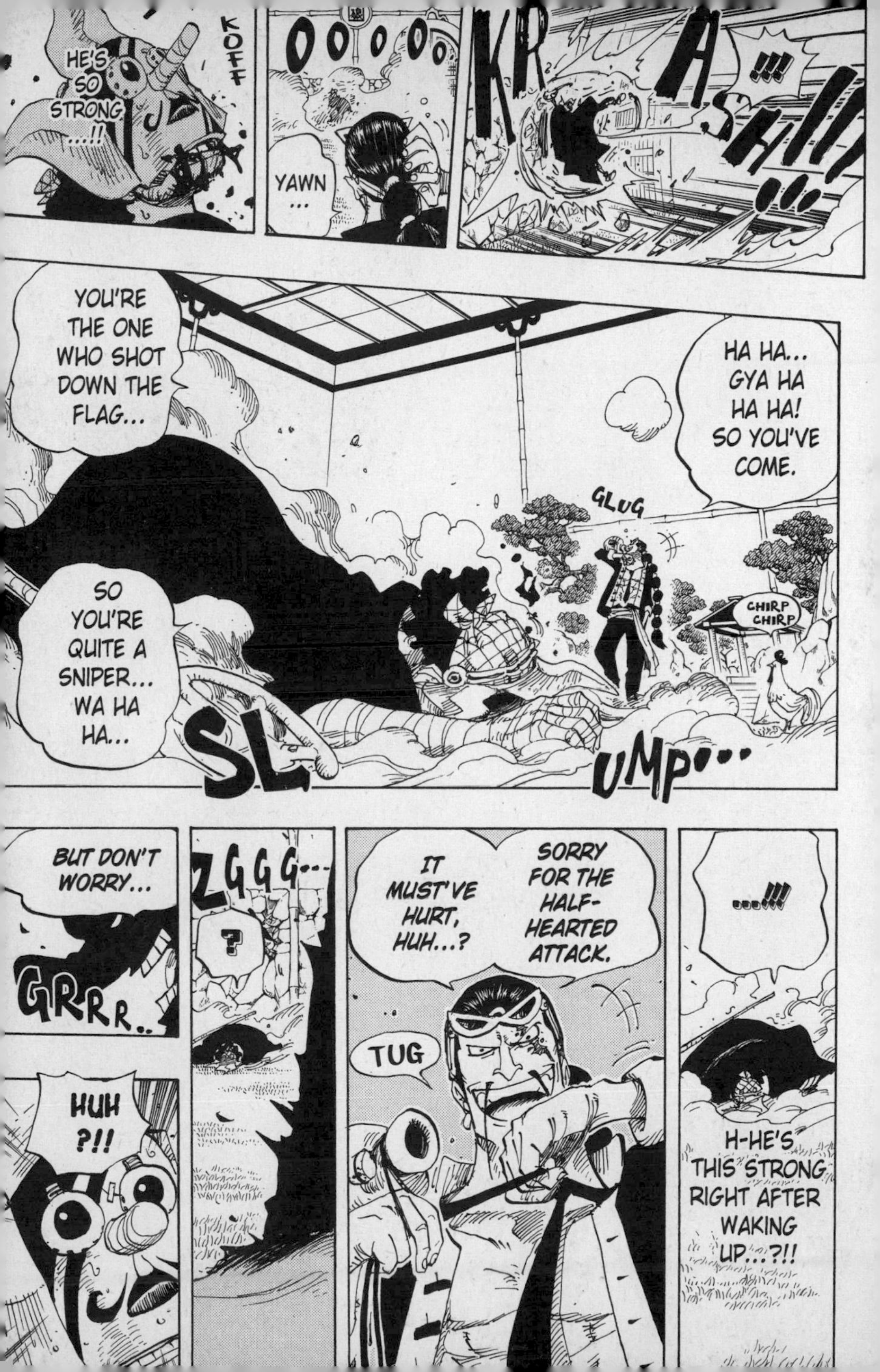
KRASH!!!
OOOOO
YAWN...
KOFF
HE'S SO STRONG...!!
HA HA... GYA HA HA HA! SO YOU'VE COME.
GLUG
CHIRP CHIRP
YOU'RE THE ONE WHO SHOT DOWN THE FLAG...
SO YOU'RE QUITE A SNIPER... WA HA HA...
SLUMP...
...!!!
H-HE'S THIS STRONG RIGHT AFTER WAKING UP...?!!
SORRY FOR THE HALF-HEARTED ATTACK.
IT MUST'VE HURT, HUH...?
TUG
ZGGG...
?
BUT DON'T WORRY...
GRRRR..
HUH ?!!

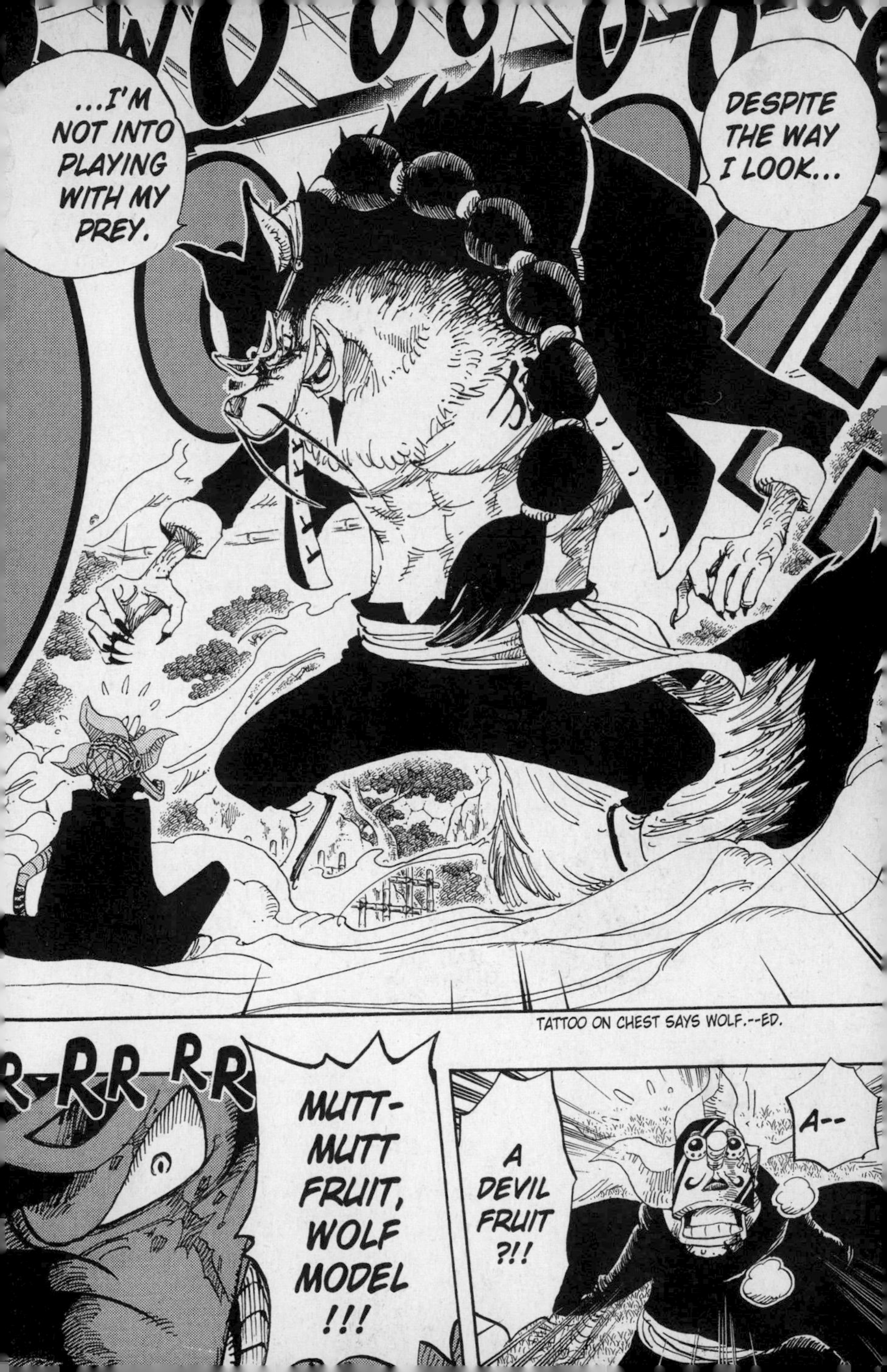
DESPITE THE WAY I LOOK...
...I'M NOT INTO PLAYING WITH MY PREY.
TATTOO ON CHEST SAYS WOLF.--ED.
A--
A DEVIL FRUIT ?!!
MUTT-MUTT FRUIT, WOLF MODEL !!!
R-RR-RR

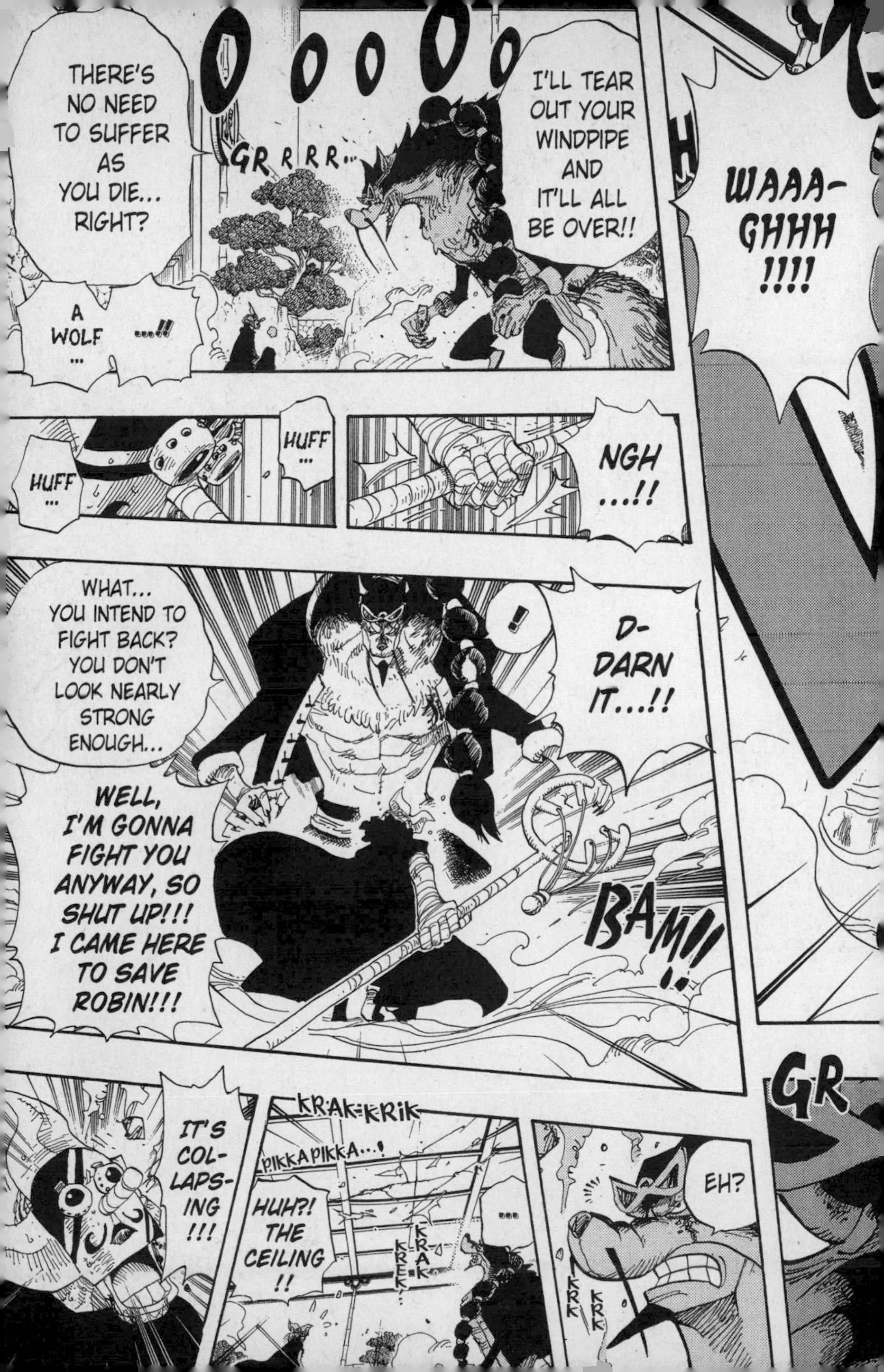
WAAA-GHHH!!!!
I'LL TEAR OUT YOUR WINDPIPE AND IT'LL ALL BE OVER!!
GRRRR...
THERE'S NO NEED TO SUFFER AS YOU DIE... RIGHT?
A WOLF ...
...!!
NGH ...!!
HUFF ...
HUFF ...
D-DARN IT...!!
!
WHAT... YOU INTEND TO FIGHT BACK? YOU DON'T LOOK NEARLY STRONG ENOUGH...
WELL, I'M GONNA FIGHT YOU ANYWAY, SO SHUT UP!!! I CAME HERE TO SAVE ROBIN!!!
BAM!!
GR
EH?
KRK KRK
KRAK-KRIK
PIKKA PIKKA...!
HUH?! THE CEILING!!
KREK KRAK
...
IT'S COL-LAPS-ING!!!

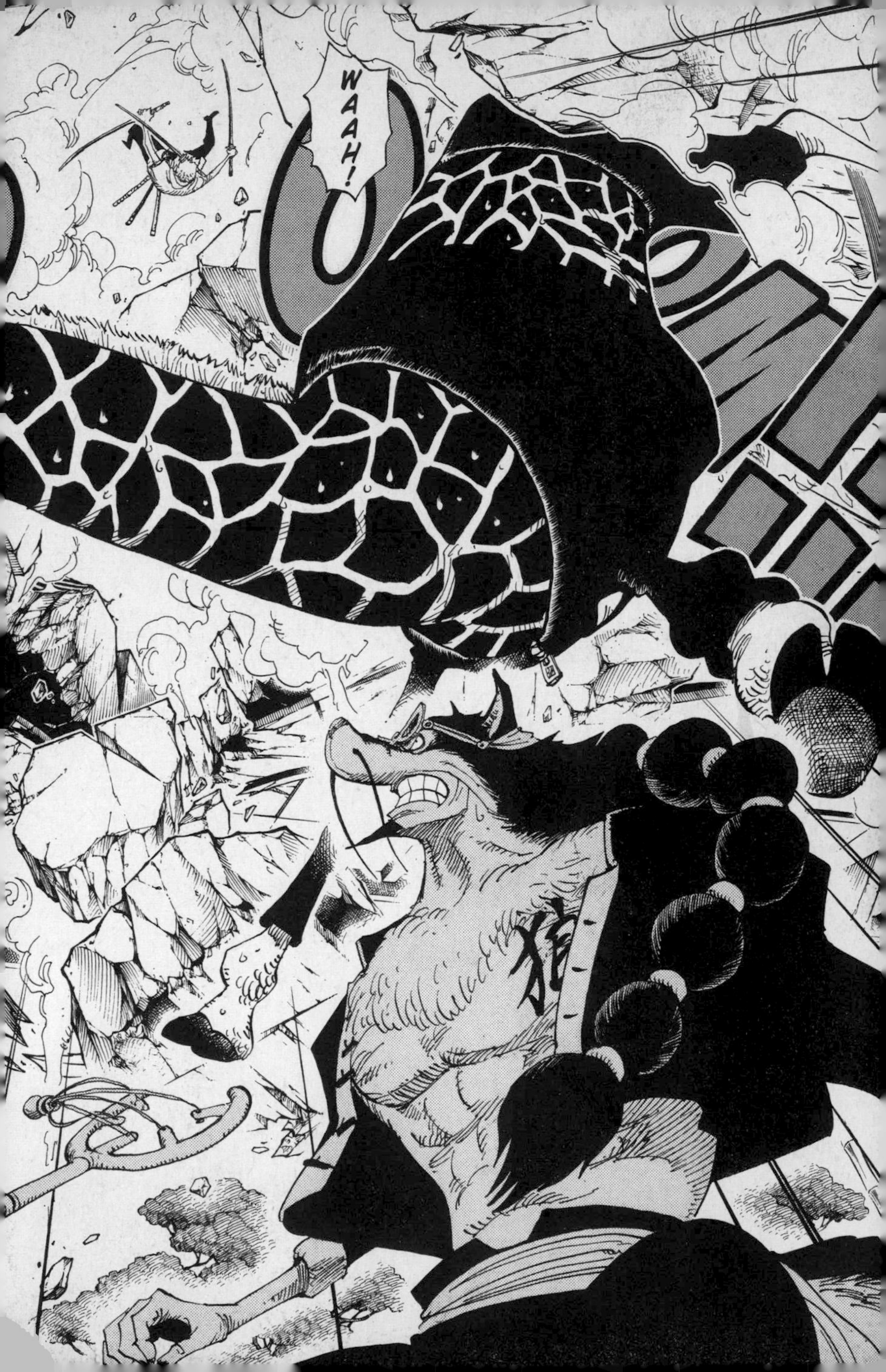
WAAH!

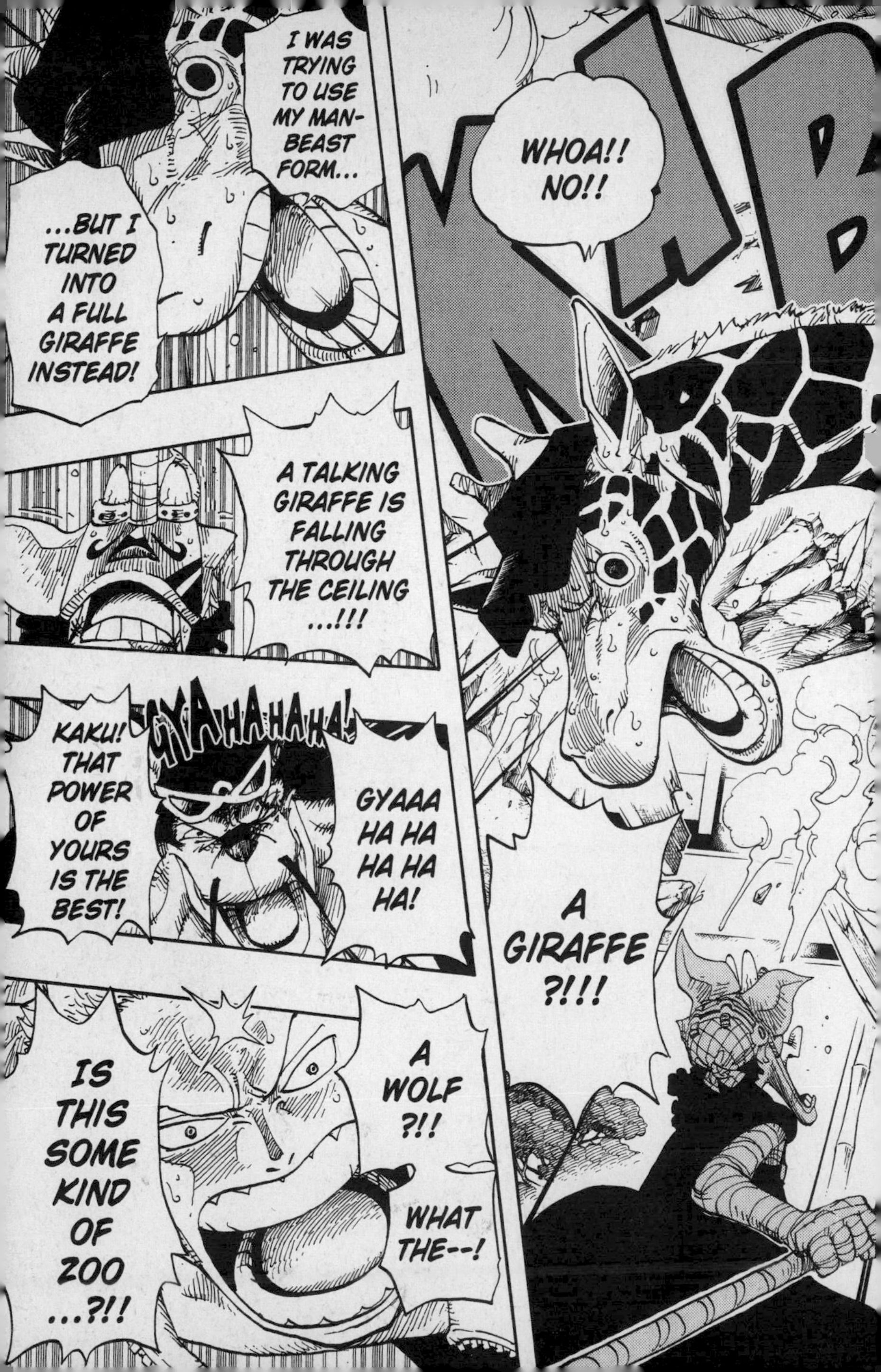
WHOA!! NO!!
A GIRAFFE ?!!!
I WAS TRYING TO USE MY MAN-BEAST FORM...
...BUT I TURNED INTO A FULL GIRAFFE INSTEAD!
A TALKING GIRAFFE IS FALLING THROUGH THE CEILING ...!!!
GYAAA HA HA HA HA HA!
GYAHAHAHAHA!
KAKU! THAT POWER OF YOURS IS THE BEST!
A WOLF ?!!
WHAT THE--!
IS THIS SOME KIND OF ZOO ...?!!

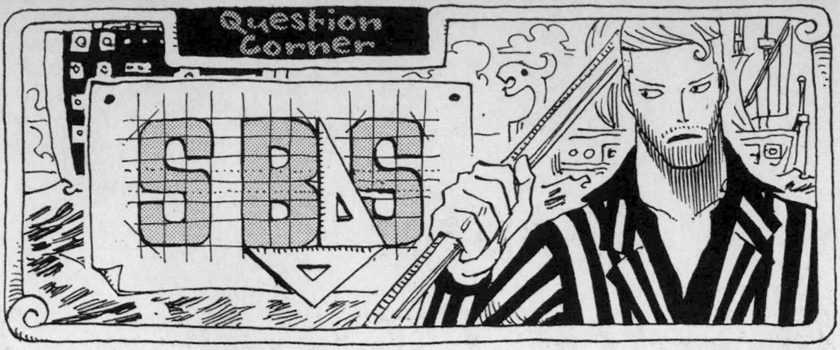
Question Corner
SBS

Reader: Otadata Sentaseita, hetallota. ♡ Ista thista hardta tota readta? Wellta, let'sta betaginta Questationta Corntaerta!!

--Tanuki ♡

Oda: What?! Tanuki?! I get it, this is written in "tanukese"! All right, let's try reading it without the "ta's"... "Hello, Oda Sensei. ♡ Is this hard to read? Well, let's begin Question Corner!!" How's that?! Anyway, ITS ALREADY BEGUN!

Q: Which is faster? Captain Kuro's "Cat-out-of-the-bag Attack" or CP9's "Shave"? Please tell me.

--Nikuou (Meat King)

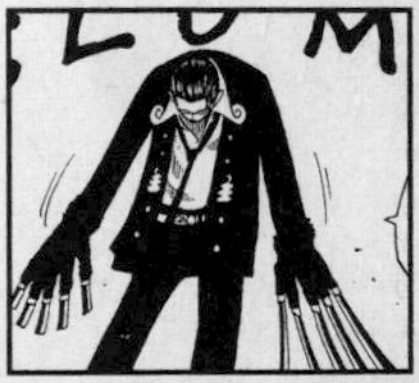

A: Yes, I received many questions about this. Captain Kuro's "Cat-out-of-the-Bag" (as seen in volume 5) was quite frightening. Speedwise, they're about the same. However, when Captain Kuro uses his technique, he's so fast he can't see who he's attacking, so that's his weakness. However, CP9 can control their speed and remain aware of their surroundings. For that reason, if they were in a battle, CP9 would win hands down.

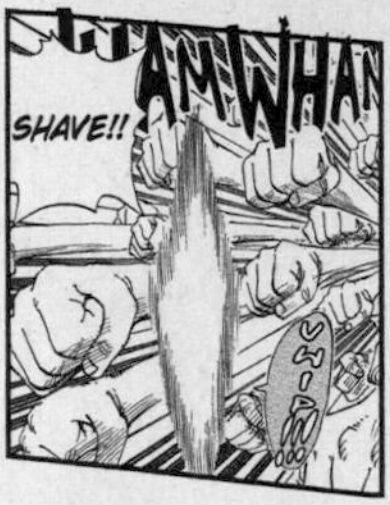
SHAVE!!

Q: Hello, Oda Sensei!! In volume 38, you said that when answers don't come to you during a test to write the word "instrumental." So I really tried it. But when I got my test back, the answers were marked wrong. Why were they marked wrong? Please tell me, Oda Sensei!

--Katsufumi Four!!

A: The test results are not the point. The courage of doing it is its own reward. (<-- ?)

Chapter 402:
HANDCUFFS No. 2

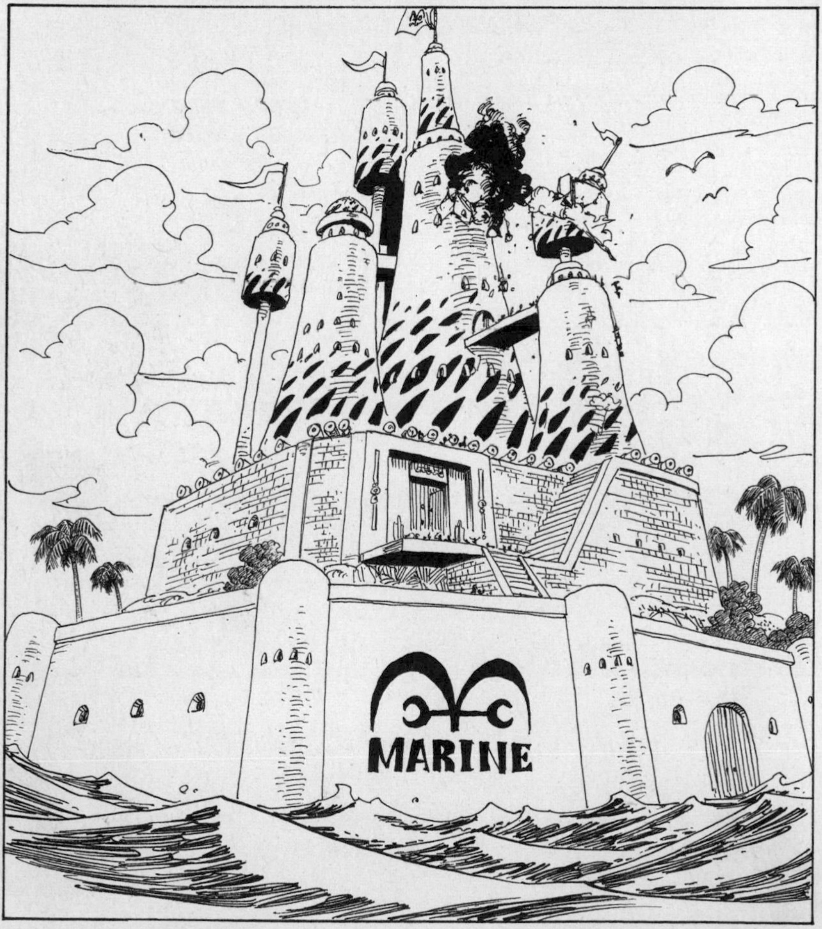
MARINE

MS. GOLDEN WEEK'S PLAN, A BAROQUE REUNION, VOL. 33:
"SIX PRISONERS+DOG MAKE THEIR ESCAPE"

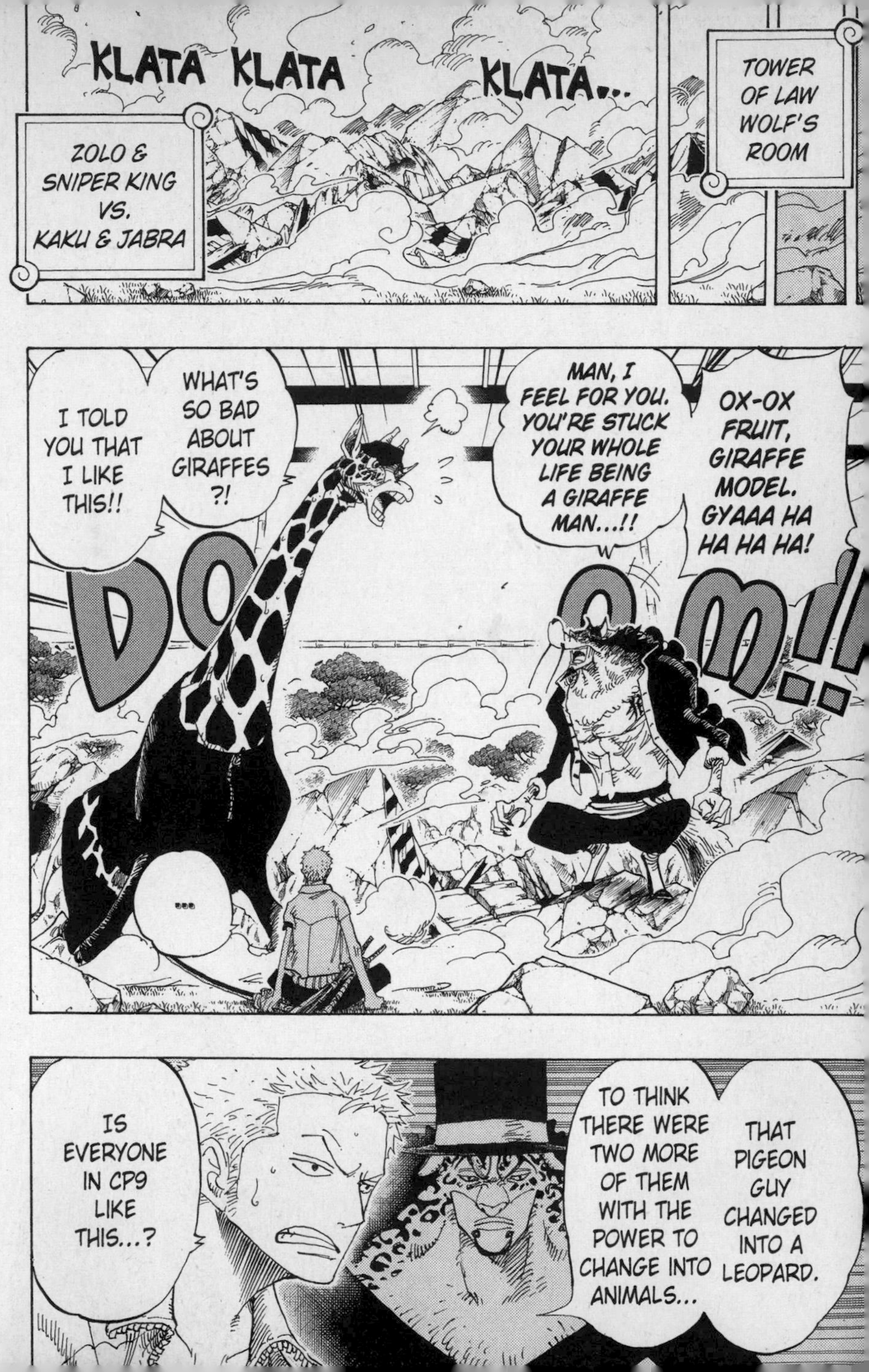
TOWER OF LAW WOLF'S ROOM
KLATA KLATA KLATA...
ZOLO & SNIPER KING VS. KAKU & JABRA
OX-OX FRUIT, GIRAFFE MODEL. GYAAA HA HA HA HA!
MAN, I FEEL FOR YOU. YOU'RE STUCK YOUR WHOLE LIFE BEING A GIRAFFE MAN...!!
DOOM!!
WHAT'S SO BAD ABOUT GIRAFFES ?!
I TOLD YOU THAT I LIKE THIS!!
...
THAT PIGEON GUY CHANGED INTO A LEOPARD.
TO THINK THERE WERE TWO MORE OF THEM WITH THE POWER TO CHANGE INTO ANIMALS...
IS EVERYONE IN CP9 LIKE THIS...?

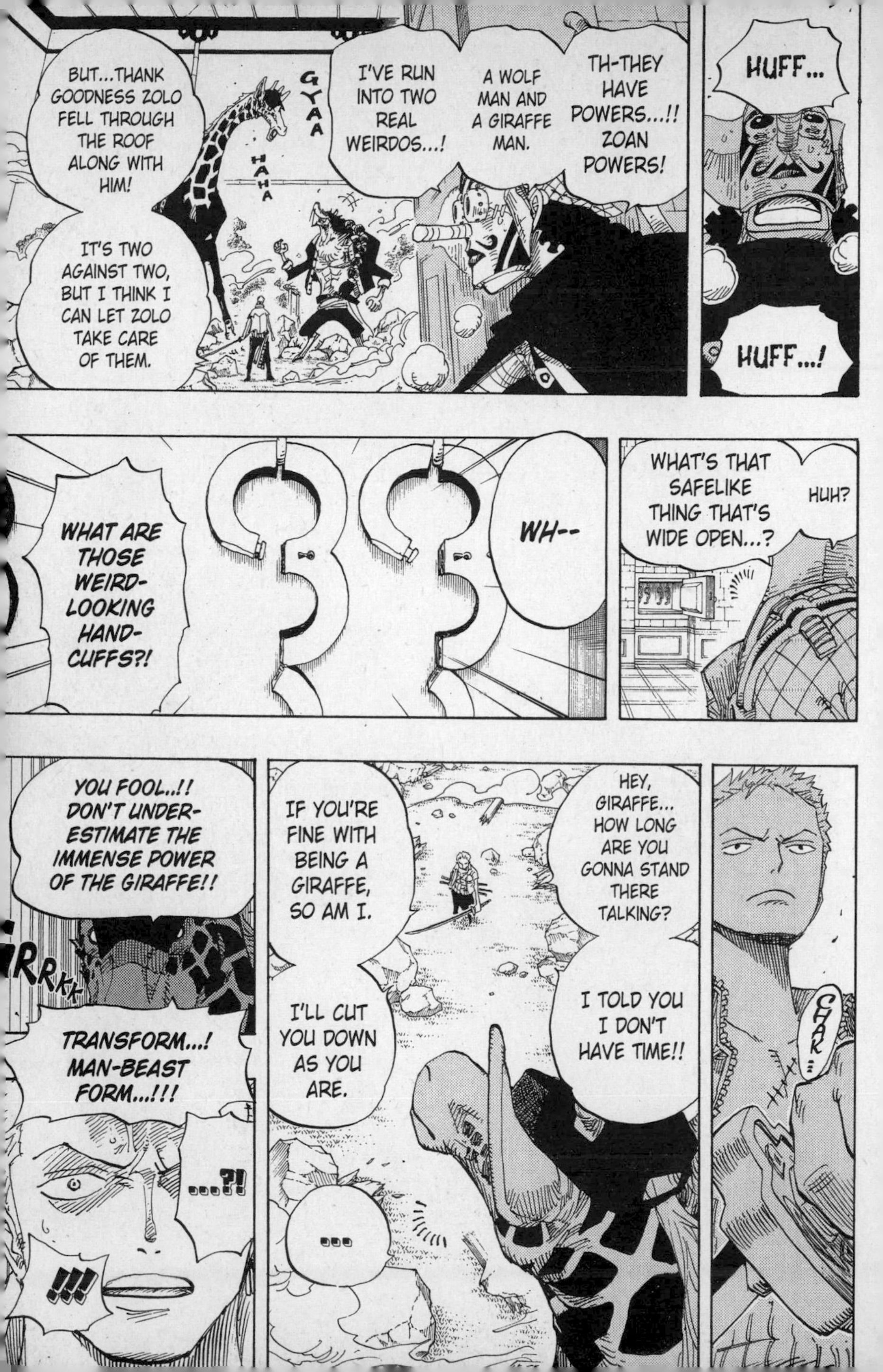
HUFF...
HUFF...!
TH-THEY HAVE POWERS...!! ZOAN POWERS!
A WOLF MAN AND A GIRAFFE MAN.
I'VE RUN INTO TWO REAL WEIRDOS...!
GYAA
HAHA
BUT...THANK GOODNESS ZOLO FELL THROUGH THE ROOF ALONG WITH HIM!
IT'S TWO AGAINST TWO, BUT I THINK I CAN LET ZOLO TAKE CARE OF THEM.
HUH?
WHAT'S THAT SAFELIKE THING THAT'S WIDE OPEN...?
WH--
WHAT ARE THOSE WEIRD-LOOKING HANDCUFFS?!
CHAK...
HEY, GIRAFFE... HOW LONG ARE YOU GONNA STAND THERE TALKING?
I TOLD YOU I DON'T HAVE TIME!!
IF YOU'RE FINE WITH BEING A GIRAFFE, SO AM I.
I'LL CUT YOU DOWN AS YOU ARE.
...
YOU FOOL..!! DON'T UNDER-ESTIMATE THE IMMENSE POWER OF THE GIRAFFE!!
RRRKK
TRANSFORM...! MAN-BEAST FORM...!!!
...?!
!!!

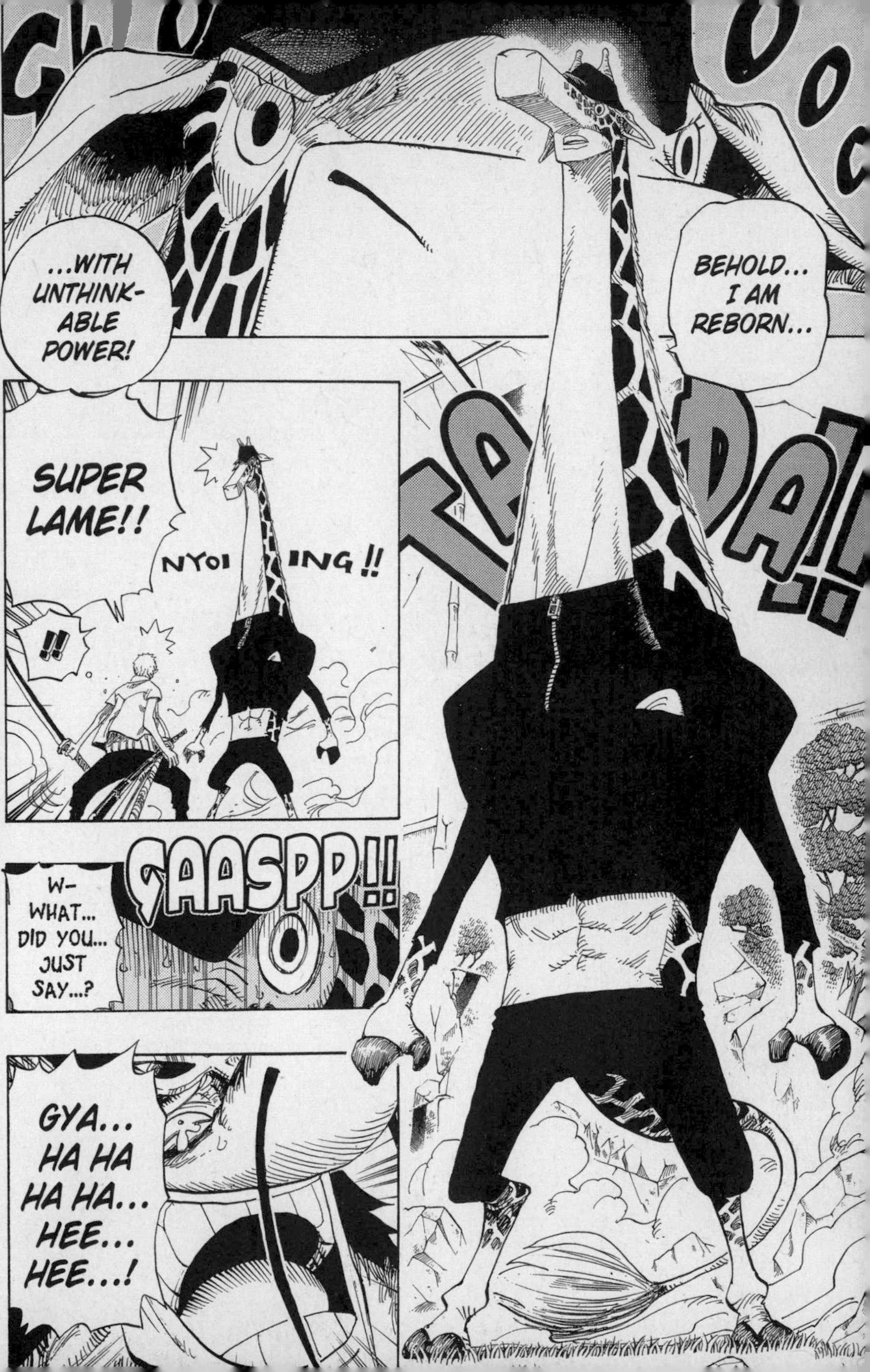
GWOOOO
BEHOLD... I AM REBORN...
...WITH UNTHINKABLE POWER!
TA DA!!
SUPER LAME!!
NYOI ING!!
!!
GAASPP!!
W-WHAT... DID YOU... JUST SAY...?
GYA... HA HA HA HA... HEE... HEE...!

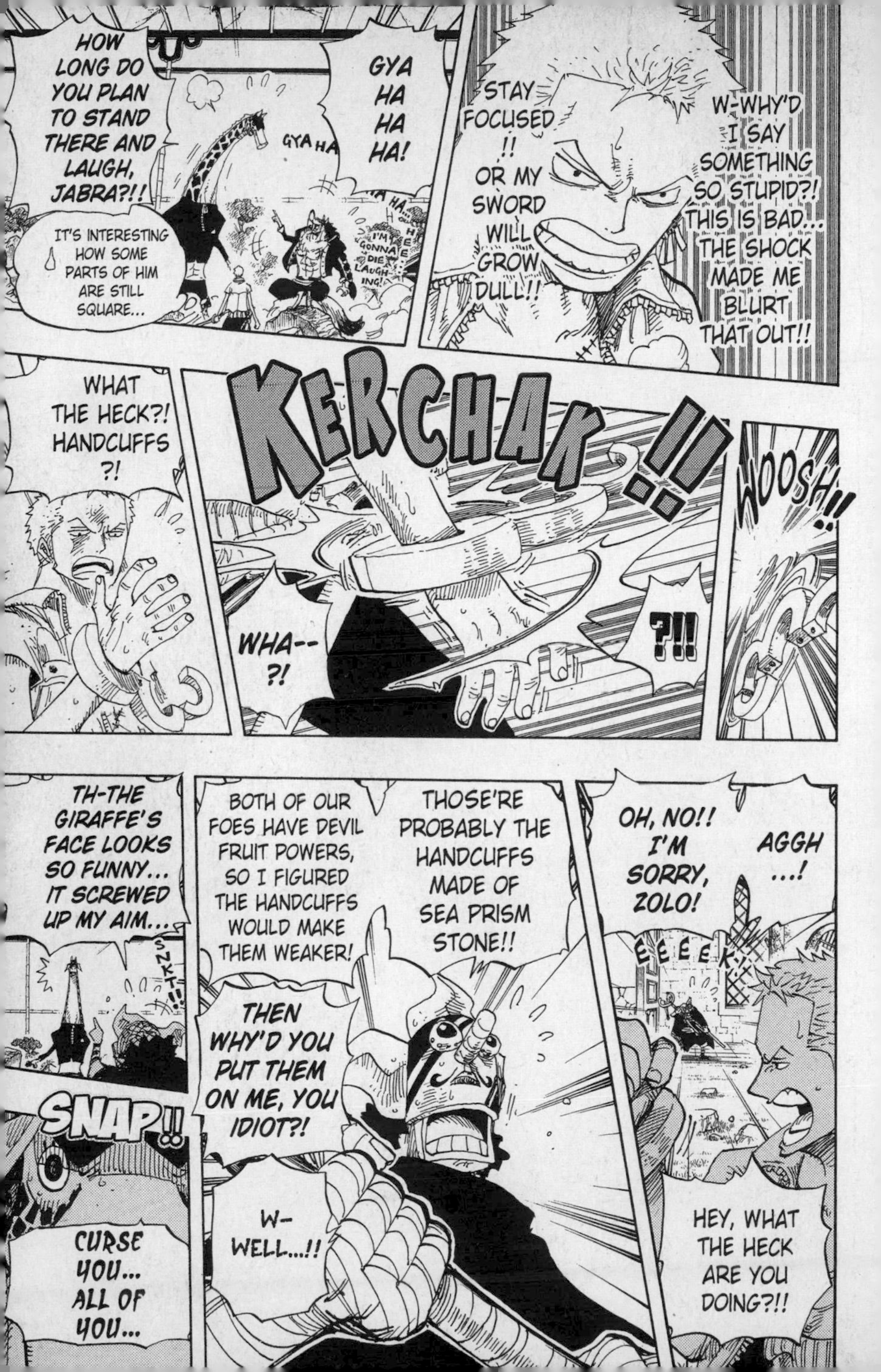
STAY FOCUSED!! OR MY SWORD WILL GROW DULL!!
W-WHY'D I SAY SOMETHING SO STUPID?! THIS IS BAD... THE SHOCK MADE ME BLURT THAT OUT!!
GYA HA HA HA!
GYA HA
HA HA
I'M GONNA DIE LAUGH-ING!
HOW LONG DO YOU PLAN TO STAND THERE AND LAUGH, JABRA?!!
IT'S INTERESTING HOW SOME PARTS OF HIM ARE STILL SQUARE...
WOOSH!!
KERCHAK!!
?!!
WHA-- ?!
WHAT THE HECK?! HANDCUFFS ?!
OH, NO!! I'M SORRY, ZOLO!
AGGH ...!
EEEEEK!!
HEY, WHAT THE HECK ARE YOU DOING?!!
THOSE'RE PROBABLY THE HANDCUFFS MADE OF SEA PRISM STONE!!
BOTH OF OUR FOES HAVE DEVIL FRUIT POWERS, SO I FIGURED THE HANDCUFFS WOULD MAKE THEM WEAKER!
THEN WHY'D YOU PUT THEM ON ME, YOU IDIOT?!
W-WELL...!!
TH-THE GIRAFFE'S FACE LOOKS SO FUNNY... IT SCREWED UP MY AIM...
SNKT!!
SNAP!!
CURSE YOU... ALL OF YOU...

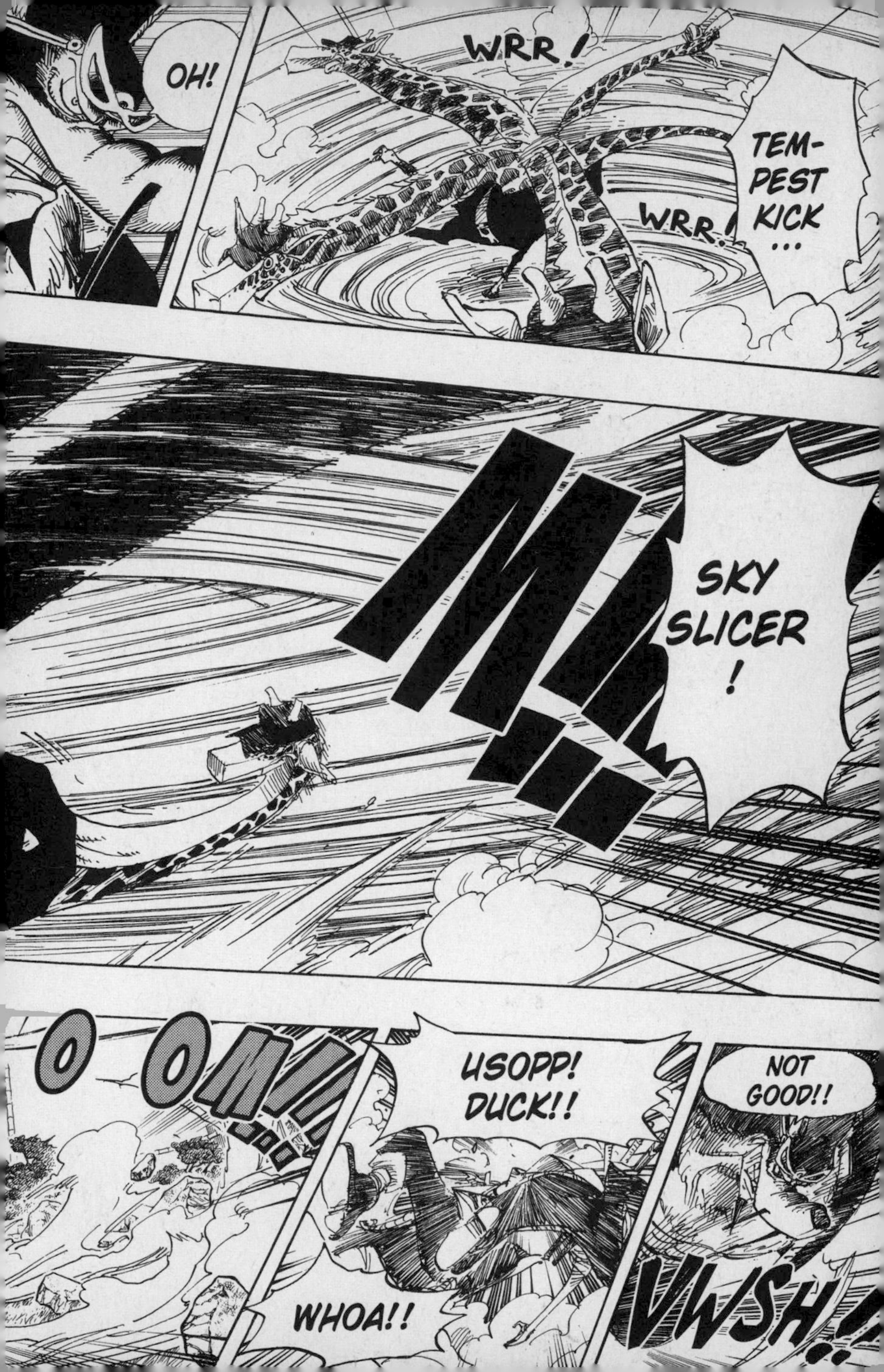
TEM-
PEST
KICK
...
WRR!
WRR.
OH!
SKY
SLICER
!
NOT
GOOD!!
VWSH!!
USOPP!
DUCK!!
WHOA!!

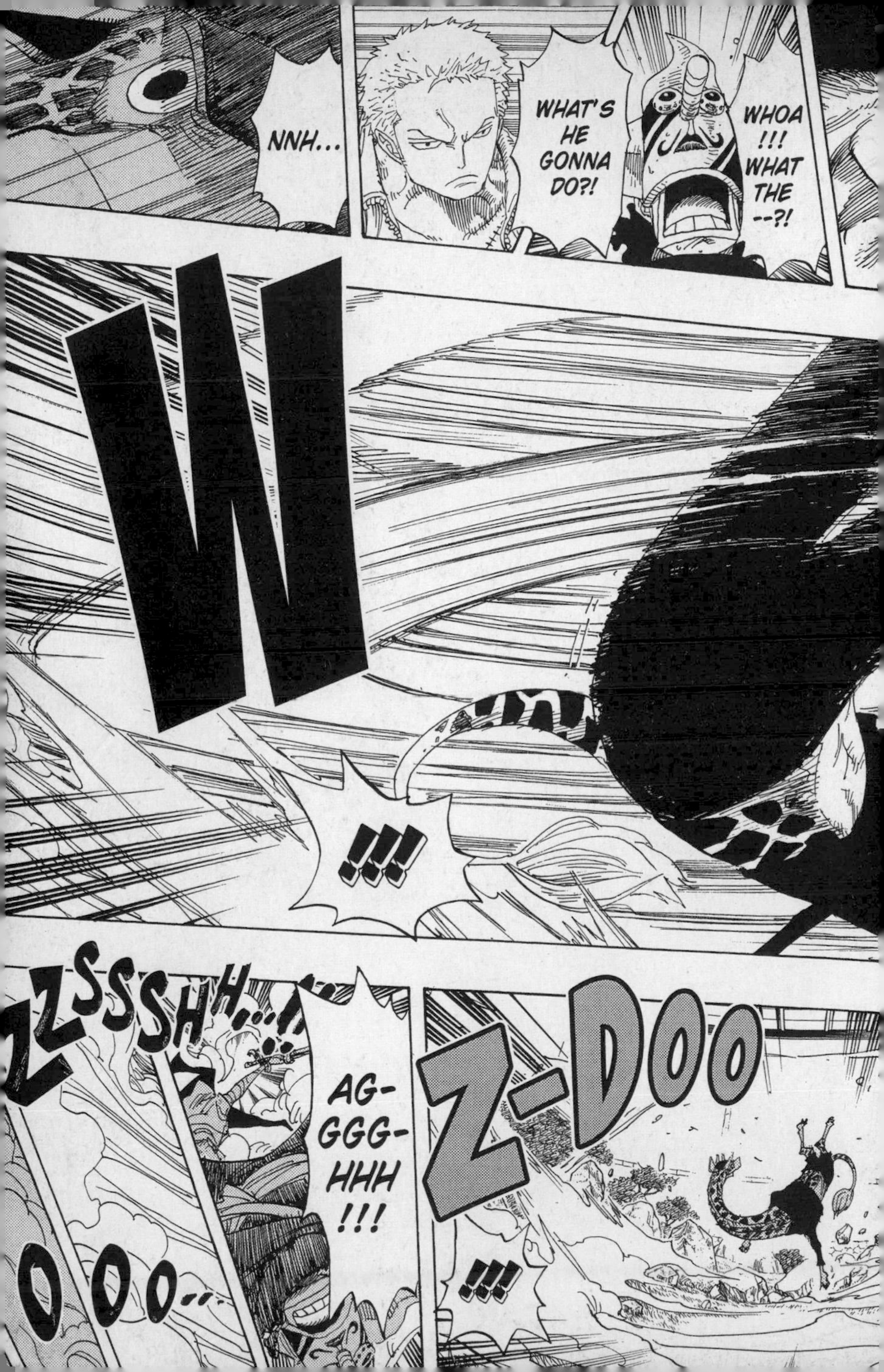
WHOA!!! WHAT THE --?!
WHAT'S HE GONNA DO?!
NNH...
W
!!!
Z-DOO
!!!
AG-GGG-HHH!!!
ZZSSSSH...!!
O O O..

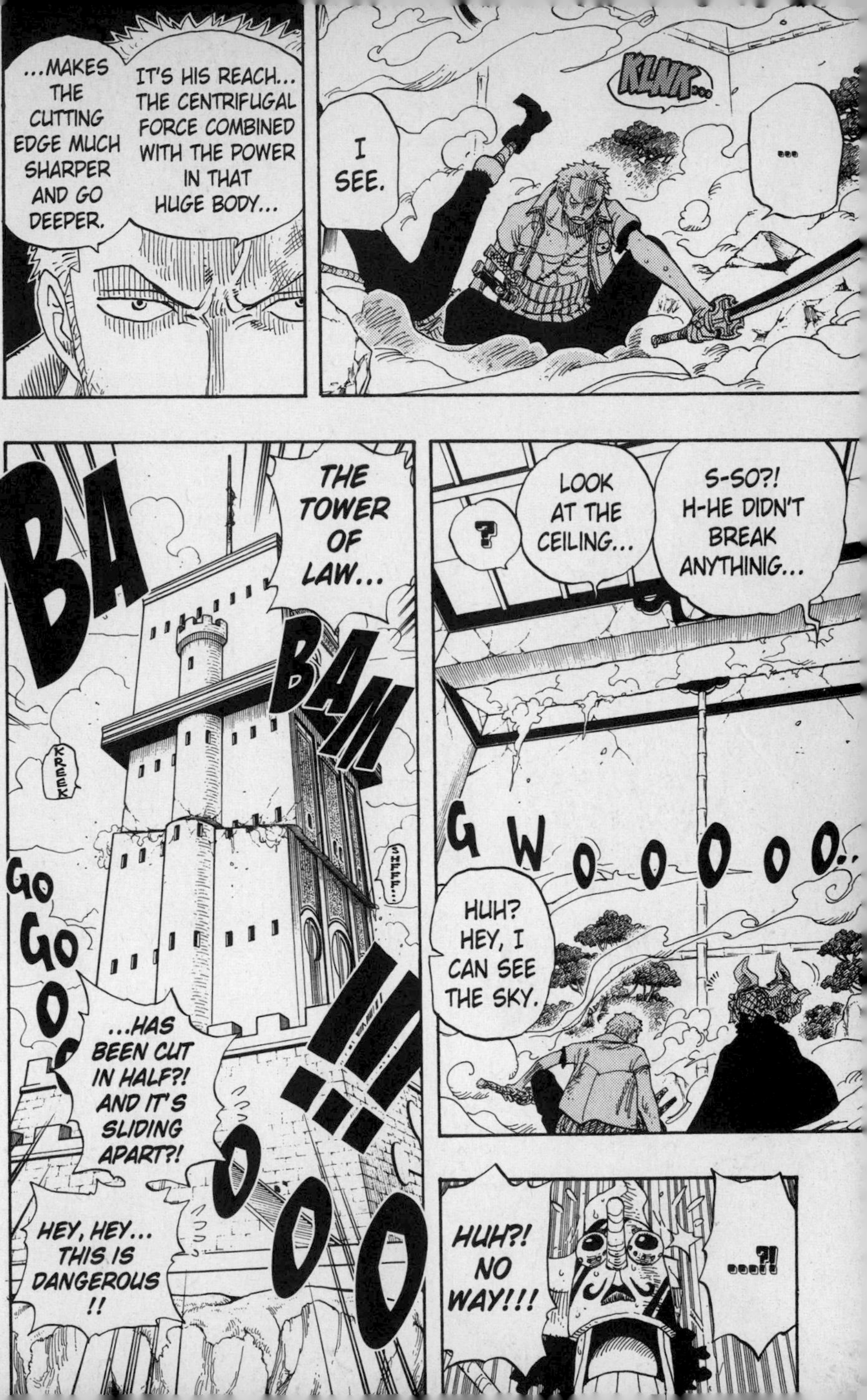
...
KLUNK...
I SEE.
IT'S HIS REACH... THE CENTRIFUGAL FORCE COMBINED WITH THE POWER IN THAT HUGE BODY...
...MAKES THE CUTTING EDGE MUCH SHARPER AND GO DEEPER.
S-SO?! H-HE DIDN'T BREAK ANYTHINIG...
LOOK AT THE CEILING...
?
GWOOOOO...
HUH? HEY, I CAN SEE THE SKY.
...?!
HUH?! NO WAY!!!
THE TOWER OF LAW...
BA
BAM
KREEK
SHFFF...
...HAS BEEN CUT IN HALF?! AND IT'S SLIDING APART?!
!!!
GO GO GO
OOO
HEY, HEY... THIS IS DANGEROUS !!

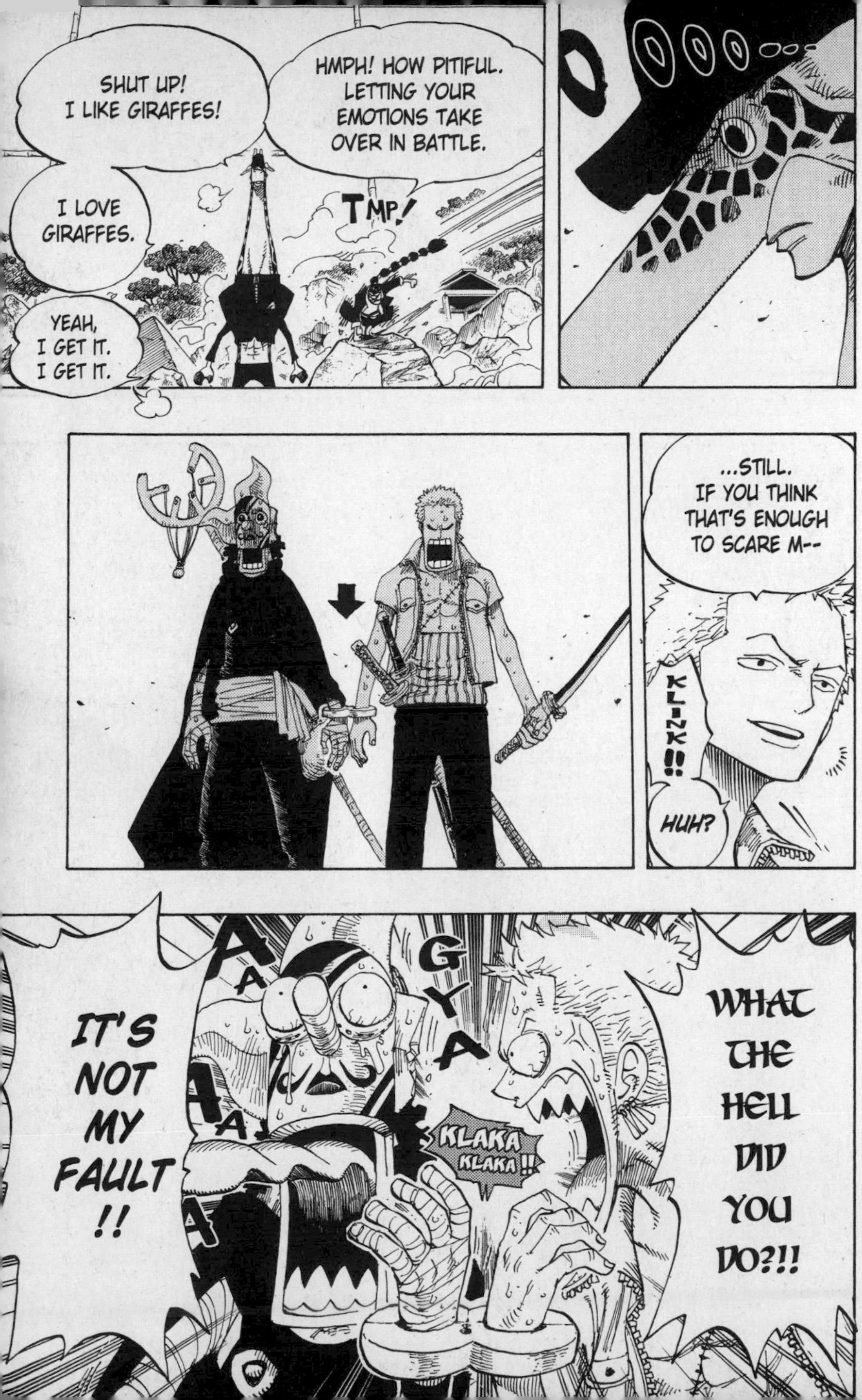
HMPH! HOW PITIFUL. LETTING YOUR EMOTIONS TAKE OVER IN BATTLE.
TMP!
SHUT UP! I LIKE GIRAFFES!
I LOVE GIRAFFES.
YEAH, I GET IT. I GET IT.
...STILL. IF YOU THINK THAT'S ENOUGH TO SCARE M--
KLINK!!
HUH?
WHAT THE HELL DID YOU DO?!!
GYA
KLAKA KLAKA!!
AAAAA
IT'S NOT MY FAULT!!

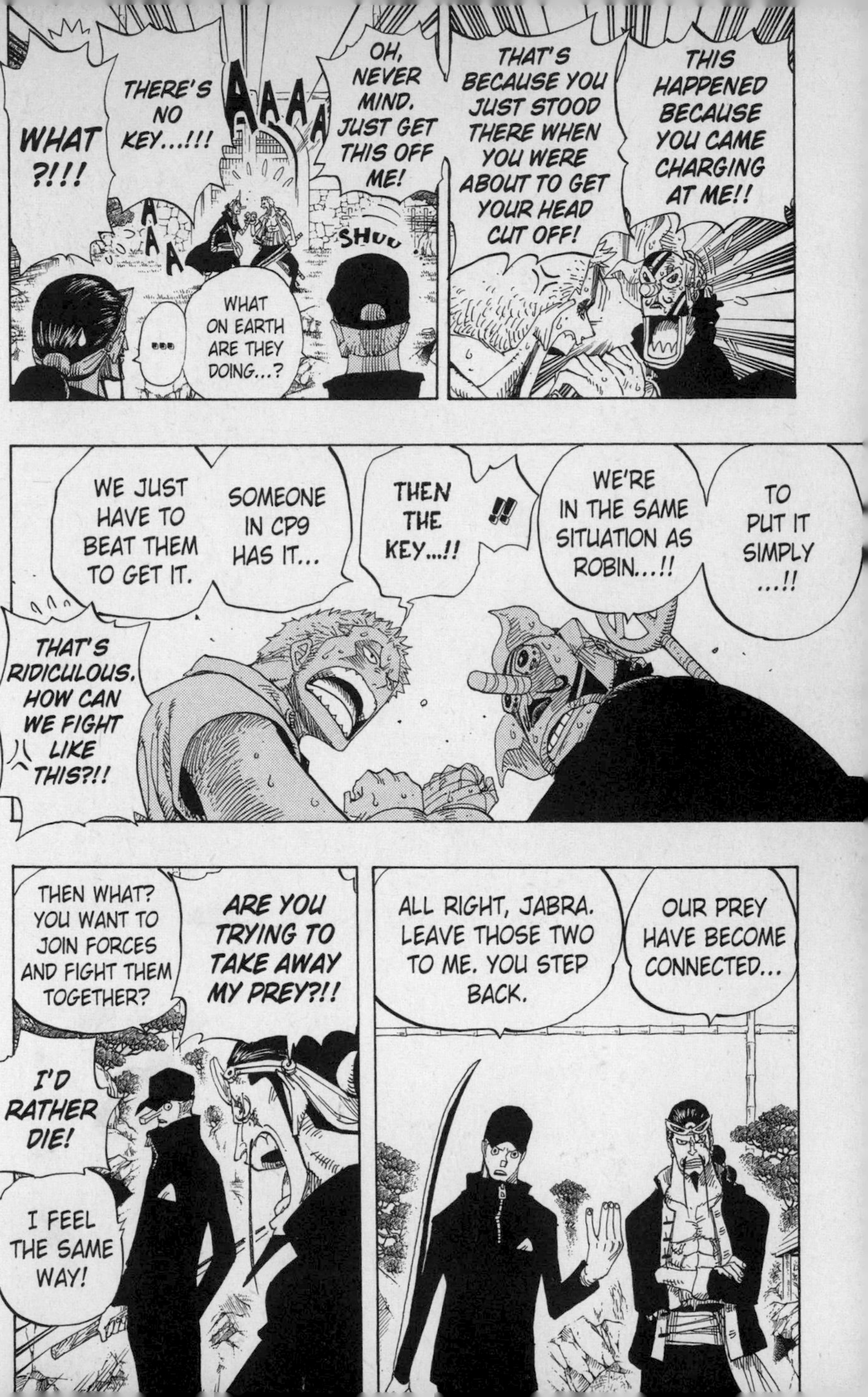

THIS HAPPENED BECAUSE YOU CAME CHARGING AT ME!!
THAT'S BECAUSE YOU JUST STOOD THERE WHEN YOU WERE ABOUT TO GET YOUR HEAD CUT OFF!
OH, NEVER MIND. JUST GET THIS OFF ME!
AAAA
THERE'S NO KEY...!!!
WHAT ?!!!
AAA
SHUU
WHAT ON EARTH ARE THEY DOING...?
...
TO PUT IT SIMPLY...!!
WE'RE IN THE SAME SITUATION AS ROBIN...!!
!!
THEN THE KEY...!!
SOMEONE IN CP9 HAS IT...
WE JUST HAVE TO BEAT THEM TO GET IT.
THAT'S RIDICULOUS. HOW CAN WE FIGHT LIKE THIS?!!
OUR PREY HAVE BECOME CONNECTED...
ALL RIGHT, JABRA. LEAVE THOSE TWO TO ME. YOU STEP BACK.
ARE YOU TRYING TO TAKE AWAY MY PREY?!!
THEN WHAT? YOU WANT TO JOIN FORCES AND FIGHT THEM TOGETHER?
I'D RATHER DIE!
I FEEL THE SAME WAY!

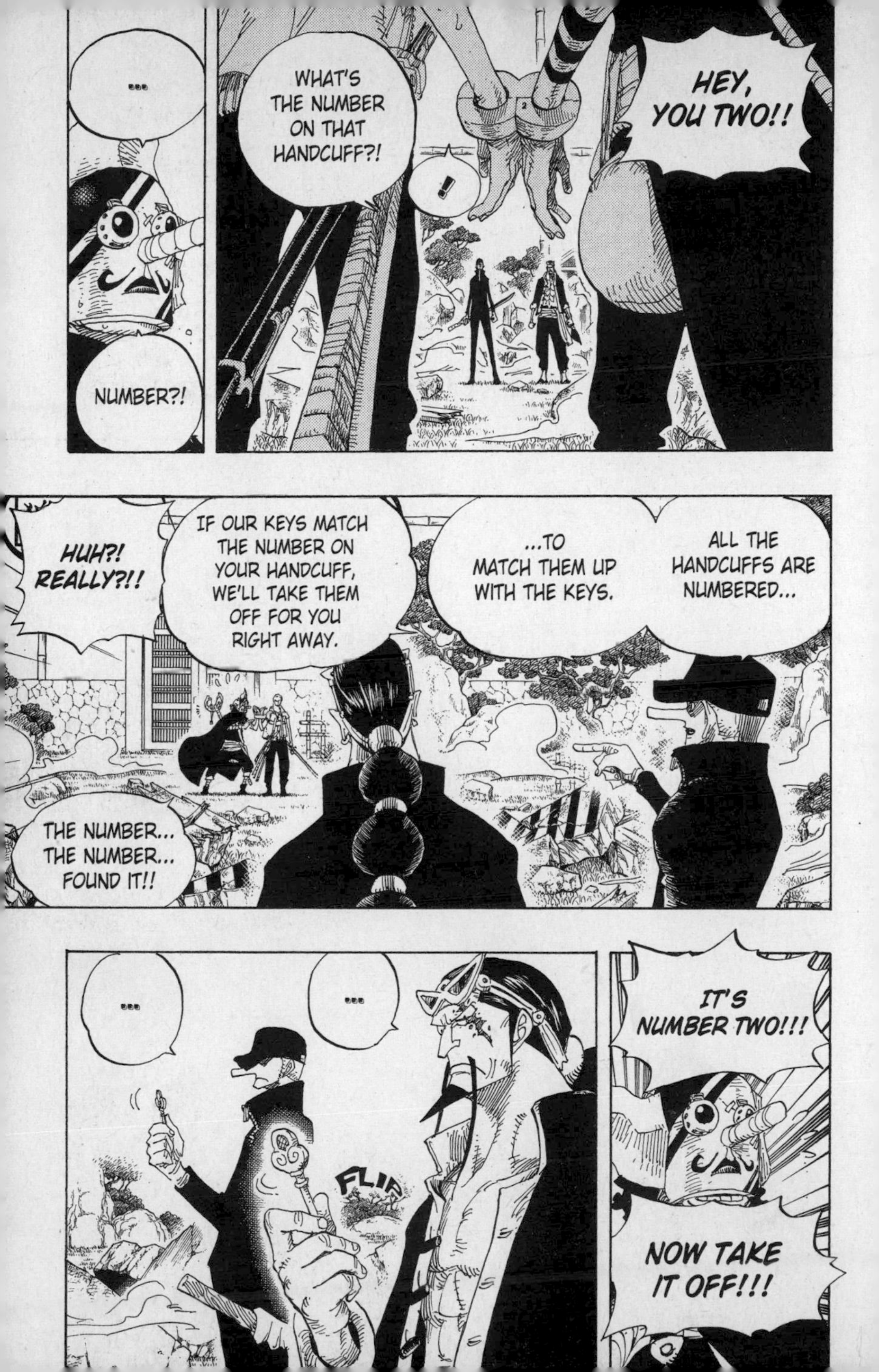
HEY, YOU TWO!!
WHAT'S THE NUMBER ON THAT HANDCUFF?!
!
...
NUMBER?!
ALL THE HANDCUFFS ARE NUMBERED...
...TO MATCH THEM UP WITH THE KEYS.
IF OUR KEYS MATCH THE NUMBER ON YOUR HANDCUFF, WE'LL TAKE THEM OFF FOR YOU RIGHT AWAY.
HUH?! REALLY?!!
THE NUMBER... THE NUMBER... FOUND IT!!
IT'S NUMBER TWO!!!
NOW TAKE IT OFF!!!
...
...
FLIP

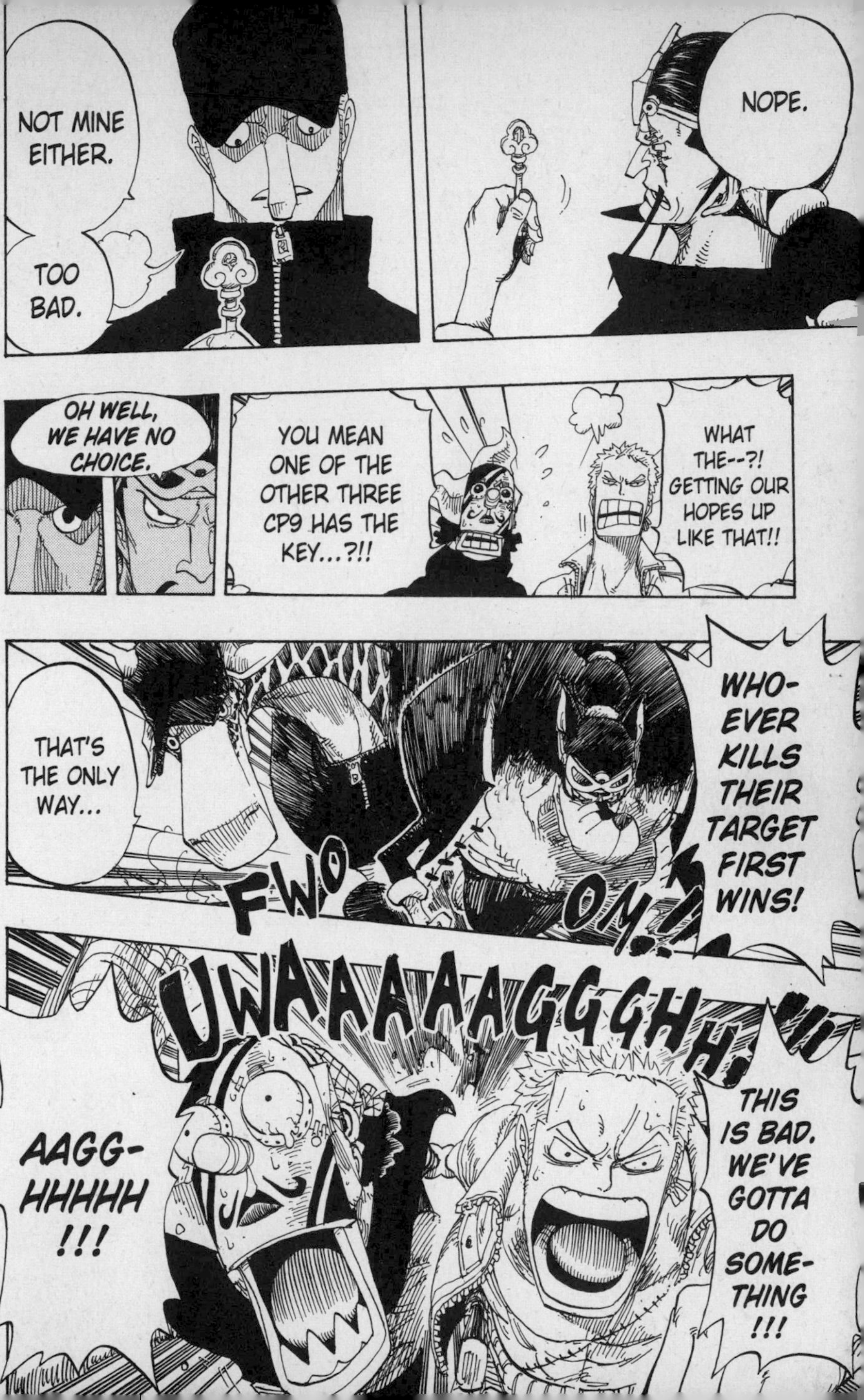
NOPE.
NOT MINE EITHER.
TOO BAD.
WHAT THE--?! GETTING OUR HOPES UP LIKE THAT!!
YOU MEAN ONE OF THE OTHER THREE CP9 HAS THE KEY...?!!
OH WELL, WE HAVE NO CHOICE.
WHO-EVER KILLS THEIR TARGET FIRST WINS!
THAT'S THE ONLY WAY...
FWOOM!!
UWAAAAAAGGGHH!!
THIS IS BAD. WE'VE GOTTA DO SOME-THING!!!
AAGG-HHHHH!!!

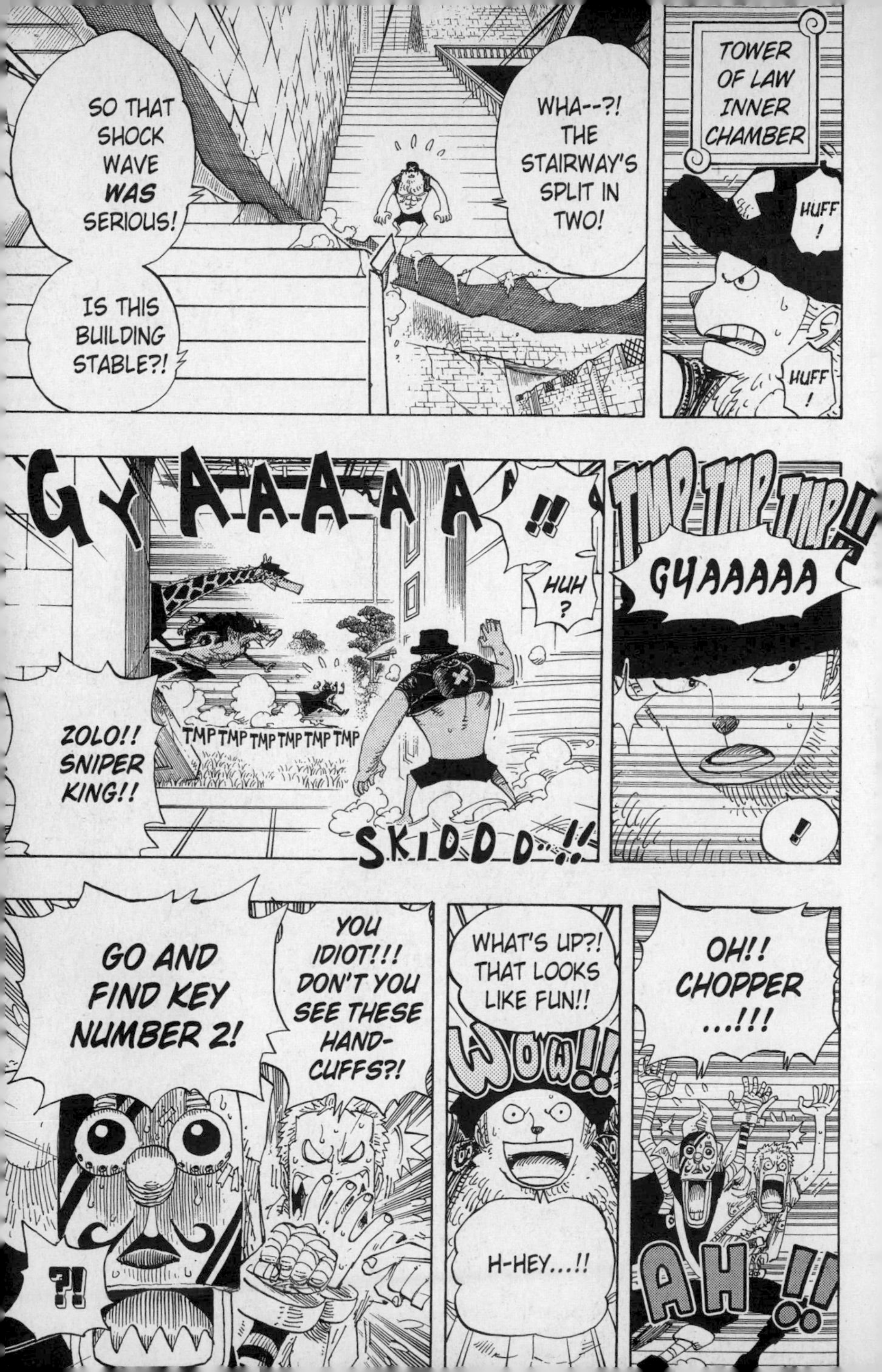
TOWER OF LAW INNER CHAMBER
HUFF!
HUFF!
WHA--?! THE STAIRWAY'S SPLIT IN TWO!
SO THAT SHOCK WAVE WAS SERIOUS!
IS THIS BUILDING STABLE?!
TMP TMP TMP!!
GYAAAAA
!
GYAAAAAA!!
HUH?
ZOLO!! SNIPER KING!!
TMP TMP TMP TMP TMP TMP
SKIDDD..!!
OH!! CHOPPER ...!!!
AH!!
WHAT'S UP?! THAT LOOKS LIKE FUN!!
WOW!!
H-HEY...!!
YOU IDIOT!!! DON'T YOU SEE THESE HAND-CUFFS?!
GO AND FIND KEY NUMBER 2!
?!

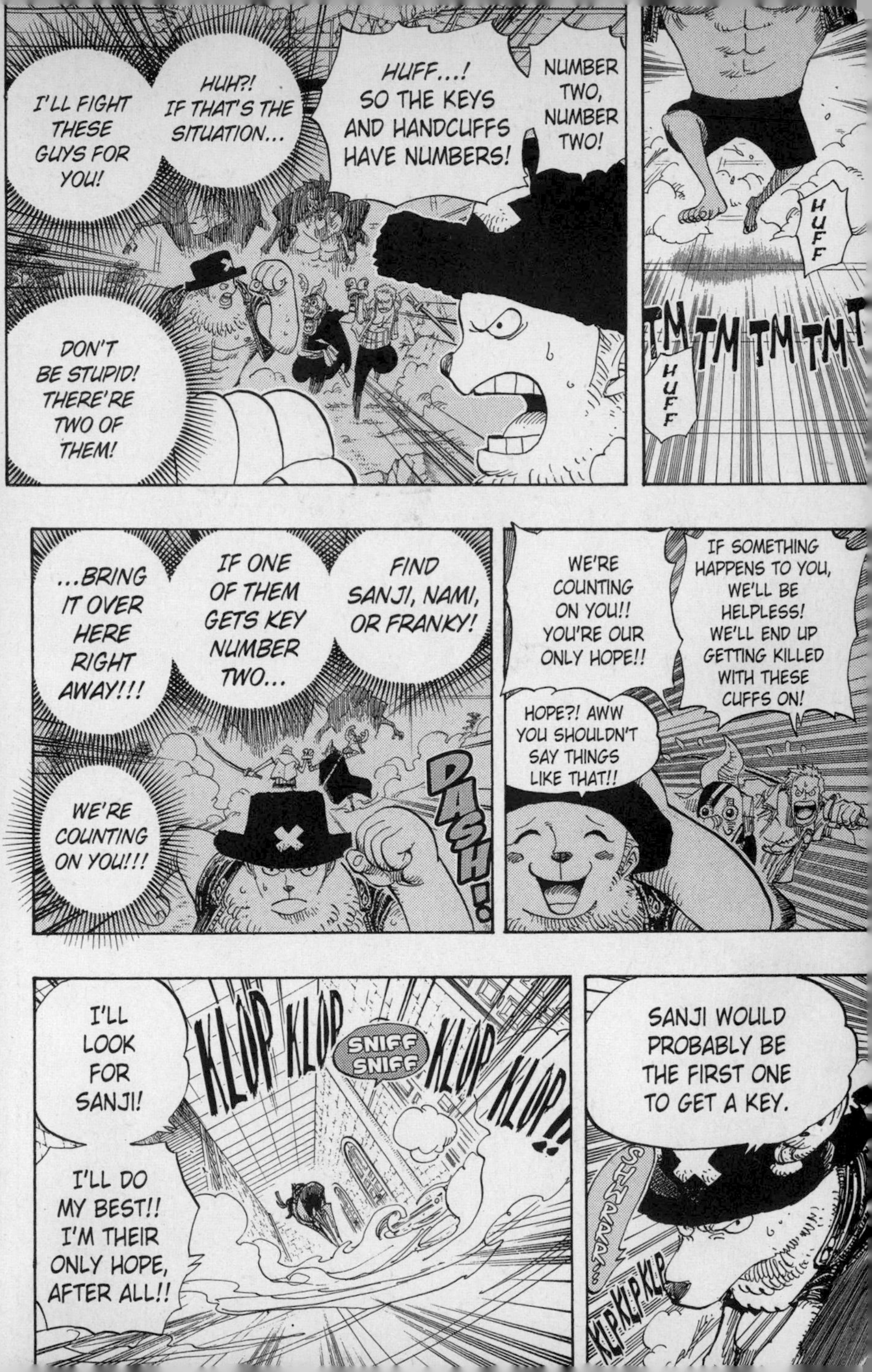
HUFF HUFF
TM TM TM TM
HUFF
NUMBER TWO, NUMBER TWO!
HUFF...! SO THE KEYS AND HANDCUFFS HAVE NUMBERS!
HUH?! IF THAT'S THE SITUATION...
I'LL FIGHT THESE GUYS FOR YOU!
DON'T BE STUPID! THERE'RE TWO OF THEM!
IF SOMETHING HAPPENS TO YOU, WE'LL BE HELPLESS! WE'LL END UP GETTING KILLED WITH THESE CUFFS ON!
WE'RE COUNTING ON YOU!! YOU'RE OUR ONLY HOPE!!
HOPE?! AWW YOU SHOULDN'T SAY THINGS LIKE THAT!!
FIND SANJI, NAMI, OR FRANKY!
IF ONE OF THEM GETS KEY NUMBER TWO...
...BRING IT OVER HERE RIGHT AWAY!!!
DASH!!
WE'RE COUNTING ON YOU!!!
SANJI WOULD PROBABLY BE THE FIRST ONE TO GET A KEY.
KLP KLP KLP
KLOP KLOP KLOP KLOP!!
SNIFF SNIFF
I'LL LOOK FOR SANJI!
I'LL DO MY BEST!! I'M THEIR ONLY HOPE, AFTER ALL!!

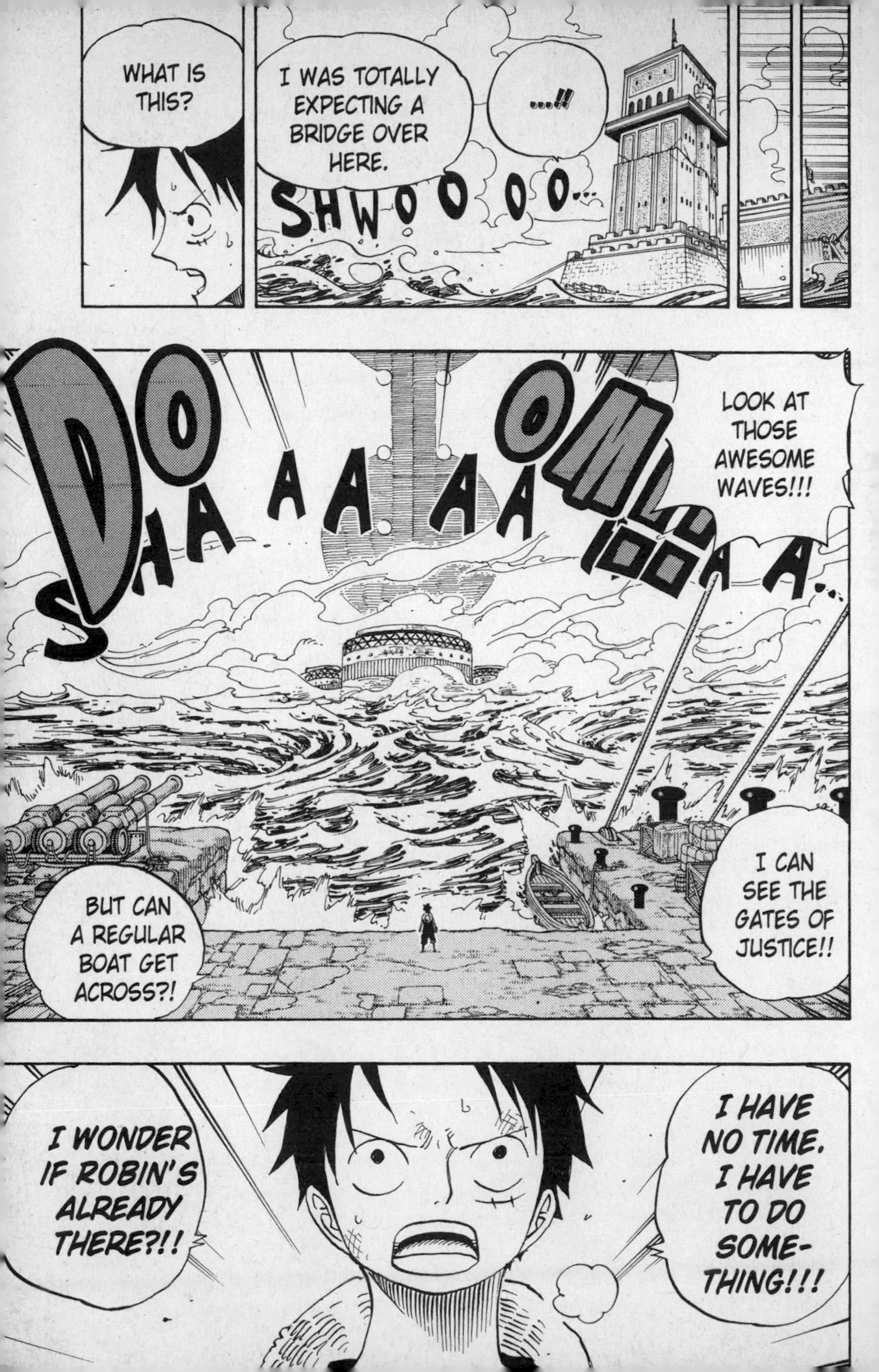
...!!
I WAS TOTALLY EXPECTING A BRIDGE OVER HERE.
SHWOOOO...
WHAT IS THIS?
LOOK AT THOSE AWESOME WAVES!!!
DOOM
SHAAAAA
I CAN SEE THE GATES OF JUSTICE!!
BUT CAN A REGULAR BOAT GET ACROSS?!
I HAVE NO TIME. I HAVE TO DO SOME-THING!!!
I WONDER IF ROBIN'S ALREADY THERE?!!

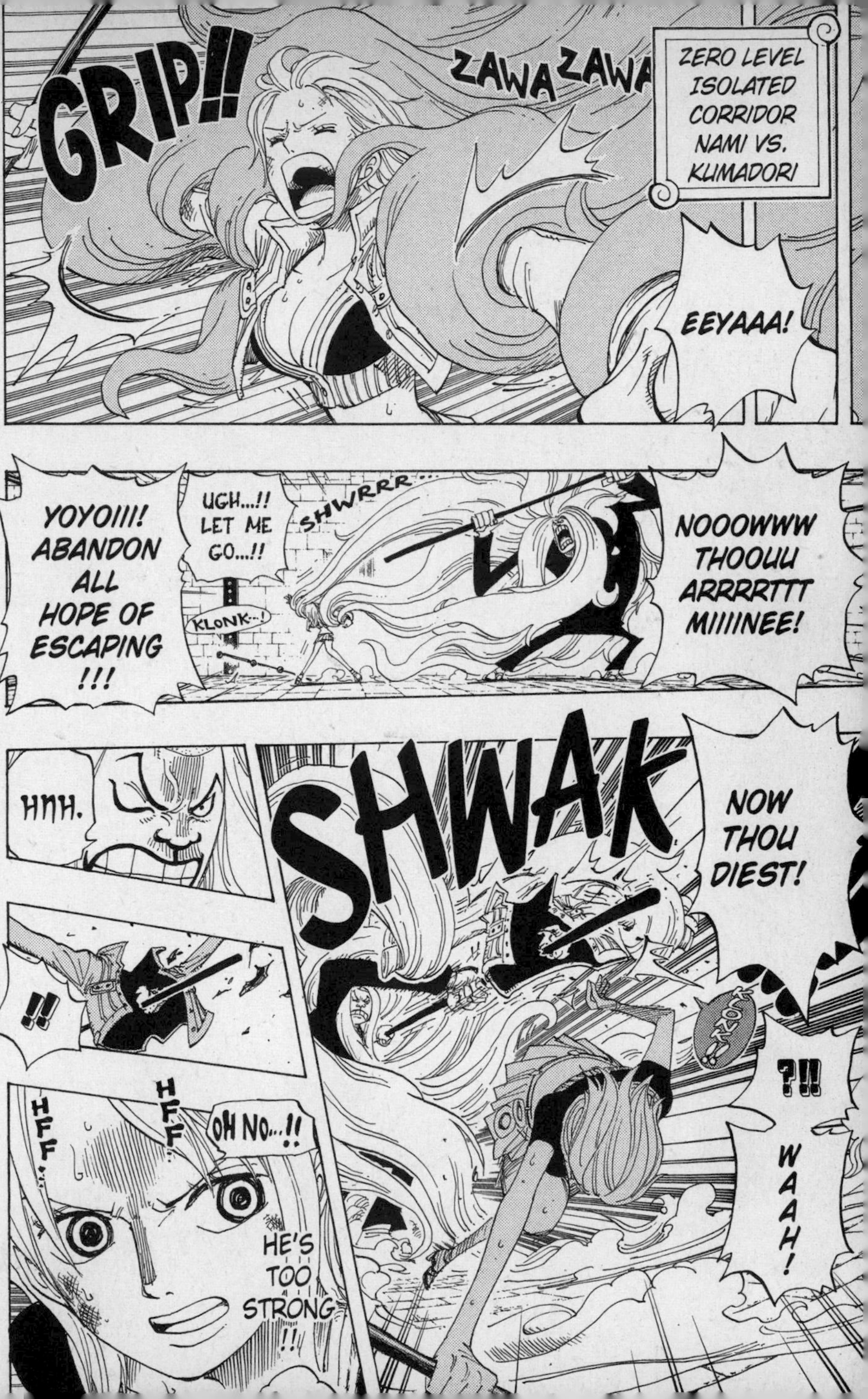
ZERO LEVEL ISOLATED CORRIDOR NAMI VS. KUMADORI
ZAWA ZAWA
EEYAAA!
GRIP!!
NOOOWWW THOOUU ARRRRTTT MIIIINEE!
SHWRRR...
UGH...!! LET ME GO...!!
KLONK...!
YOYOIIII! ABANDON ALL HOPE OF ESCAPING!!!
SHWAK
NOW THOU DIEST!
?!!
WAAH!
HNH.
!!
OH NO...!!
HFF
HFF
HE'S TOO STRONG!!

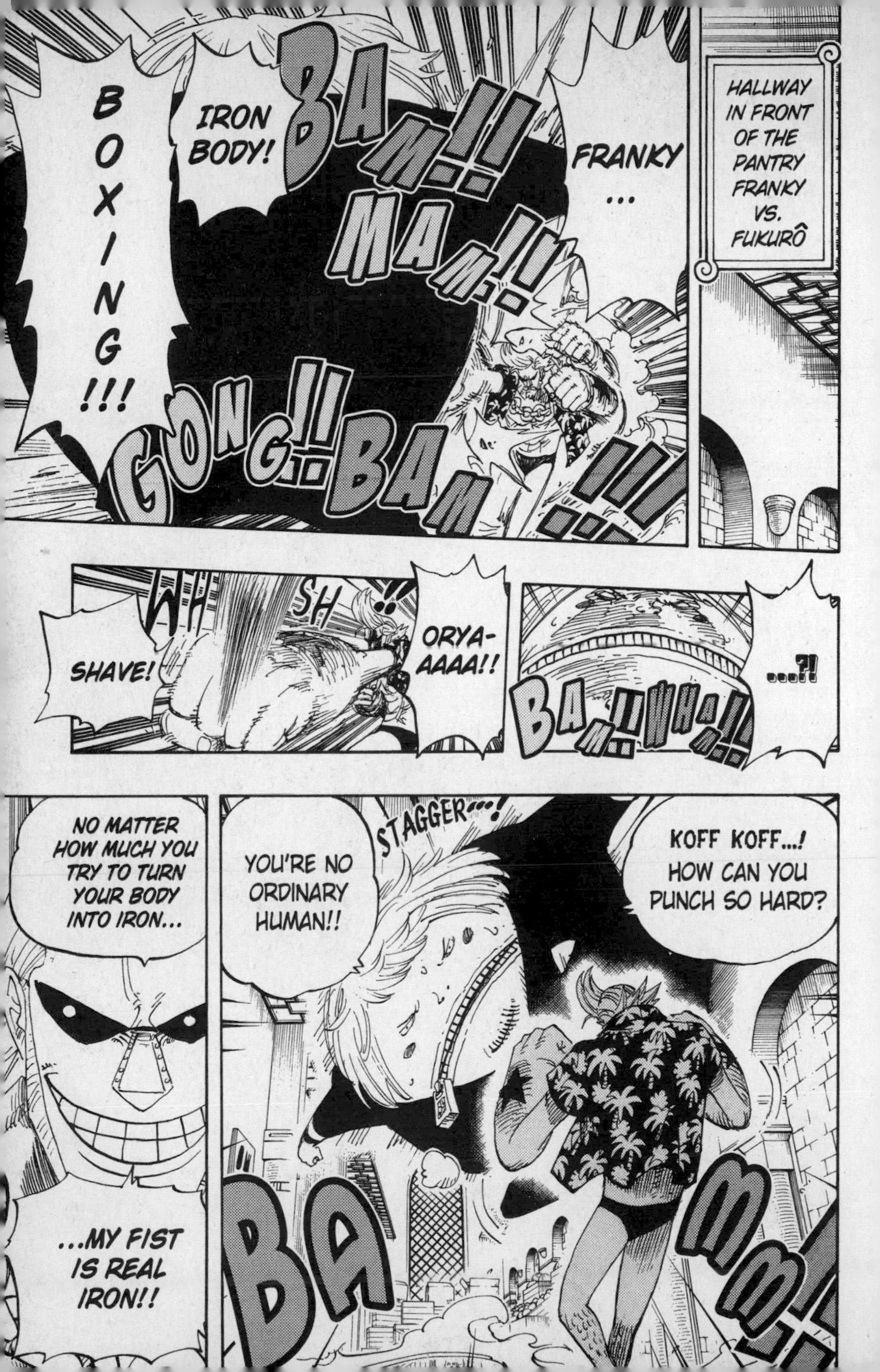
HALLWAY IN FRONT OF THE PANTRY FRANKY VS. FUKURÔ
FRANKY ...
BAM!!
MAM!!
IRON BODY!
BOXING!!!
GONG!!
BAM!!
...?!
BAM!! WHAM!!
ORYA-AAAA!!
WH
SH
SHAVE!
KOFF KOFF...! HOW CAN YOU PUNCH SO HARD?
STAGGER...!
YOU'RE NO ORDINARY HUMAN!!
BA
NO MATTER HOW MUCH YOU TRY TO TURN YOUR BODY INTO IRON...
...MY FIST IS REAL IRON!!

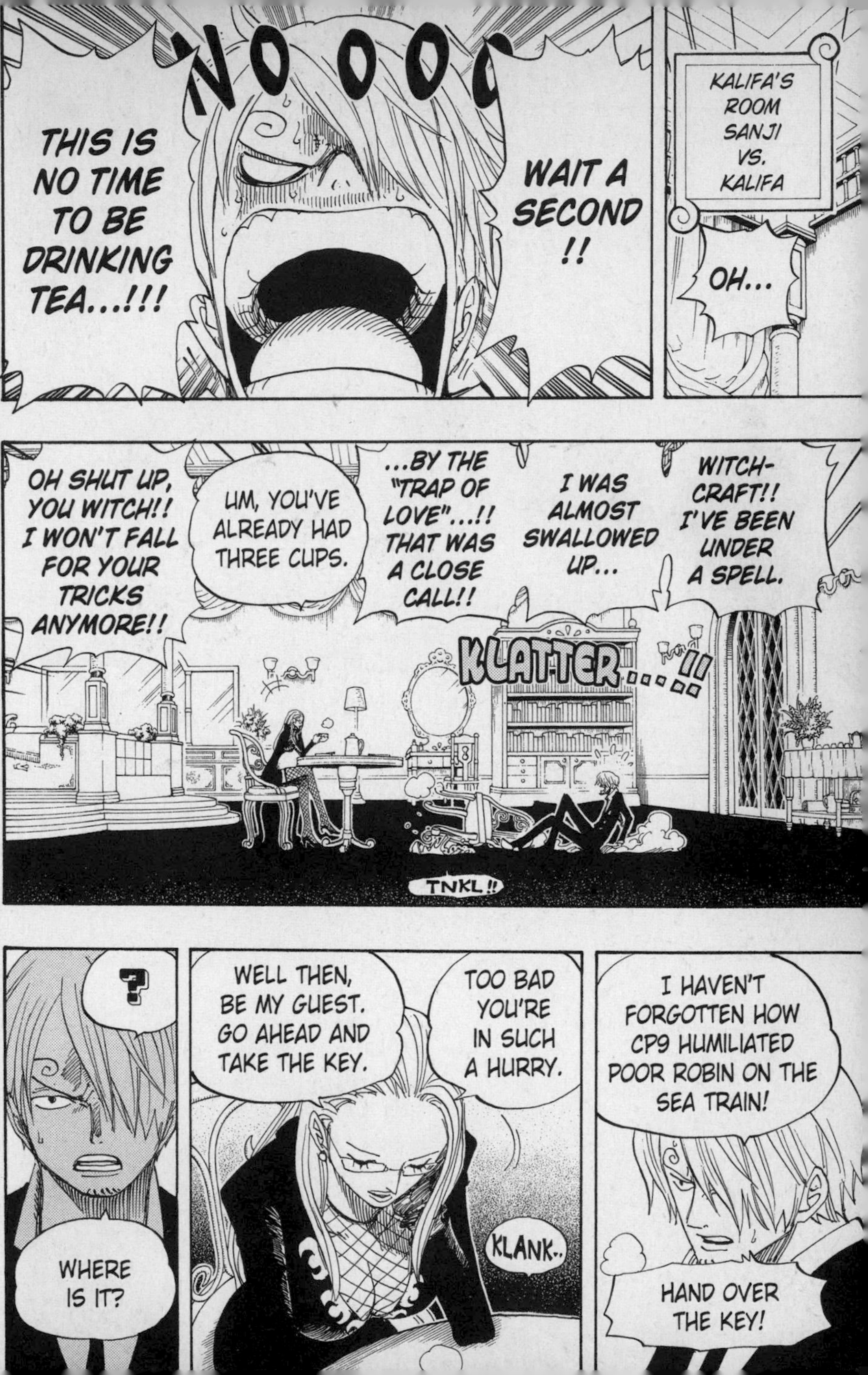
KALIFA'S ROOM SANJI VS. KALIFA
OH...
WAIT A SECOND !!
NOOOO
THIS IS NO TIME TO BE DRINKING TEA...!!!
WITCH-CRAFT!! I'VE BEEN UNDER A SPELL.
I WAS ALMOST SWALLOWED UP...
...BY THE "TRAP OF LOVE"...!! THAT WAS A CLOSE CALL!!
UM, YOU'VE ALREADY HAD THREE CUPS.
OH SHUT UP, YOU WITCH!! I WON'T FALL FOR YOUR TRICKS ANYMORE!!
KLATTER....!!
TNKL!!
I HAVEN'T FORGOTTEN HOW CP9 HUMILIATED POOR ROBIN ON THE SEA TRAIN!
HAND OVER THE KEY!
TOO BAD YOU'RE IN SUCH A HURRY.
WELL THEN, BE MY GUEST. GO AHEAD AND TAKE THE KEY.
KLANK..
?
WHERE IS IT?

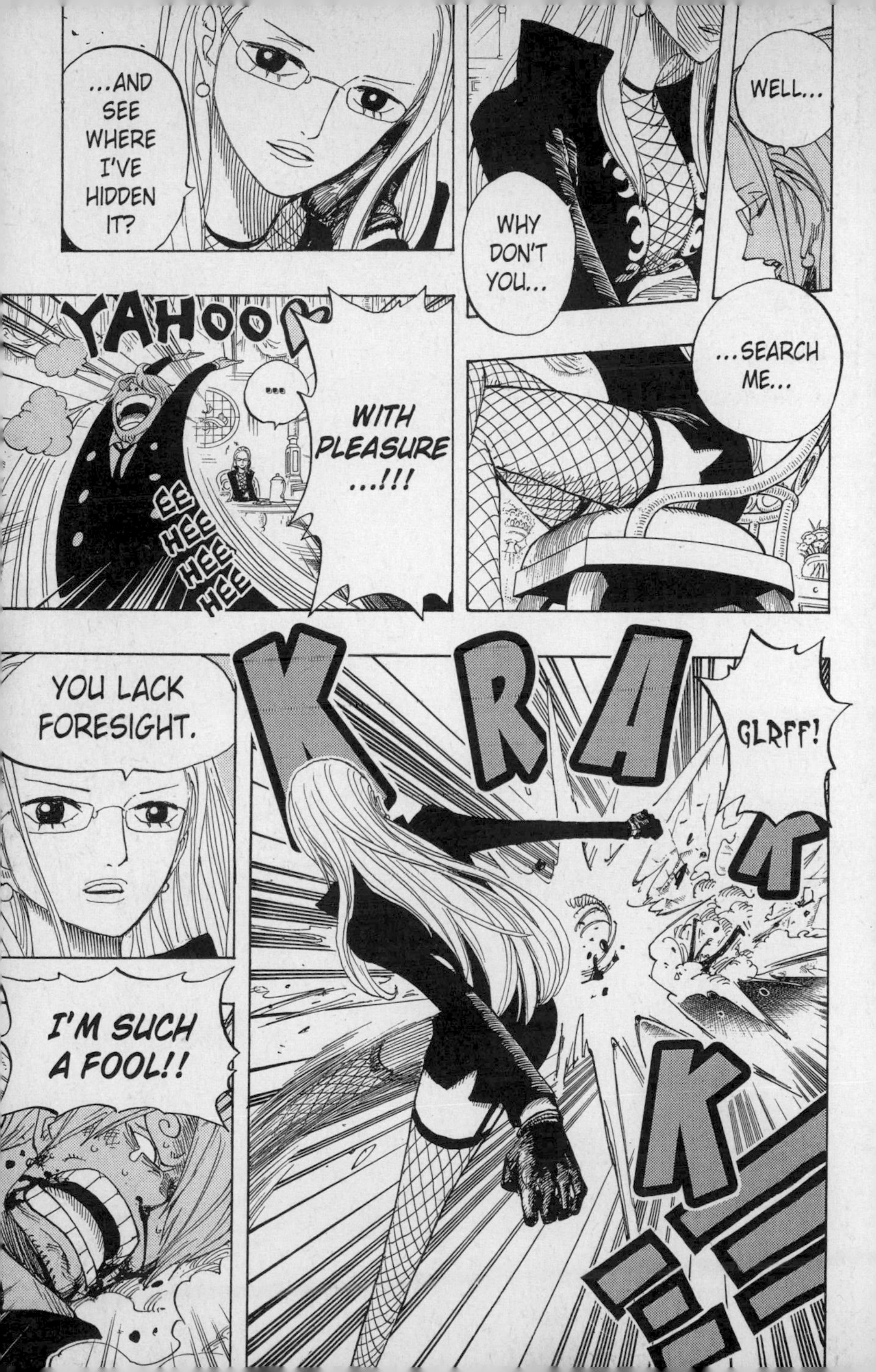
WELL...
WHY DON'T YOU...
...SEARCH ME...
...AND SEE WHERE I'VE HIDDEN IT?
YAHOO
...
WITH PLEASURE ...!!!
EE HEE HEE HEE
KRAKK
GLRFF!
YOU LACK FORESIGHT.
I'M SUCH A FOOL!!

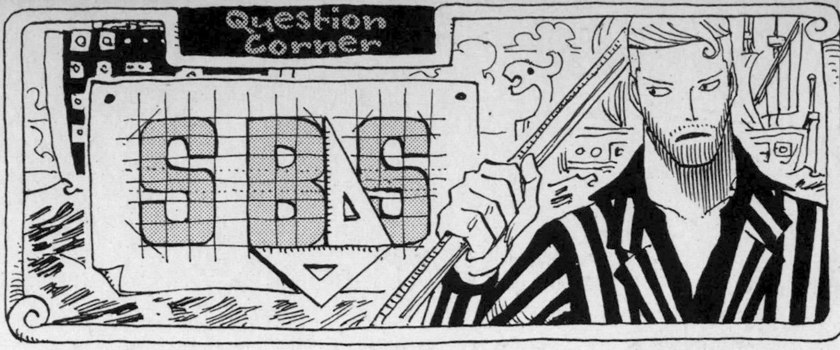
Question Corner
SBS

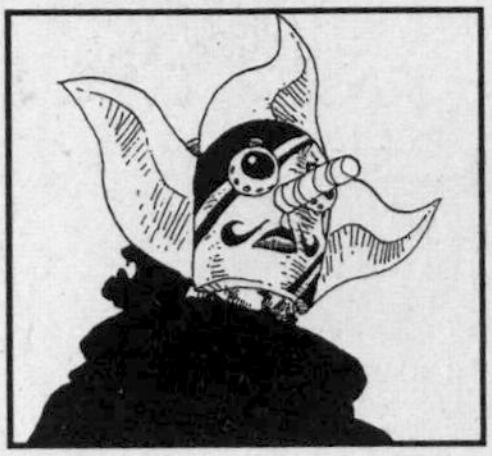

Q: Oda Sensei!! Please help me!! My dad, my kid brother and I are hooked on Sniper King!! No matter where or when, we start singing "On Sniper Island…♪"! You know what this is? Yup, it's the "We'll die without Sniper King" disease!! Please tell us what to do!! Sniiiipe! --Megaking

A: I see. All right! Now Sniper King!! Solve this for them!!

SK: Ah...you seem troubled. You'll die without me, you say? Never fear! I'm not going anywhere! After all, as I always say..."Sniper Island is in your heart"!

A: Okay, okay. That's enough. On to the next question.

SK: What do you mean, "that's enough"?

A: Okay, okay, okay.

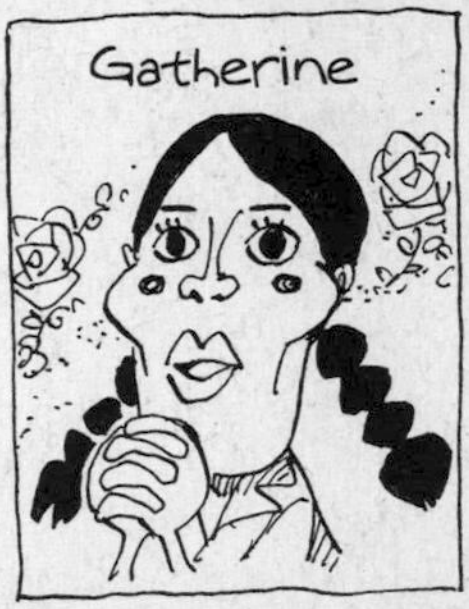
Gatherine

Q: I have a question, Oda Sensei. The waitress Gatherine, who turned down Jabra on volume 40, page 36 (Chapter 379: Power Level)… What type of guys does she like? Or does she already have a boyfriend? I can't sleep at night when I think about this… --Recycle Shogun

A: It seems Gatherine, the idol of Enies Lobby, has an unrequited love. This is what she said when she turned down Jabra: "I'm sorry. I love Lucci!! After all, a man's face is everything!" Countless men have suffered an honorable defeat by Gatherine's pure love. Hang in there, Jabra!

Chapter 403:

MR. CHIVALRY

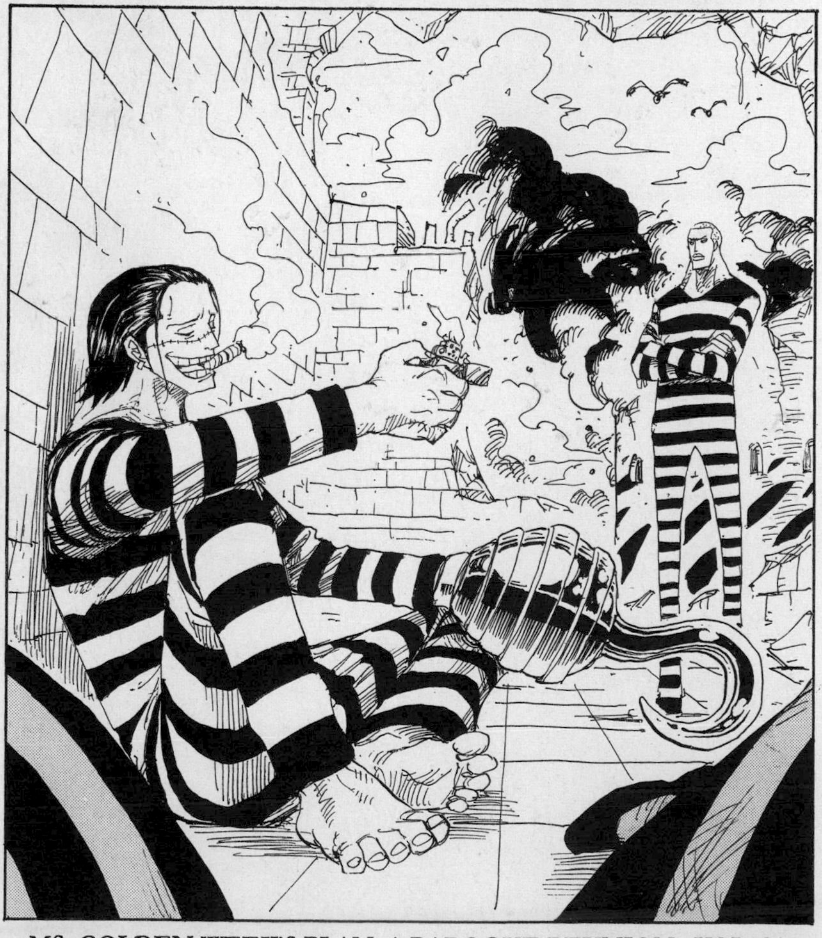

MS. GOLDEN WEEK'S PLAN, A BAROQUE REUNION, VOL. 34:
"DECLINING THE ESCAPE. JUST NOT IN THE MOOD"

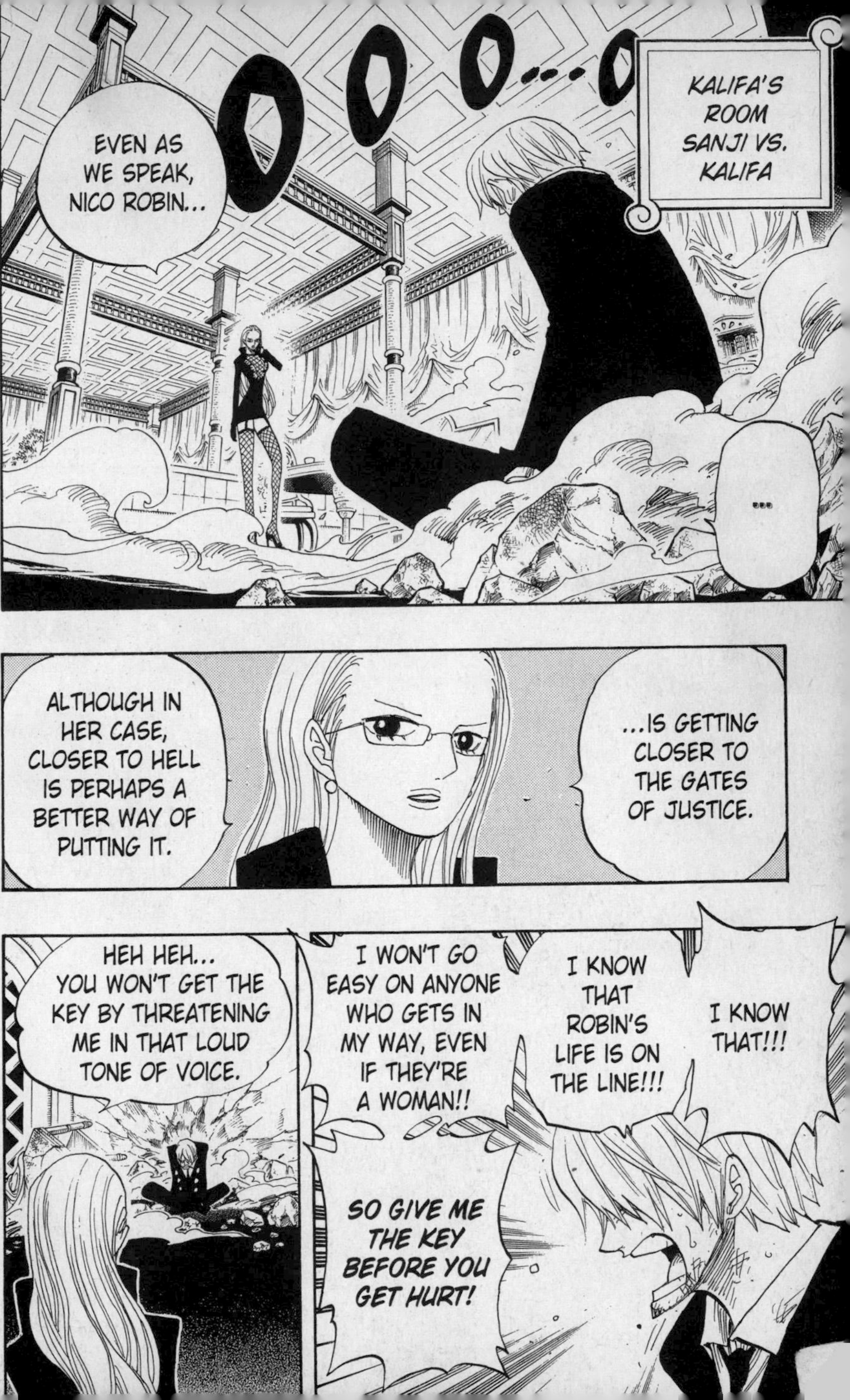
KALIFA'S ROOM SANJI VS. KALIFA
EVEN AS WE SPEAK, NICO ROBIN...
...
...IS GETTING CLOSER TO THE GATES OF JUSTICE.
ALTHOUGH IN HER CASE, CLOSER TO HELL IS PERHAPS A BETTER WAY OF PUTTING IT.
I KNOW THAT!!!
I KNOW THAT ROBIN'S LIFE IS ON THE LINE!!!
I WON'T GO EASY ON ANYONE WHO GETS IN MY WAY, EVEN IF THEY'RE A WOMAN!!
SO GIVE ME THE KEY BEFORE YOU GET HURT!
HEH HEH... YOU WON'T GET THE KEY BY THREATENING ME IN THAT LOUD TONE OF VOICE.

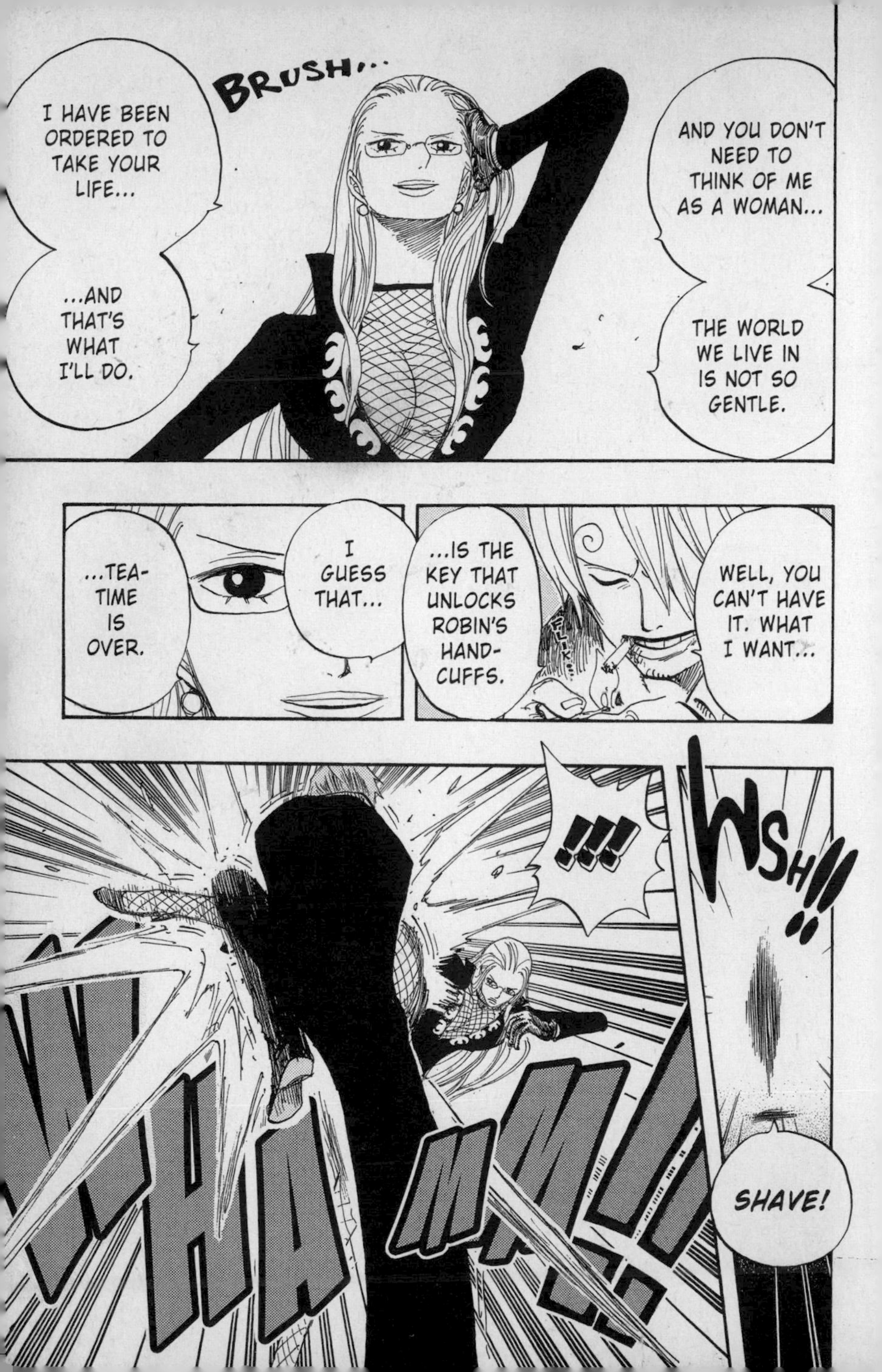
AND YOU DON'T NEED TO THINK OF ME AS A WOMAN...
THE WORLD WE LIVE IN IS NOT SO GENTLE.
BRUSH...
I HAVE BEEN ORDERED TO TAKE YOUR LIFE...
...AND THAT'S WHAT I'LL DO.
WELL, YOU CAN'T HAVE IT. WHAT I WANT...
FLIK...
...IS THE KEY THAT UNLOCKS ROBIN'S HAND-CUFFS.
I GUESS THAT...
...TEA-TIME IS OVER.
WSH!!
SHAVE!
!!!
WHAM!!

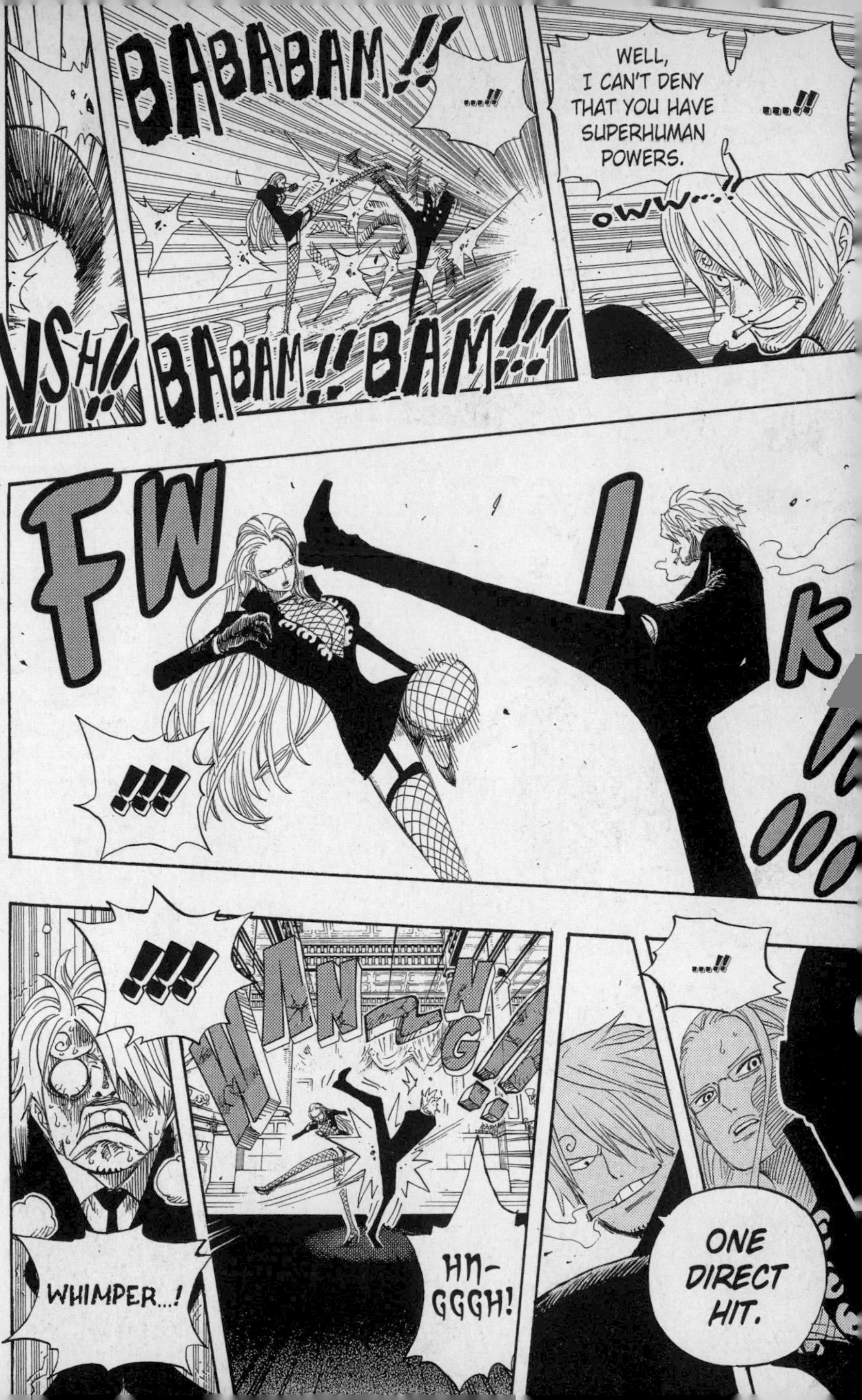
WELL, I CAN'T DENY THAT YOU HAVE SUPERHUMAN POWERS.
...!!
OWW...!!
BABABAM!!
...!!
BABAM!! BAM!!!
VSH!!
!!!
...!!
ONE DIRECT HIT.
HN-GGGH!
!!!
WHIMPER...!

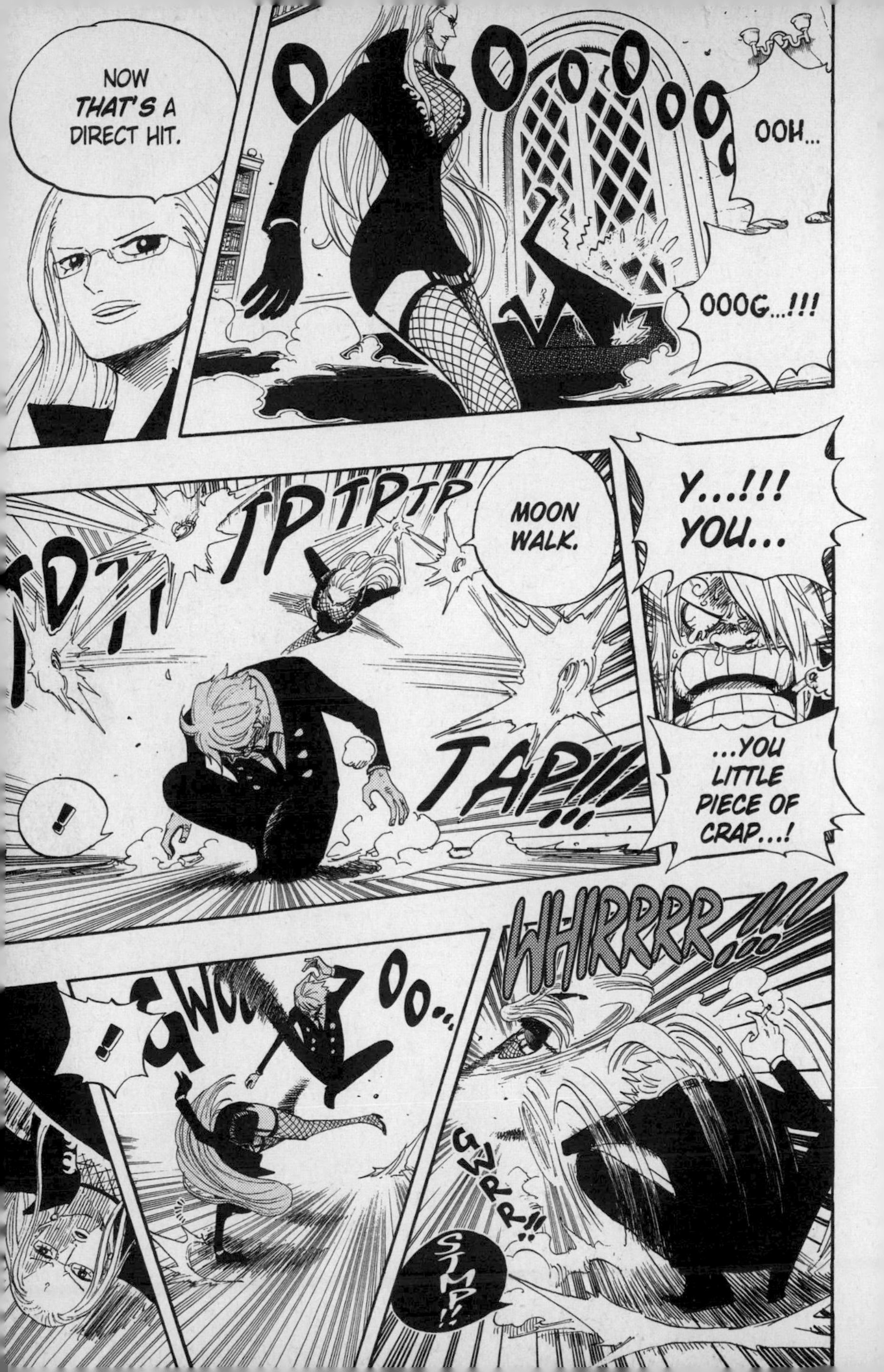
OOH...
OOOG...!!!
NOW THAT'S A DIRECT HIT.
Y...!!! YOU...
...YOU LITTLE PIECE OF CRAP...!
MOON WALK.
TP TP TP TP
TAP!!!
!
WHIRRRR!!!
GWRRR!!
STMP!!
GWOO OO...
!

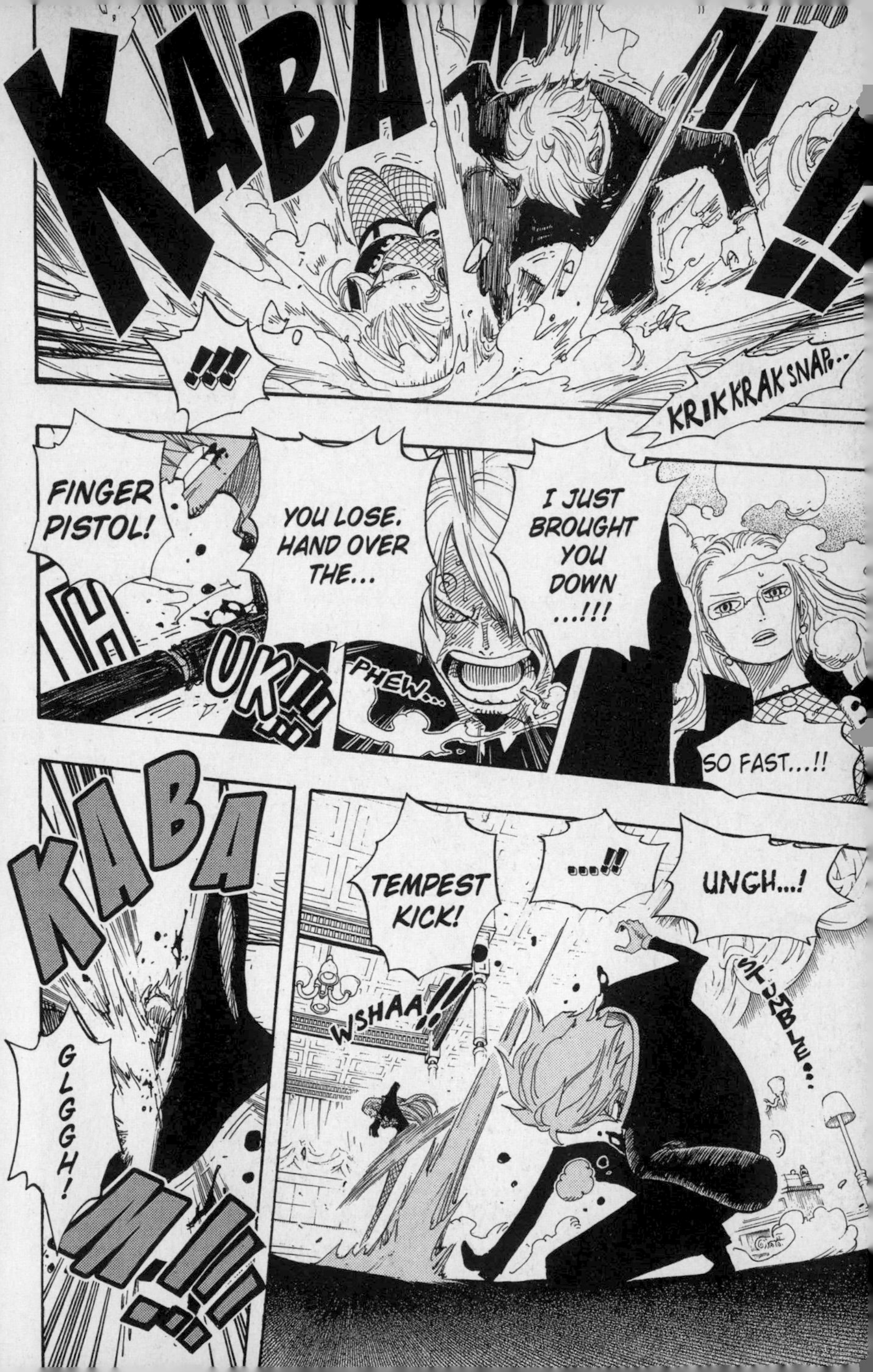
KABAM!!
!!!
KRIKKRAK SNAP...
SO FAST...!!
I JUST BROUGHT YOU DOWN ...!!!
YOU LOSE. HAND OVER THE...
PHEW...
FINGER PISTOL!
UK!!!...
UNGH...!
...!!
TEMPEST KICK!
STUMBLE...
WSHAA!!
KABA
M!!!...
GLGGH!

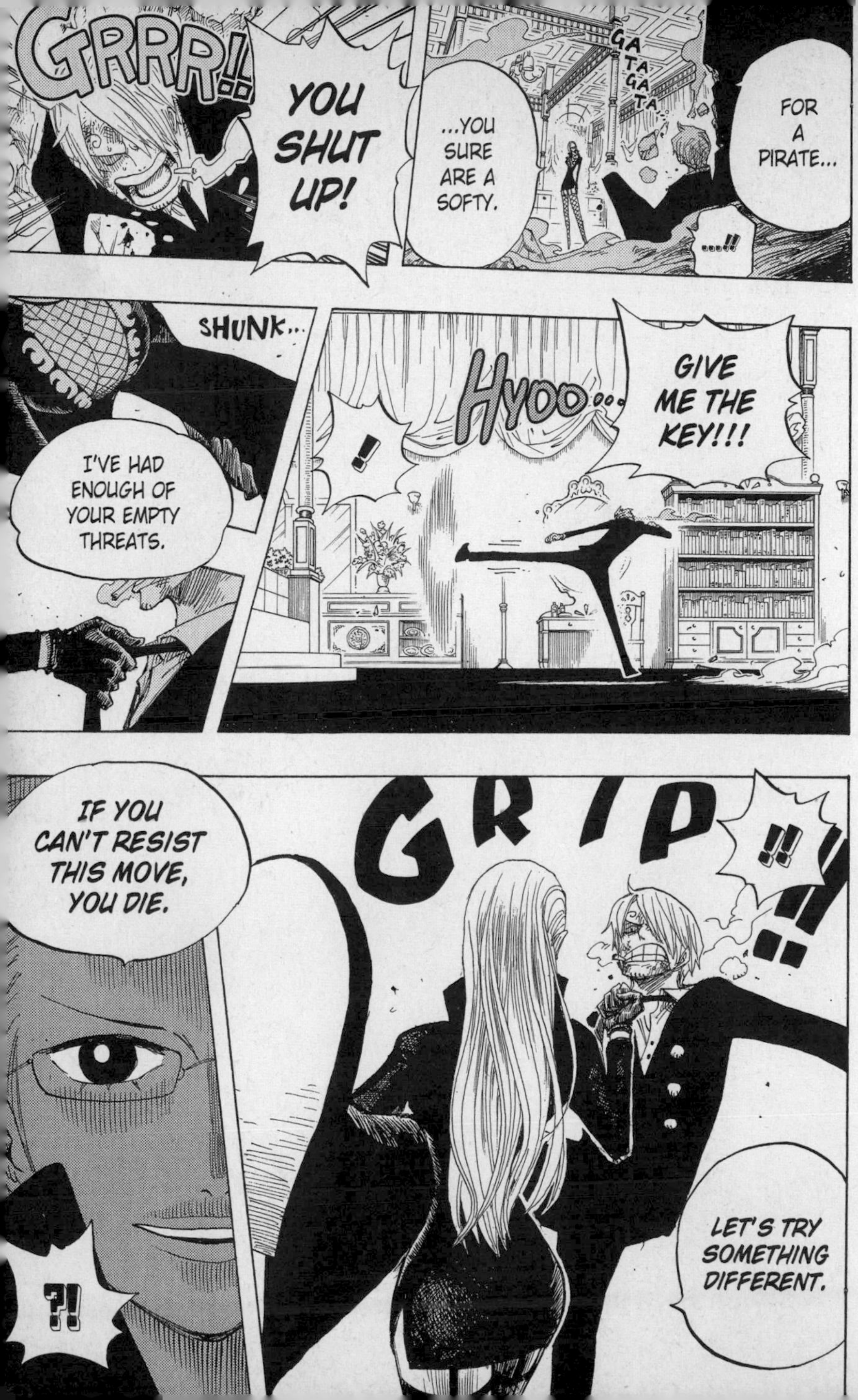
FOR A PIRATE...
...!!
GATAGATA...
...YOU SURE ARE A SOFTY.
YOU SHUT UP!
GRRR!!
GIVE ME THE KEY!!!
HYOO...
!
SHUNK...
I'VE HAD ENOUGH OF YOUR EMPTY THREATS.
GRIP
!!
!!
LET'S TRY SOMETHING DIFFERENT.
IF YOU CAN'T RESIST THIS MOVE, YOU DIE.
?!

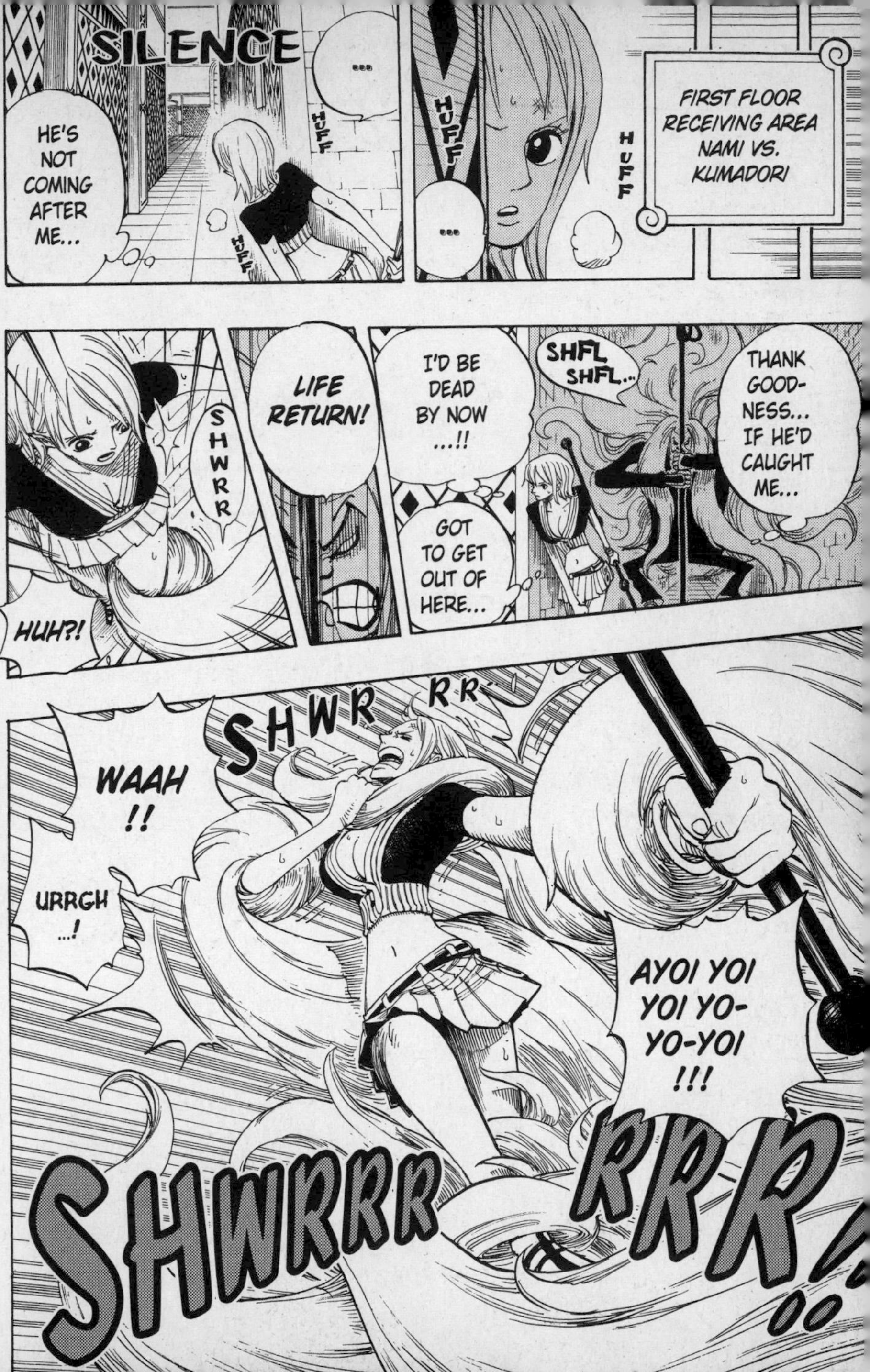
FIRST FLOOR RECEIVING AREA NAMI VS. KUMADORI
HUFF
HUFF
...
SILENCE
...
HUFF
HUFF
HE'S NOT COMING AFTER ME...
THANK GOODNESS... IF HE'D CAUGHT ME...
SHFL SHFL...
I'D BE DEAD BY NOW ...!!
GOT TO GET OUT OF HERE...
LIFE RETURN!
SHWRR
HUH?!
AYOI YOI YOI YO-YO-YOI !!!
SHWR RR
WAAH !!
URRGH ...!
SHWRRR RRR!!

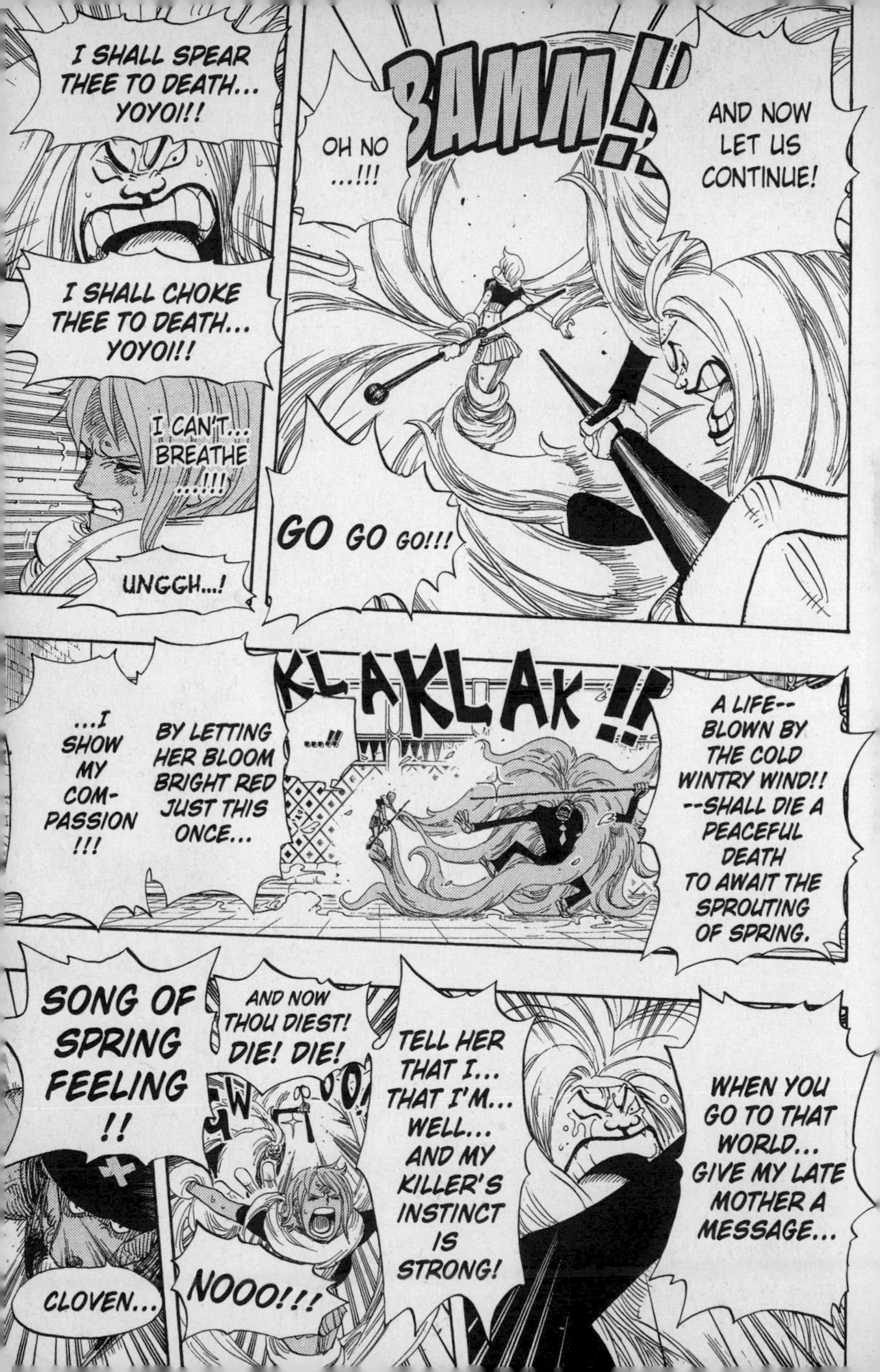
BAMM!!
AND NOW LET US CONTINUE!
OH NO ...!!!
GO GO GO!!!
I SHALL SPEAR THEE TO DEATH... YOYOI!!
I SHALL CHOKE THEE TO DEATH... YOYOI!!
I CAN'T... BREATHE ...!!!
UNGGH...!
KLAKLAK!!
A LIFE-- BLOWN BY THE COLD WINTRY WIND!! --SHALL DIE A PEACEFUL DEATH TO AWAIT THE SPROUTING OF SPRING.
...!!
BY LETTING HER BLOOM BRIGHT RED JUST THIS ONCE...
...I SHOW MY COM- PASSION !!!
WHEN YOU GO TO THAT WORLD... GIVE MY LATE MOTHER A MESSAGE...
TELL HER THAT I... THAT I'M... WELL... AND MY KILLER'S INSTINCT IS STRONG!
AND NOW THOU DIEST! DIE! DIE!
NOOO!!!
SONG OF SPRING FEELING !!
CLOVEN...

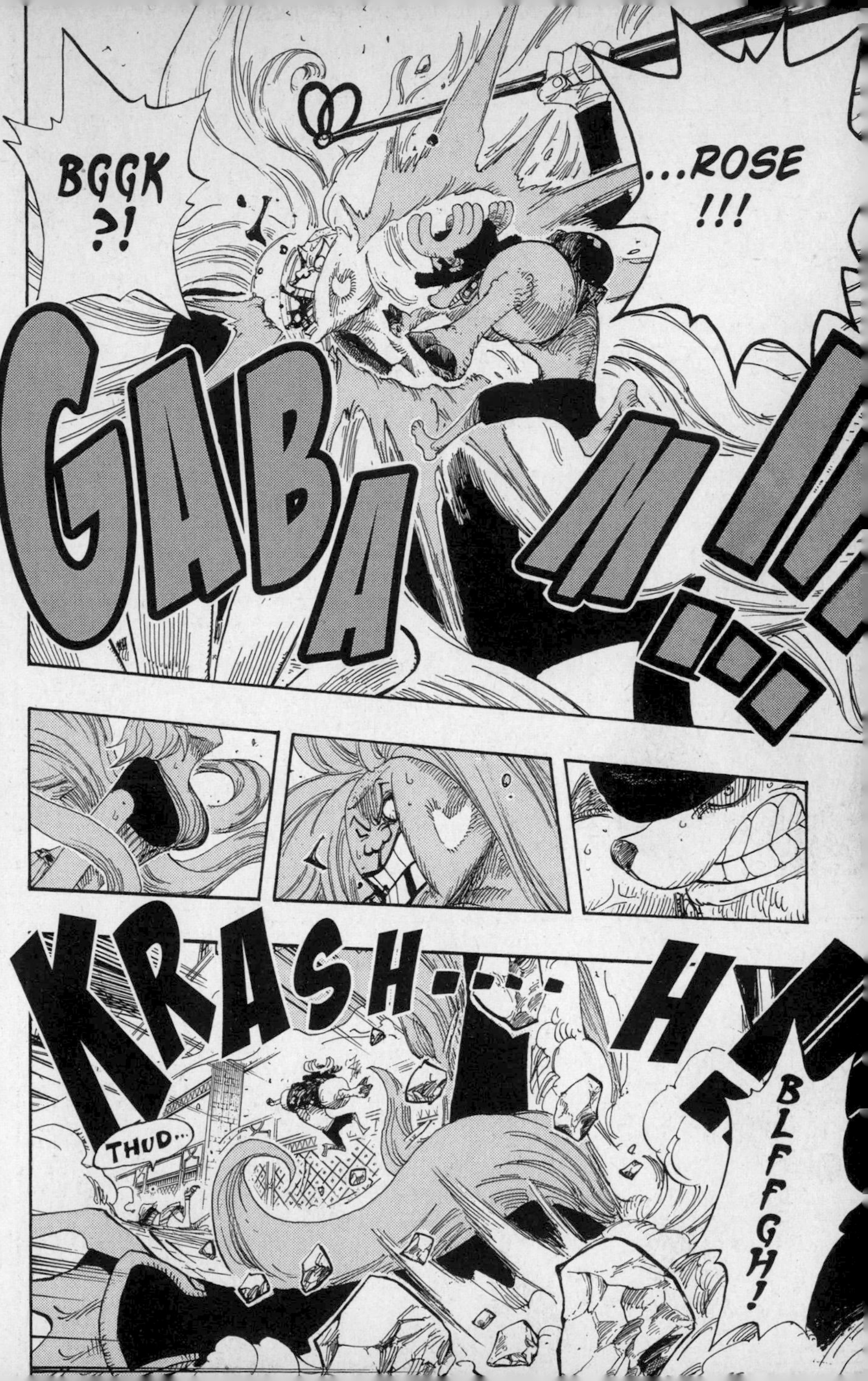
...ROSE !!!
BGGK ?!
GABAN!!
BLFFGH!
KRASH...H
THUD...

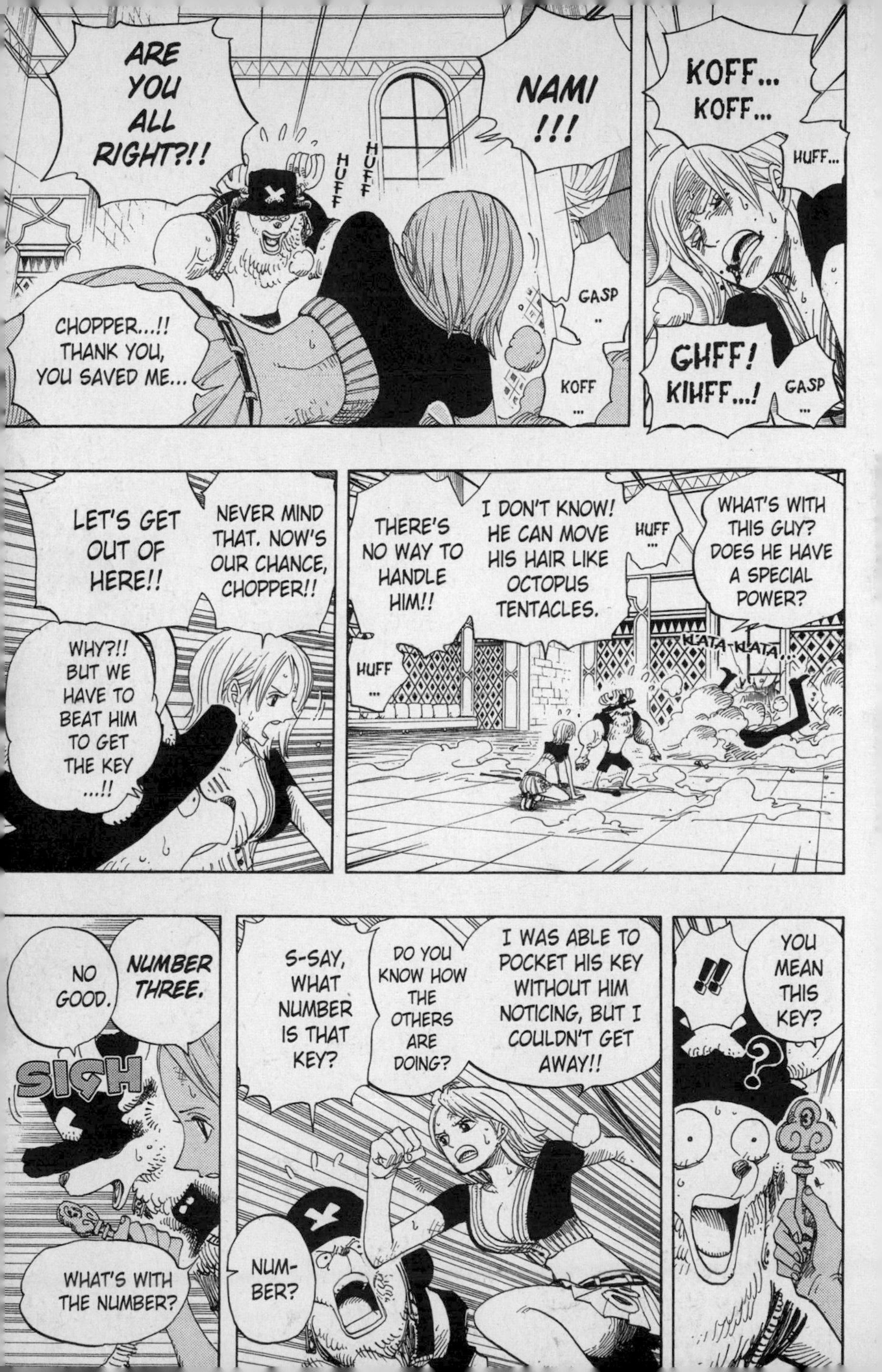
KOFF... KOFF...
HUFF...
GHFF! KIHFF...!
GASP...
NAMI!!!
ARE YOU ALL RIGHT?!!
HUFF HUFF
GASP...
CHOPPER...!! THANK YOU, YOU SAVED ME...
KOFF...
WHAT'S WITH THIS GUY? DOES HE HAVE A SPECIAL POWER?
HUFF...
I DON'T KNOW! HE CAN MOVE HIS HAIR LIKE OCTOPUS TENTACLES.
THERE'S NO WAY TO HANDLE HIM!!
KLATA-KLATA...
HUFF...
NEVER MIND THAT. NOW'S OUR CHANCE, CHOPPER!!
LET'S GET OUT OF HERE!!
WHY?!! BUT WE HAVE TO BEAT HIM TO GET THE KEY ...!!
YOU MEAN THIS KEY?
!!
?
I WAS ABLE TO POCKET HIS KEY WITHOUT HIM NOTICING, BUT I COULDN'T GET AWAY!!
DO YOU KNOW HOW THE OTHERS ARE DOING?
S-SAY, WHAT NUMBER IS THAT KEY?
NUM-BER?
NUMBER THREE.
NO GOOD.
SIGH
WHAT'S WITH THE NUMBER?

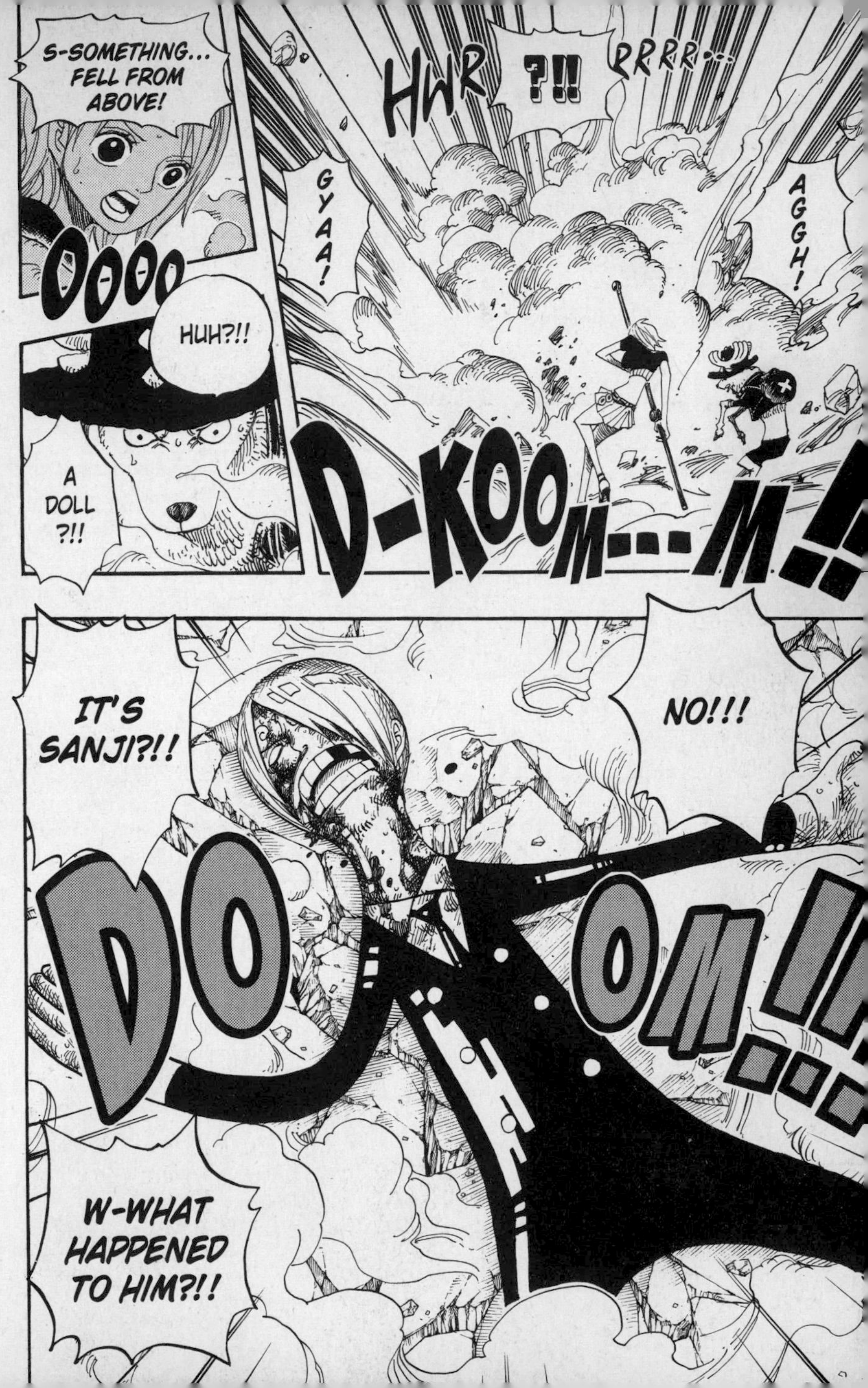

RRRR...
?!!
HWR
AGGH!
GYAA!
D-KOOM... M!!
S-SOMETHING... FELL FROM ABOVE!
OOOO
HUH?!!
A DOLL ?!!
NO!!!
IT'S SANJI?!!
DO OM!!...
W-WHAT HAPPENED TO HIM?!!

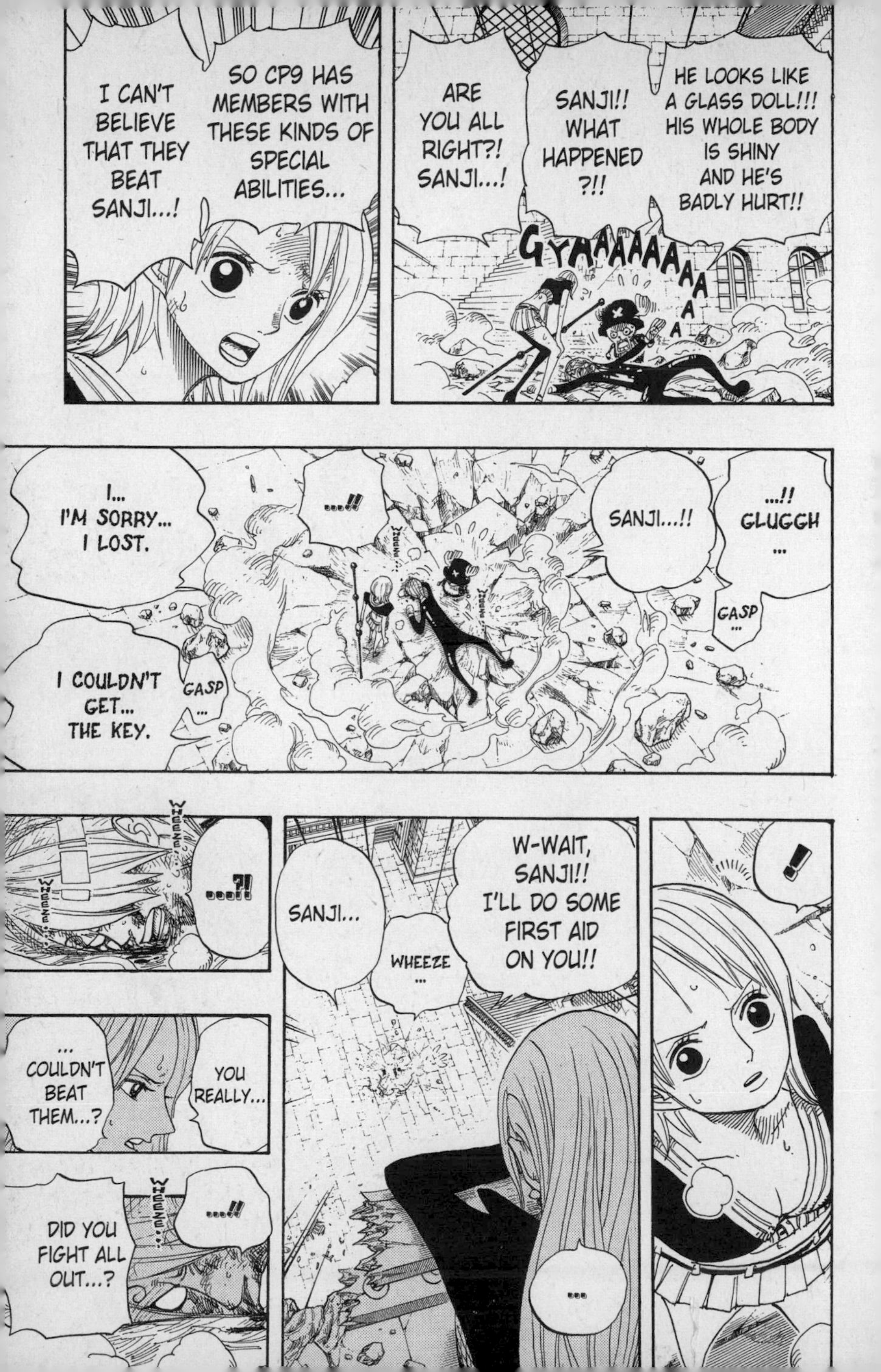
HE LOOKS LIKE A GLASS DOLL!!! HIS WHOLE BODY IS SHINY AND HE'S BADLY HURT!!
SANJI!! WHAT HAPPENED ?!!
ARE YOU ALL RIGHT?! SANJI...!
GYAAAAAAAAA
SO CP9 HAS MEMBERS WITH THESE KINDS OF SPECIAL ABILITIES...
I CAN'T BELIEVE THAT THEY BEAT SANJI...!
...!! GLUGGH ...
SANJI...!!
GASP ...
WHEEZE
...!!
I... I'M SORRY... I LOST.
GASP ...
I COULDN'T GET... THE KEY.
!
...
W-WAIT, SANJI!! I'LL DO SOME FIRST AID ON YOU!!
SANJI...
WHEEZE ...
...?!
WHEEZE
YOU REALLY...
... COULDN'T BEAT THEM...?
...!!
WHEEZE
DID YOU FIGHT ALL OUT...?

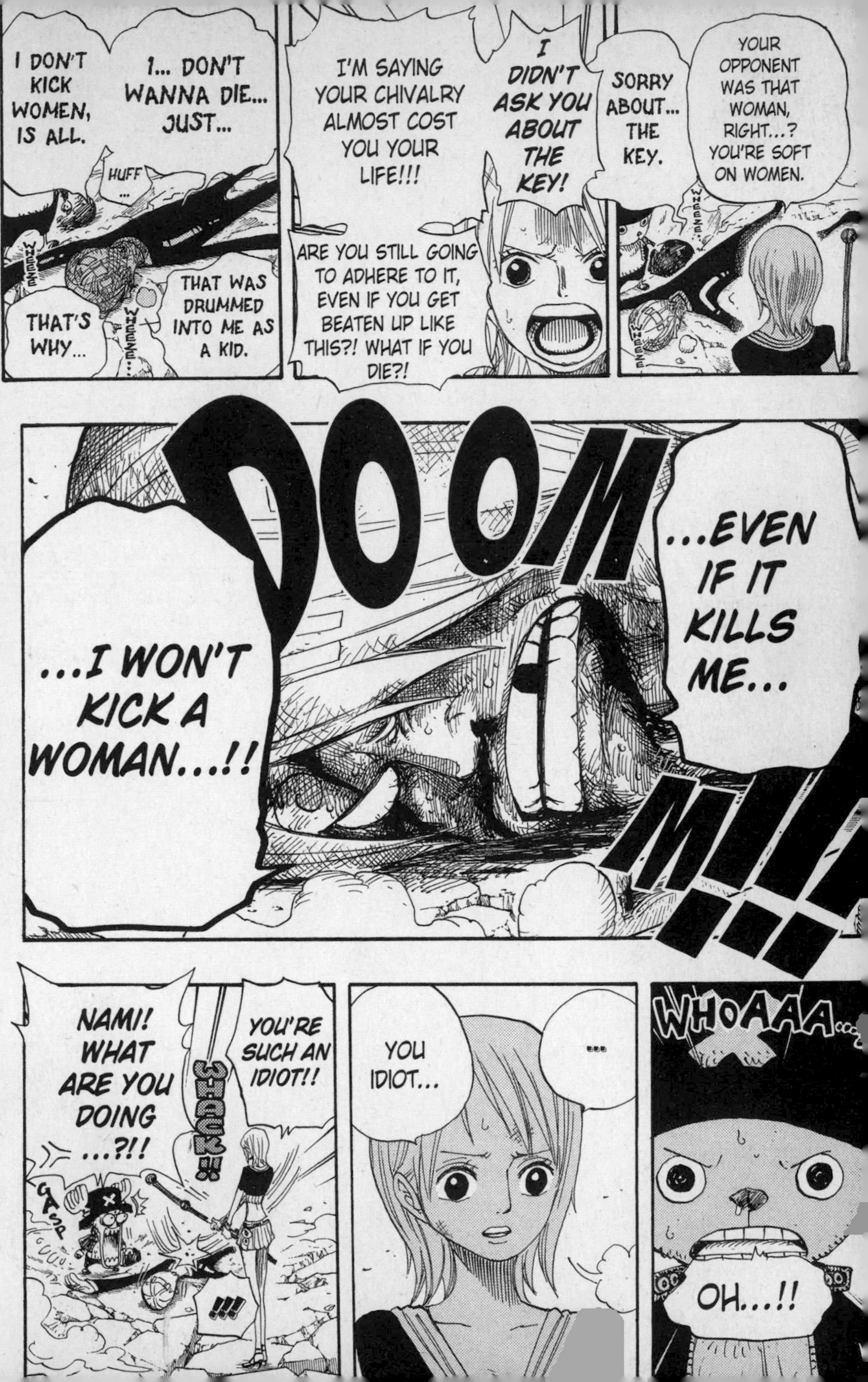
YOUR OPPONENT WAS THAT WOMAN, RIGHT...? YOU'RE SOFT ON WOMEN.
WHEEZE
WHEEZE
SORRY ABOUT... THE KEY.
I DIDN'T ASK YOU ABOUT THE KEY!
I'M SAYING YOUR CHIVALRY ALMOST COST YOU YOUR LIFE!!!
ARE YOU STILL GOING TO ADHERE TO IT, EVEN IF YOU GET BEATEN UP LIKE THIS?! WHAT IF YOU DIE?!
I... DON'T WANNA DIE... JUST...
I DON'T KICK WOMEN, IS ALL.
HUFF ...
THAT WAS DRUMMED INTO ME AS A KID.
THAT'S WHY...
WHEEZE
WHEEZE...
...EVEN IF IT KILLS ME...
DOOM
...I WON'T KICK A WOMAN...!!
M!!!
WHOAAA...
OH...!!
...
YOU IDIOT...
YOU'RE SUCH AN IDIOT!!
WHACK!!
NAMI! WHAT ARE YOU DOING ...?!!
GASP
!!!

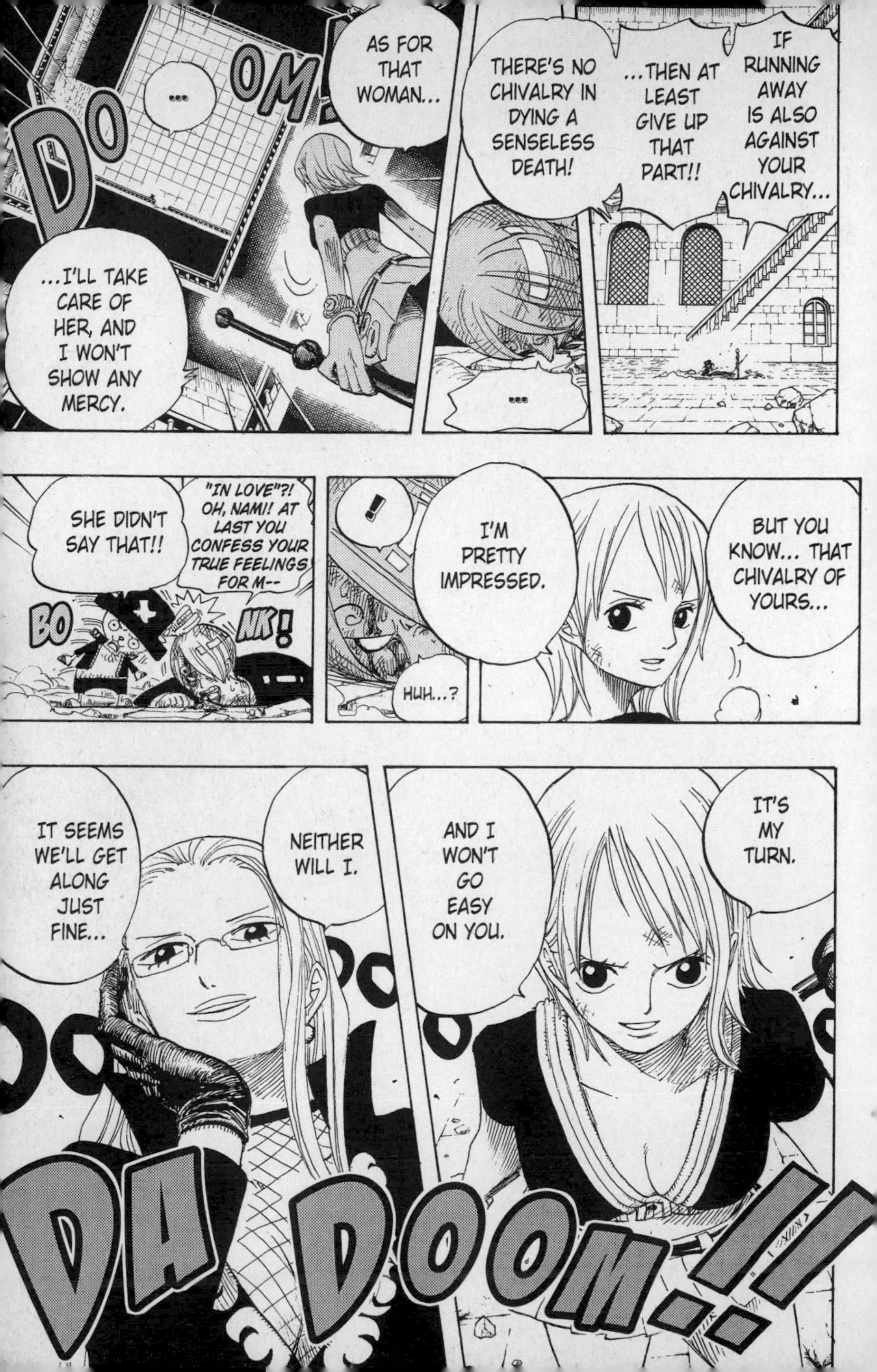
IF RUNNING AWAY IS ALSO AGAINST YOUR CHIVALRY...
...THEN AT LEAST GIVE UP THAT PART!!
THERE'S NO CHIVALRY IN DYING A SENSELESS DEATH!
...
AS FOR THAT WOMAN...
...
DOOM
...I'LL TAKE CARE OF HER, AND I WON'T SHOW ANY MERCY.
BUT YOU KNOW... THAT CHIVALRY OF YOURS...
I'M PRETTY IMPRESSED.
!
HUH...?
"IN LOVE"?! OH, NAMI! AT LAST YOU CONFESS YOUR TRUE FEELINGS FOR M--
SHE DIDN'T SAY THAT!!
BONK!
IT'S MY TURN.
AND I WON'T GO EASY ON YOU.
NEITHER WILL I.
IT SEEMS WE'LL GET ALONG JUST FINE...
DA DOOM..!!

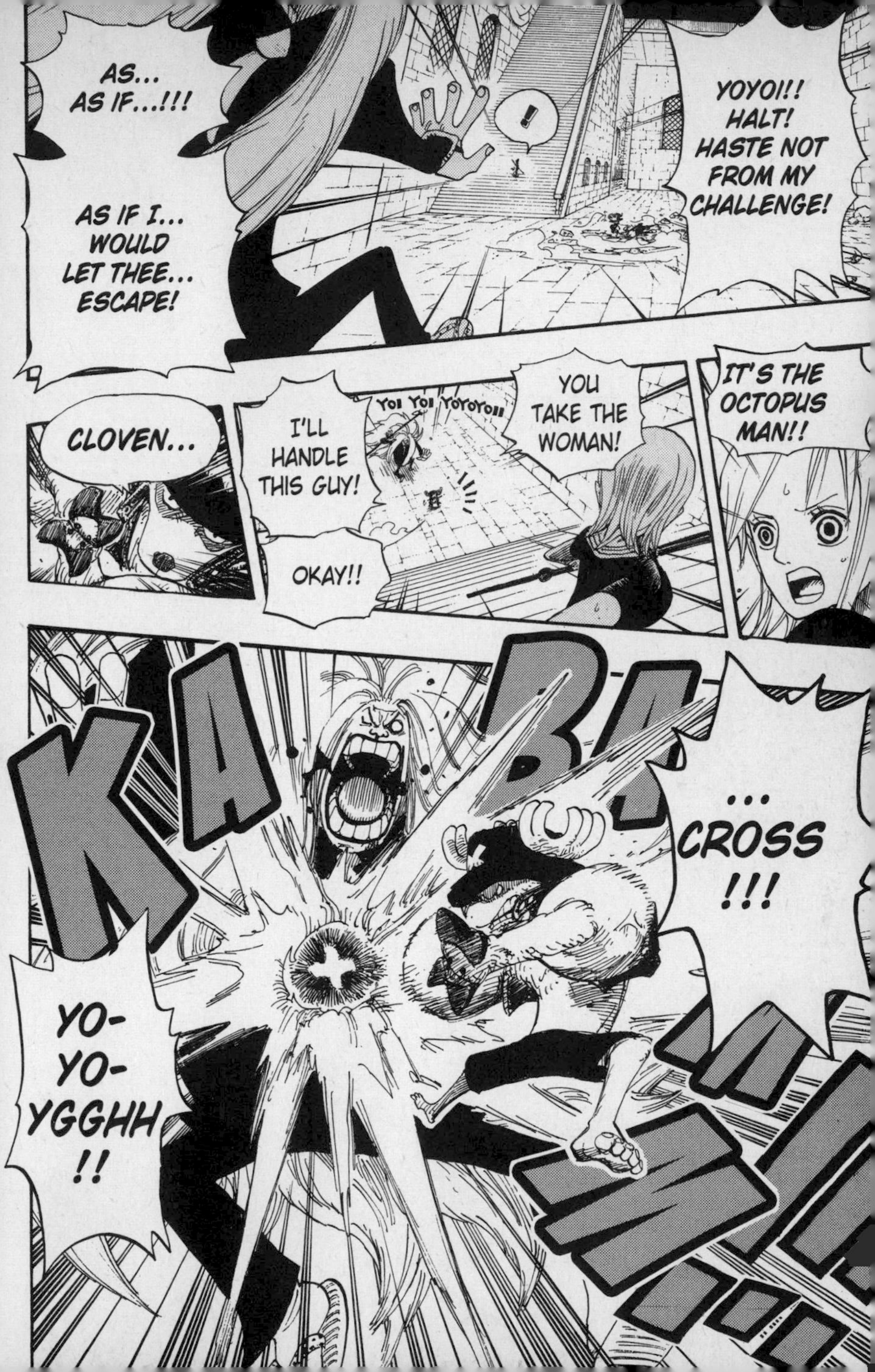
YOYOI!! HALT! HASTE NOT FROM MY CHALLENGE!
!
AS... AS IF...!!!
AS IF I... WOULD LET THEE... ESCAPE!
IT'S THE OCTOPUS MAN!!
YOU TAKE THE WOMAN!
YOI YOI YOYOYOI!!
I'LL HANDLE THIS GUY!
OKAY!!
CLOVEN...
...CROSS!!!
KABA
YO-YO-YGGHH!!

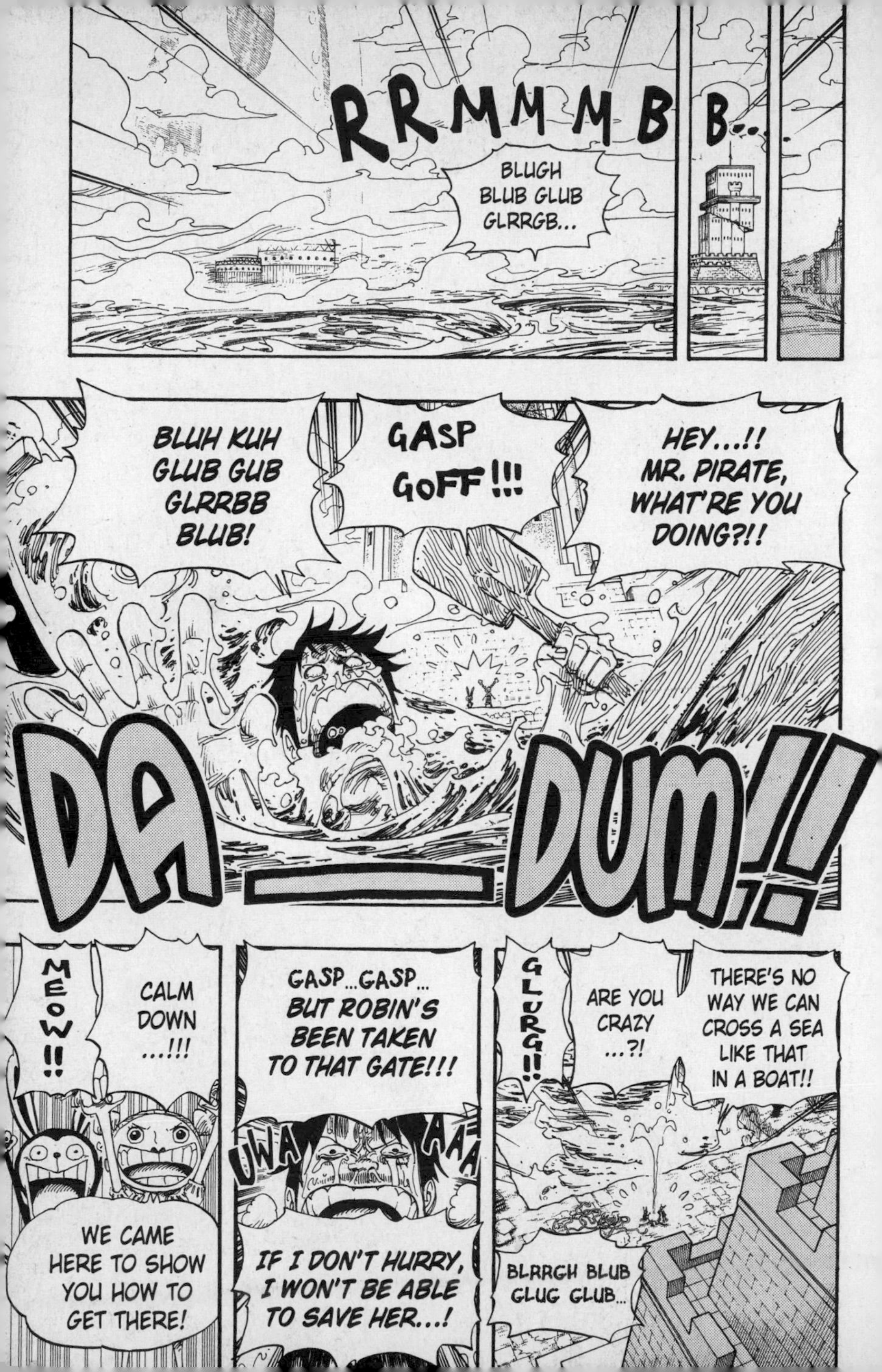

RRMMMBB...
BLUGH BLUB GLUB GLRRGB...
HEY...!! MR. PIRATE, WHAT'RE YOU DOING?!!
GASP GoFF!!!
BLUH KUH GLUB GUB GLRRBB BLUB!
DA—DUM!!
THERE'S NO WAY WE CAN CROSS A SEA LIKE THAT IN A BOAT!!
ARE YOU CRAZY ...?!
GLURG!!
BLRRGH BLUB GLUG GLUB...
GASP...GASP... BUT ROBIN'S BEEN TAKEN TO THAT GATE!!!
UWAAAA
IF I DON'T HURRY, I WON'T BE ABLE TO SAVE HER...!
CALM DOWN ...!!!
MEOW!!
WE CAME HERE TO SHOW YOU HOW TO GET THERE!

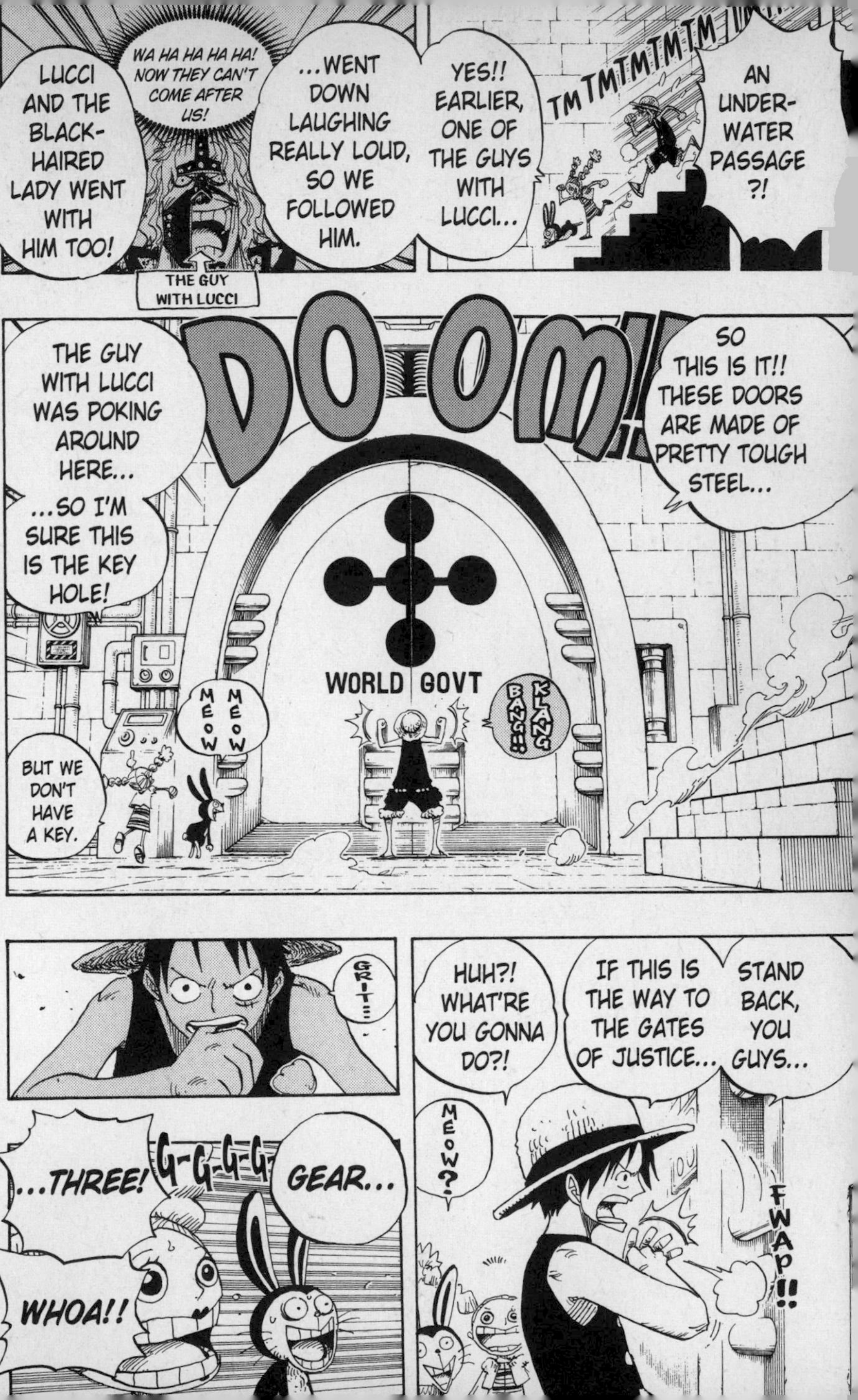
AN UNDER-WATER PASSAGE?!
TM TM TM TM TM TM
YES!! EARLIER, ONE OF THE GUYS WITH LUCCI...
...WENT DOWN LAUGHING REALLY LOUD, SO WE FOLLOWED HIM.
WA HA HA HA HA! NOW THEY CAN'T COME AFTER US!
LUCCI AND THE BLACK-HAIRED LADY WENT WITH HIM TOO!
THE GUY WITH LUCCI
DOOM!!
SO THIS IS IT!! THESE DOORS ARE MADE OF PRETTY TOUGH STEEL...
KLANG BANG!!
WORLD GOVT
THE GUY WITH LUCCI WAS POKING AROUND HERE...
...SO I'M SURE THIS IS THE KEY HOLE!
MEOW MEOW
BUT WE DON'T HAVE A KEY.
STAND BACK, YOU GUYS...
IF THIS IS THE WAY TO THE GATES OF JUSTICE...
HUH?! WHAT'RE YOU GONNA DO?!
MEOW?
FWAP!!
GRIT...
GEAR...
G-G-G-G
...THREE!
WHOA!!

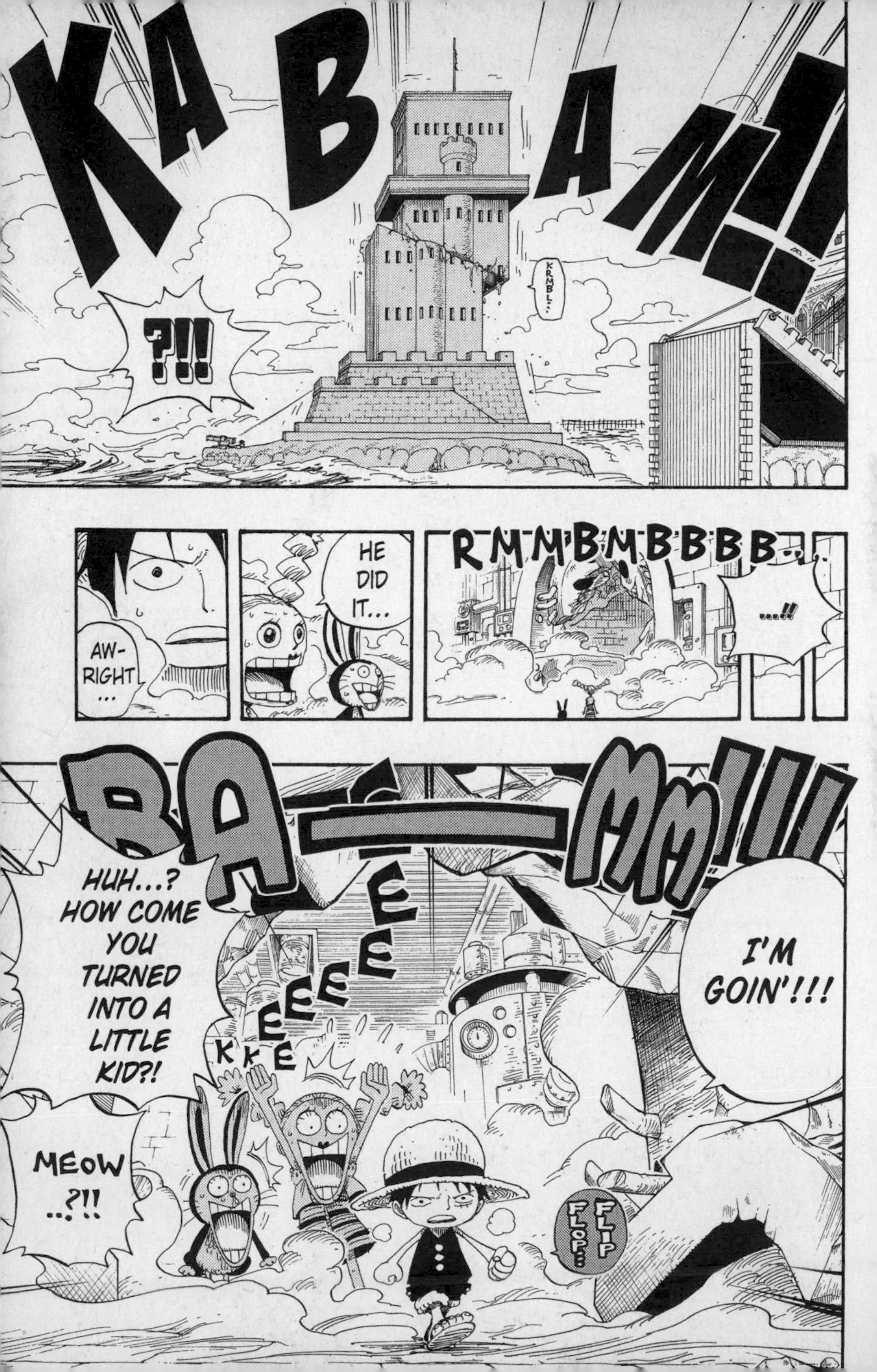

KABAM!!
KRMBL...
?!!
RMMBMBBBB...
...!!
HE DID IT...
AW-RIGHT...
BA—M!!!!
I'M GOIN'!!!
KKEEEEEE
HUH...? HOW COME YOU TURNED INTO A LITTLE KID?!
FLIP FLOP
MEOW ...?!!

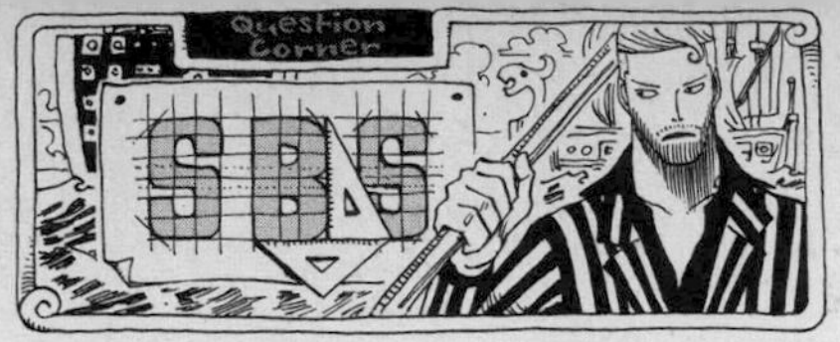
Question Corner
SBS

Oda: Let's start right away with something new!

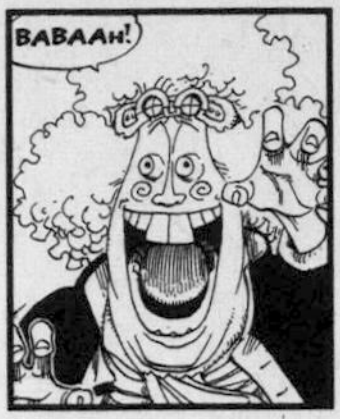
BABAAH!

This time, I'll show you some rough sketches I found which show the development of Wanze's face!! Take a look!

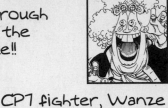

CP7 fighter, Wanze

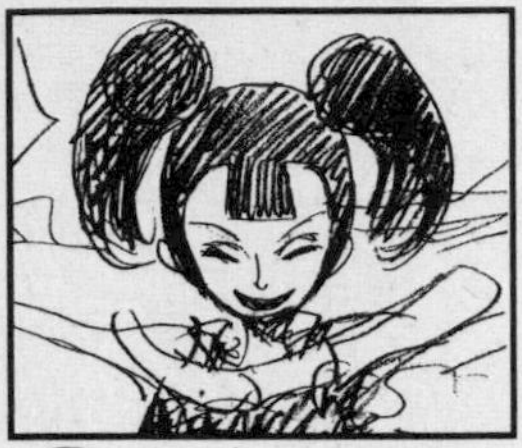

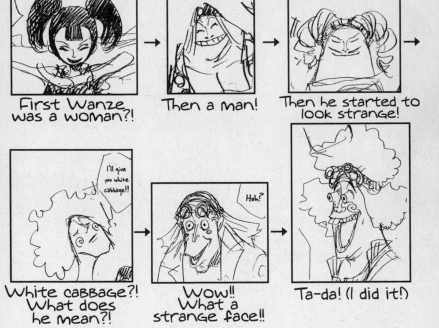

First Wanze was a woman?!

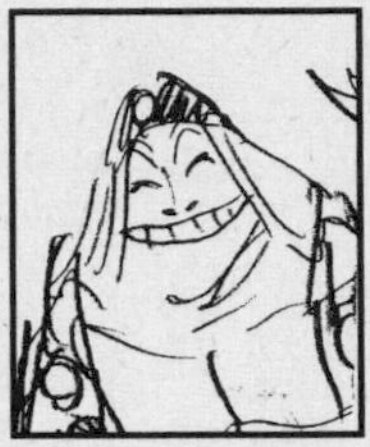

Then a man!

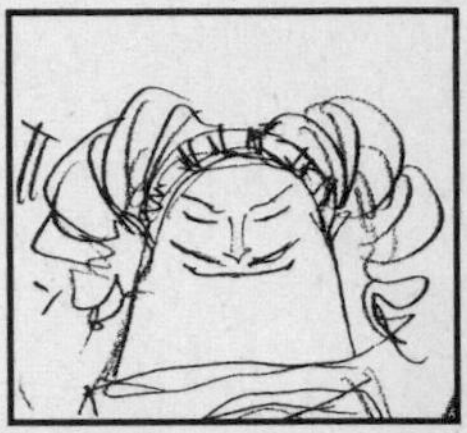

Then he started to look strange!

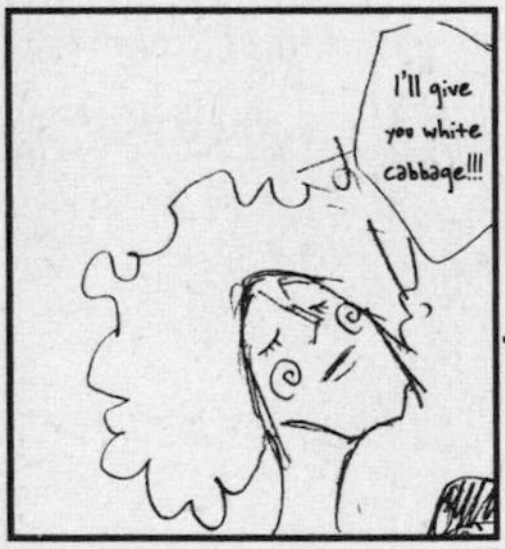
I'll give you white cabbage!!!

White cabbage?! What does he mean?!

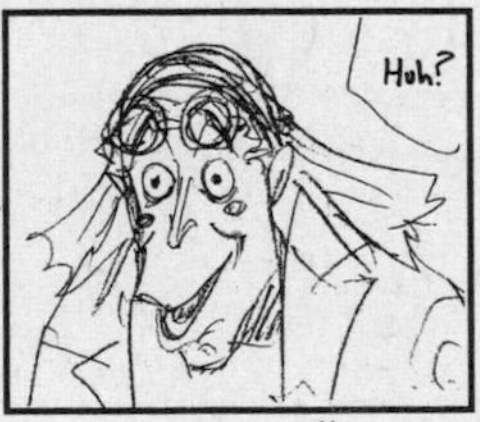
Huh?

Wow!! What a strange face!!

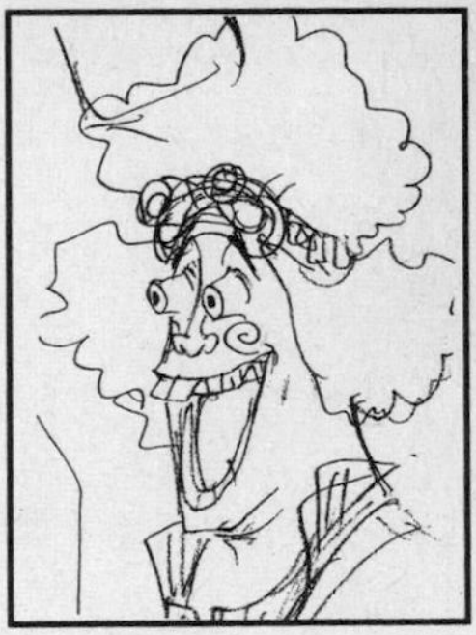

Ta-da! (I did it!)

Chapter 404:
FRANKY VS. FUKURÔ

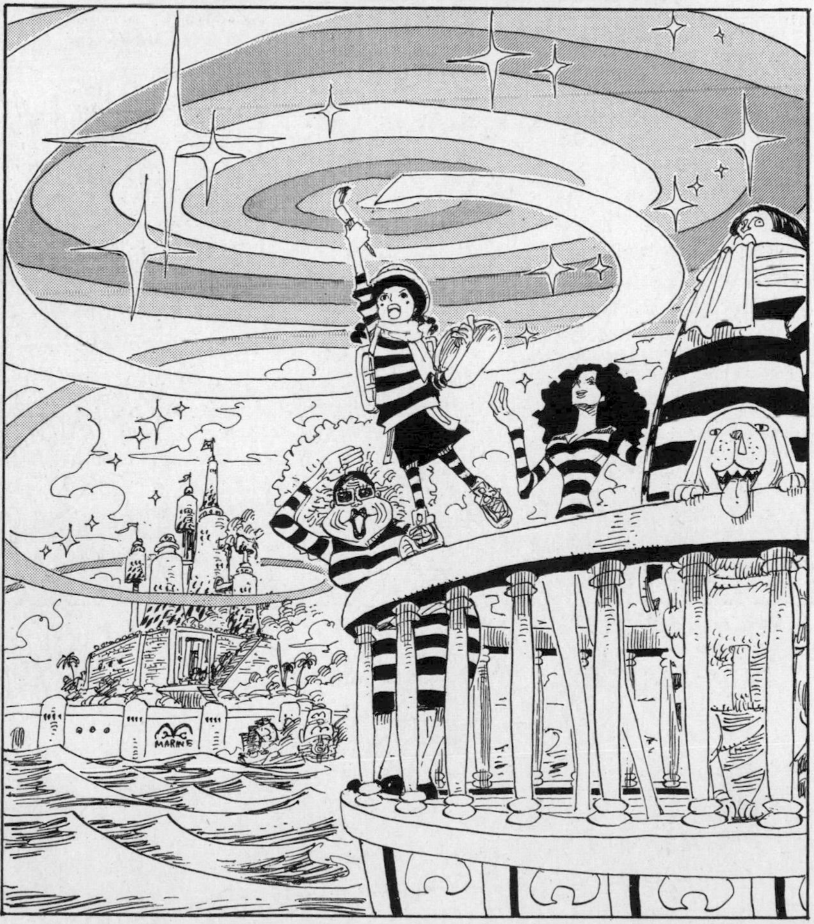
MARINE

MS. GOLDEN WEEK'S PLAN, A BAROQUE REUNION, VOL. 35:
"COLOR TRAP: RAINBOW-COLORED DREAMS!
THE IDEAL TRANSFORMATION!"

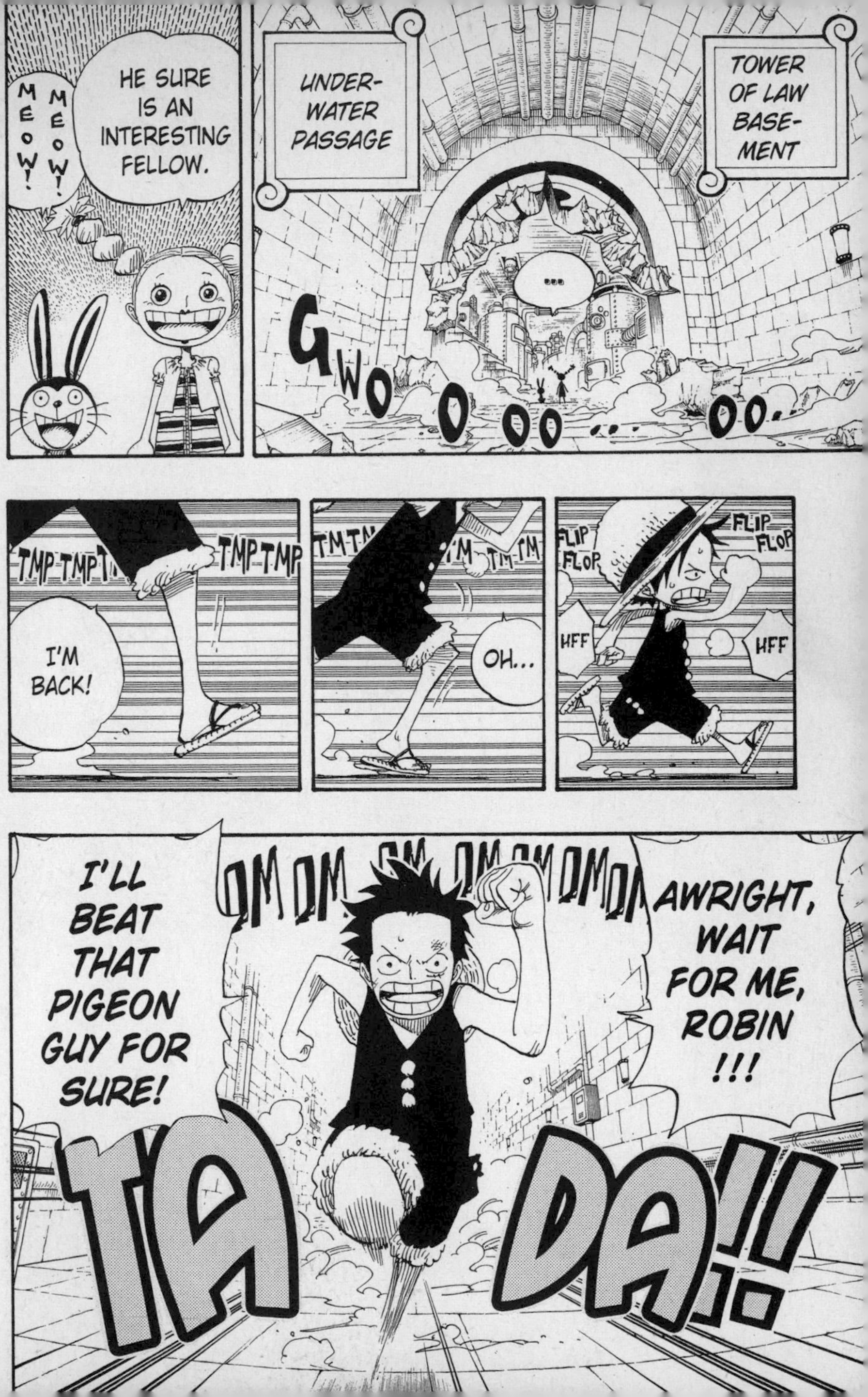
TOWER OF LAW BASEMENT
UNDERWATER PASSAGE
...
GWOOOOOO...
HE SURE IS AN INTERESTING FELLOW.
MEOW! MEOW!
FLIP FLOP
FLIP FLOP
HFF
HFF
TM-TM
TM TM-TM
OH...
TMP TMP
TMP TMP
I'M BACK!
AWRIGHT, WAIT FOR ME, ROBIN !!!
OM OM OM OM OM OM
I'LL BEAT THAT PIGEON GUY FOR SURE!
TA DA!!

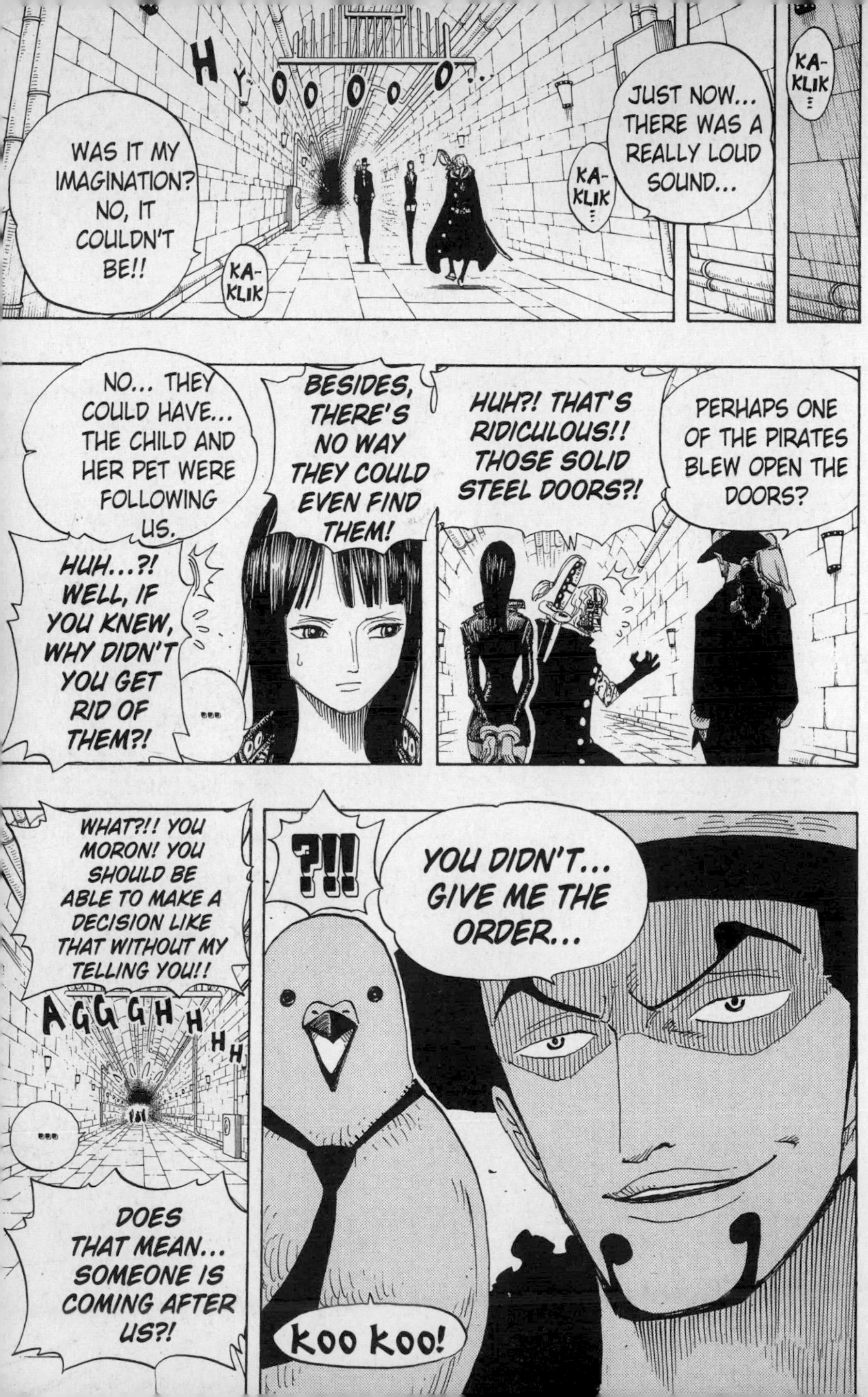
KA-KLIK
JUST NOW... THERE WAS A REALLY LOUD SOUND...
KA-KLIK
HYOOOOO...
WAS IT MY IMAGINATION? NO, IT COULDN'T BE!!
KA-KLIK
PERHAPS ONE OF THE PIRATES BLEW OPEN THE DOORS?
HUH?! THAT'S RIDICULOUS!! THOSE SOLID STEEL DOORS?!
BESIDES, THERE'S NO WAY THEY COULD EVEN FIND THEM!
NO... THEY COULD HAVE... THE CHILD AND HER PET WERE FOLLOWING US.
HUH...?! WELL, IF YOU KNEW, WHY DIDN'T YOU GET RID OF THEM?!
...
?!!
YOU DIDN'T... GIVE ME THE ORDER...
KOO KOO!
WHAT?!! YOU MORON! YOU SHOULD BE ABLE TO MAKE A DECISION LIKE THAT WITHOUT MY TELLING YOU!!
AGGGHHHH
...
DOES THAT MEAN... SOMEONE IS COMING AFTER US?!

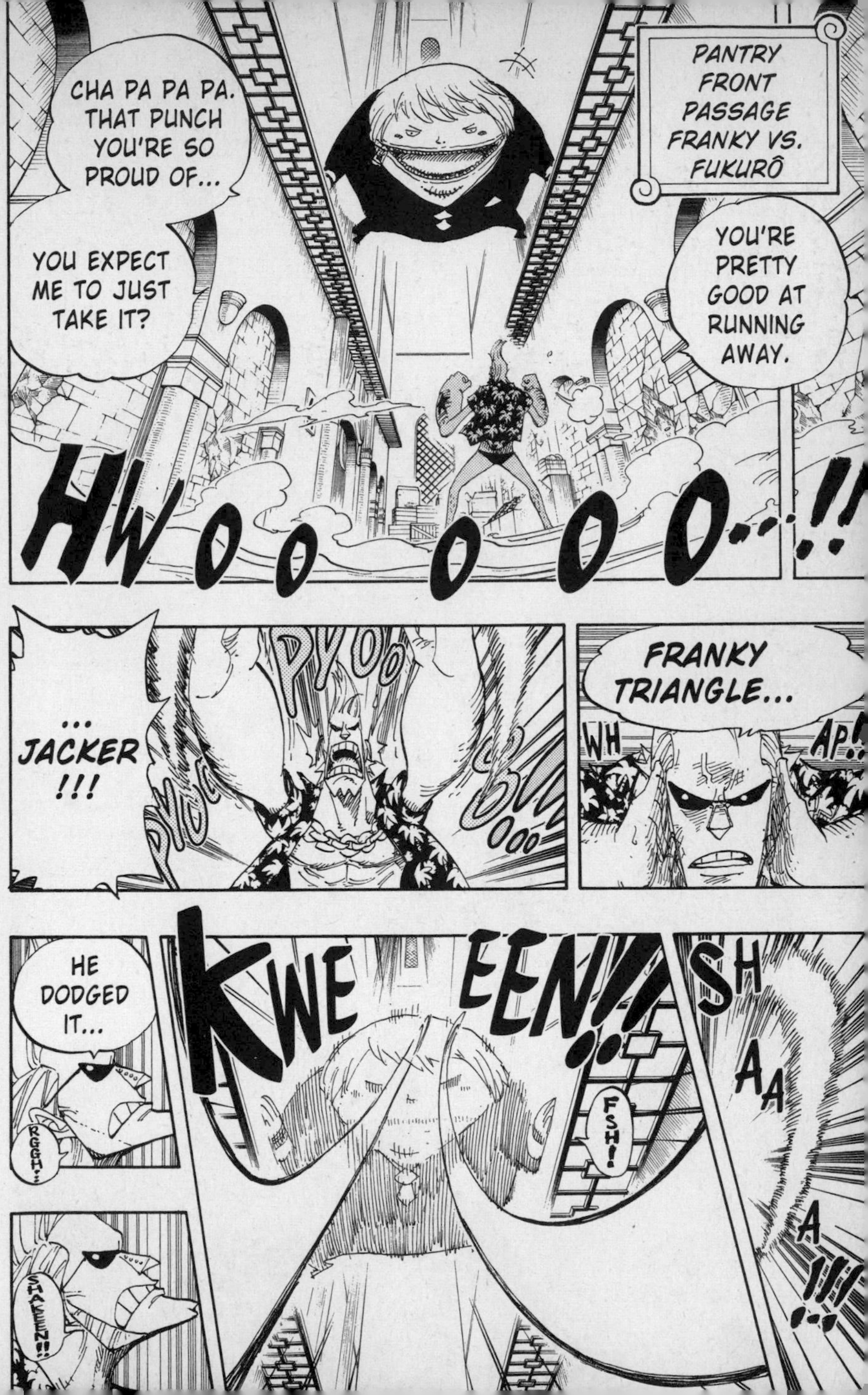
PANTRY FRONT PASSAGE FRANKY VS. FUKURÔ
YOU'RE PRETTY GOOD AT RUNNING AWAY.
CHA PA PA PA. THAT PUNCH YOU'RE SO PROUD OF...
YOU EXPECT ME TO JUST TAKE IT?
HWOOOOO...!!
FRANKY TRIANGLE...
WHAP!
PYOOOO
... JACKER !!!
SHAAAA!!!
KWEEEN!!
FSH!
HE DODGED IT...
RGGH!!
SHAKEEN!!

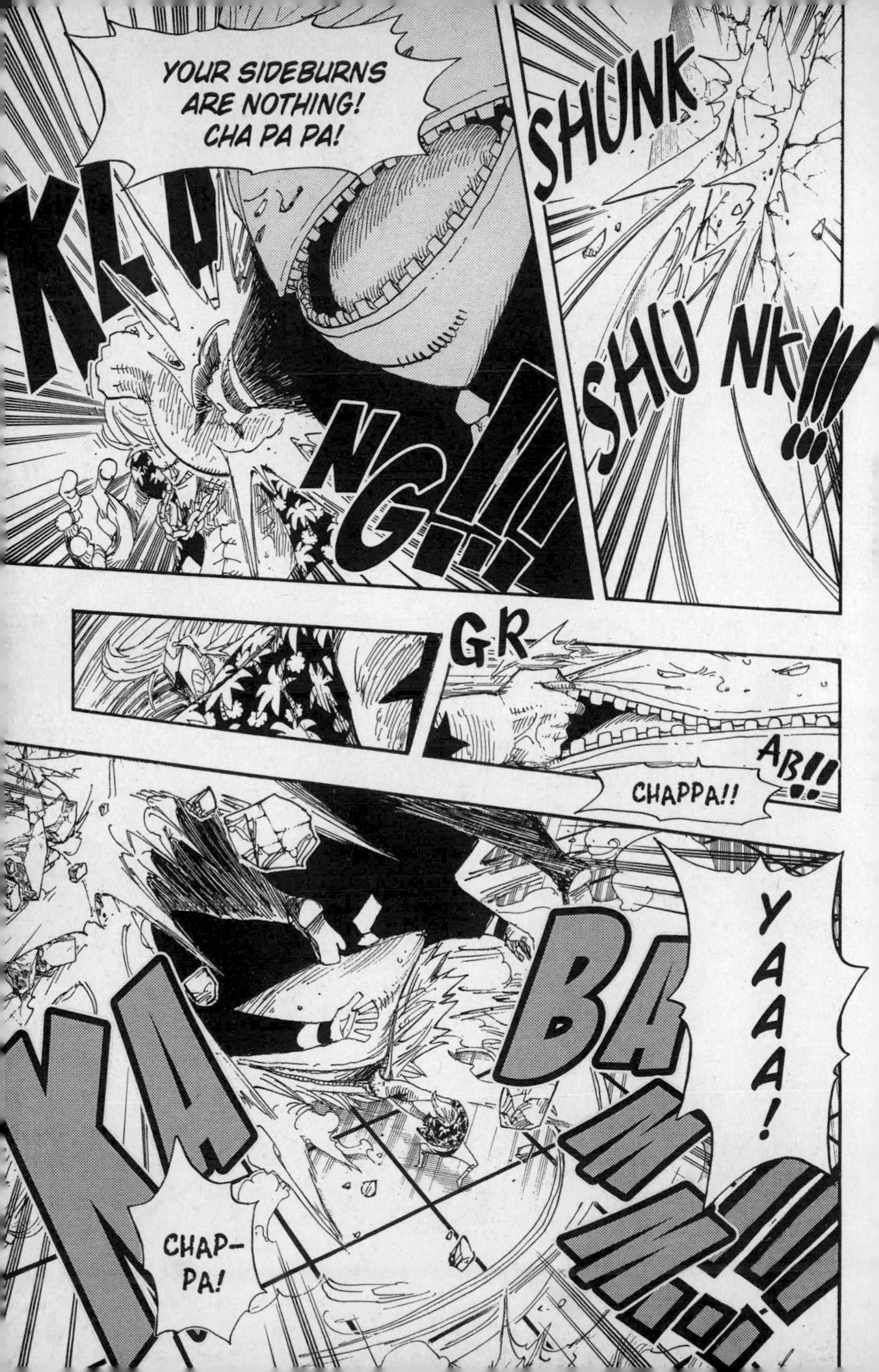
SHUNK
SHU NK!!!
YOUR SIDEBURNS ARE NOTHING! CHA PA PA!
KLA
NG!!!
GR
AB!!
CHAPPA!!
YAAAA!
BA
KA
CHAP-PA!

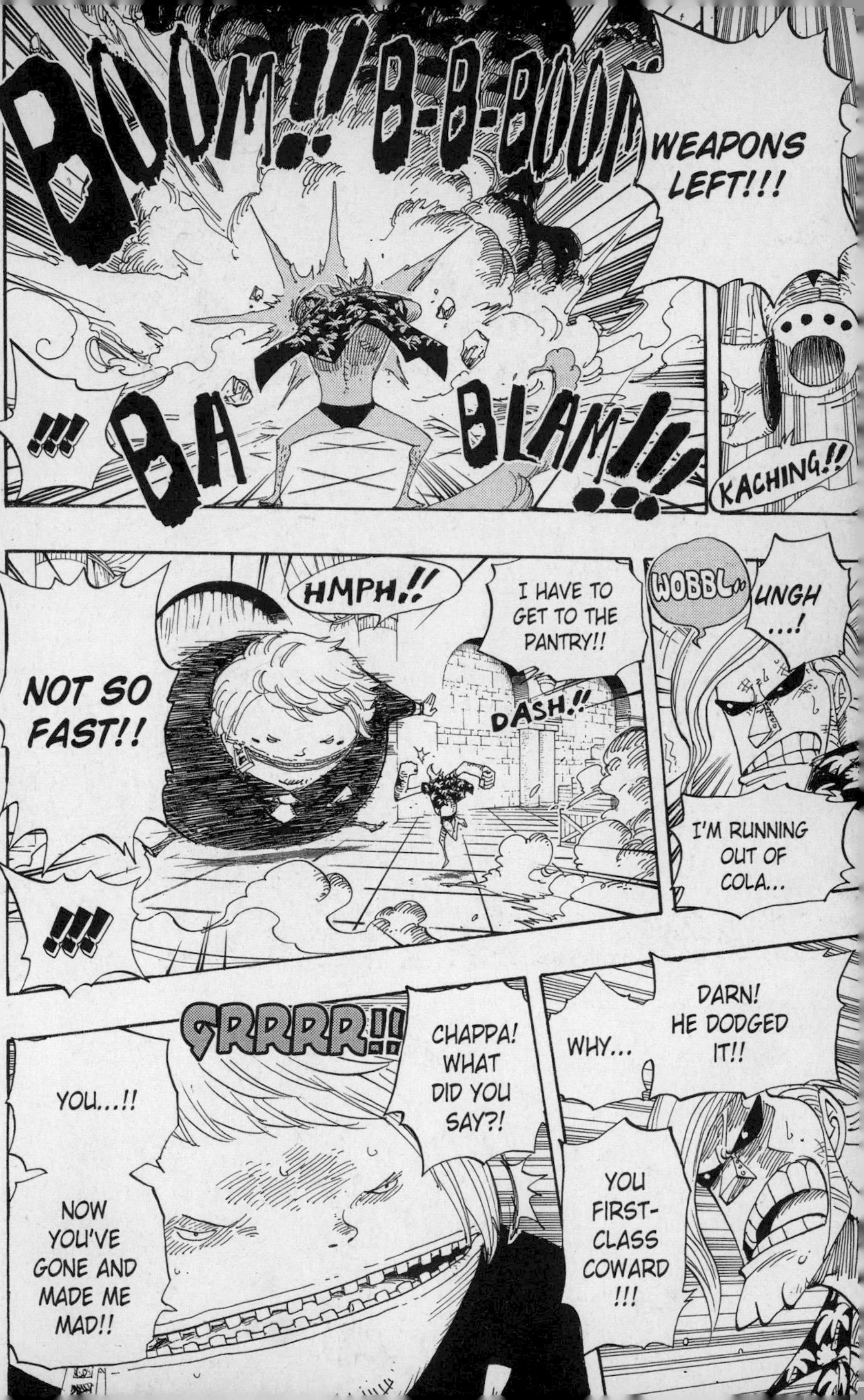
WEAPONS LEFT!!!
KACHING!!
BOOM!! B-B-BOOM
!!!
BA BLAM!!!
WOBBL..
UNGH ...!
I'M RUNNING OUT OF COLA...
HMPH.!!
I HAVE TO GET TO THE PANTRY!!
DASH!!
NOT SO FAST!!
!!!
DARN! HE DODGED IT!!
WHY...
YOU FIRST-CLASS COWARD !!!
GRRRR!!
CHAPPA! WHAT DID YOU SAY?!
YOU...!!
NOW YOU'VE GONE AND MADE ME MAD!!

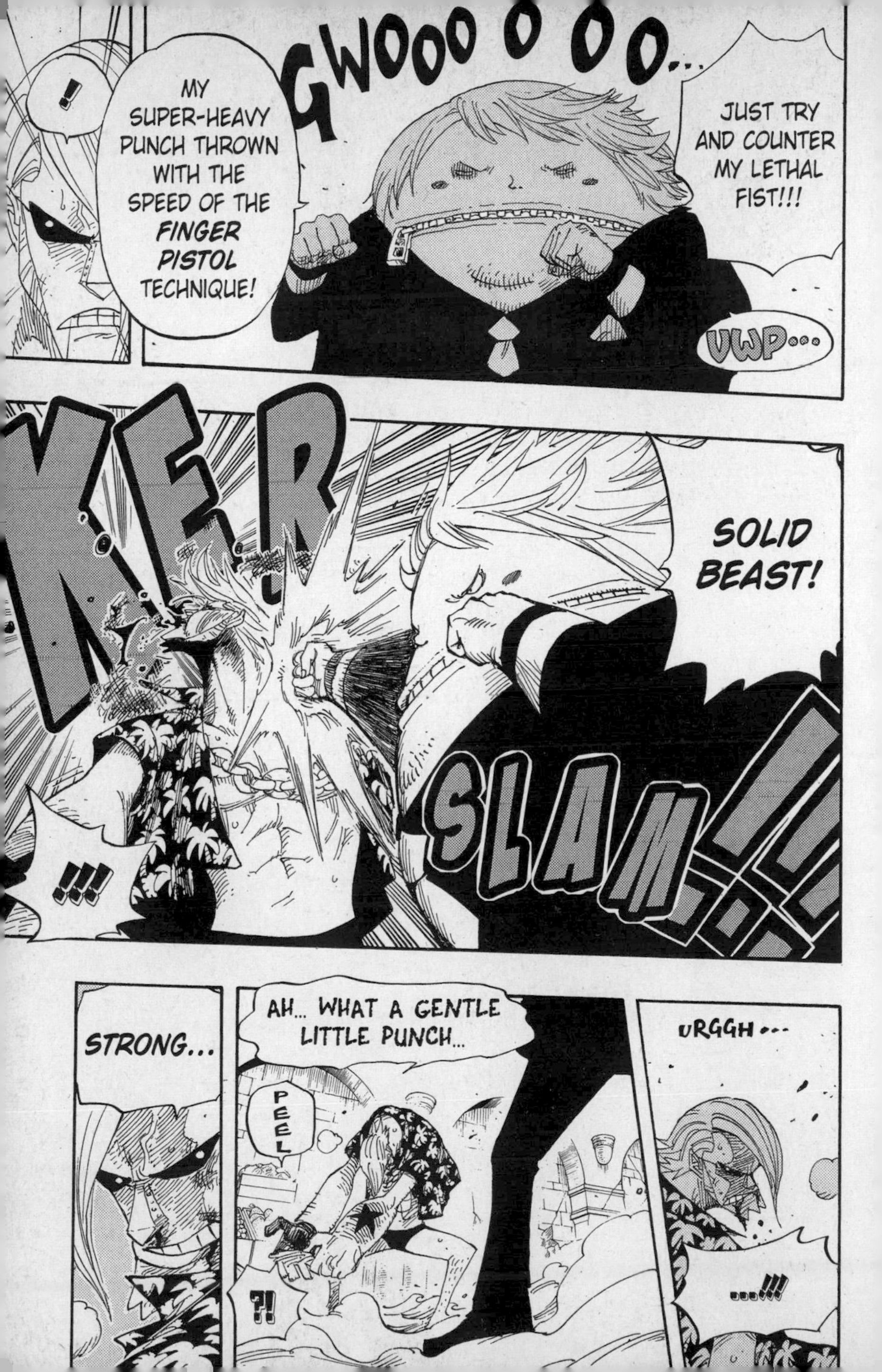
JUST TRY AND COUNTER MY LETHAL FIST!!!
GWOOO O O O...
MY SUPER-HEAVY PUNCH THROWN WITH THE SPEED OF THE FINGER PISTOL TECHNIQUE!
UWP...
!
SOLID BEAST!
KER
SLAM!!!
!!!
URGGH...
...!!!
AH... WHAT A GENTLE LITTLE PUNCH...
PEEL
?!
STRONG...

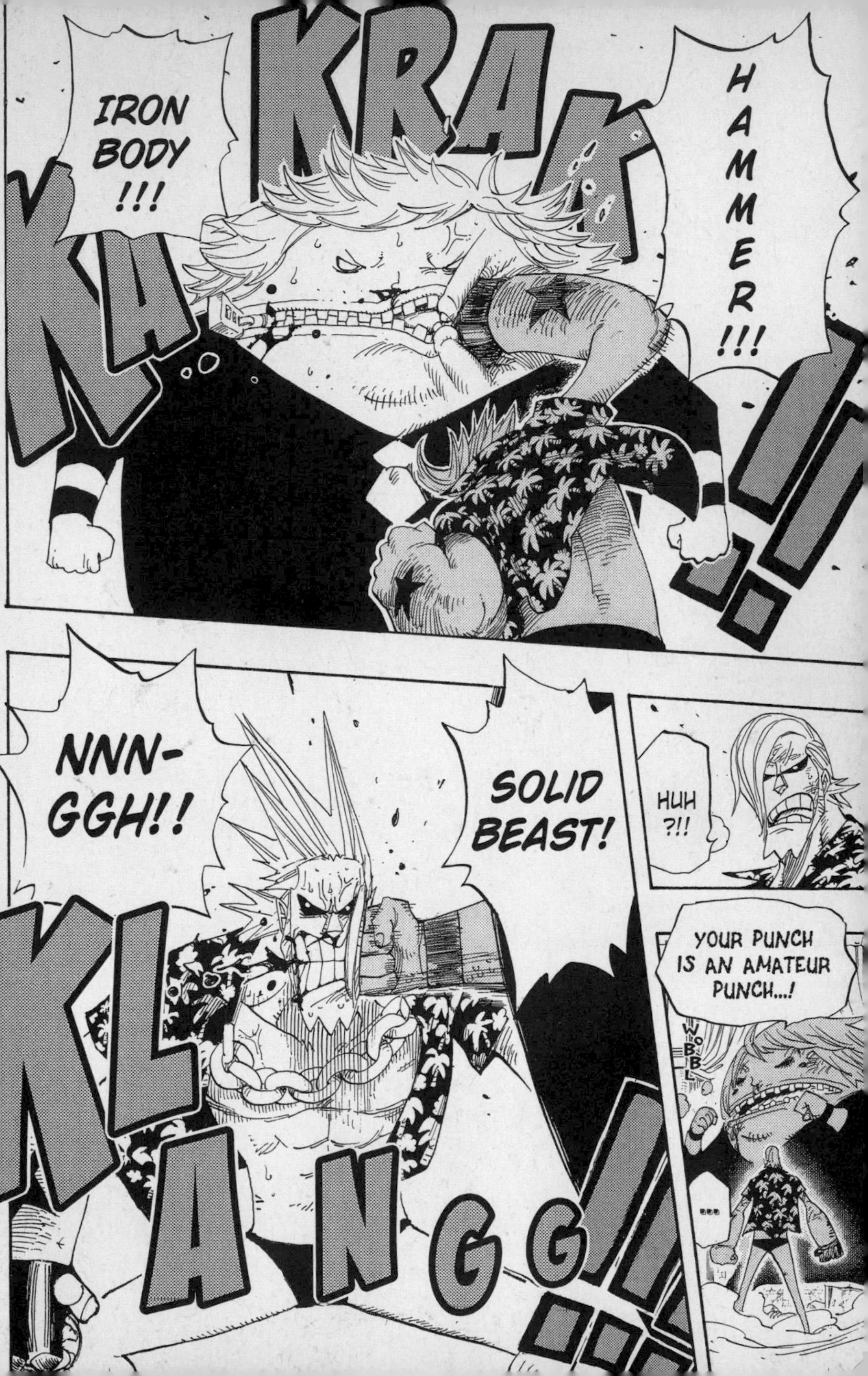
HAMMER!!!
KRAK
IRON BODY!!!
HUH?!!
YOUR PUNCH IS AN AMATEUR PUNCH...!
WOBBL
...
SOLID BEAST!
NNN-GGH!!
KLANGG

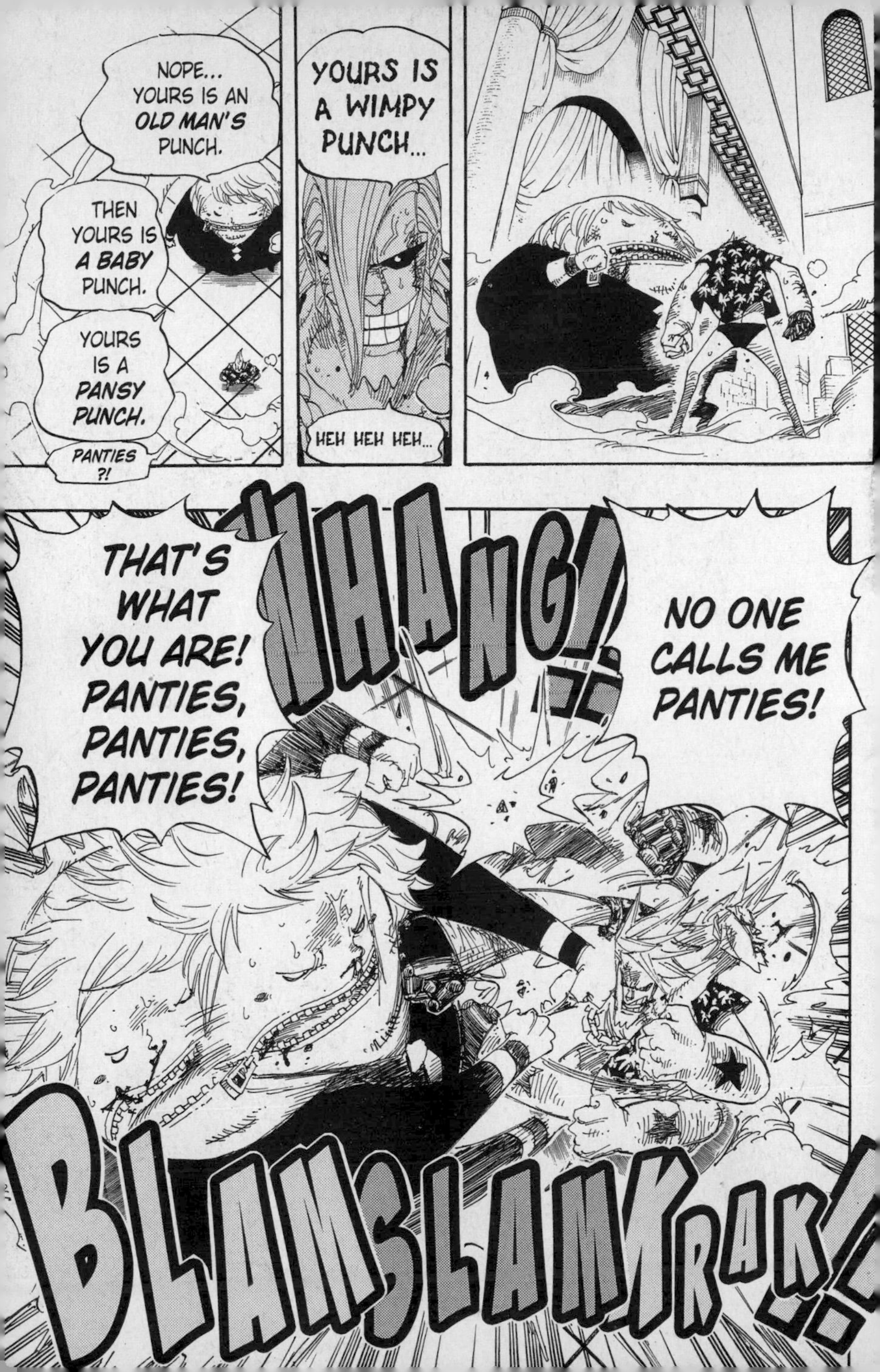
YOURS IS A WIMPY PUNCH...
HEH HEH HEH...
NOPE... YOURS IS AN OLD MAN'S PUNCH.
THEN YOURS IS A BABY PUNCH.
YOURS IS A PANSY PUNCH.
PANTIES ?!
NO ONE CALLS ME PANTIES!
WHANG!
THAT'S WHAT YOU ARE! PANTIES, PANTIES, PANTIES!
BLAMSLAMKRAK!!

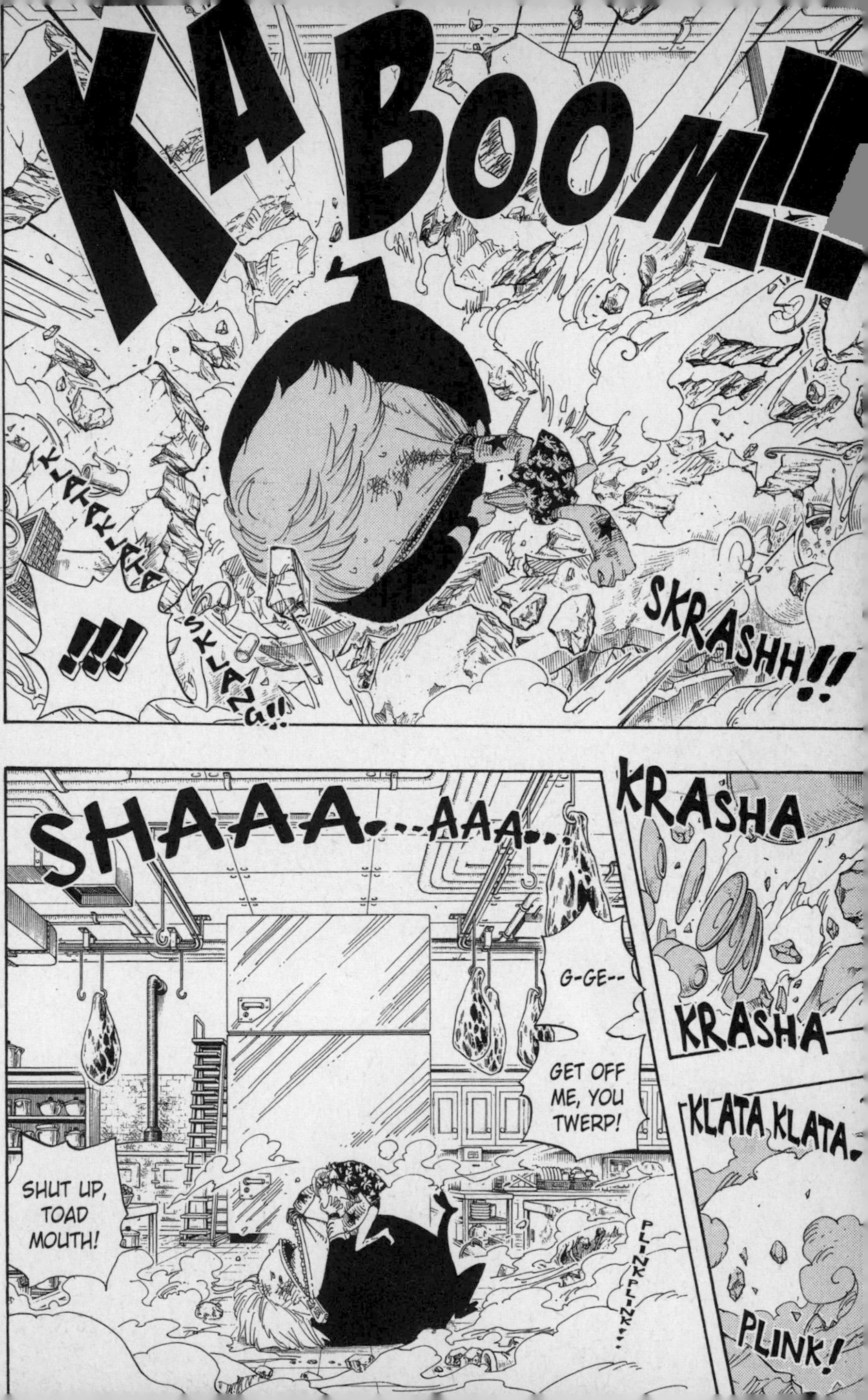
KABOOM!!!
SKRASHH!!
SKLANG!!
KLAKKLATA!!!
KRASHA
KRASHA
KLATA KLATA...
PLINK!
SHAAA...AAA...
G-GE--
GET OFF ME, YOU TWERP!
SHUT UP, TOAD MOUTH!
PLINK PLINK...

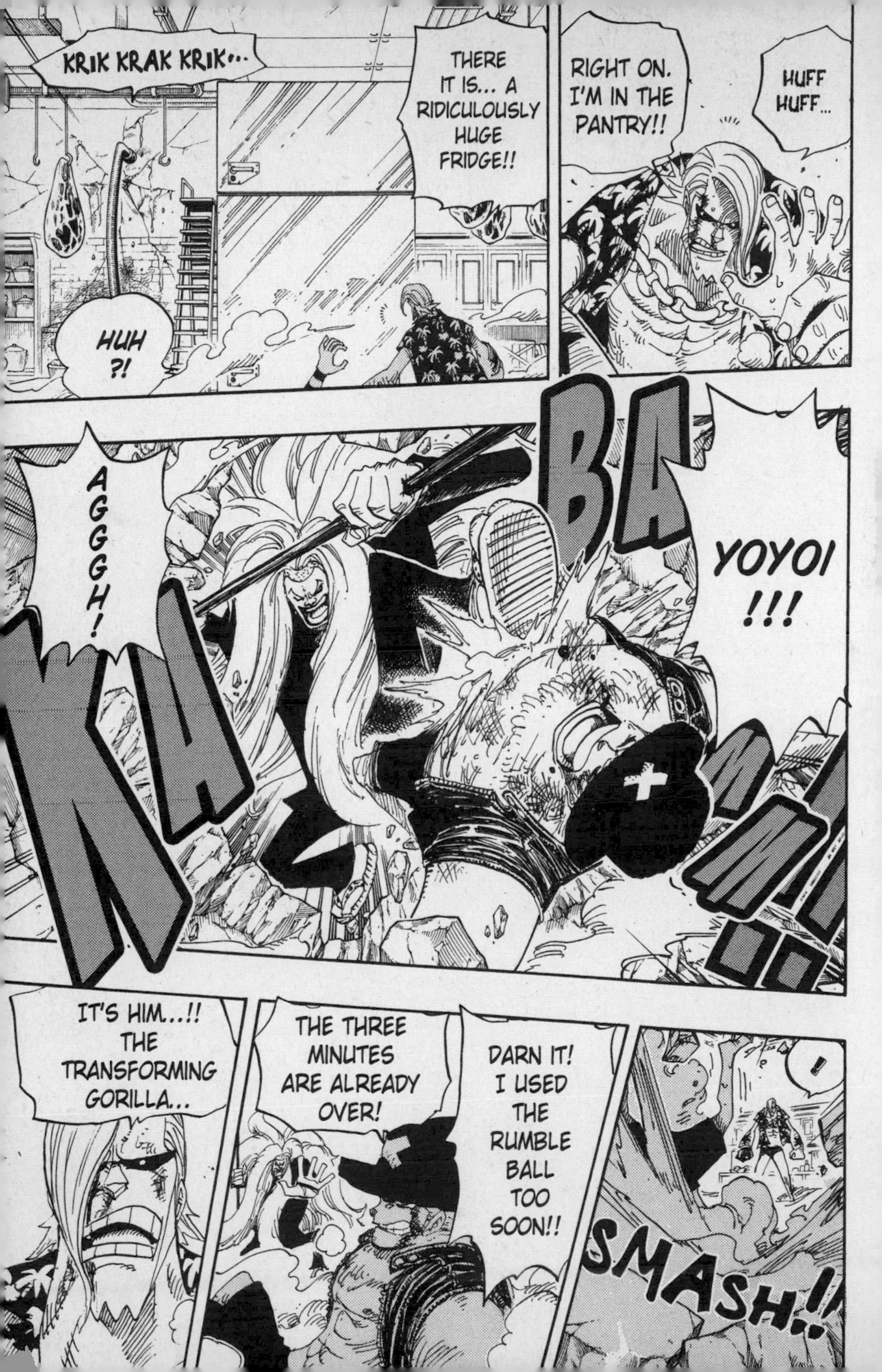
HUFF HUFF...
RIGHT ON. I'M IN THE PANTRY!!
THERE IT IS... A RIDICULOUSLY HUGE FRIDGE!!
KRIK KRAK KRIK...
HUH ?!
YOYOI !!!
AGGGH!
!
SMASH!!
DARN IT! I USED THE RUMBLE BALL TOO SOON!!
THE THREE MINUTES ARE ALREADY OVER!
IT'S HIM...!! THE TRANSFORMING GORILLA...

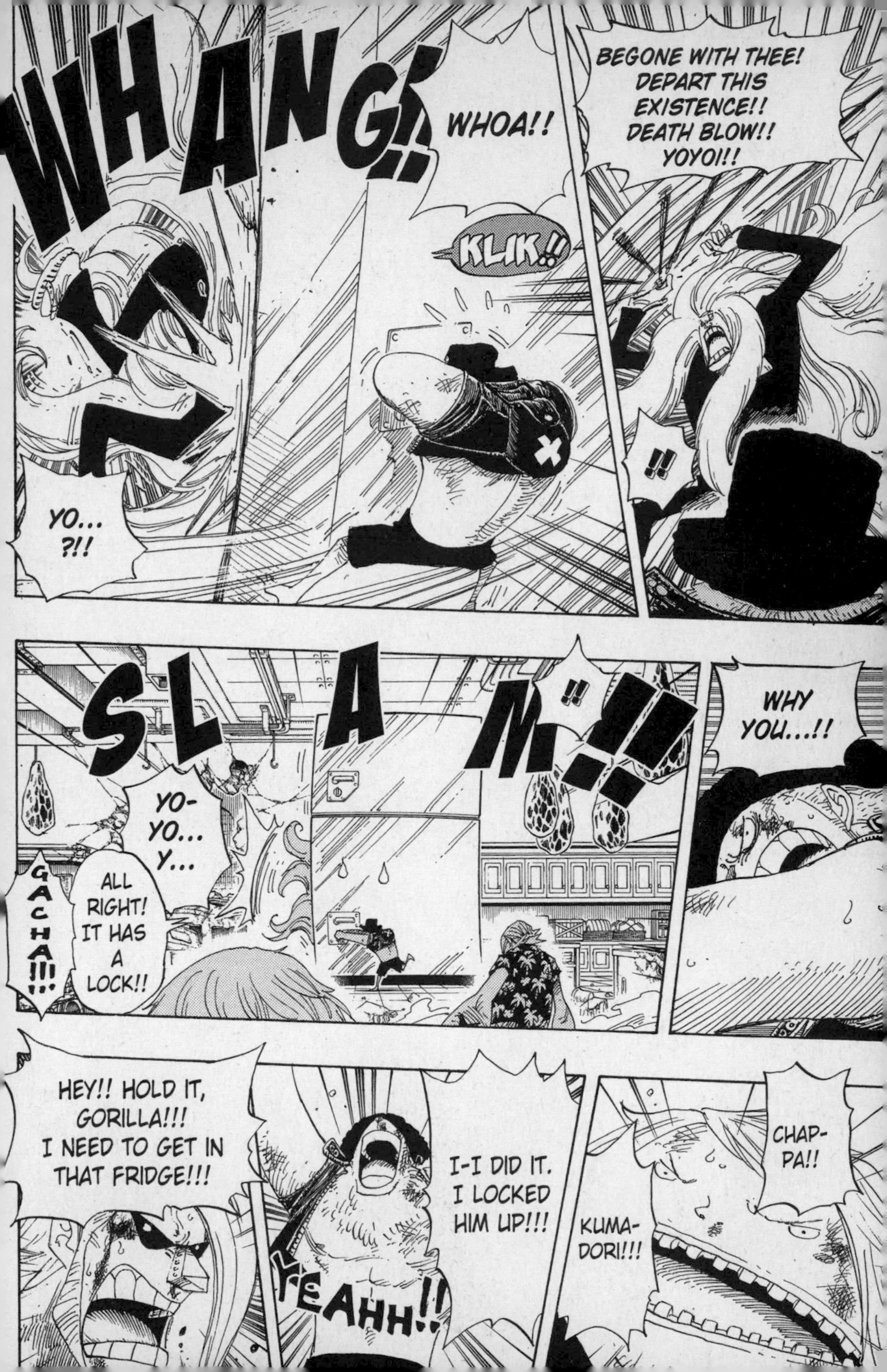

BEGONE WITH THEE! DEPART THIS EXISTENCE!! DEATH BLOW!! YOYOI!!
!!
WHOA!!
KLIK!!
WHANG!!
YO... ?!!
WHY YOU...!!
SLAM!!
YO-YO... Y...
ALL RIGHT! IT HAS A LOCK!!
GACHA!!!
CHAP-PA!!
KUMA-DORI!!!
I-I DID IT. I LOCKED HIM UP!!!
YEAHH!!
HEY!! HOLD IT, GORILLA!!! I NEED TO GET IN THAT FRIDGE!!!

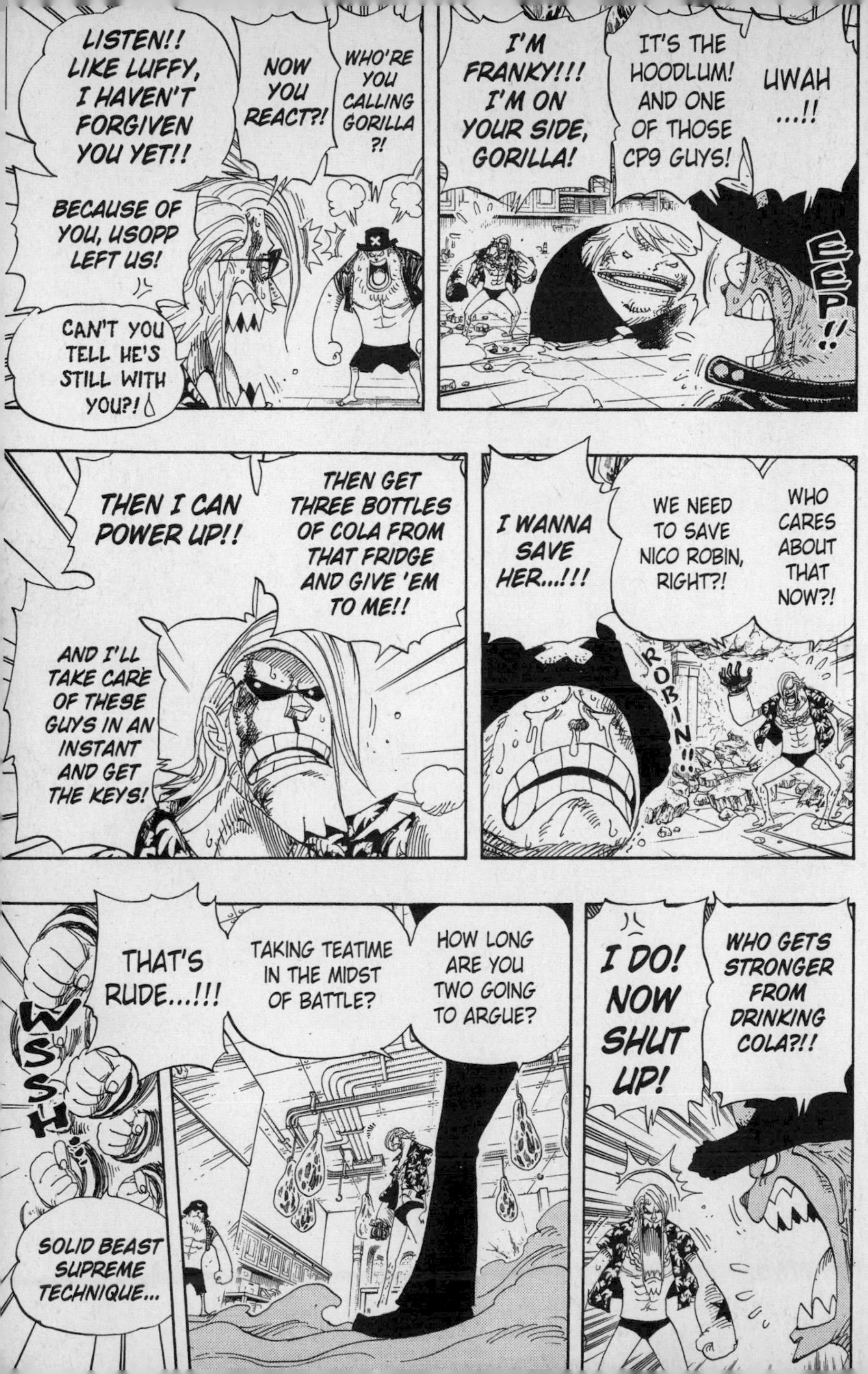
UWAH ...!!
IT'S THE HOODLUM! AND ONE OF THOSE CP9 GUYS!
I'M FRANKY!!! I'M ON YOUR SIDE, GORILLA!
EEEP!!
WHO'RE YOU CALLING GORILLA?!
NOW YOU REACT?!
LISTEN!! LIKE LUFFY, I HAVEN'T FORGIVEN YOU YET!!
BECAUSE OF YOU, USOPP LEFT US!
CAN'T YOU TELL HE'S STILL WITH YOU?!
WHO CARES ABOUT THAT NOW?!
WE NEED TO SAVE NICO ROBIN, RIGHT?!
I WANNA SAVE HER...!!!
ROBIN!!
THEN GET THREE BOTTLES OF COLA FROM THAT FRIDGE AND GIVE 'EM TO ME!!
THEN I CAN POWER UP!!
AND I'LL TAKE CARE OF THESE GUYS IN AN INSTANT AND GET THE KEYS!
WHO GETS STRONGER FROM DRINKING COLA?!!
I DO! NOW SHUT UP!
HOW LONG ARE YOU TWO GOING TO ARGUE?
TAKING TEATIME IN THE MIDST OF BATTLE?
THAT'S RUDE...!!!
WSSH!
SOLID BEAST SUPREME TECHNIQUE...

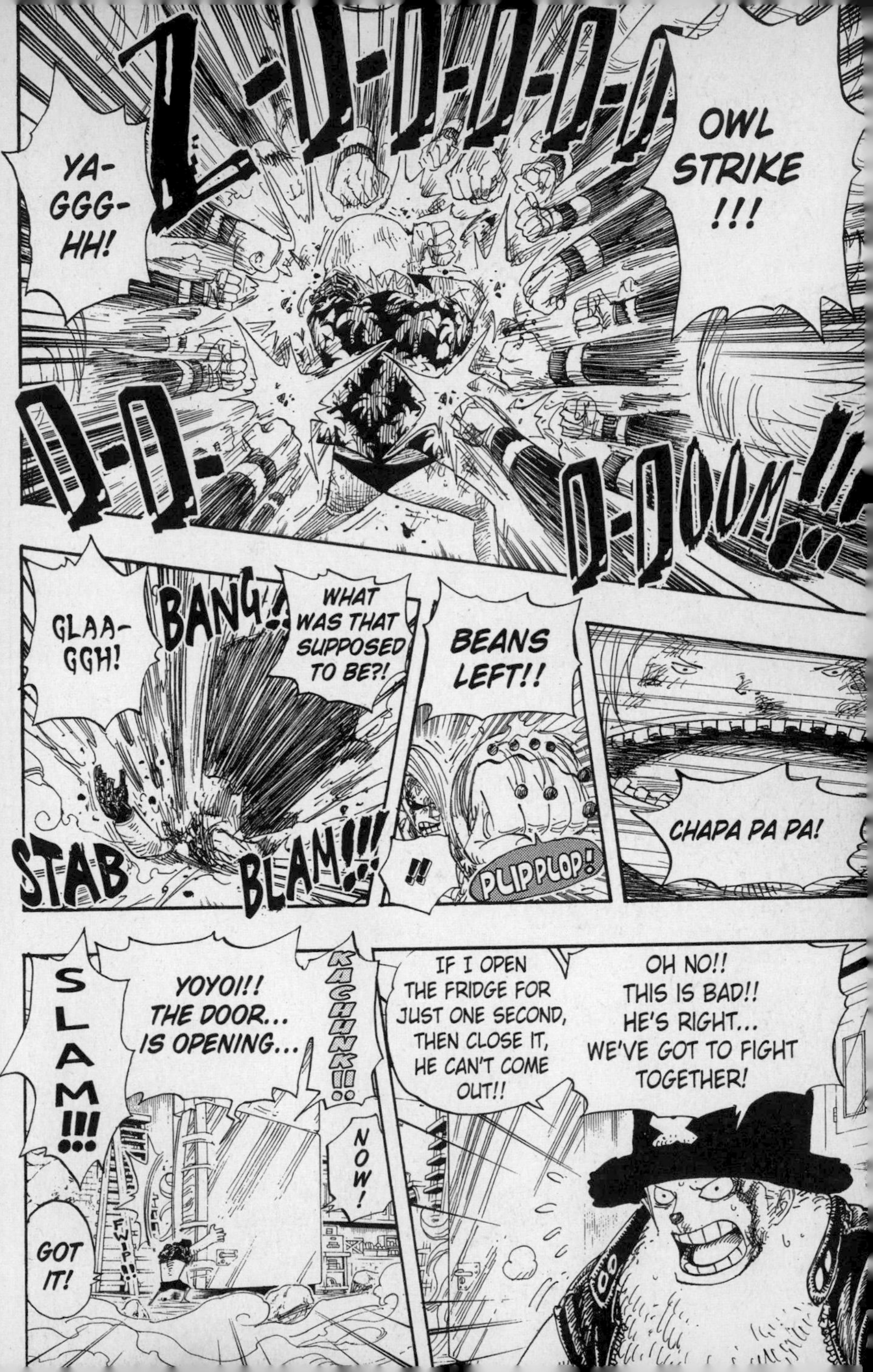

OWL STRIKE!!!
Z-D-D-D-D-D-D
YA-GGG-HH!
D-D-D-
D-DOOM!!
CHAPA PA PA!
BEANS LEFT!!
PLIPPLOP!
!!
WHAT WAS THAT SUPPOSED TO BE?!
BANG!!
GLAA-GGH!
BLAM!!!
STAB
OH NO!! THIS IS BAD!! HE'S RIGHT... WE'VE GOT TO FIGHT TOGETHER!
IF I OPEN THE FRIDGE FOR JUST ONE SECOND, THEN CLOSE IT, HE CAN'T COME OUT!!
NOW!
KACHUNK!!
YOYOI!! THE DOOR... IS OPENING...
SLAM!!!
FWIP!!
GOT IT!

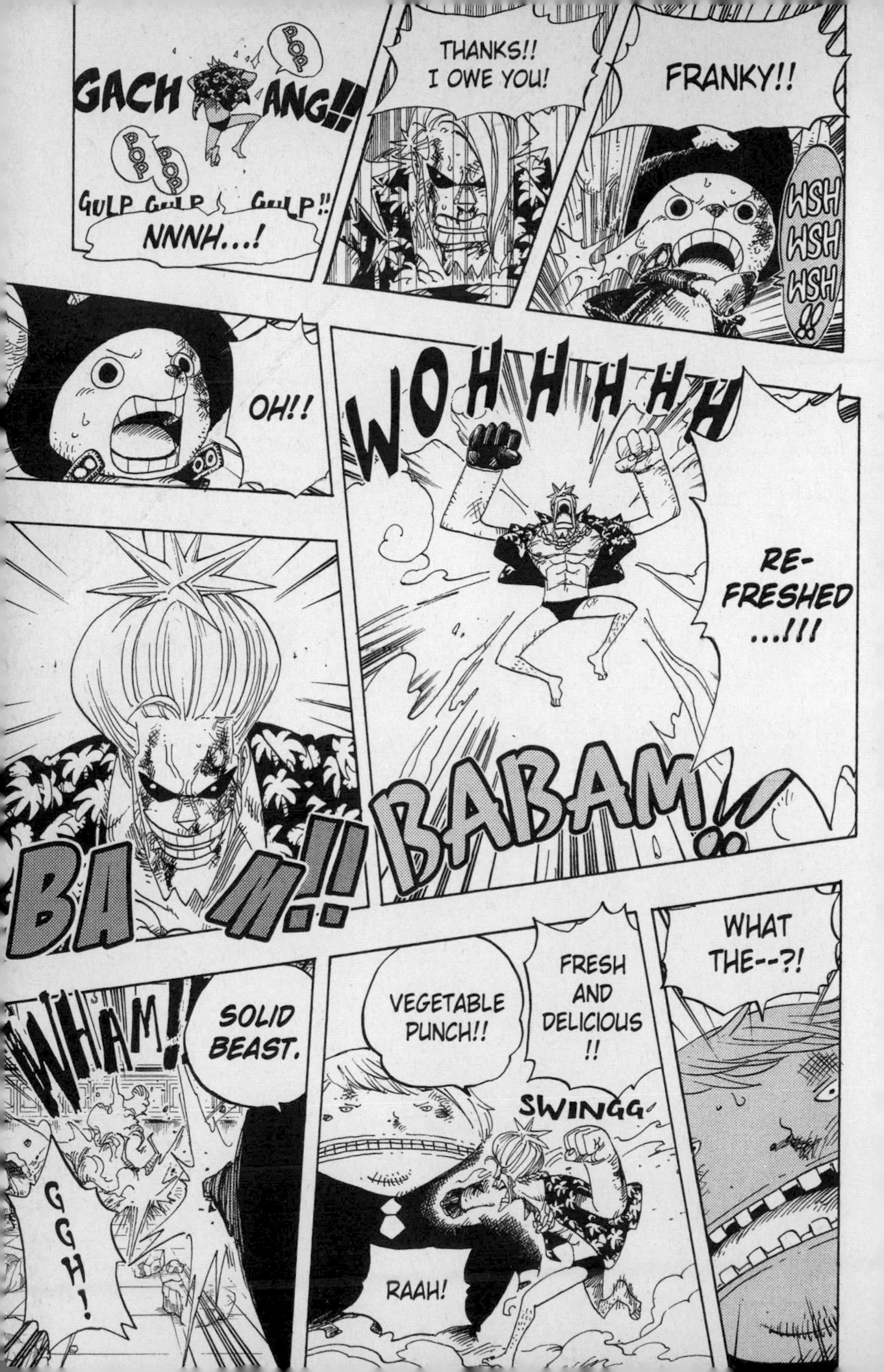
FRANKY!!
WSH WSH WSH!!
THANKS!! I OWE YOU!
GACH ANG!!
POP
POP
POP
GULP GULP GULP!!
NNNH...!
WOHHHHHH
RE-FRESHED...!!!
BABAM!!
OH!!
BA M!!
WHAT THE--?!
FRESH AND DELICIOUS!!
VEGETABLE PUNCH!!
SWINGG
RAAH!
SOLID BEAST.
WHAM!
GGH!

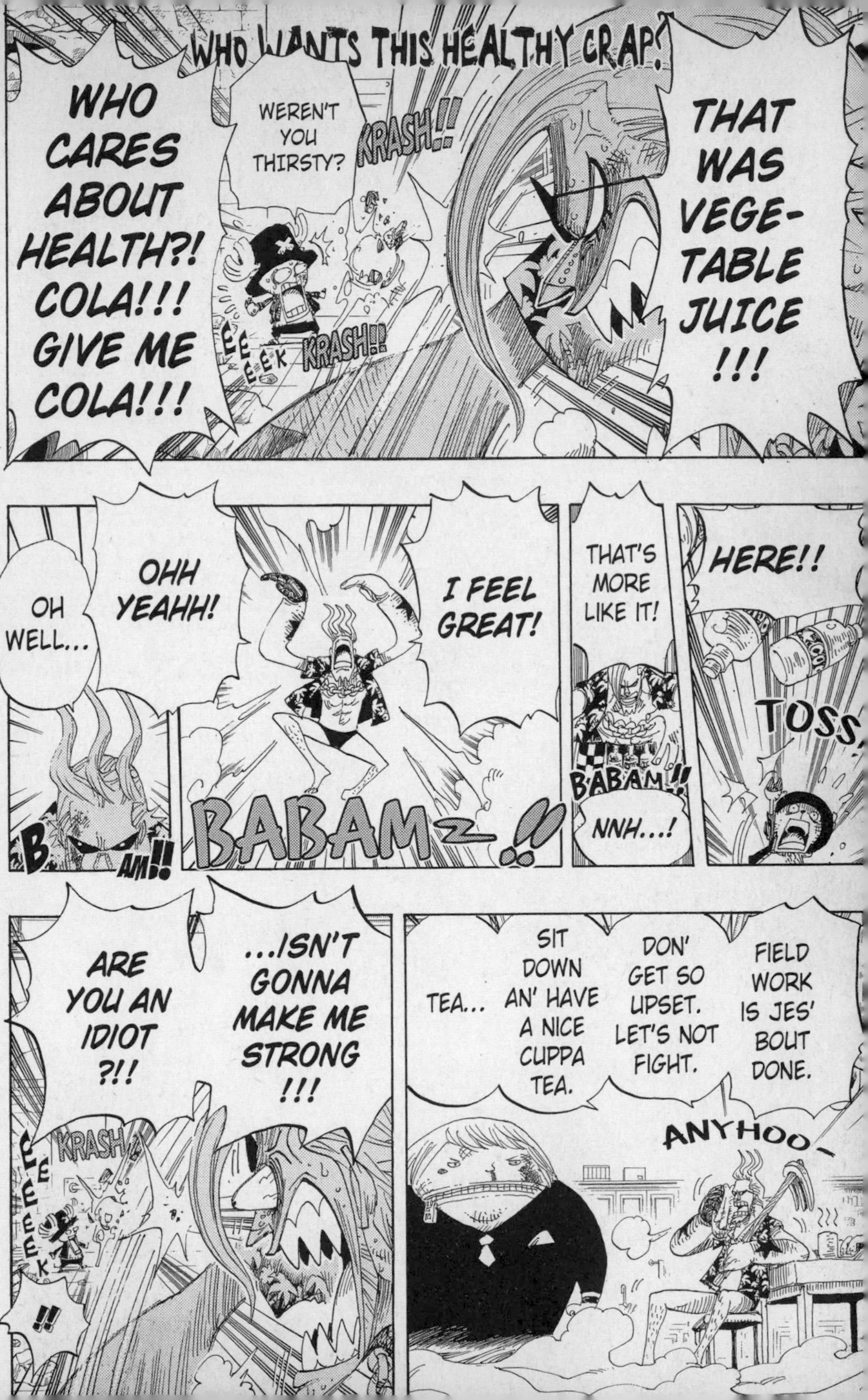

THAT WAS VEGETABLE JUICE!!!
WHO WANTS THIS HEALTHY CRAP?
KRASH!!
WEREN'T YOU THIRSTY?
WHO CARES ABOUT HEALTH?! COLA!!! GIVE ME COLA!!!
KRASH!!
EEEEK
HERE!!
TOSS
THAT'S MORE LIKE IT!
BABAM!!
NNH...!
I FEEL GREAT!
OHH YEAHH!
BABAMz!!
OH WELL...
BAM!!
FIELD WORK IS JES' BOUT DONE.
DON' GET SO UPSET. LET'S NOT FIGHT.
SIT DOWN AN' HAVE A NICE CUPPA TEA.
TEA...
ANYHOO~
...ISN'T GONNA MAKE ME STRONG!!!
ARE YOU AN IDIOT?!!
KRASH!!
EEEEEK!!

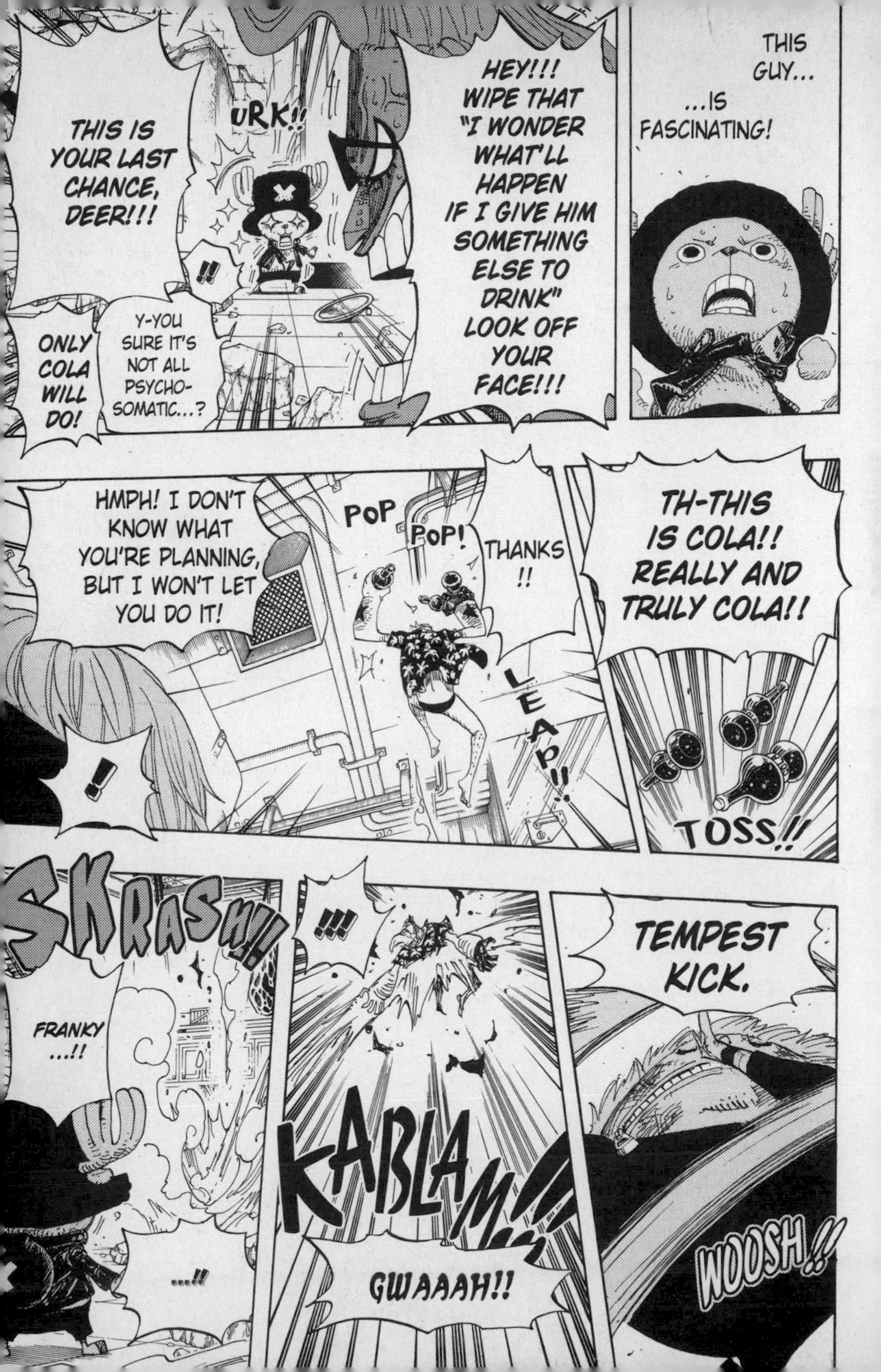
THIS GUY...
...IS FASCINATING!
HEY!!! WIPE THAT "I WONDER WHAT'LL HAPPEN IF I GIVE HIM SOMETHING ELSE TO DRINK" LOOK OFF YOUR FACE!!!
URK!!
THIS IS YOUR LAST CHANCE, DEER!!!
!!
Y-YOU SURE IT'S NOT ALL PSYCHO-SOMATIC...?
ONLY COLA WILL DO!
TH-THIS IS COLA!! REALLY AND TRULY COLA!!
TOSS!!
THANKS!!
POP
POP!
HMPH! I DON'T KNOW WHAT YOU'RE PLANNING, BUT I WON'T LET YOU DO IT!
LEAP!!
!
TEMPEST KICK.
WOOSH!!
!!!
KABLAM!!
GWAAAH!!
SKRASH!!
FRANKY...!!
...!!

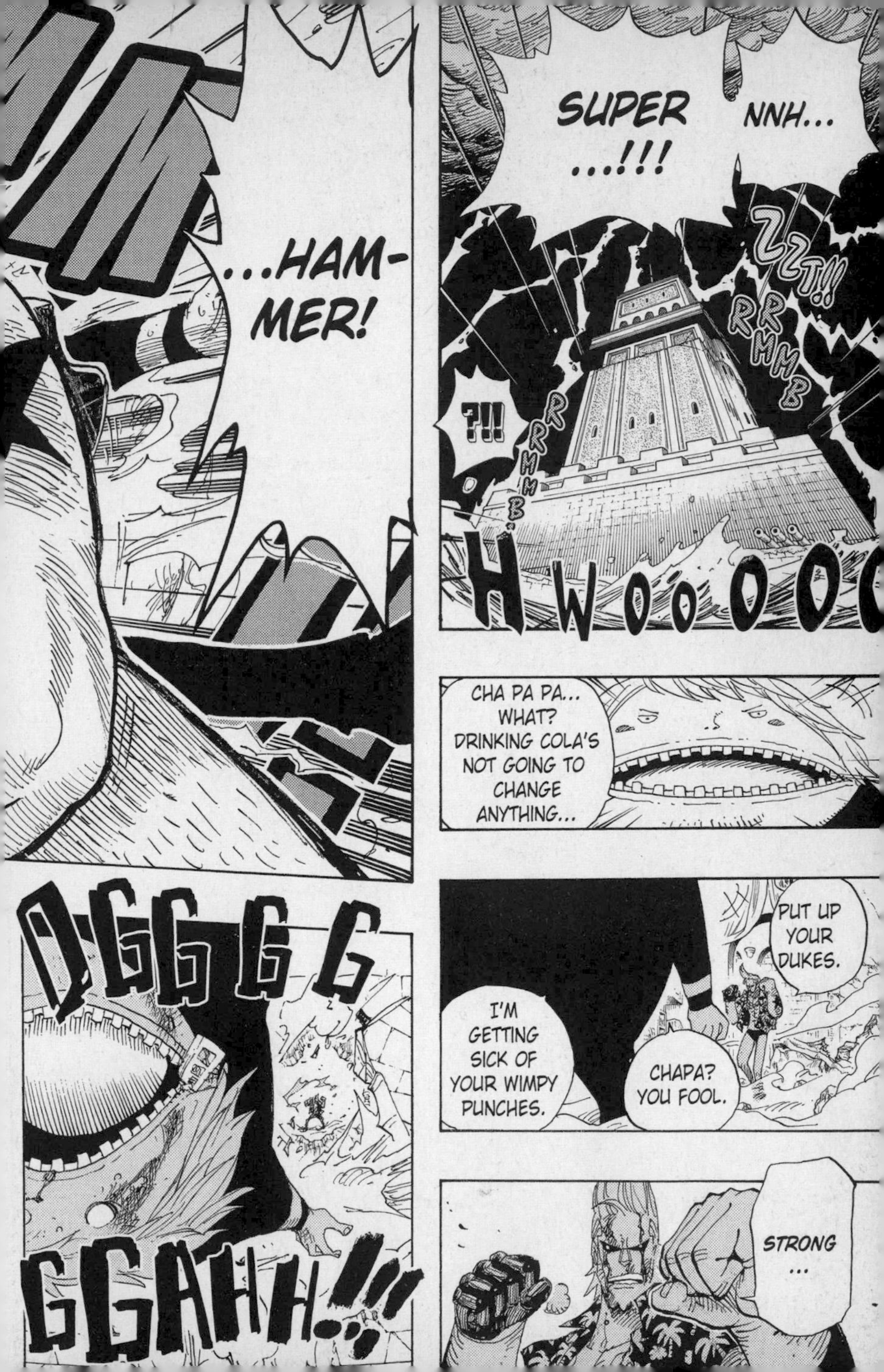
SUPER ...!!!
NNH...
ZZT!!
RRRMMB
?!!
RRRMMB
HWOOOOO
CHA PA PA... WHAT? DRINKING COLA'S NOT GOING TO CHANGE ANYTHING...
...HAM-MER!
PUT UP YOUR DUKES.
I'M GETTING SICK OF YOUR WIMPY PUNCHES.
CHAPA? YOU FOOL.
STRONG ...
DGGGG
GGAHH!!!

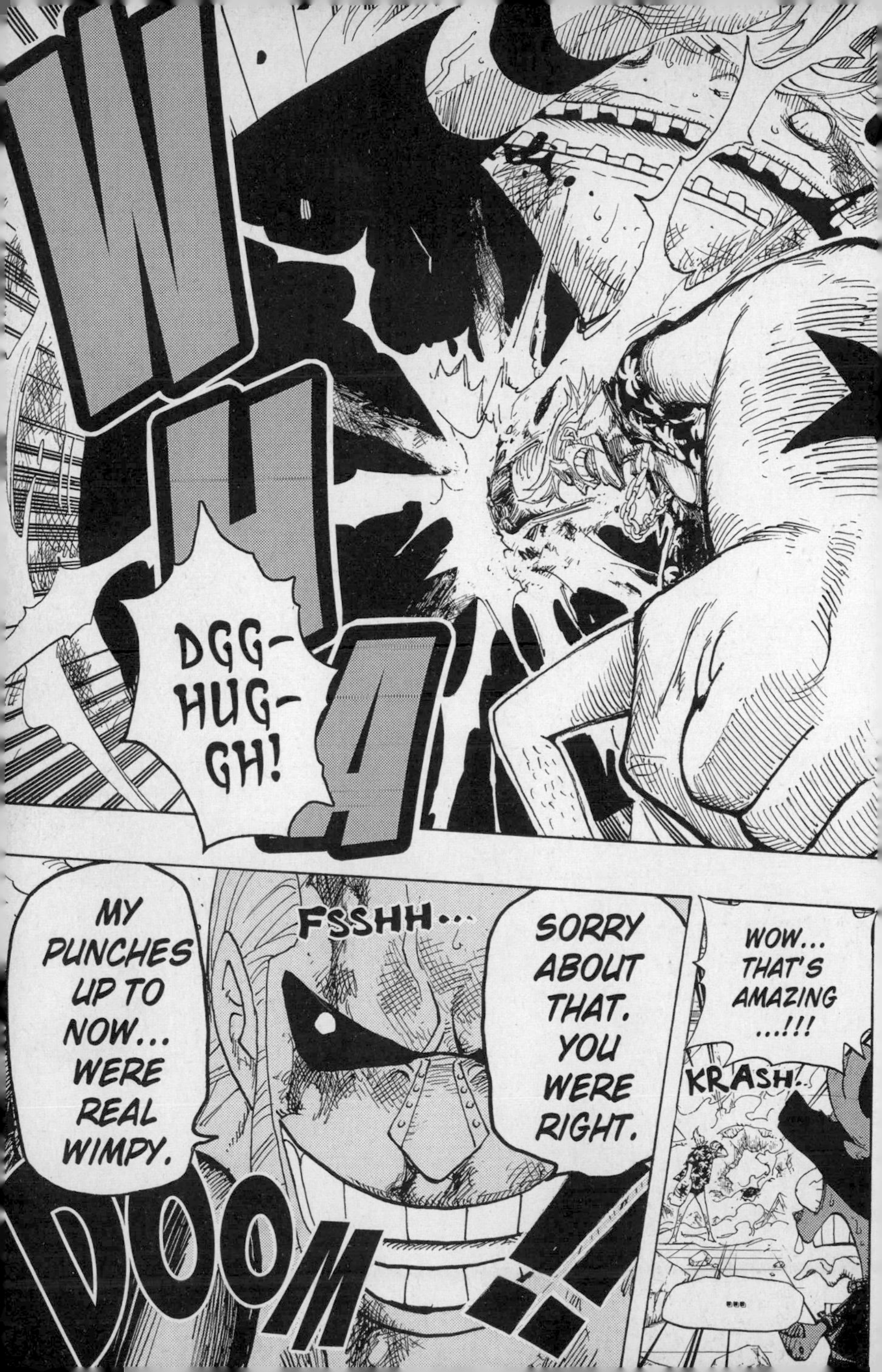
DGG-HUG-GH!
WOW... THAT'S AMAZING ...!!!
KRASH!!
SORRY ABOUT THAT. YOU WERE RIGHT.
FSSHH...
MY PUNCHES UP TO NOW... WERE REAL WIMPY.
DOOM!!

Chapter 405: POWER

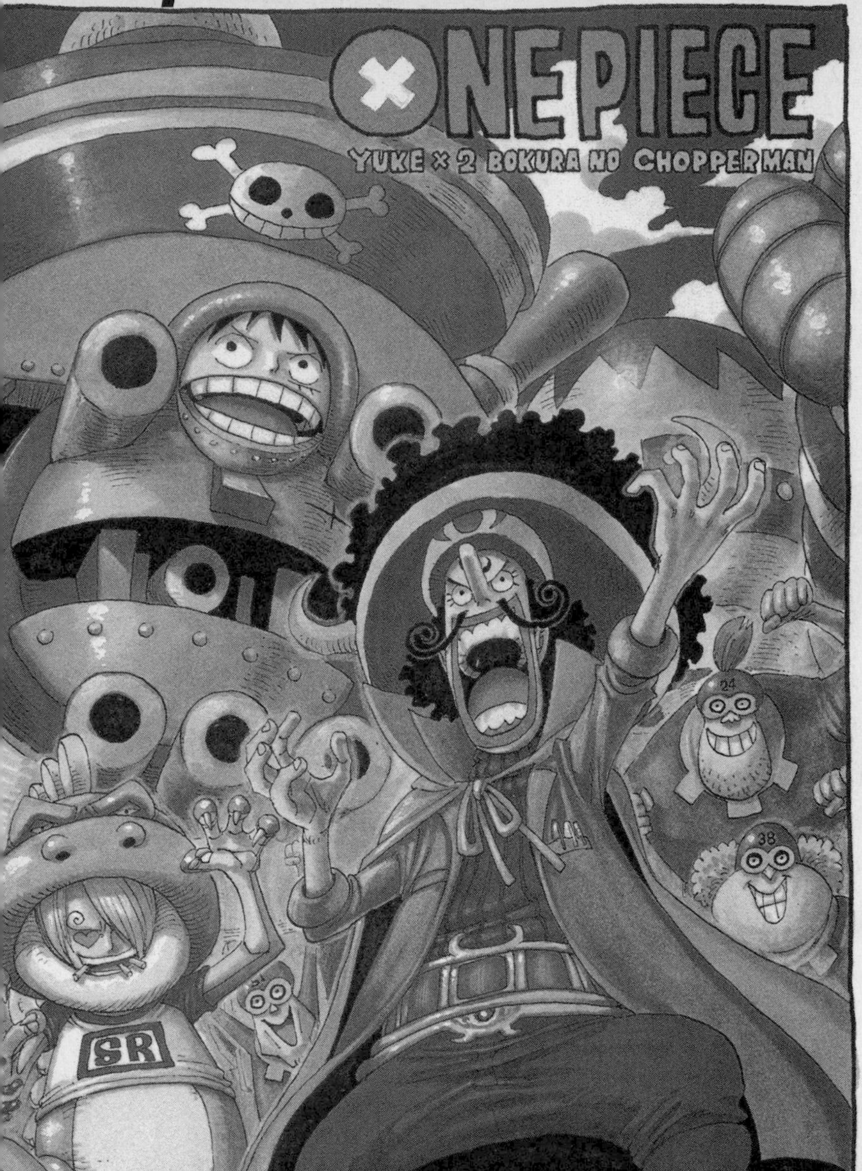
ONE PIECE
YUKE × 2 BOKURA NO CHOPPERMAN
SR

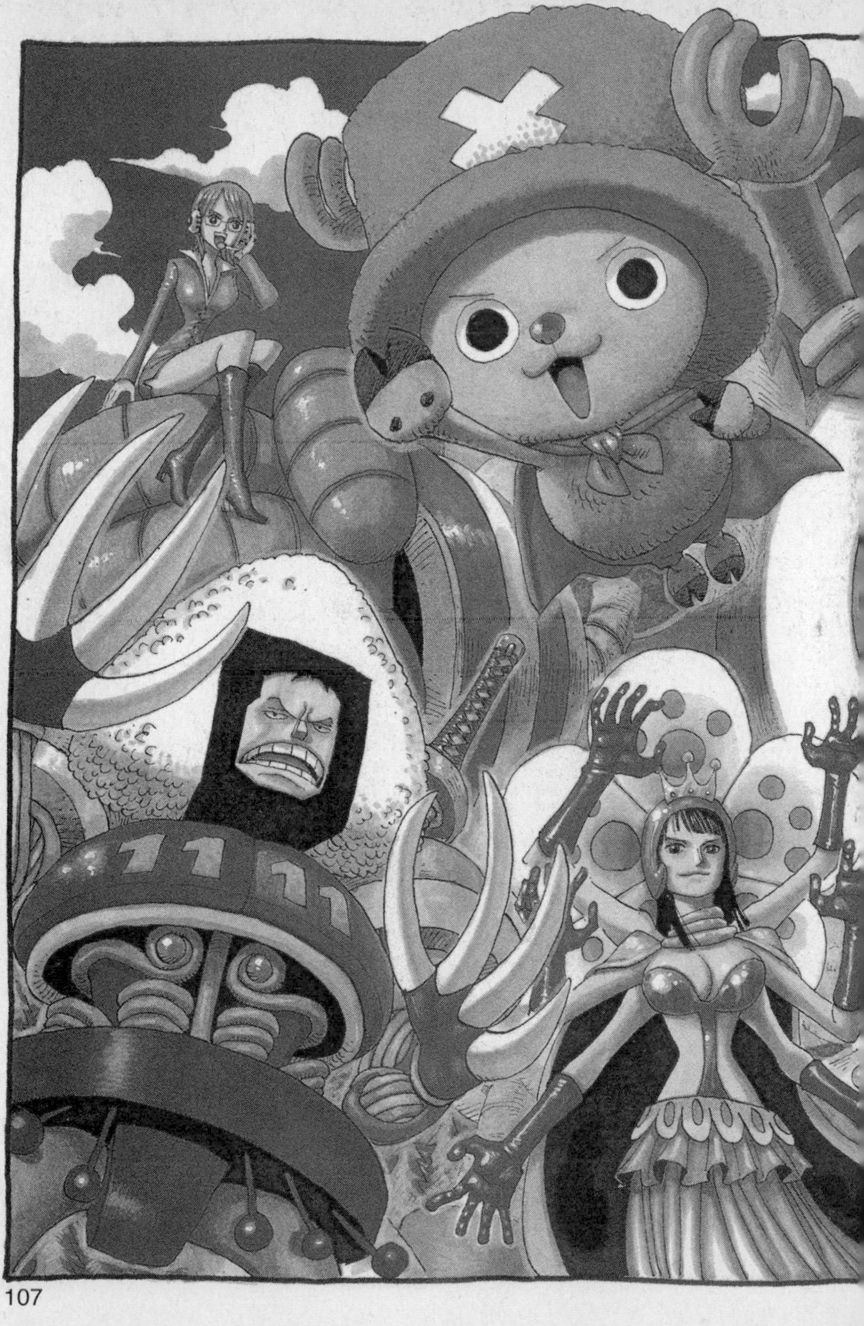

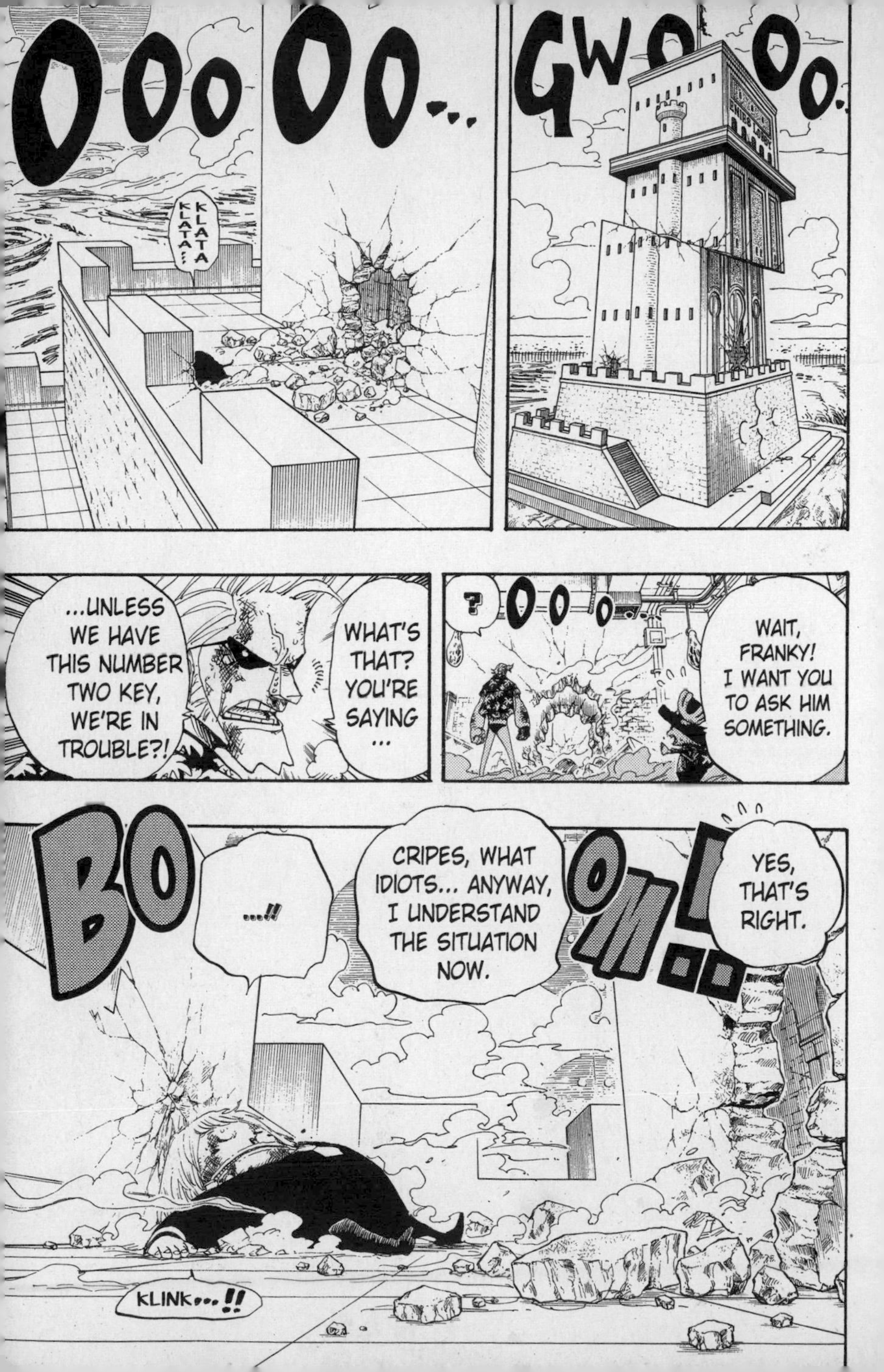
GWO... OO...
OOOOOO...
KLATA KLATA...
WAIT, FRANKY! I WANT YOU TO ASK HIM SOMETHING.
? OOO...
WHAT'S THAT? YOU'RE SAYING ...
...UNLESS WE HAVE THIS NUMBER TWO KEY, WE'RE IN TROUBLE?!
YES, THAT'S RIGHT.
BOOM..!
CRIPES, WHAT IDIOTS... ANYWAY, I UNDERSTAND THE SITUATION NOW.
...!!
KLINK...!!

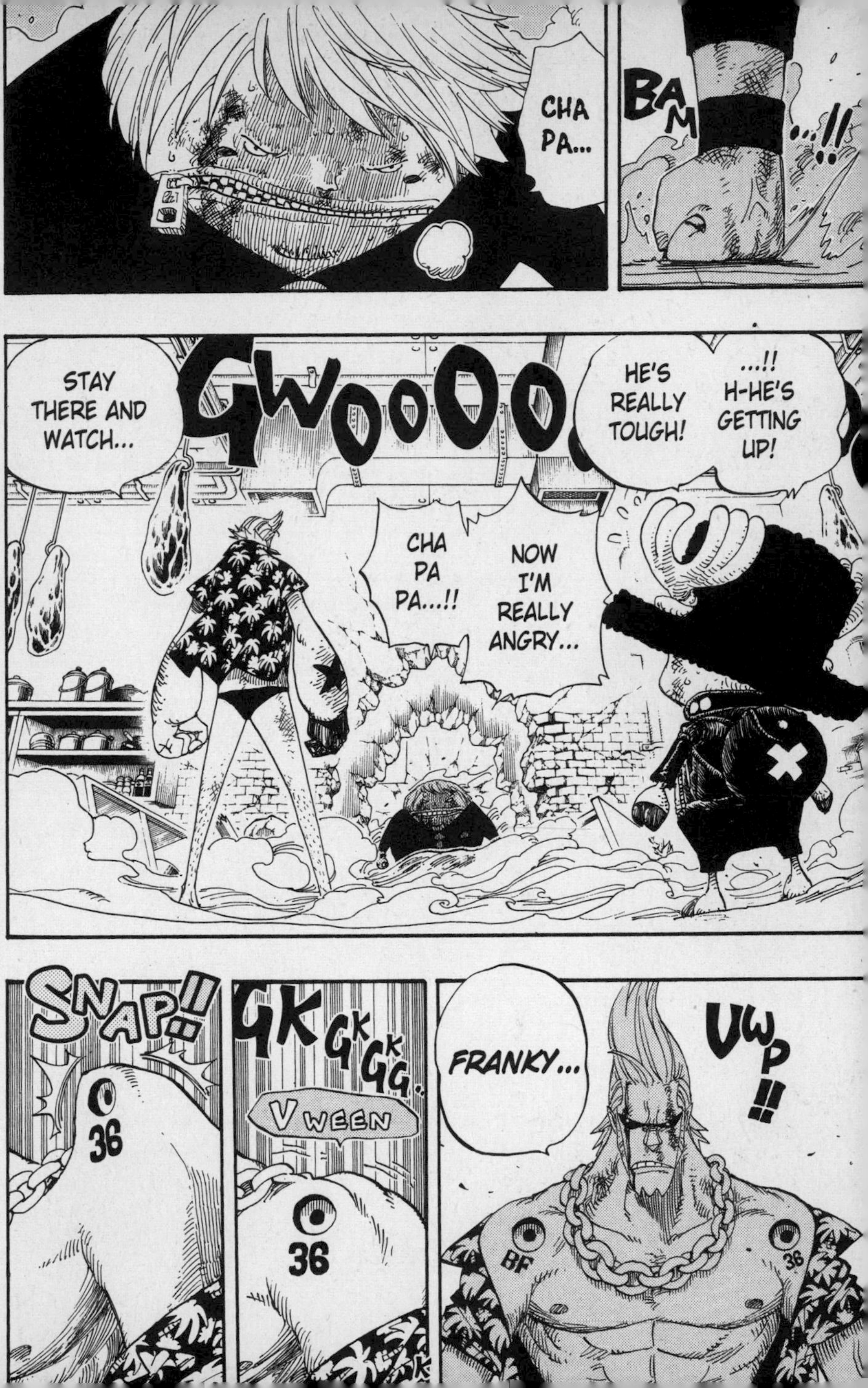
BAM
...!!
CHA PA...
...!! H-HE'S GETTING UP!
HE'S REALLY TOUGH!
GWOOOO
NOW I'M REALLY ANGRY...
CHA PA PA...!!
STAY THERE AND WATCH...
UWP!!
FRANKY...
GKGKGG..
VWEEN
SNAP!!

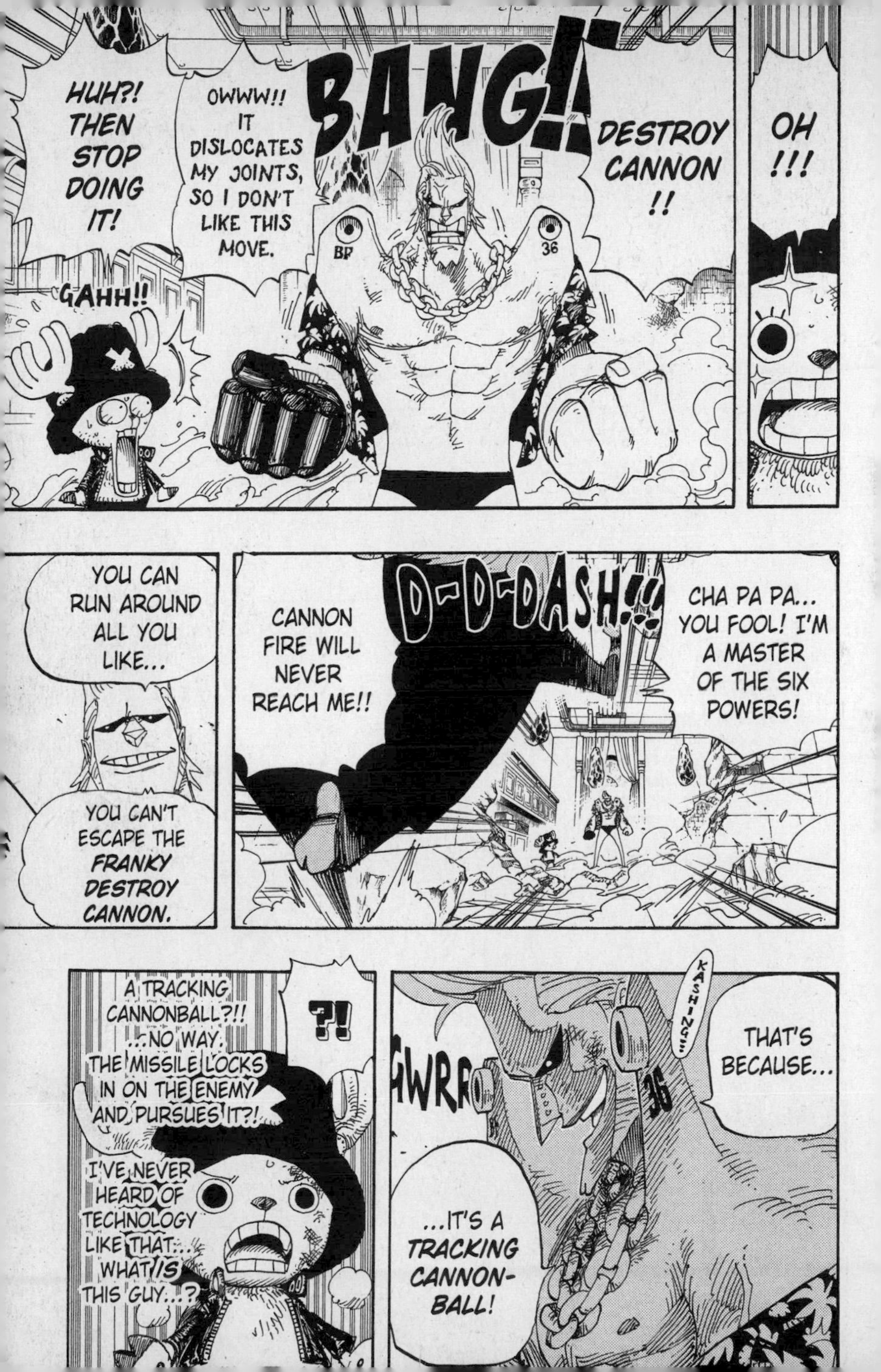
OH !!!
DESTROY CANNON !!
BANG!!
OWWW!! IT DISLOCATES MY JOINTS, SO I DON'T LIKE THIS MOVE.
HUH?! THEN STOP DOING IT!
GAHH!!
CHA PA PA... YOU FOOL! I'M A MASTER OF THE SIX POWERS!
D-D-DASH!!!
CANNON FIRE WILL NEVER REACH ME!!
YOU CAN RUN AROUND ALL YOU LIKE...
YOU CAN'T ESCAPE THE *FRANKY DESTROY CANNON.*
KASHING!!!
THAT'S BECAUSE...
GWRR
...IT'S A *TRACKING CANNONBALL!*
?!
A TRACKING CANNONBALL?!! ...NO WAY. THE MISSILE LOCKS IN ON THE ENEMY AND PURSUES IT?!
I'VE NEVER HEARD OF TECHNOLOGY LIKE THAT... WHAT *IS* THIS GUY...?

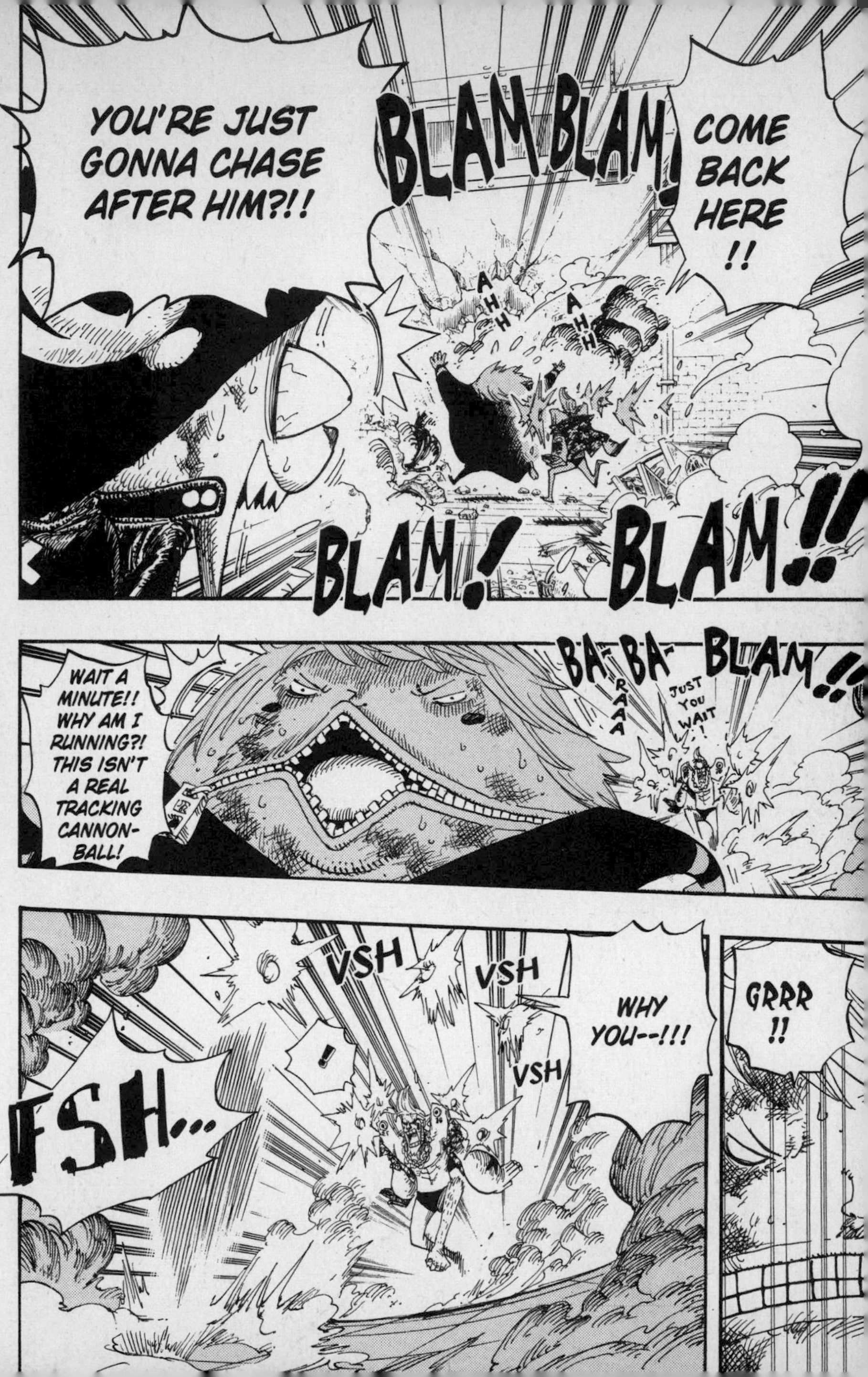
COME BACK HERE !!
BLAM BLAM!
YOU'RE JUST GONNA CHASE AFTER HIM?!!
AHH
AHH
BLAM!!
BLAM!
BA- BA- BLAM!!
JUST YOU WAIT!
RAAA
WAIT A MINUTE!! WHY AM I RUNNING?! THIS ISN'T A REAL TRACKING CANNON-BALL!
GRRR !!
WHY YOU--!!!
VSH
VSH
VSH
!
FSH...

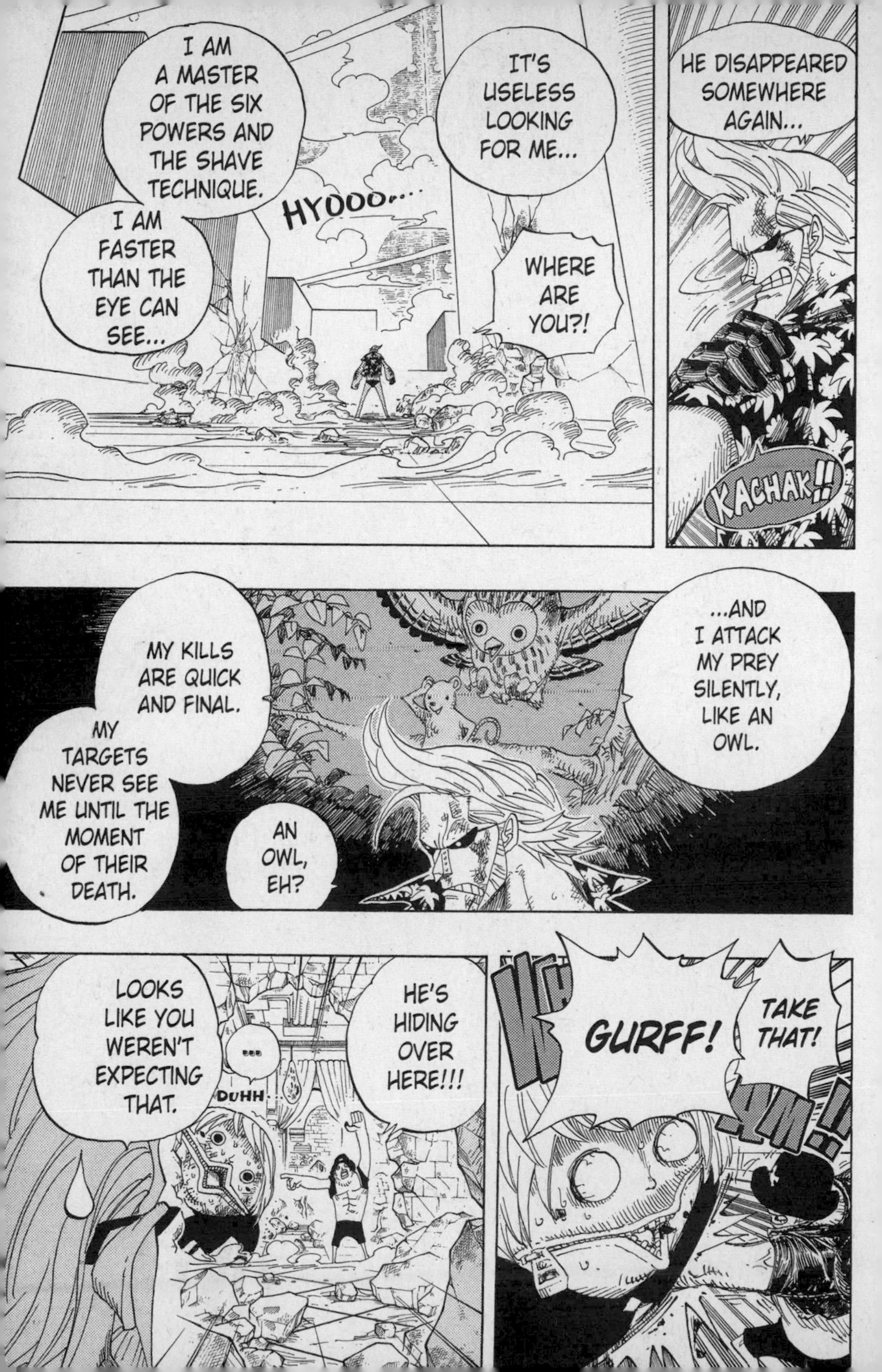
HE DISAPPEARED SOMEWHERE AGAIN...
KACHAK!!
IT'S USELESS LOOKING FOR ME...
I AM A MASTER OF THE SIX POWERS AND THE SHAVE TECHNIQUE.
HYOOO...
I AM FASTER THAN THE EYE CAN SEE...
WHERE ARE YOU?!
...AND I ATTACK MY PREY SILENTLY, LIKE AN OWL.
MY KILLS ARE QUICK AND FINAL.
MY TARGETS NEVER SEE ME UNTIL THE MOMENT OF THEIR DEATH.
AN OWL, EH?
TAKE THAT!
GURFF!
HE'S HIDING OVER HERE!!!
...
DUHH...
LOOKS LIKE YOU WEREN'T EXPECTING THAT.

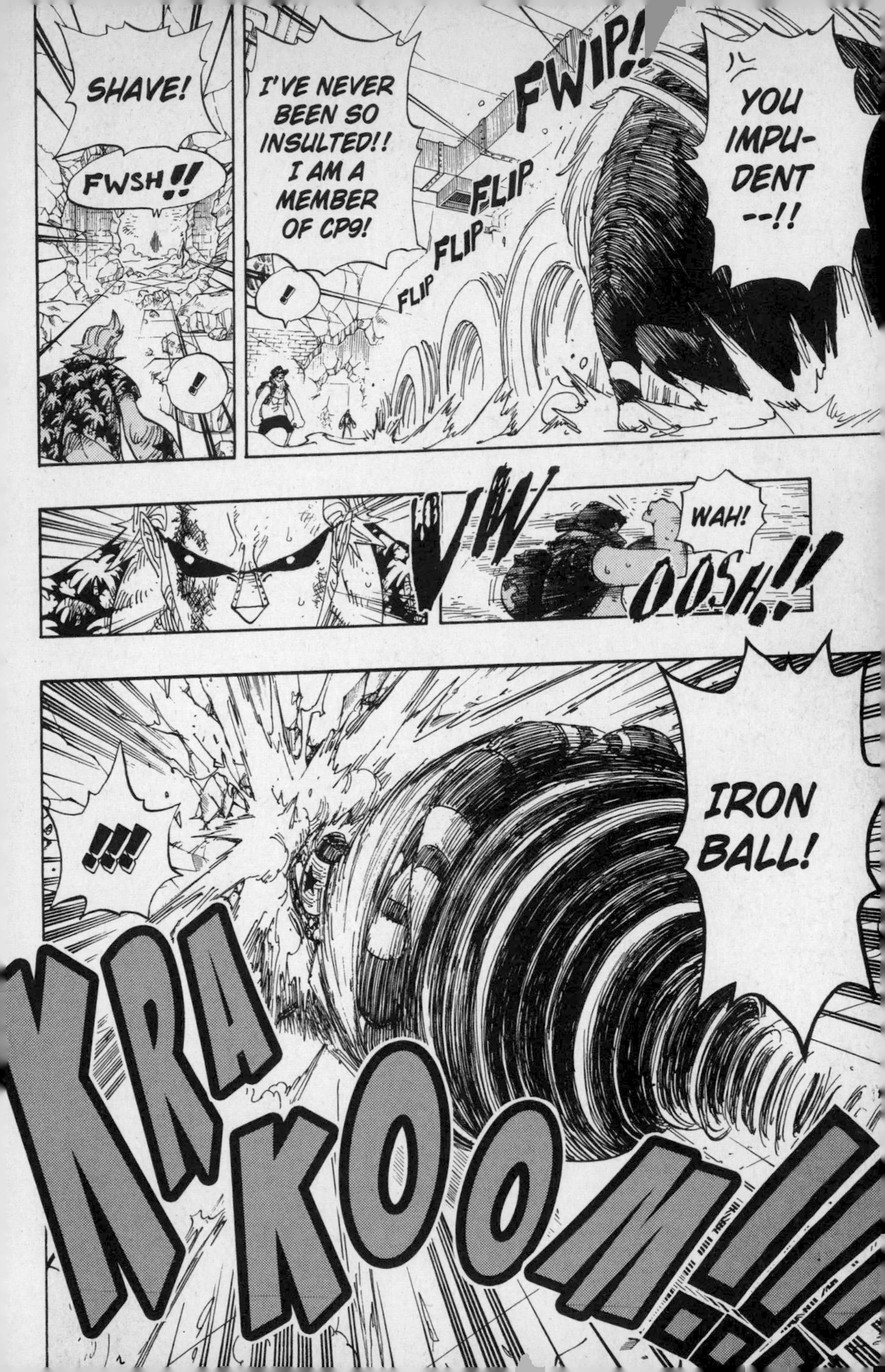
FWIP!!
YOU IMPUDENT--!!
I'VE NEVER BEEN SO INSULTED!! I AM A MEMBER OF CP9!
FLIP FLIP FLIP
!
SHAVE!
FWSH!!
!
WAH!
VWOOSH!!
IRON BALL!
!!!
KRA KOOM!!

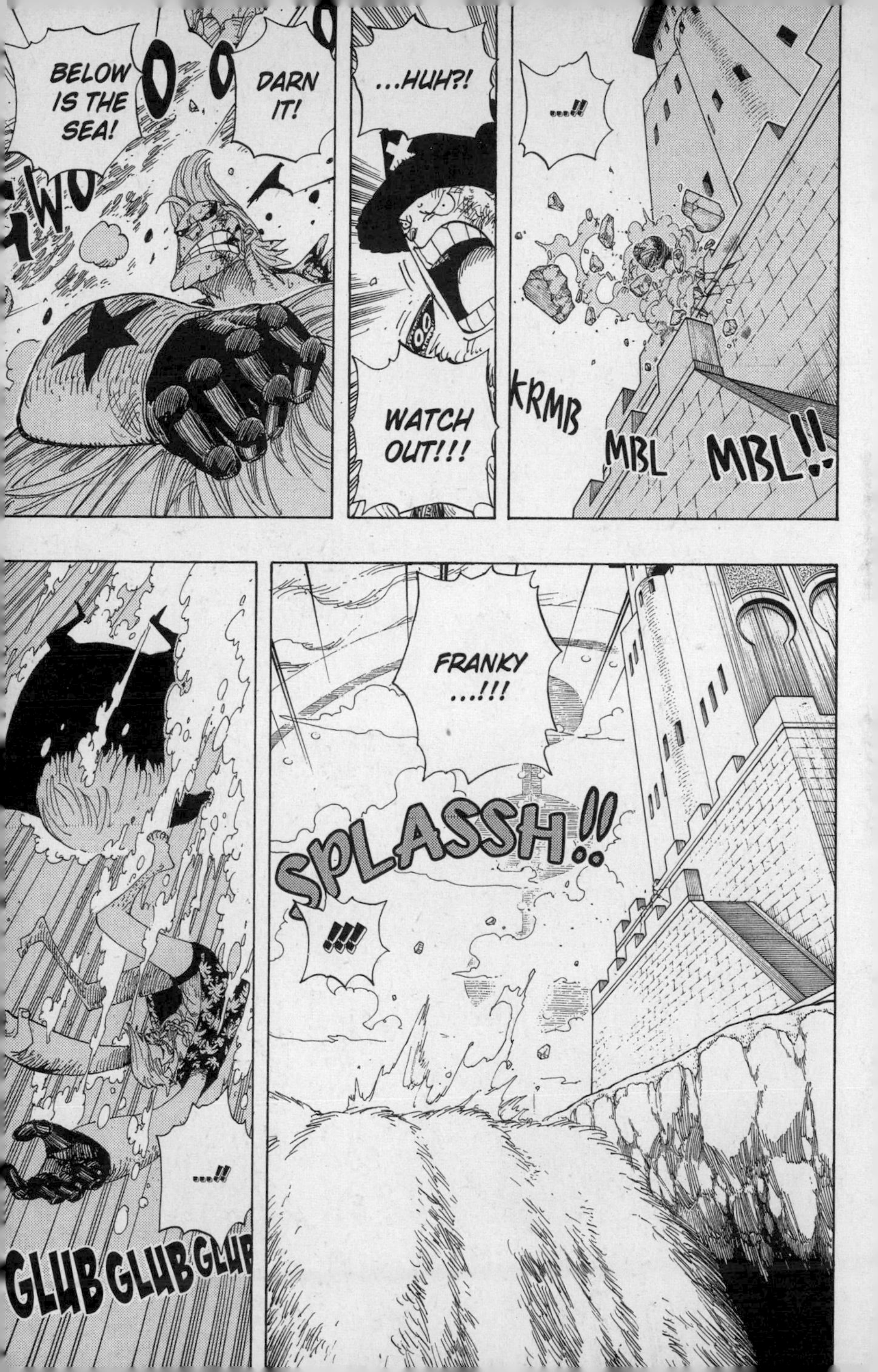
...!!
KRMB
MBL
MBL!!
...HUH?!
WATCH OUT!!!
DARN IT!
BELOW IS THE SEA!
FRANKY ...!!!
SPLASSH!!
!!!
...!!
GLUB GLUB GLUB

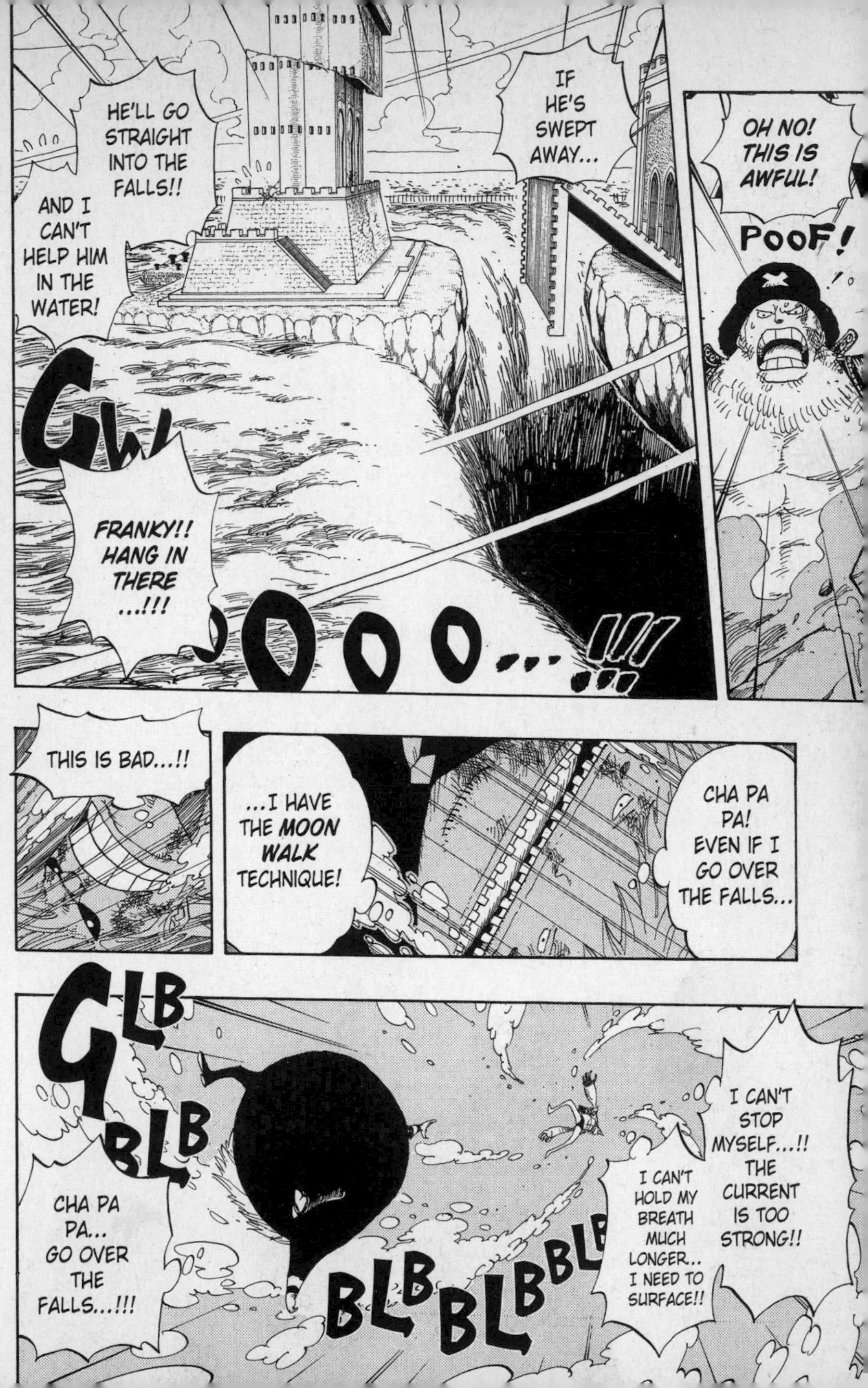
OH NO! THIS IS AWFUL!
POOF!
IF HE'S SWEPT AWAY...
HE'LL GO STRAIGHT INTO THE FALLS!!
AND I CAN'T HELP HIM IN THE WATER!
GWOOOO...!!!
FRANKY!! HANG IN THERE...!!!
CHA PA PA! EVEN IF I GO OVER THE FALLS...
...I HAVE THE MOON WALK TECHNIQUE!
THIS IS BAD...!!
I CAN'T STOP MYSELF...!! THE CURRENT IS TOO STRONG!!
I CAN'T HOLD MY BREATH MUCH LONGER.. I NEED TO SURFACE!!
BLB BLB BLB
CHA PA PA... GO OVER THE FALLS...!!!
GLB BLB

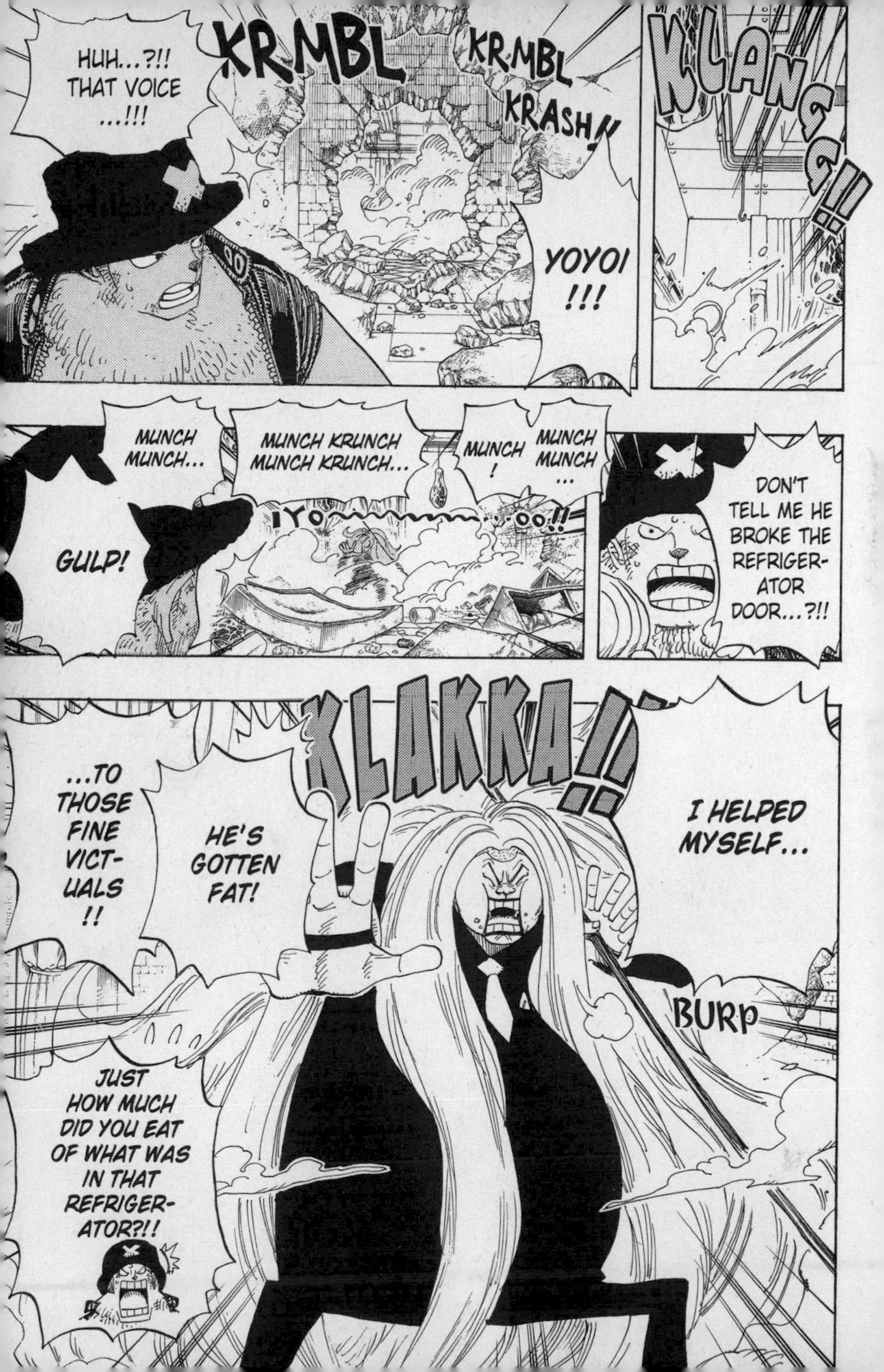
KLANG!!
KRMBL
KRASH!!
KRMBL
YOYOI!!!
HUH...?!! THAT VOICE ...!!!
DON'T TELL ME HE BROKE THE REFRIGER-ATOR DOOR...?!!
MUNCH MUNCH ...
MUNCH !
MUNCH KRUNCH MUNCH KRUNCH...
MUNCH MUNCH...
IYO~~~...OO!!
GULP!
KLAKKA!!
I HELPED MYSELF...
BURP
...TO THOSE FINE VICT-UALS !!
HE'S GOTTEN FAT!
JUST HOW MUCH DID YOU EAT OF WHAT WAS IN THAT REFRIGER-ATOR?!!

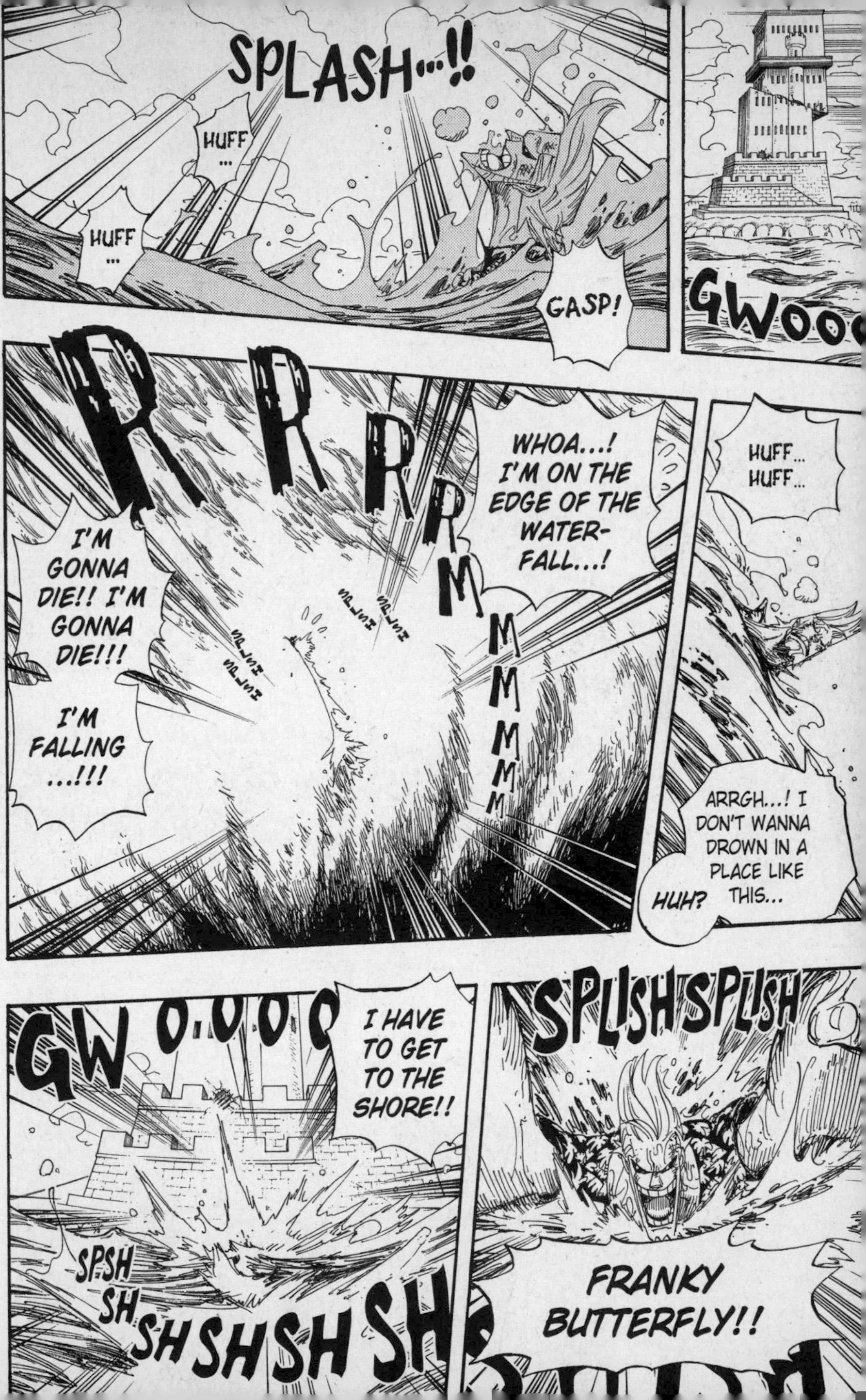
GWOO
SPLASH...!!
HUFF...
HUFF...
GASP!
HUFF... HUFF...
ARRGH...! I DON'T WANNA DROWN IN A PLACE LIKE THIS...
HUH?
RRRRRMMMMM
WHOA...! I'M ON THE EDGE OF THE WATER-FALL...!
I'M GONNA DIE!! I'M GONNA DIE!!!
I'M FALLING...!!!
SPLISH SPLISH
FRANKY BUTTERFLY!!
GWOOOO
I HAVE TO GET TO THE SHORE!!
SPSH SH SH SH SH SH

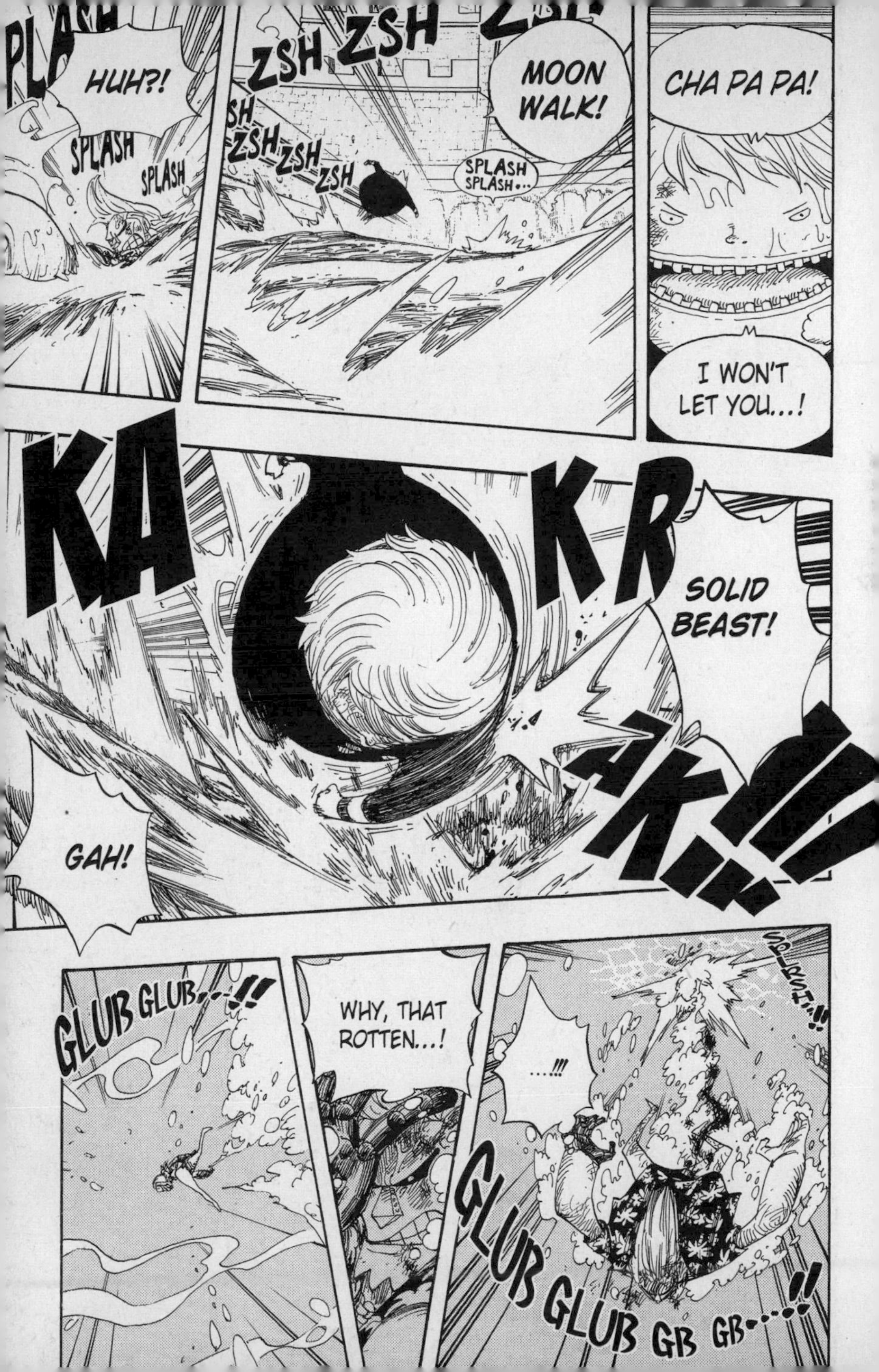
CHA PA PA!
I WON'T LET YOU...!
ZSH ZSH
MOON WALK!
SH ZSH ZSH ZSH
SPLASH SPLASH...
PLASH
HUH?!
SPLASH
SPLASH
KA
KR
SOLID BEAST!
AK...!!!
GAH!
SPLASH...!!
...!!!
GLUB GLUB GB GB...!!
WHY, THAT ROTTEN...!
GLUB GLUB...!!

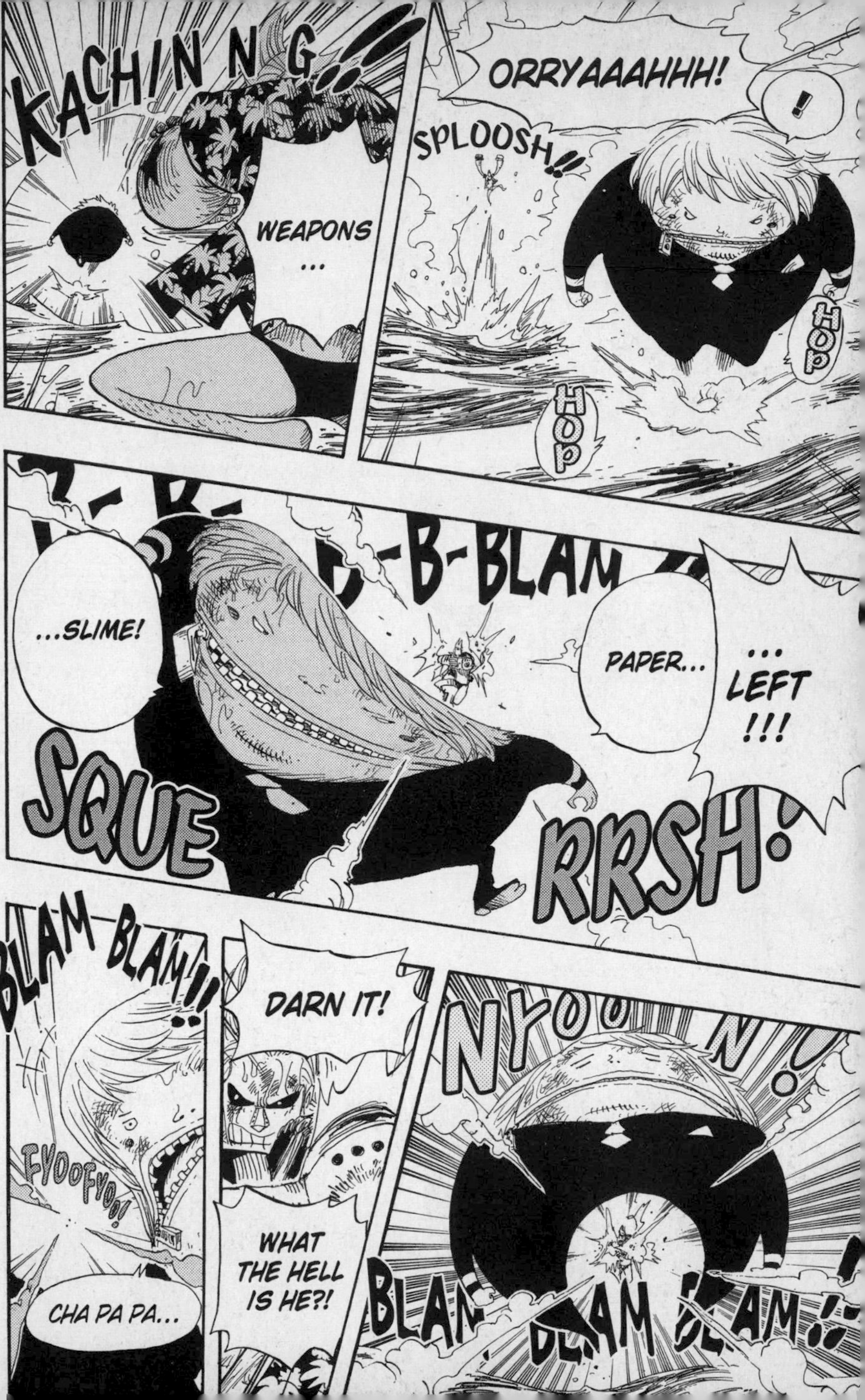
ORRYAAAHHH!
!
SPLOOSH!!
HOP
HOP
KACHIN NG..!!
WEAPONS ...
... LEFT !!!
PAPER...
B-B-BLAM
...SLIME!
SQUE RRSH!
NYOO N!
BLAM BLAM BLAM!!
DARN IT!
WHAT THE HELL IS HE?!
BLAM BLAM!!
FYOOFYOO!
CHA PA PA...

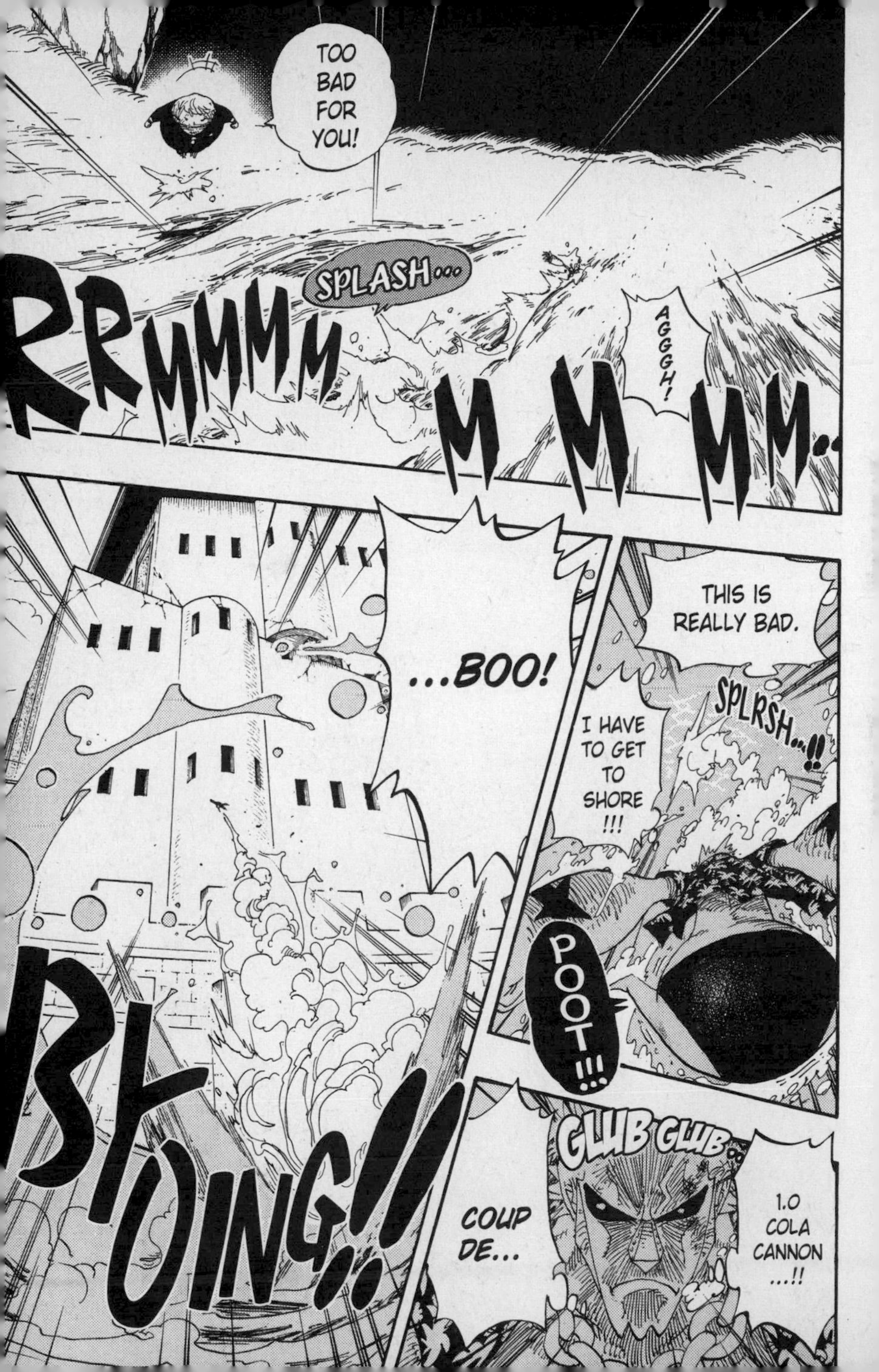
TOO BAD FOR YOU!
AGGGH!
SPLASH...
RRUMMMMM M M MM...
THIS IS REALLY BAD.
SPLRSH...!!
I HAVE TO GET TO SHORE !!!
POOT!!!
GLUB GLUB...
1.0 COLA CANNON ...!!
COUP DE...
...BOO!
BYOING!!

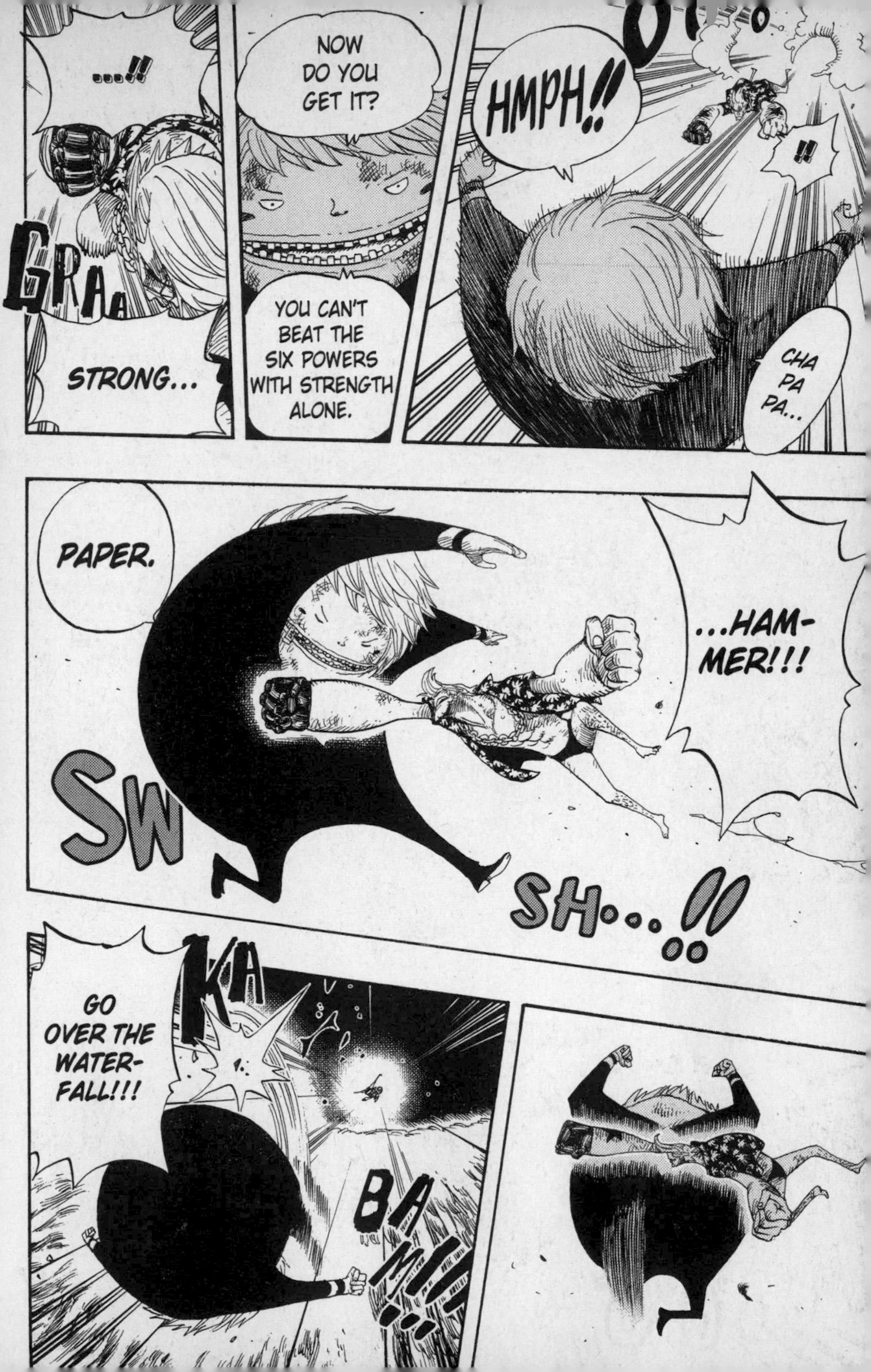
HMPH!!
!!
CHA PA PA...
NOW DO YOU GET IT?
YOU CAN'T BEAT THE SIX POWERS WITH STRENGTH ALONE.
...!!
GRAA
STRONG...
...HAM-MER!!!
PAPER.
SW
SH...!!
GO OVER THE WATER-FALL!!!
KA
BAM!!

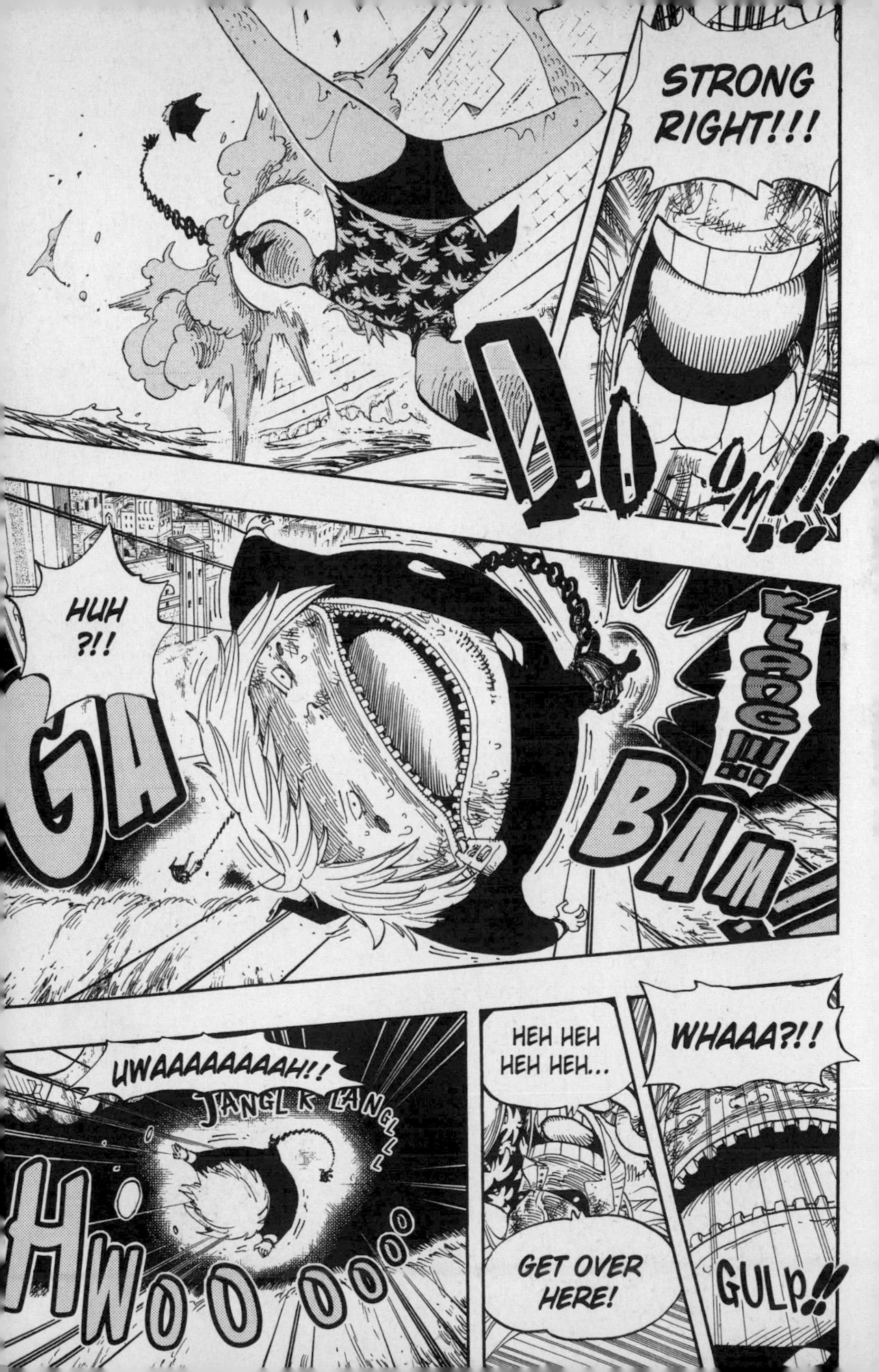

STRONG RIGHT!!!
DOOM!!!
KLANG!!!
BAM!!
HUH ?!!
GA
WHAAA?!!
HEH HEH HEH HEH...
GET OVER HERE!
GULP!!
UWAAAAAAAAH!!
JANGL KLANGLL
HWOOOOOO

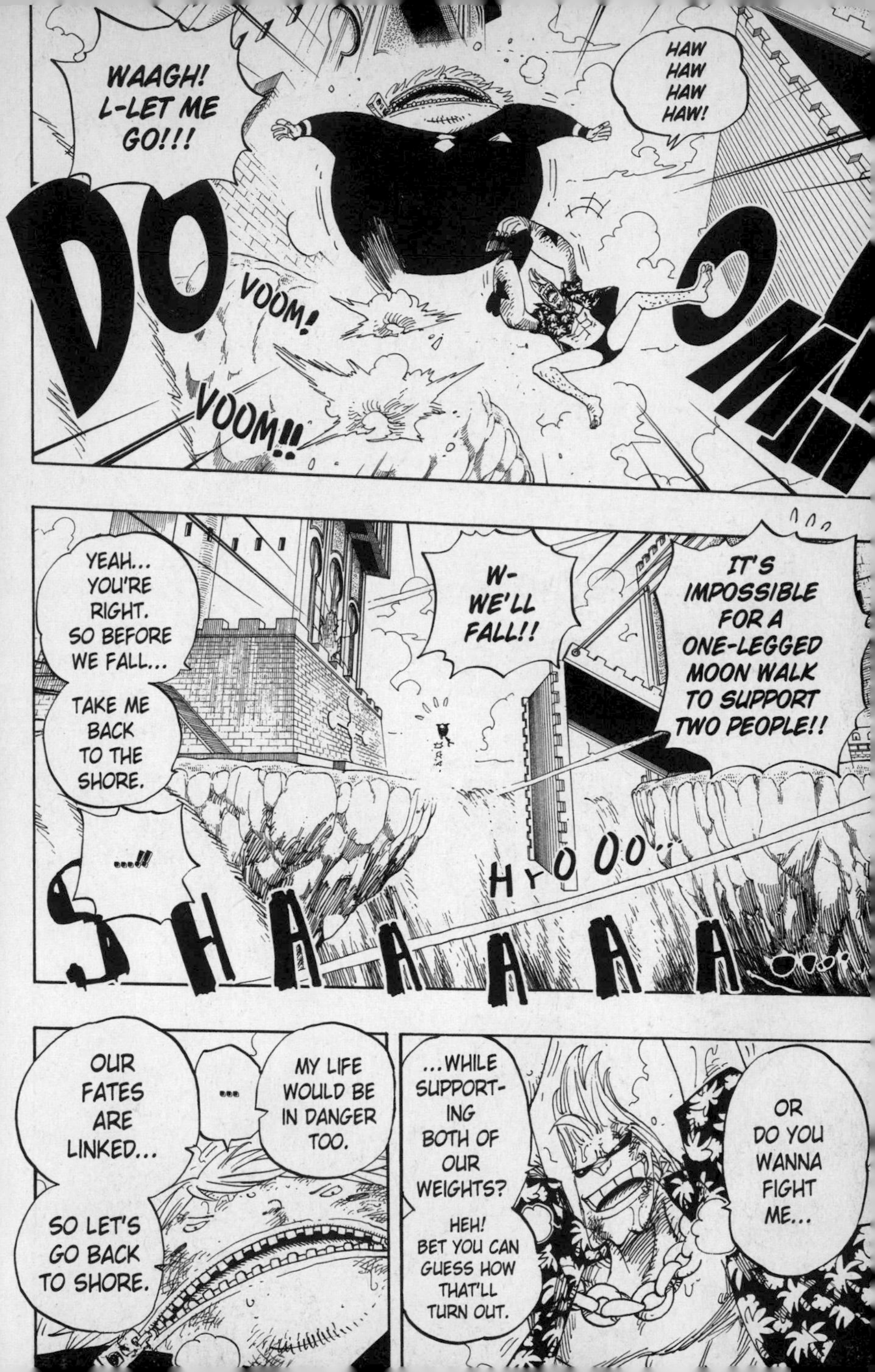
HAW HAW HAW HAW!
WAAGH! L-LET ME GO!!!
DO OM
VOOM!
VOOM!!
IT'S IMPOSSIBLE FOR A ONE-LEGGED MOON WALK TO SUPPORT TWO PEOPLE!!
W-WE'LL FALL!!
YEAH... YOU'RE RIGHT. SO BEFORE WE FALL...
TAKE ME BACK TO THE SHORE.
...!!
HYOOO..
SHAAAAA...
OR DO YOU WANNA FIGHT ME...
...WHILE SUPPORTING BOTH OF OUR WEIGHTS?
HEH! BET YOU CAN GUESS HOW THAT'LL TURN OUT.
MY LIFE WOULD BE IN DANGER TOO.
...
OUR FATES ARE LINKED...
SO LET'S GO BACK TO SHORE.

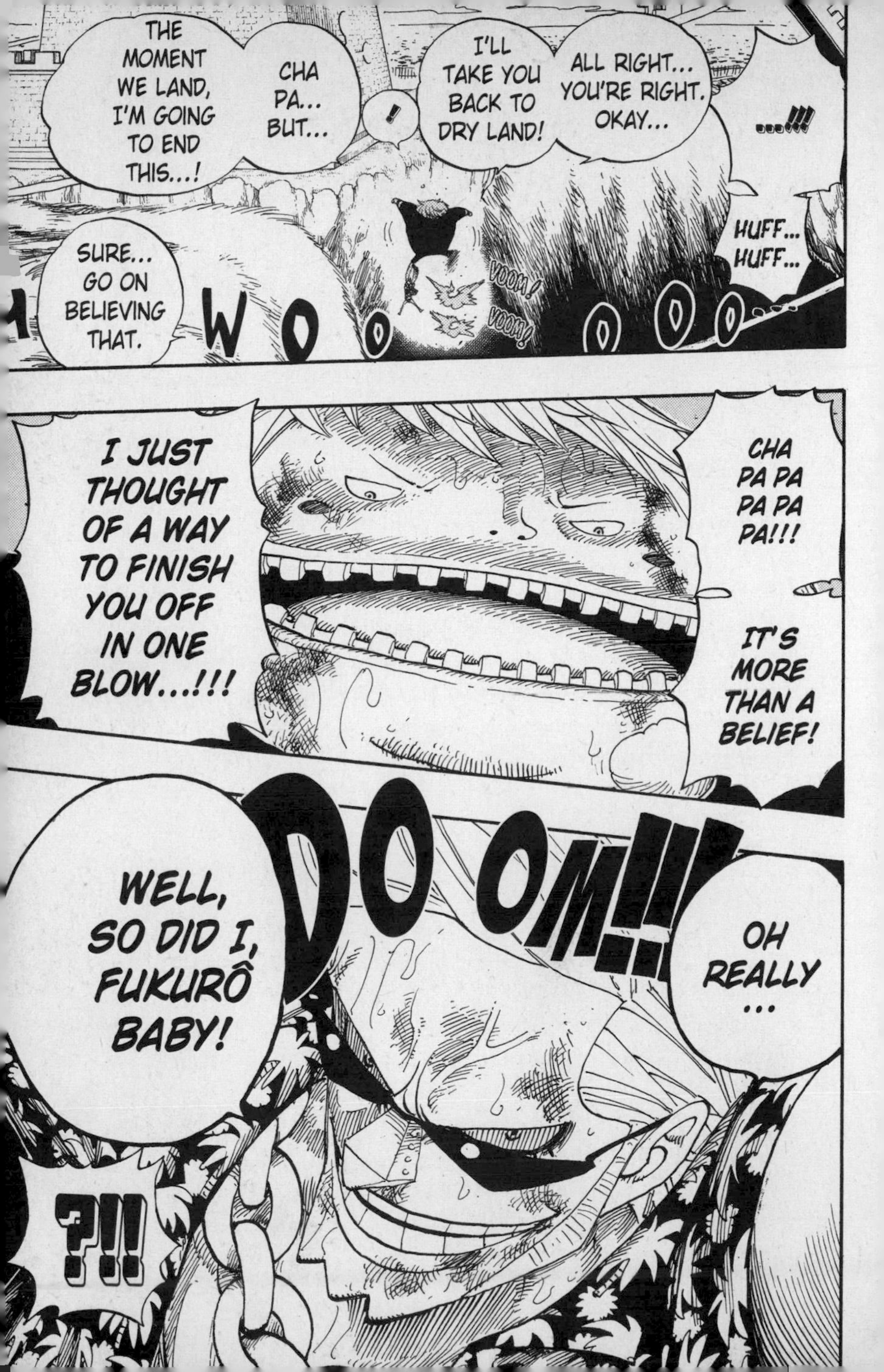
...!!!
HUFF... HUFF...
ALL RIGHT... YOU'RE RIGHT. OKAY...
I'LL TAKE YOU BACK TO DRY LAND!
!
CHA PA... BUT...
THE MOMENT WE LAND, I'M GOING TO END THIS...!
VOOM!
VOOM!
SURE... GO ON BELIEVING THAT.
CHA PA PA PA PA PA!!!
IT'S MORE THAN A BELIEF!
I JUST THOUGHT OF A WAY TO FINISH YOU OFF IN ONE BLOW...!!!
OH REALLY...
DOOM!!!
WELL, SO DID I, FUKURÔ BABY!
?!!

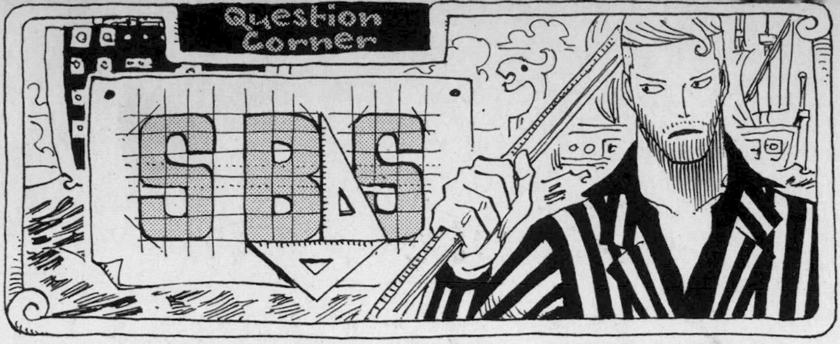
Question Corner
SBS

Q: **Don't take the sauce, you idiot!!!** --Sunny-side-up Eggs Need Salt Faction

A: Okay. Let's keep 'em coming.

Q: Hello, Oda Sensei! This is a serious question. *One Piece* has been running for quite some time, right? Have you thought of bringing it to an end? Personally, I want it to continue forever. *One Piece* is the best!!! --From Mac

A: I answered this question during some interview, but One Piece was originally to be a five-year story. I've always had the last chapter clear in my mind, but it's taken longer than five years to build up the storyline. (Ha ha ha!) And so, the pirates have been on a nine-year adventure, and I don't know how much longer it will take. ("Hey!")

Q: Hello, Odacci. Last month, I bought the video game **One Piece: Pirates' Carnival**. So here is my question…

A: Hey!!! Is that it?! Where's your question?!!

Q: In a Question Corner in volume 41, you talked about Wanze's goggles, remember? Actually, you tear up when chopping onions because of an ingredient that goes up your nose. So wearing goggles has no effect. So please tell Wanze, "When you chop onions, stuff your goggles into your nostrils." --Home Ec Year One Student

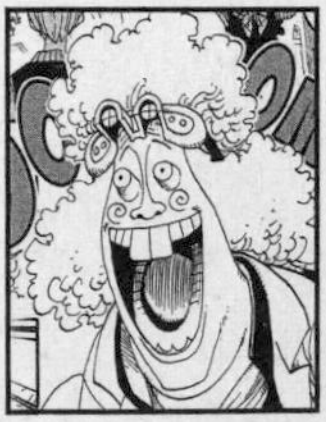

A: I see. So that's it. He messed up! That crazy Wanze! Point taken. Thank you!

Chapter 406:
LIFE RETURN

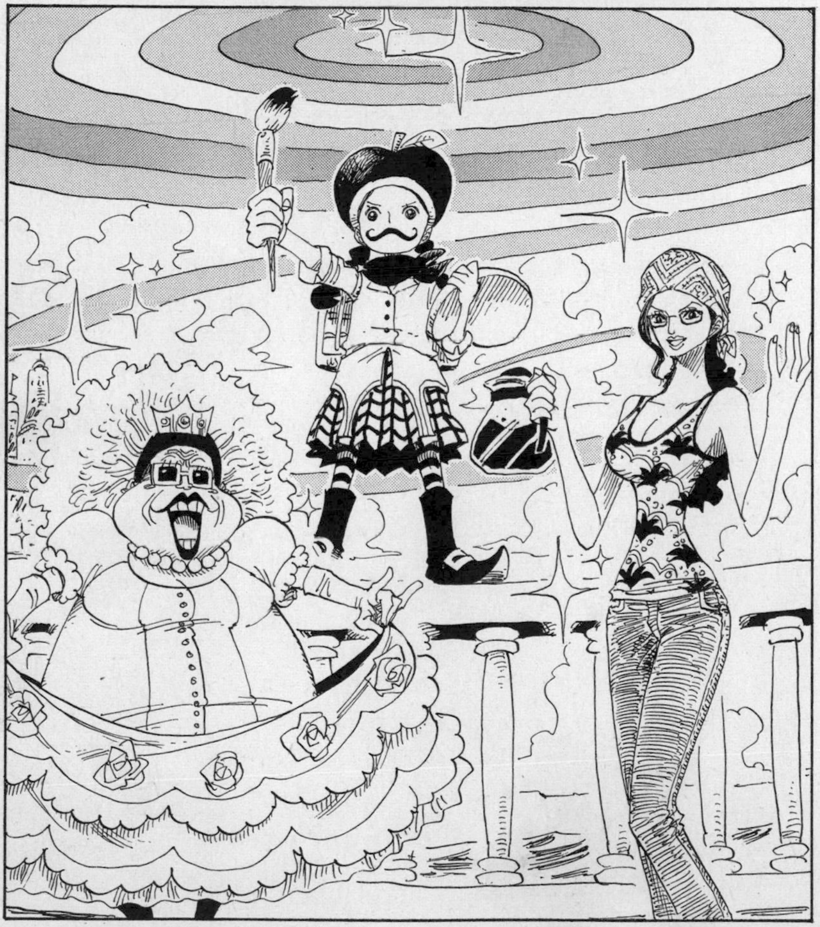

MS. GOLDEN WEEK'S PLAN, A BAROQUE REUNION, VOL. 36:
"TRANSFORMATION! A PRINCESS, AN ARTIST
AND PAULA FROM THE PUB"

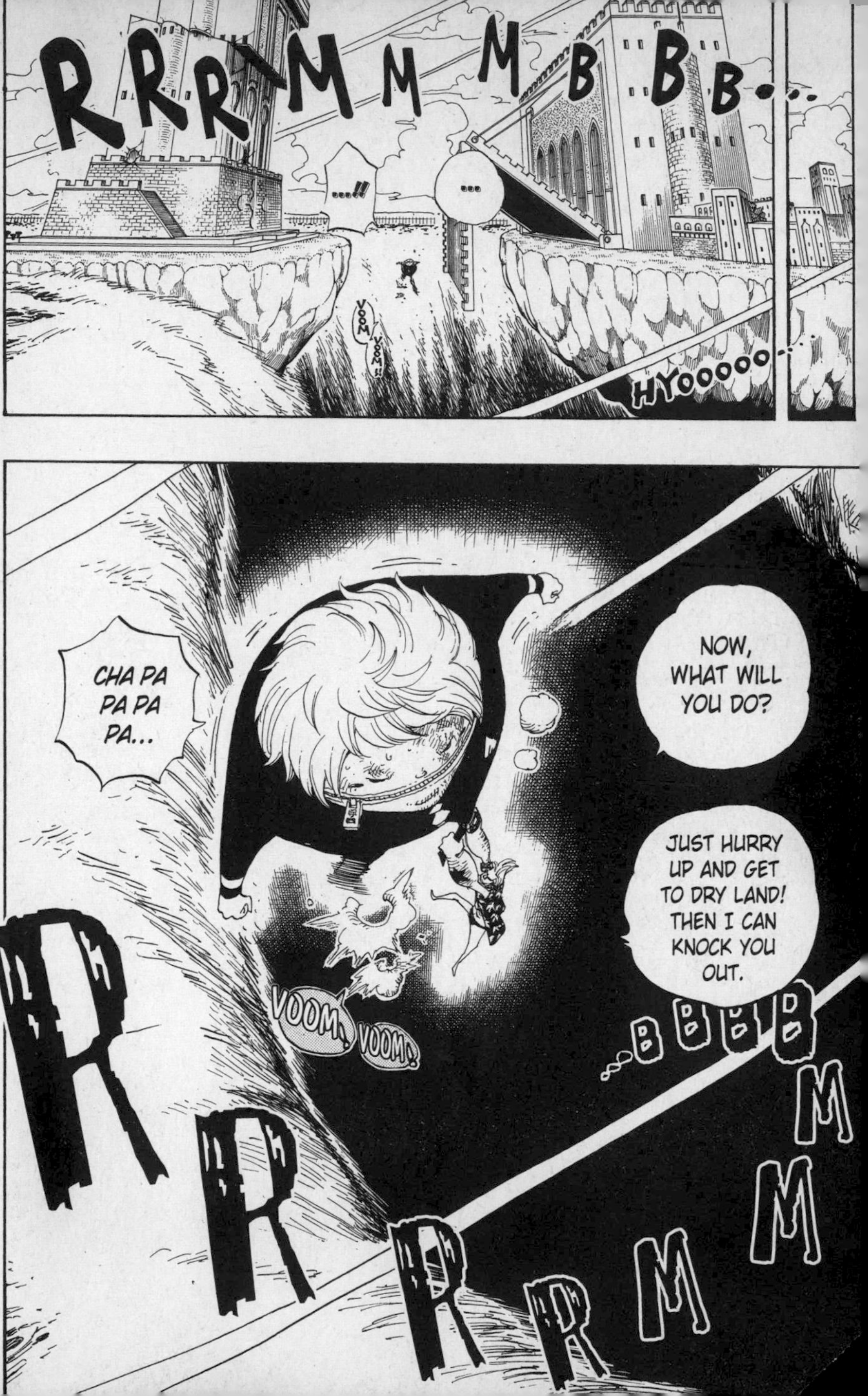
RRRMMMMBBB...
...
...!!
VOOM VOOM!!
HYOOOOO...
NOW, WHAT WILL YOU DO?
JUST HURRY UP AND GET TO DRY LAND! THEN I CAN KNOCK YOU OUT.
CHA PA PA PA PA...
VOOM! VOOM!
RRRRMMMMBBBB...

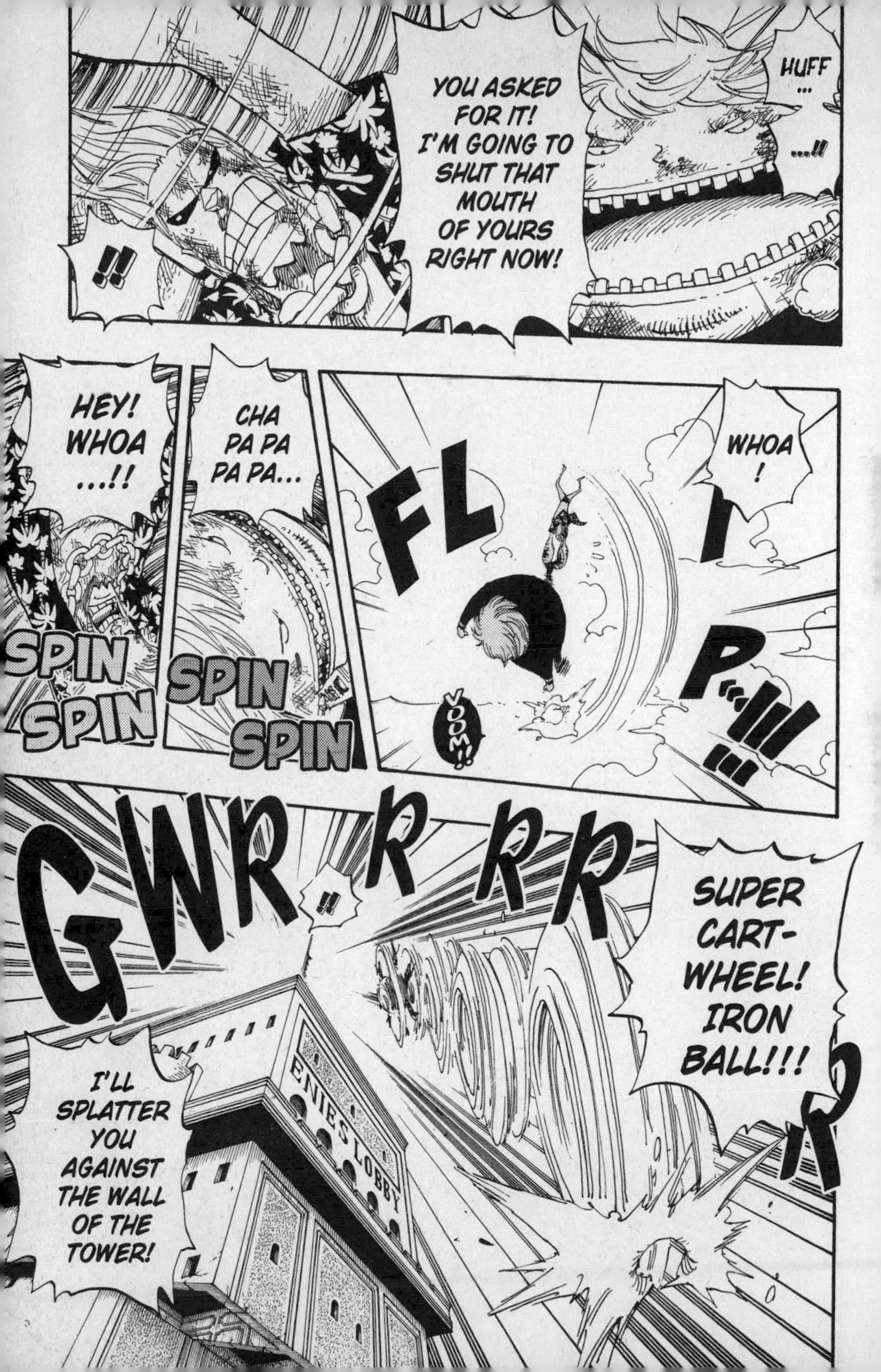
HUFF ...
...!!
YOU ASKED FOR IT! I'M GOING TO SHUT THAT MOUTH OF YOURS RIGHT NOW!
!!
FLIP!!!
WHOA!
VOOM!!
CHA PA PA PA PA...
SPIN SPIN
HEY! WHOA ...!!
SPIN SPIN
SUPER CART-WHEEL! IRON BALL!!!
GWRRRRRR
!!
I'LL SPLATTER YOU AGAINST THE WALL OF THE TOWER!
ENIES LOBBY

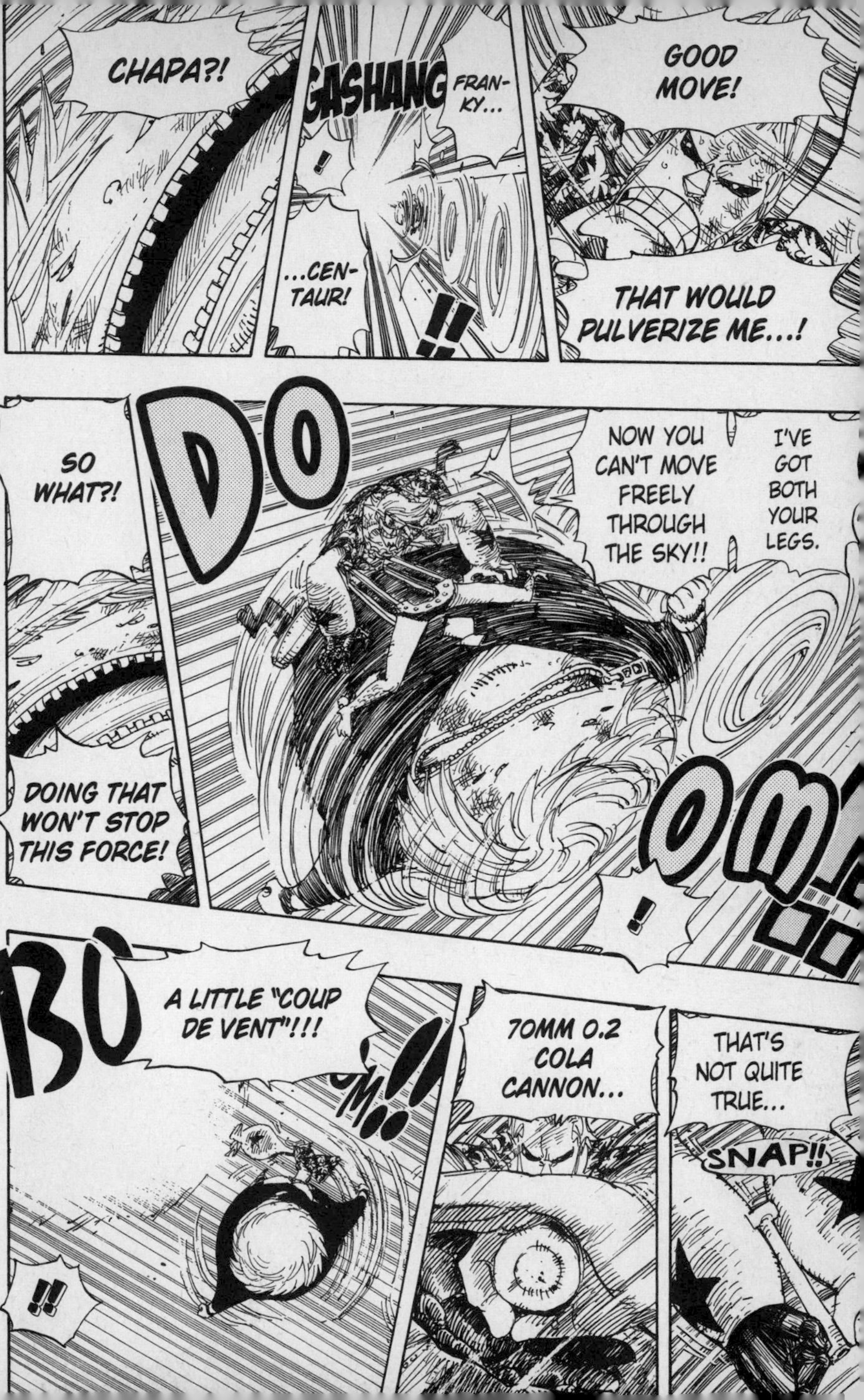
GOOD MOVE!
THAT WOULD PULVERIZE ME...!
FRAN-KY...
GASHANG
!
...CEN-TAUR!
!!
CHAPA?!
I'VE GOT BOTH YOUR LEGS.
NOW YOU CAN'T MOVE FREELY THROUGH THE SKY!!
DO
OM
!
SO WHAT?!
DOING THAT WON'T STOP THIS FORCE!
THAT'S NOT QUITE TRUE...
SNAP!!
70MM 0.2 COLA CANNON...
BO
A LITTLE "COUP DE VENT"!!!
OM!!
!!

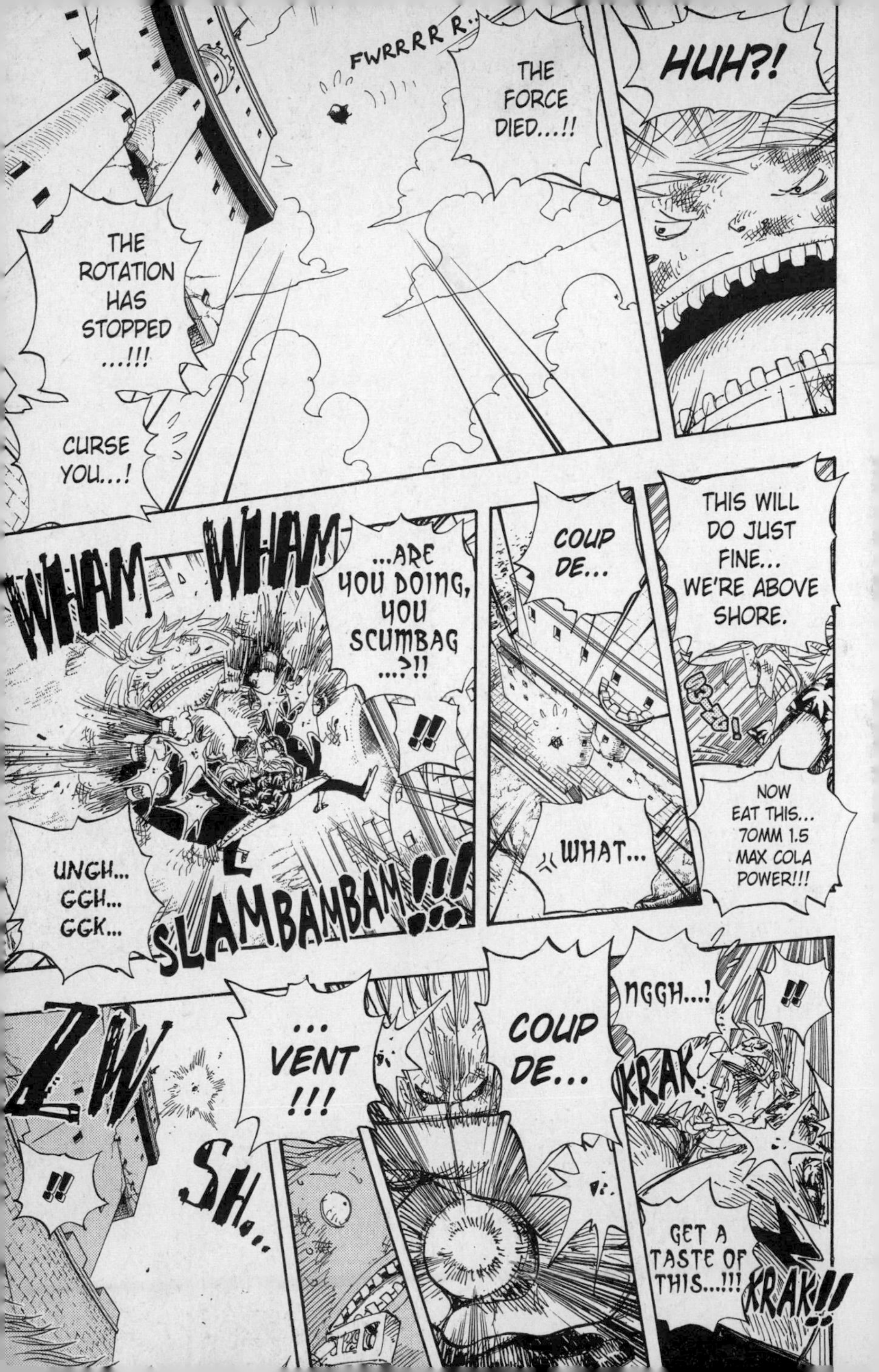
HUH?!
FWRRRR R...
THE FORCE DIED...!!
THE ROTATION HAS STOPPED ...!!!
CURSE YOU...!
THIS WILL DO JUST FINE... WE'RE ABOVE SHORE.
NOW EAT THIS... 70MM 1.5 MAX COLA POWER!!!
COUP DE...
WHAT...
WHAM
WHAM
...ARE YOU DOING, YOU SCUMBAG ...?!!
!!
UNGH... GGH... GGK...
SLAMBAMBAM!!!
NGGH...!
!!
KRAK
GET A TASTE OF THIS...!!!
KRAK!!
COUP DE...
... VENT !!!
ZW
SH...
!!

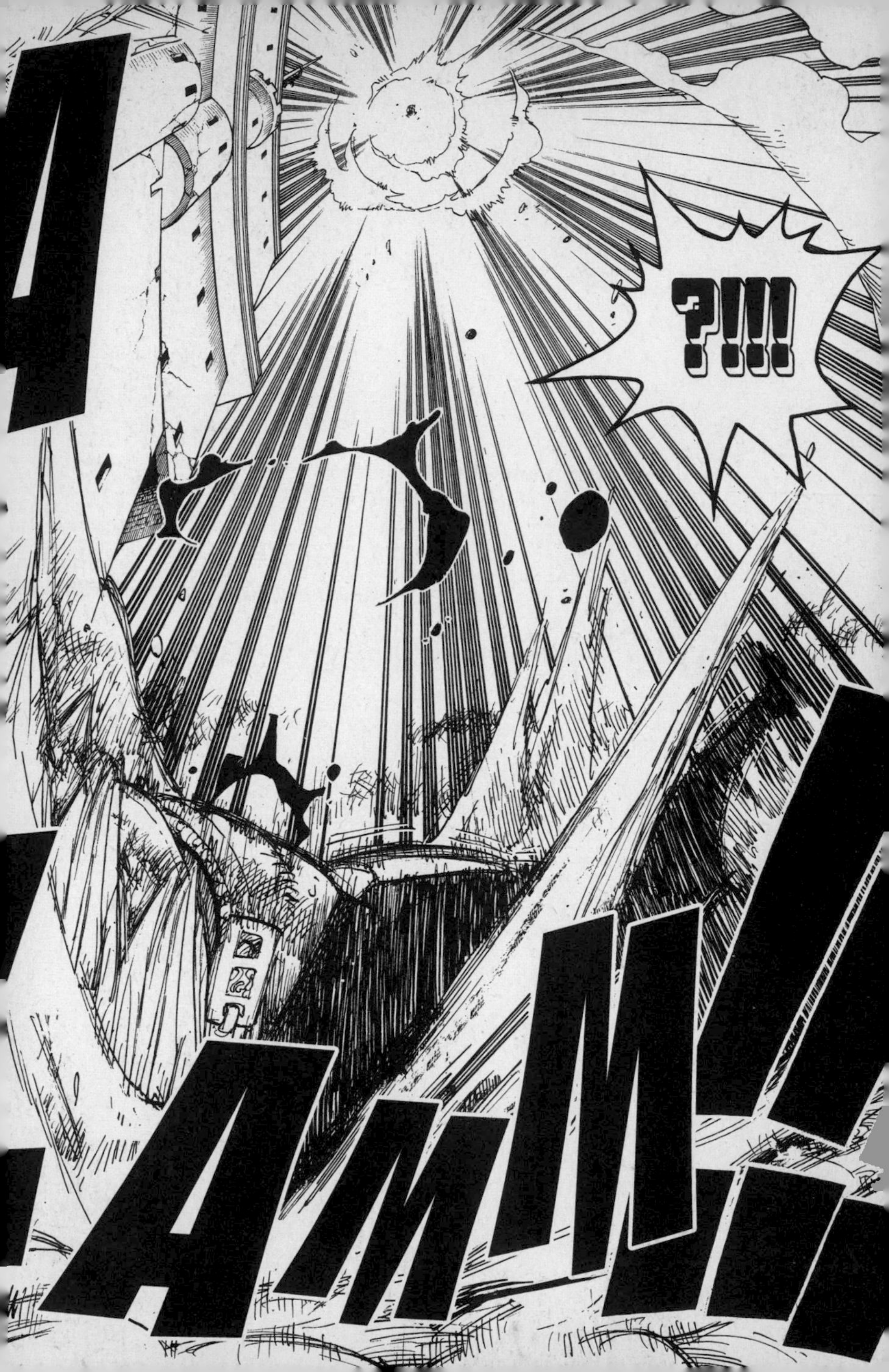
?!!!

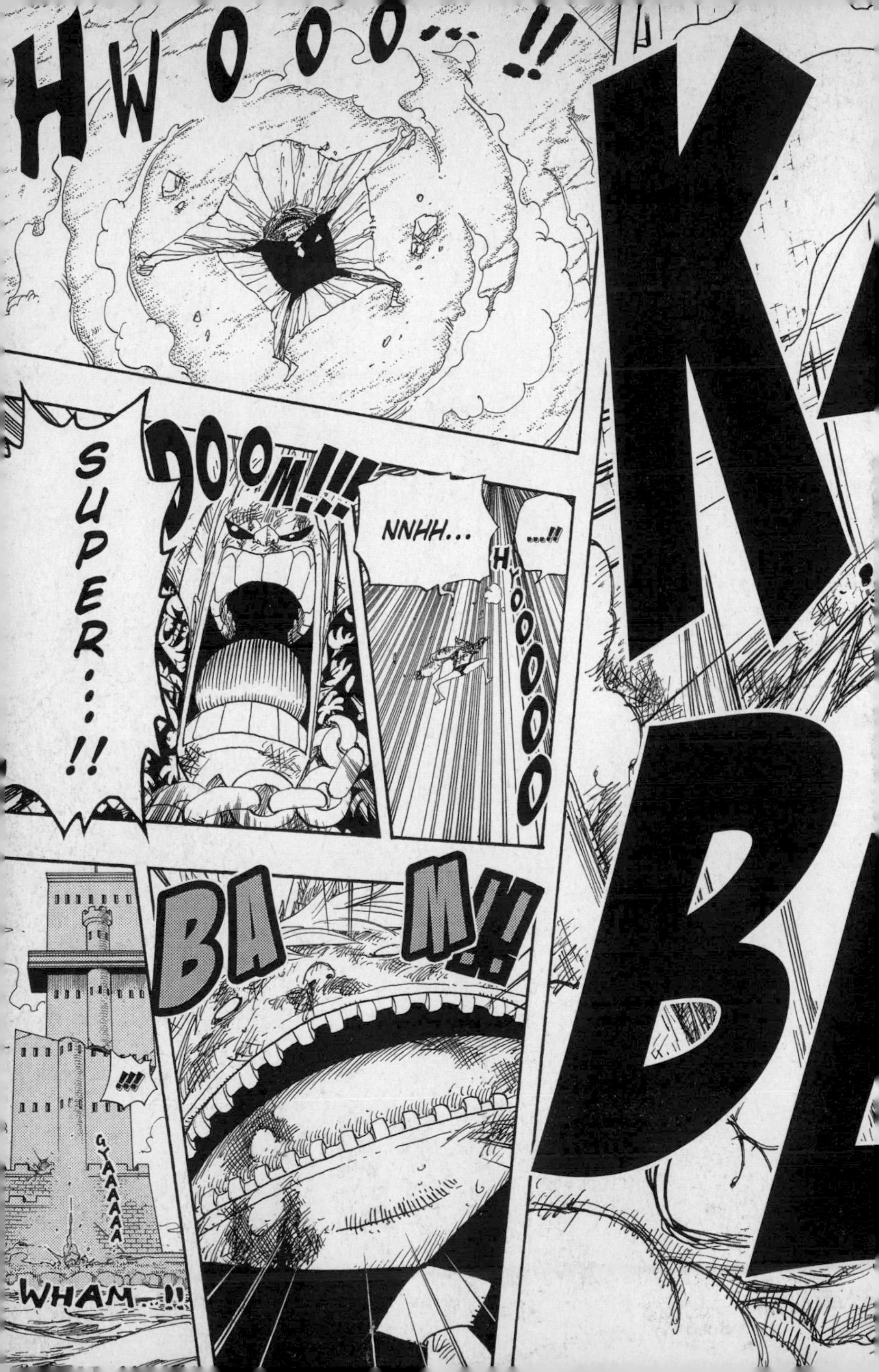
HWOOO...!!
KABAM
DOOM!!!
SUPER...!!
NNHH...
...!!
HYOOOOOOO
BAM!!
!!!
GYAAAAAA
WHAM...!!

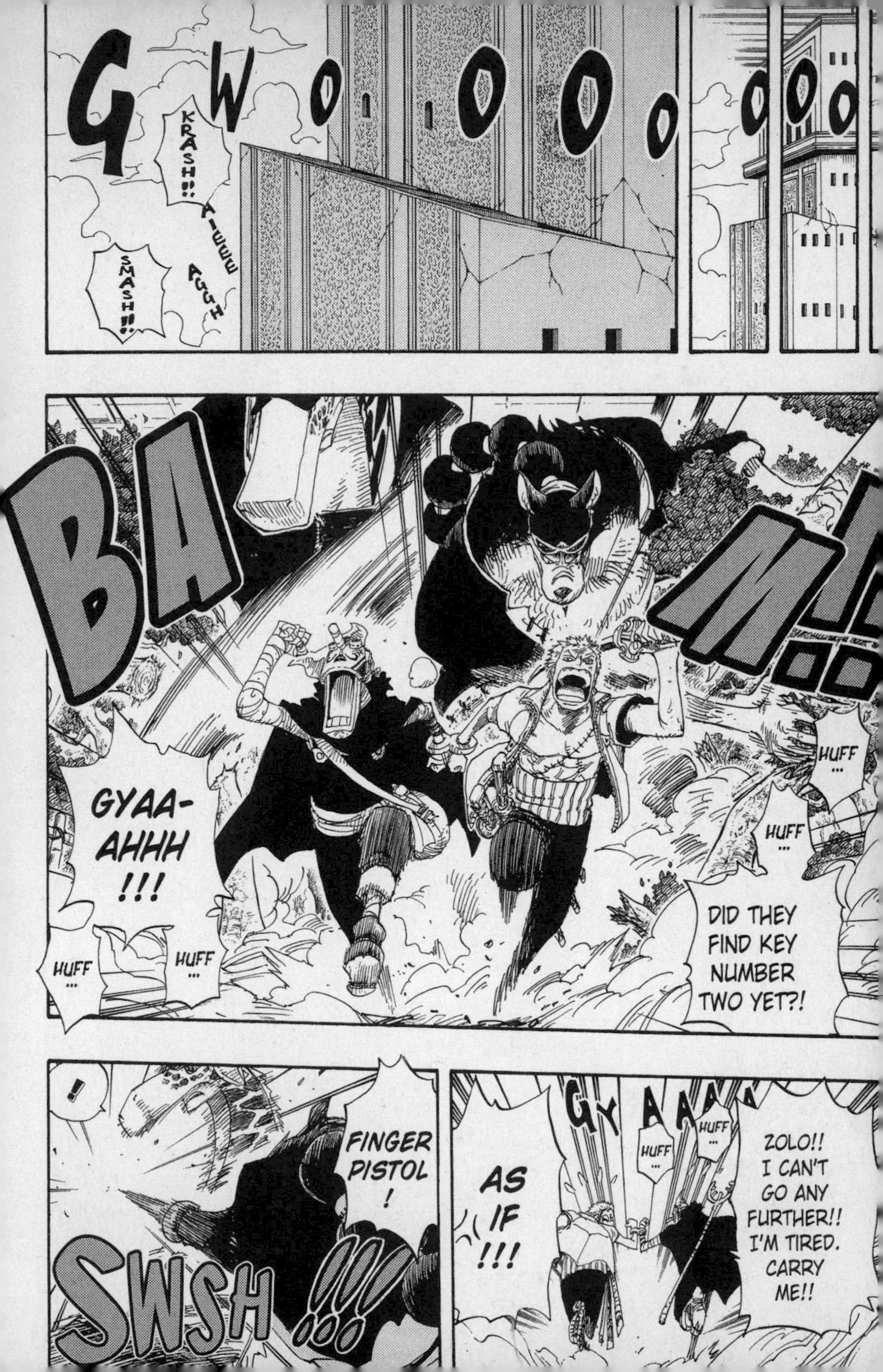
GWOOOOOOOO
KRASH!!
AIEEE
AUGH
SMASH!!
BAM!!
HUFF...
HUFF...
DID THEY FIND KEY NUMBER TWO YET?!
GYAA-AHHH!!!
HUFF...
HUFF...
GYAAAA
ZOLO!! I CAN'T GO ANY FURTHER!! I'M TIRED. CARRY ME!!
HUFF...
HUFF...
AS IF!!!
!
FINGER PISTOL!
SWSH!!!

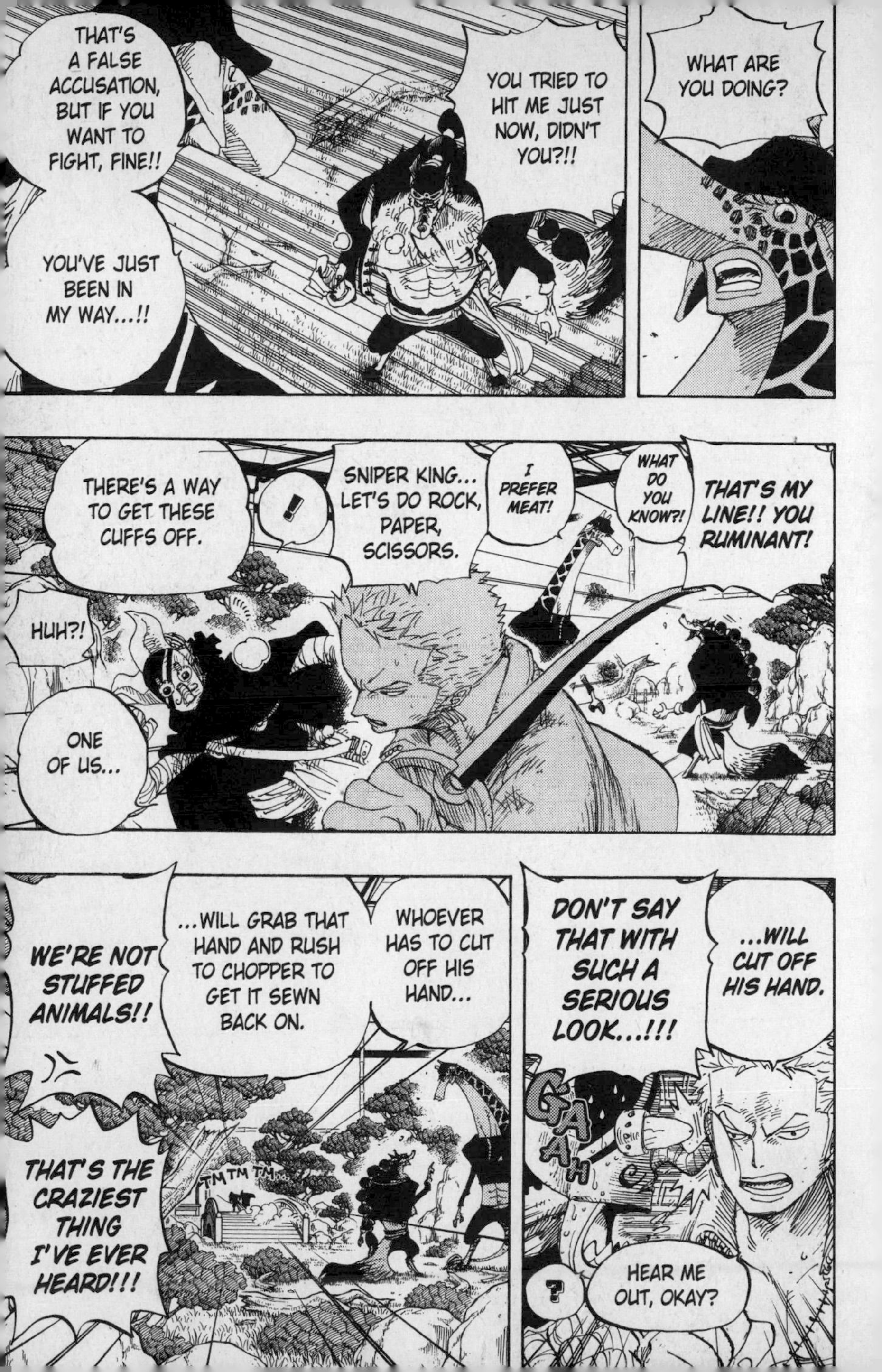
WHAT ARE YOU DOING?
YOU TRIED TO HIT ME JUST NOW, DIDN'T YOU?!!
THAT'S A FALSE ACCUSATION, BUT IF YOU WANT TO FIGHT, FINE!!
YOU'VE JUST BEEN IN MY WAY...!!
THAT'S MY LINE!! YOU RUMINANT!
WHAT DO YOU KNOW?!
I PREFER MEAT!
SNIPER KING... LET'S DO ROCK, PAPER, SCISSORS.
!
THERE'S A WAY TO GET THESE CUFFS OFF.
HUH?!
ONE OF US...
...WILL CUT OFF HIS HAND.
DON'T SAY THAT WITH SUCH A SERIOUS LOOK...!!!
GAAH
HEAR ME OUT, OKAY?
?
WHOEVER HAS TO CUT OFF HIS HAND...
...WILL GRAB THAT HAND AND RUSH TO CHOPPER TO GET IT SEWN BACK ON.
WE'RE NOT STUFFED ANIMALS!!
TM TM TM...
THAT'S THE CRAZIEST THING I'VE EVER HEARD!!!

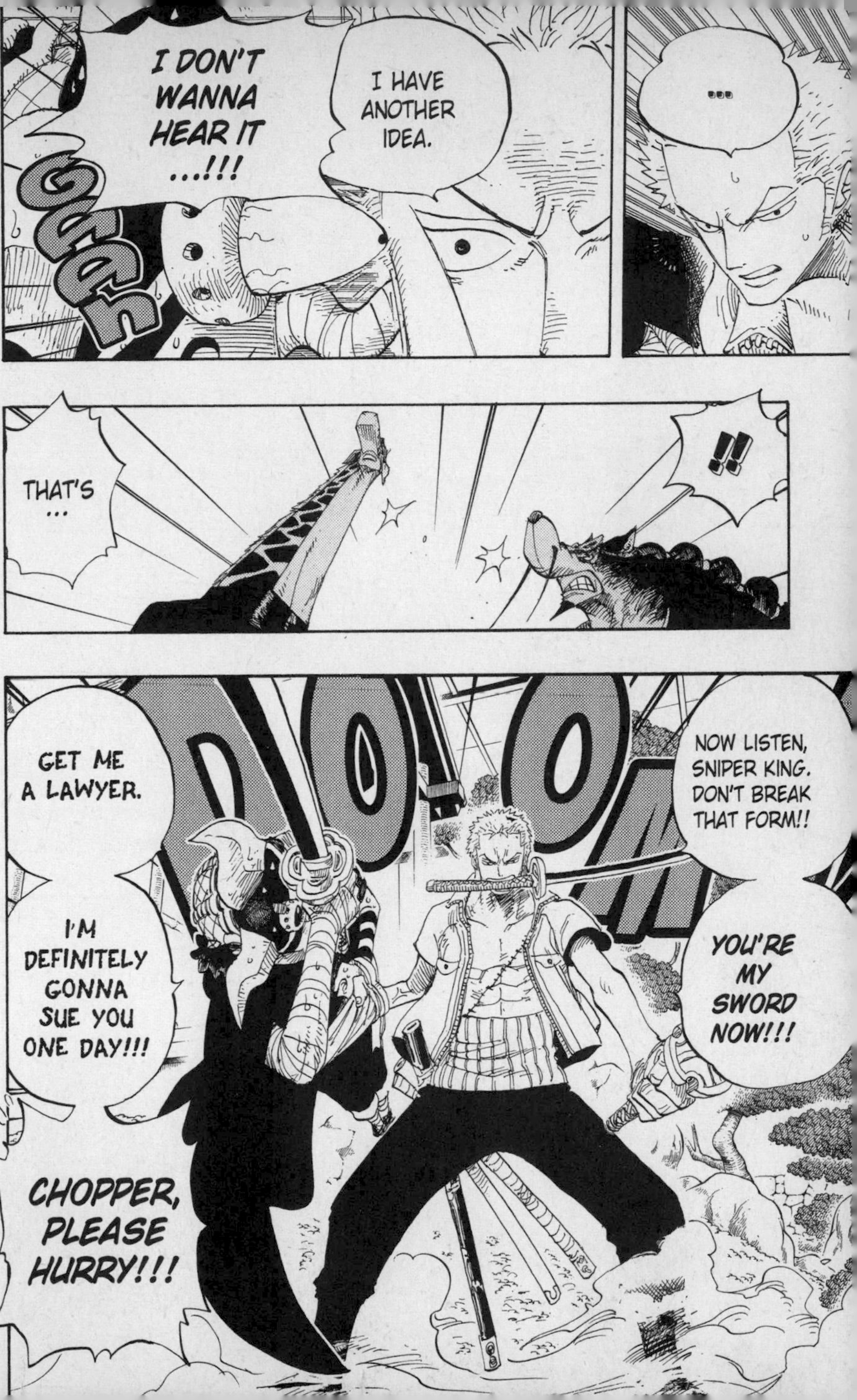
...
I HAVE ANOTHER IDEA.
I DON'T WANNA HEAR IT ...!!!
GUAH
!!
THAT'S ...
NOW LISTEN, SNIPER KING. DON'T BREAK THAT FORM!!
YOU'RE MY SWORD NOW!!!
GET ME A LAWYER.
I'M DEFINITELY GONNA SUE YOU ONE DAY!!!
CHOPPER, PLEASE HURRY!!!

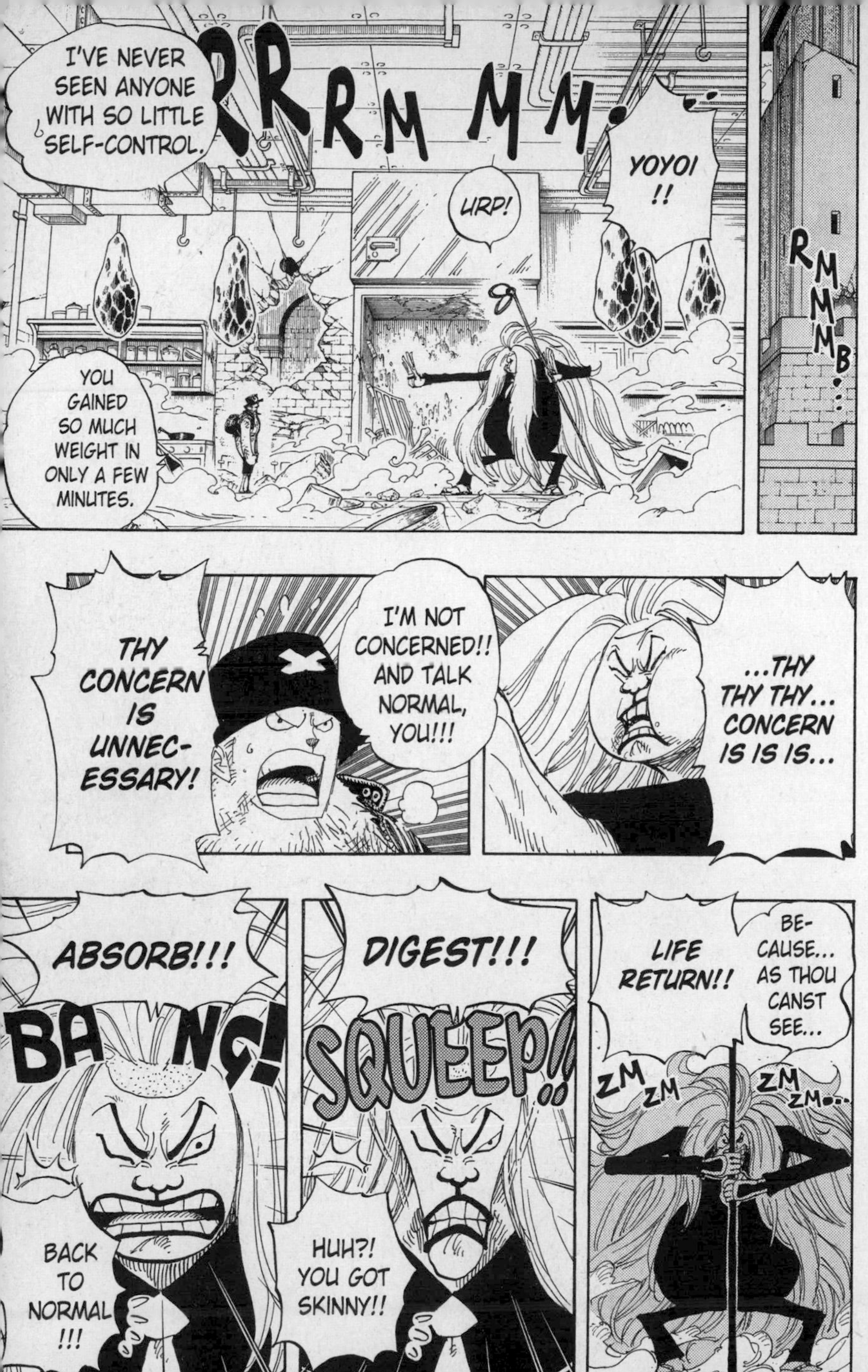
RMMMB...
RRRMMM...
YOYOI !!
URP!
I'VE NEVER SEEN ANYONE WITH SO LITTLE SELF-CONTROL.
YOU GAINED SO MUCH WEIGHT IN ONLY A FEW MINUTES.
...THY THY THY... CONCERN IS IS IS...
I'M NOT CONCERNED!! AND TALK NORMAL, YOU!!!
THY CONCERN IS UNNEC-ESSARY!
BE-CAUSE... AS THOU CANST SEE...
LIFE RETURN!!
ZM ZM
ZM ZM...
DIGEST!!!
SQUEEP!!
HUH?! YOU GOT SKINNY!!
ABSORB!!!
BANG!
BACK TO NORMAL !!!

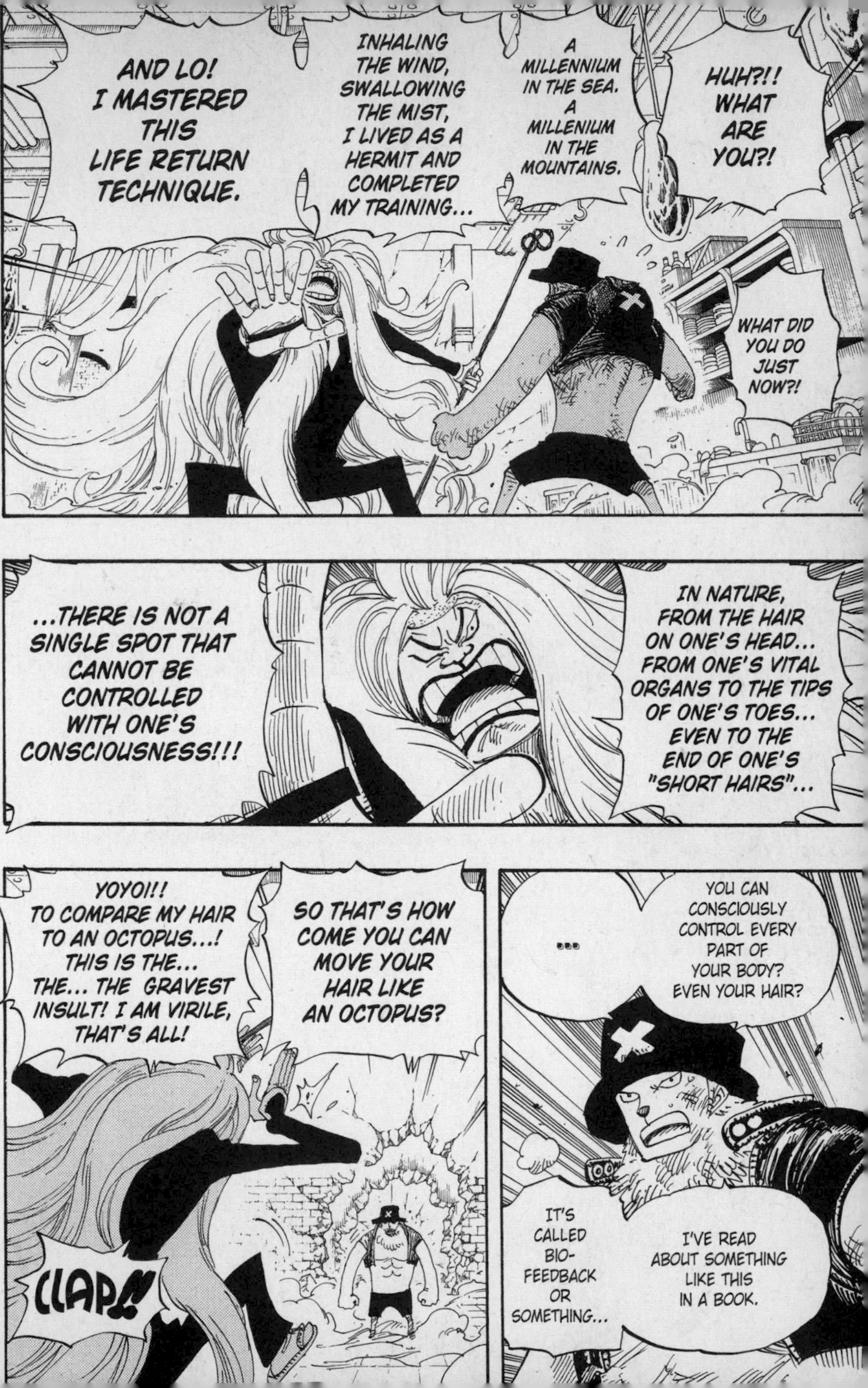
HUH?!! WHAT ARE YOU?!
WHAT DID YOU DO JUST NOW?!
A MILLENNIUM IN THE SEA. A MILLENIUM IN THE MOUNTAINS.
INHALING THE WIND, SWALLOWING THE MIST, I LIVED AS A HERMIT AND COMPLETED MY TRAINING...
AND LO! I MASTERED THIS LIFE RETURN TECHNIQUE.
IN NATURE, FROM THE HAIR ON ONE'S HEAD... FROM ONE'S VITAL ORGANS TO THE TIPS OF ONE'S TOES... EVEN TO THE END OF ONE'S "SHORT HAIRS"...
...THERE IS NOT A SINGLE SPOT THAT CANNOT BE CONTROLLED WITH ONE'S CONSCIOUSNESS!!!
YOU CAN CONSCIOUSLY CONTROL EVERY PART OF YOUR BODY? EVEN YOUR HAIR?
...
I'VE READ ABOUT SOMETHING LIKE THIS IN A BOOK.
IT'S CALLED BIO-FEEDBACK OR SOMETHING...
SO THAT'S HOW COME YOU CAN MOVE YOUR HAIR LIKE AN OCTOPUS?
YOYOI!! TO COMPARE MY HAIR TO AN OCTOPUS...! THIS IS THE... THE... THE GRAVEST INSULT! I AM VIRILE, THAT'S ALL!
CLAP!!

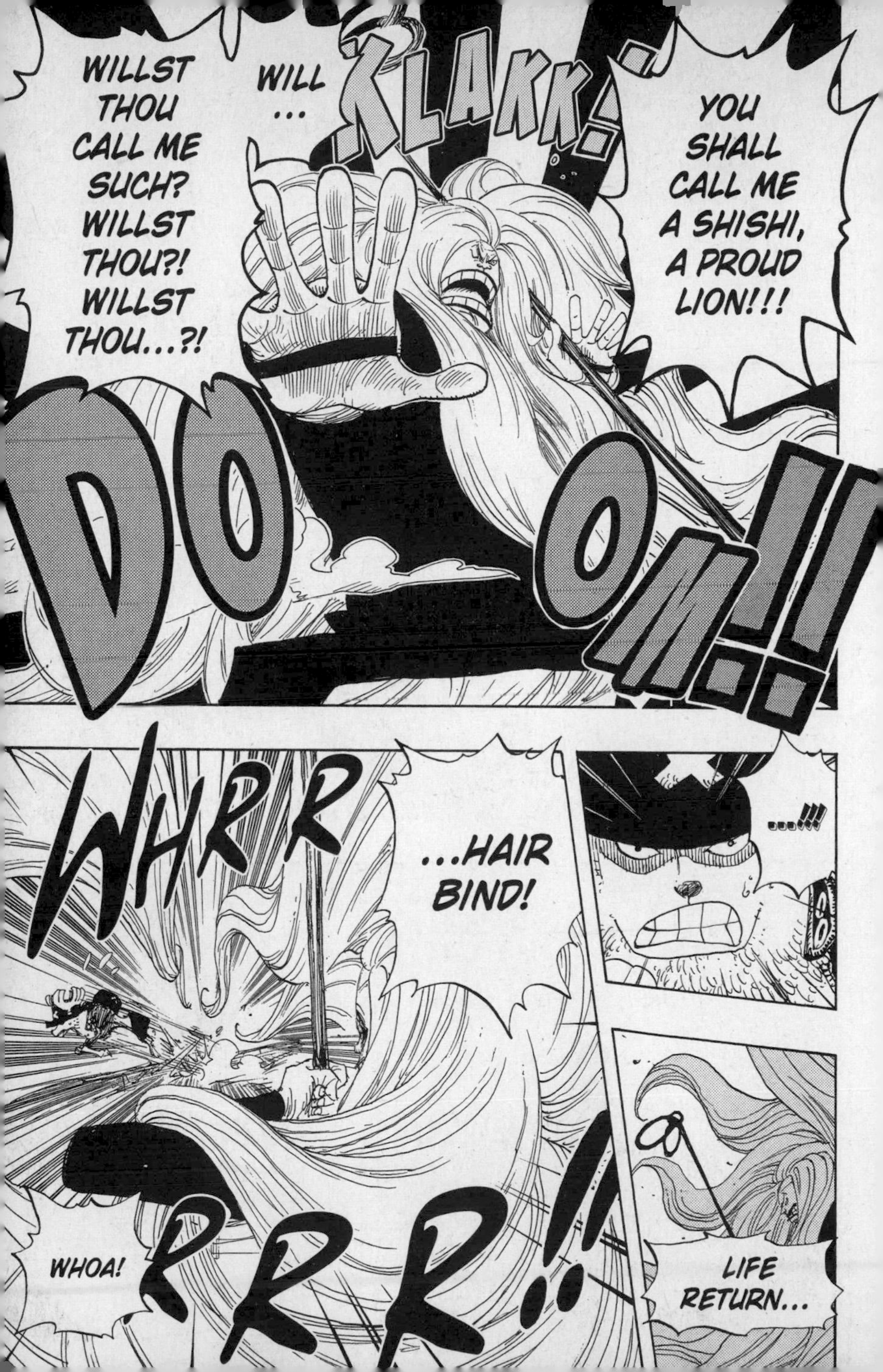
YOU SHALL CALL ME A SHISHI, A PROUD LION!!!
KLAKK!
WILL ...
WILLST THOU CALL ME SUCH? WILLST THOU?! WILLST THOU...?!
DOOM!!
...!!!
LIFE RETURN...
...HAIR BIND!
WHRRRRR!!
WHOA!

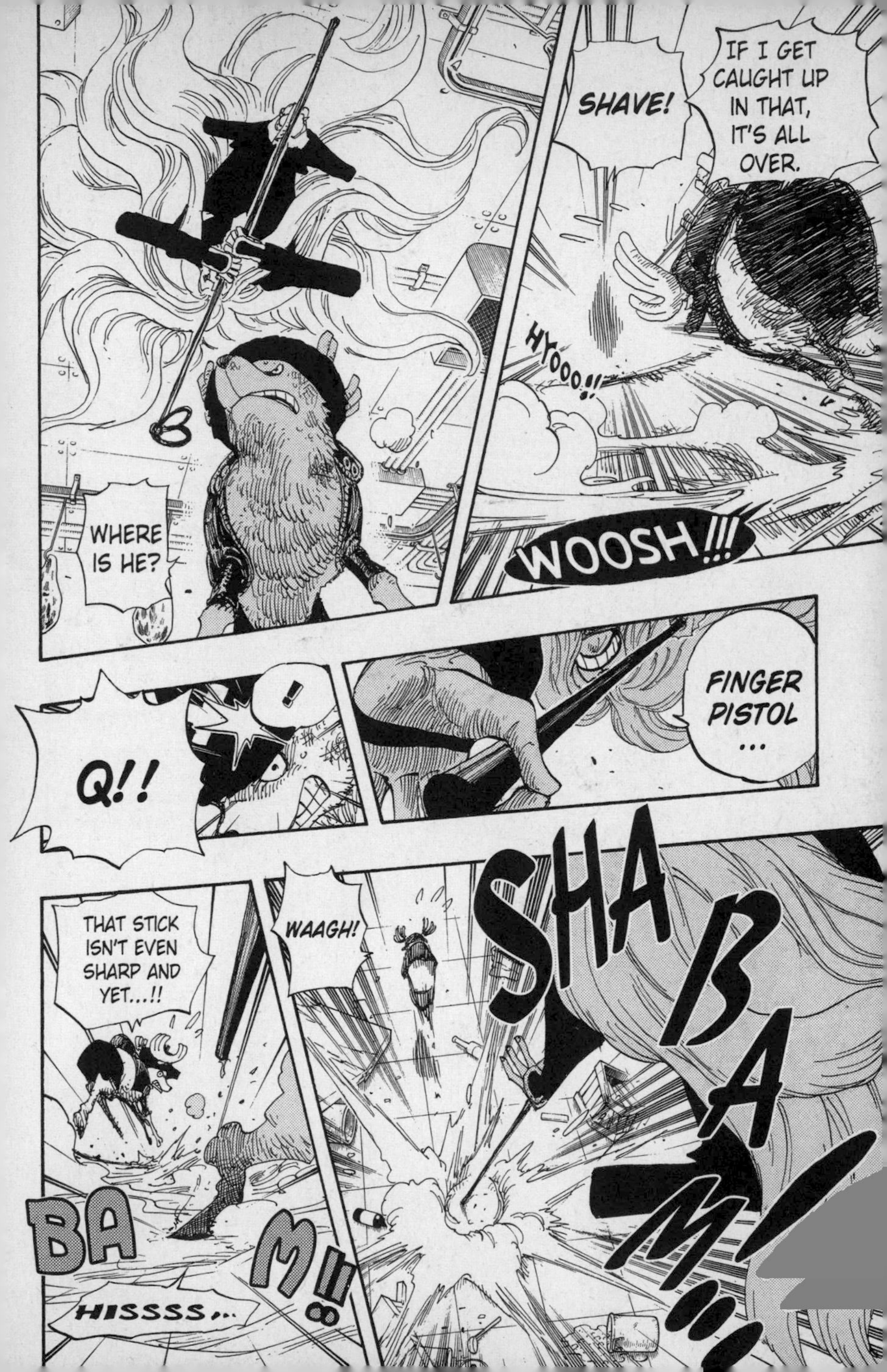
IF I GET CAUGHT UP IN THAT, IT'S ALL OVER.
SHAVE!
HYOOO!!
WOOSH!!!
WHERE IS HE?
FINGER PISTOL ...
!
Q!!
SHABAM!!!
WAAGH!
THAT STICK ISN'T EVEN SHARP AND YET...!!
BAM!!
HISSSS...

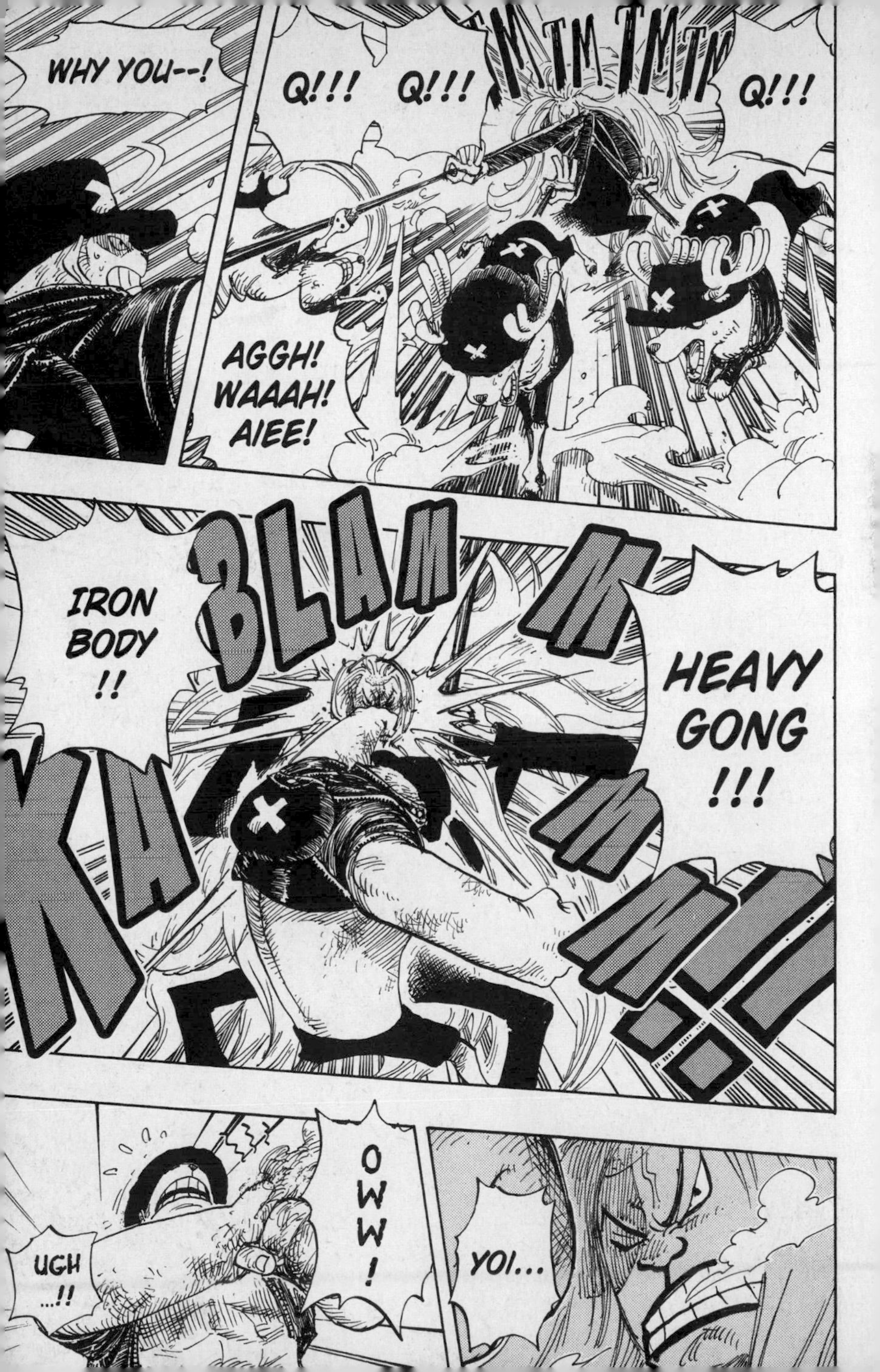
Q!!!
Q!!! Q!!!
AGGH! WAAAH! AIEE!
WHY YOU--!
HEAVY GONG !!!
BLAM
IRON BODY !!
YOI...
OWW!
UGH ...!!

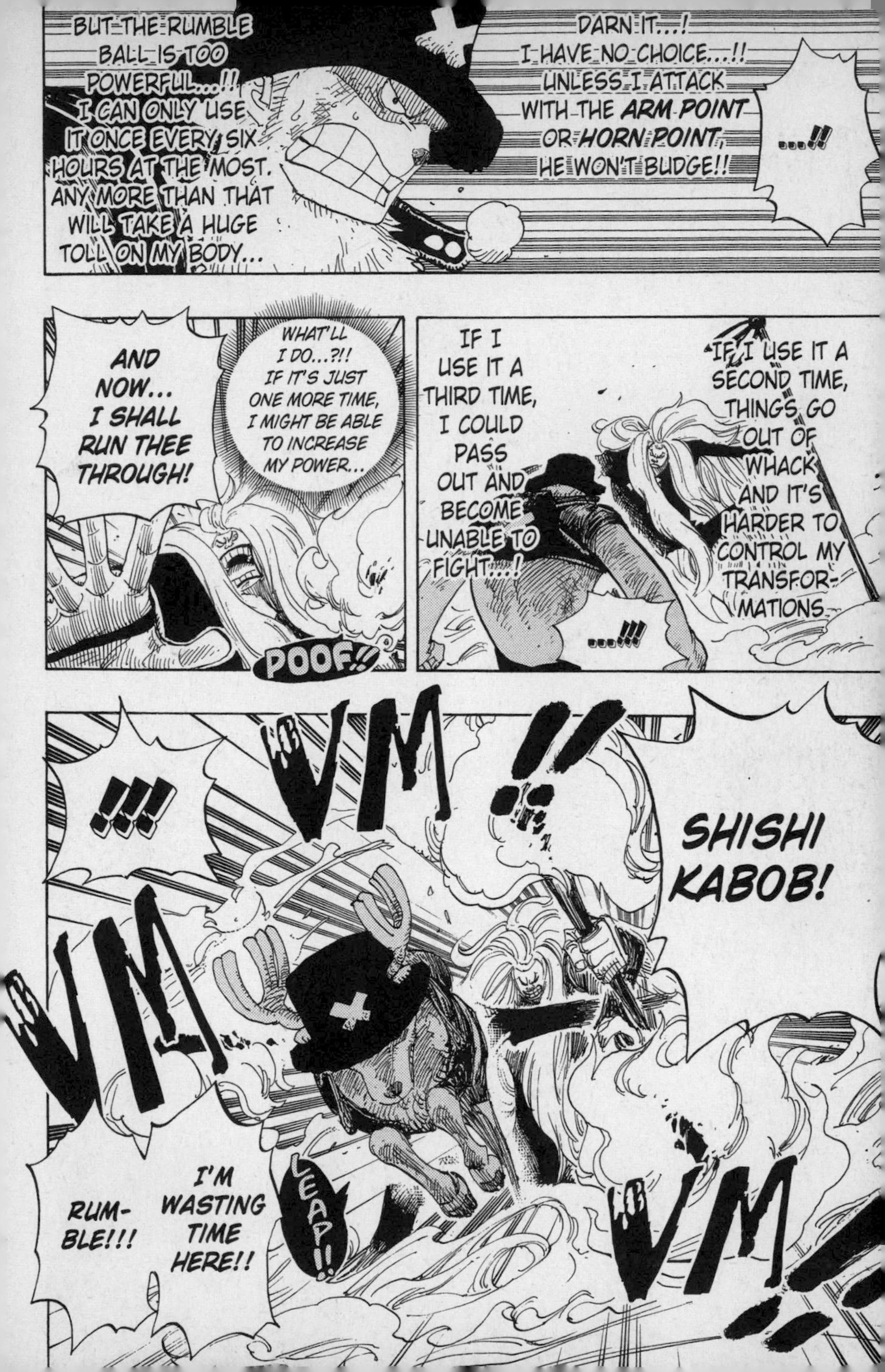
...!!
DARN IT...! I HAVE NO CHOICE...!! UNLESS I ATTACK WITH THE **ARM POINT** OR **HORN POINT**, HE WON'T BUDGE!!
BUT THE RUMBLE BALL IS TOO POWERFUL...!! I CAN ONLY USE IT ONCE EVERY SIX HOURS AT THE MOST. ANY MORE THAN THAT WILL TAKE A HUGE TOLL ON MY BODY...
IF I USE IT A SECOND TIME, THINGS GO OUT OF WHACK AND IT'S HARDER TO CONTROL MY TRANSFORMATIONS.
IF I USE IT A THIRD TIME, I COULD PASS OUT AND BECOME UNABLE TO FIGHT...!
...!!!
WHAT'LL I DO...?!! IF IT'S JUST ONE MORE TIME, I MIGHT BE ABLE TO INCREASE MY POWER...
AND NOW... I SHALL RUN THEE THROUGH!
POOF!!
SHISHI KABOB!
VM!!
!!!!
VM
VM!!
LEAP!!
I'M WASTING TIME HERE!!
RUM-BLE!!!

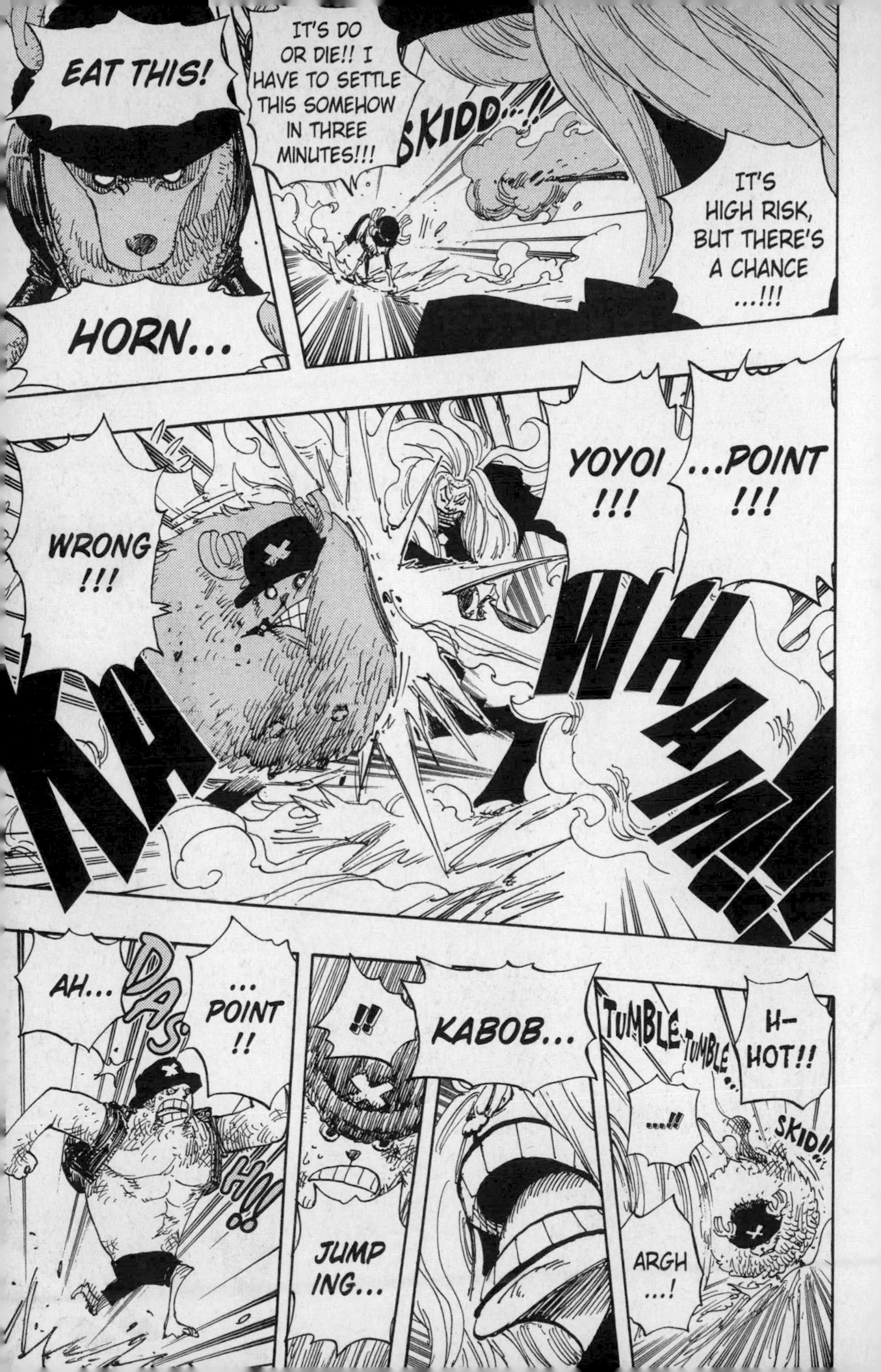
IT'S HIGH RISK, BUT THERE'S A CHANCE ...!!!
IT'S DO OR DIE!! I HAVE TO SETTLE THIS SOMEHOW IN THREE MINUTES!!!
SKIDD...!!
EAT THIS!
HORN...
...POINT !!!
YOYOI !!!
WHAM!!
WRONG !!!
H-HOT!!
TUMBLE TUMBLE...
SKID!!
...!!
ARGH ...!
KABOB...
!!
JUMP ING...
... POINT !!
AH...
DASH!!

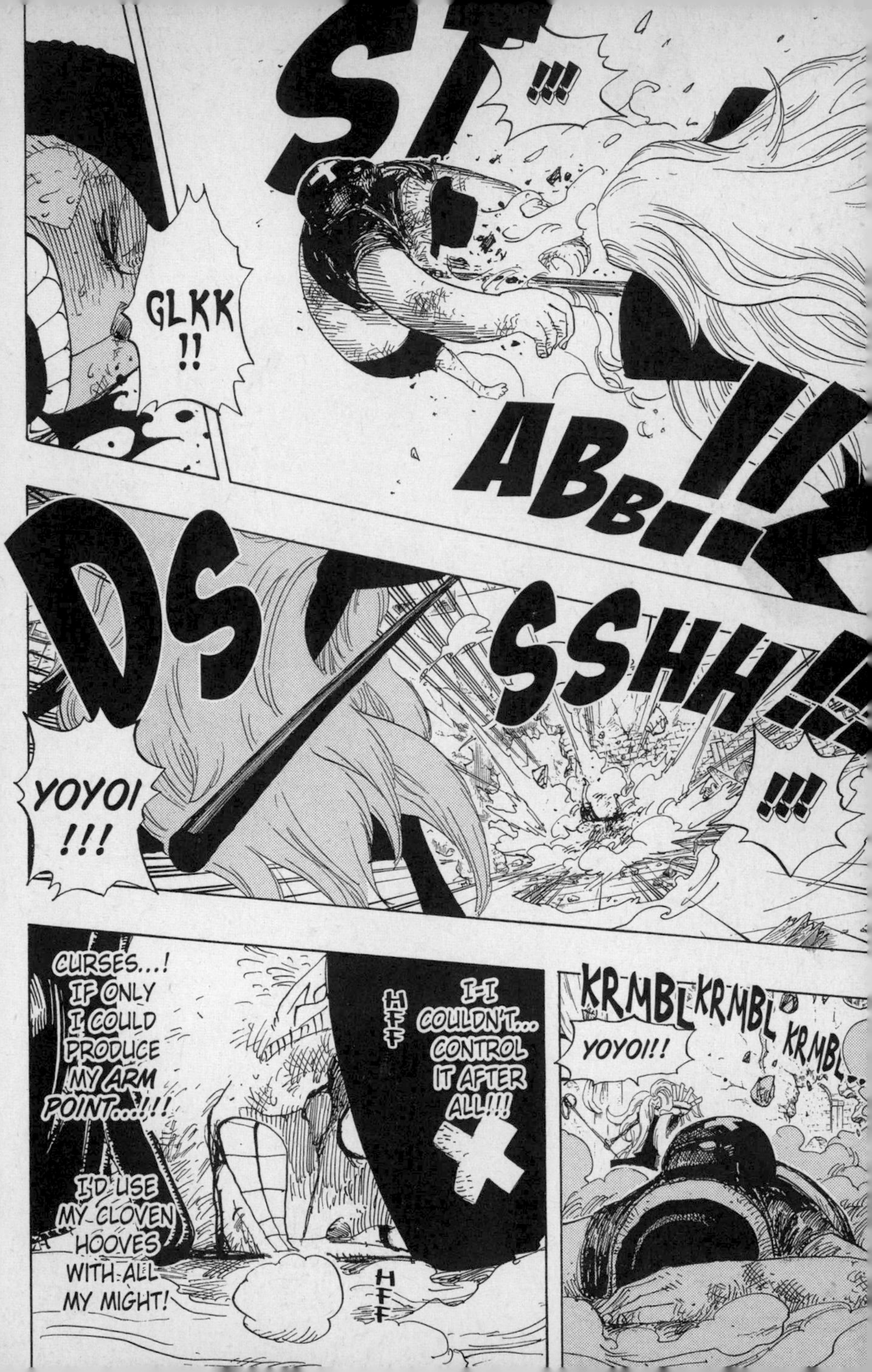
ST!!!
ABB!!
GLKK !!
DS SSHH!!!
YOYOI !!!
KRMBL KRMBL KRMBL
YOYOI!!
HFF
I-I COULDN'T... CONTROL IT AFTER ALL!!!
HFF
CURSES...! IF ONLY I COULD PRODUCE MY ARM POINT...!!!
I'D USE MY CLOVEN HOOVES WITH ALL MY MIGHT!

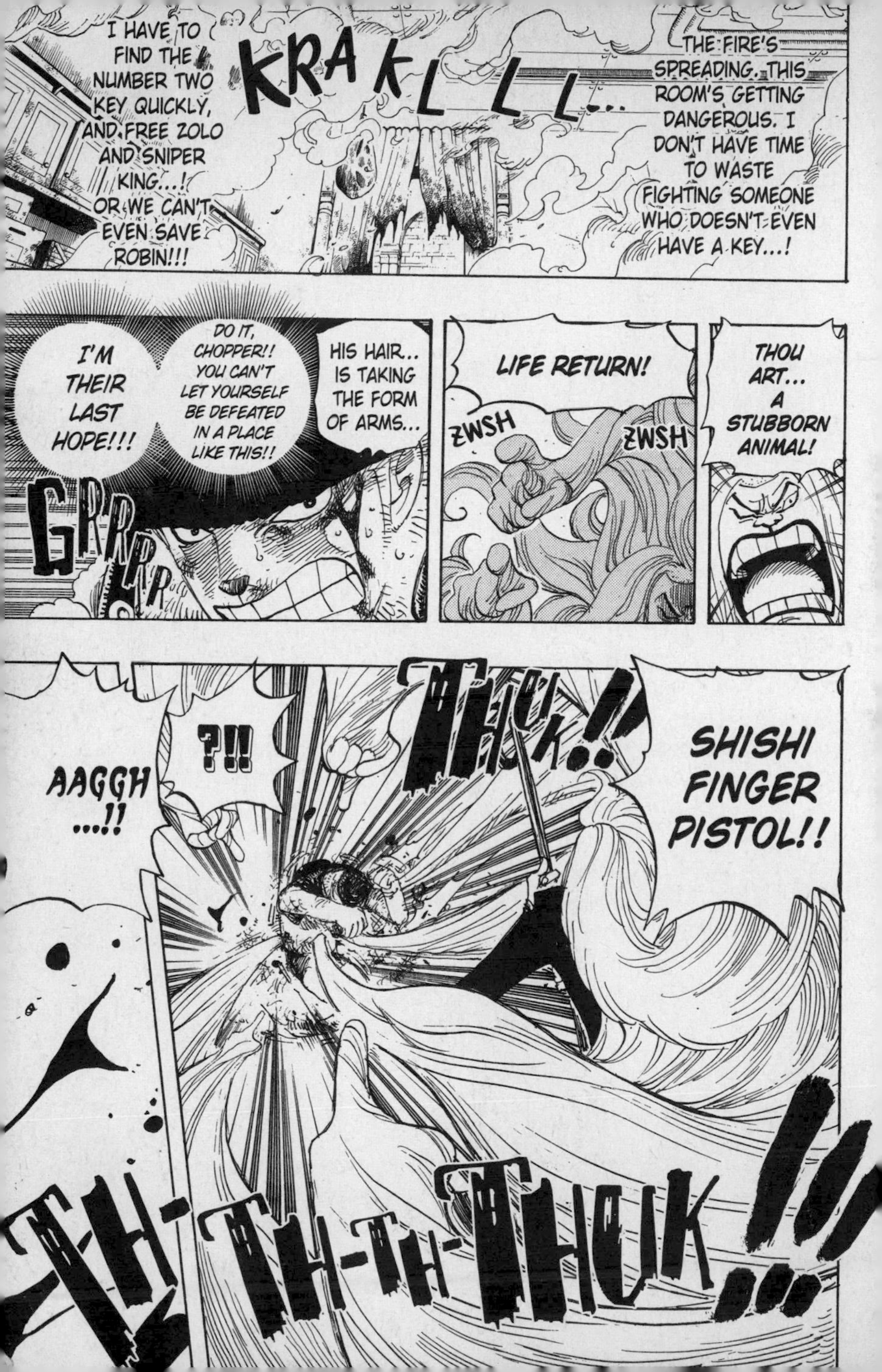
THE FIRE'S SPREADING. THIS ROOM'S GETTING DANGEROUS. I DON'T HAVE TIME TO WASTE FIGHTING SOMEONE WHO DOESN'T EVEN HAVE A KEY...!
KRA K L L L...
I HAVE TO FIND THE NUMBER TWO KEY QUICKLY, AND FREE ZOLO AND SNIPER KING...! OR WE CAN'T EVEN SAVE ROBIN!!!
THOU ART... A STUBBORN ANIMAL!
LIFE RETURN!
ZWSH
ZWSH
HIS HAIR... IS TAKING THE FORM OF ARMS...
DO IT, CHOPPER!! YOU CAN'T LET YOURSELF BE DEFEATED IN A PLACE LIKE THIS!!
I'M THEIR LAST HOPE!!!
GRRRRR
SHISHI FINGER PISTOL!!
THUCK!!
?!!
AAGGH ...!!
TH-TH-TH-TH-THUCK...!!

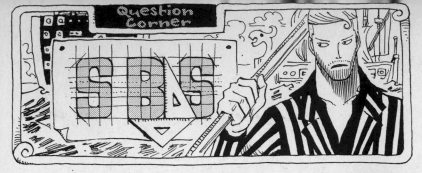

Q: Hello, Oda Sensei. It's nice to meet you, I always enjoy reading *One Piece*. Anyway, here's a kind of serious question. In class the other day, I learned that the word "Rob" means "to steal." That got me curious, and I looked up "Lucci" (lucchi) and found out that it means "light" in Italian. Together,  they become "steal the light." It hit me very hard as I realized that, throughout the entire story, the verb "to steal" plays a very important part in *One Piece*. So did you name him from the start knowing that? —Reflect

A: Uh.... Uh.... Well. Uh-huh. Y-Y...Yes. (anxiousness) You know me. I always come up with names that have deep meanings. Yup. I sure do. "Rob Lucci" means "to steal the light," or so I hear. (<-- I didn't know)

Q: I am Miss Sniper King, and I support good health for young boys. ♡ This is for all the healthy boys throughout this country!! Remember in volume 41's Question Corner, there was a question about Nami's cup size?! According to my scope, Nami's underbust  size is 65. From that, I calculated that her bust size is 95, which makes her an I-cup!!! (DOOM!!) That's huge!!! Personally, I'm a D-cup… Boys… Are you satisfied??

A: Well, regarding this matter, I received many answers from my female readers. Thank you for your detailed analysis and explanations. But young boys won't read complicated explanations, so let me sum up the consensus: Nami and Robin are both I-cups! Wow!

Chapter 407: MONSTER

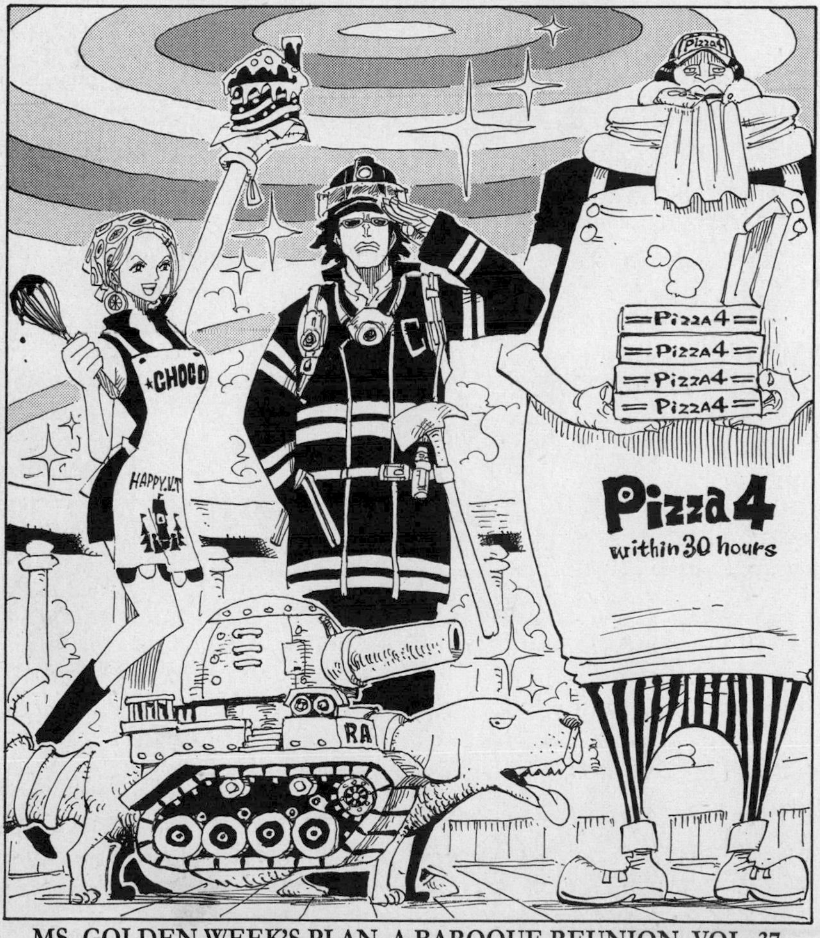
Pizza4
Pizza4
Pizza4
Pizza4
Pizza4
★CHOCO
HAPPY.V.T
C
Pizza4
within 30 hours
RA

MS. GOLDEN WEEK'S PLAN, A BAROQUE REUNION, VOL. 37:
"A CHOCOLATIER, A FIREMAN,
A PIZZA DELIVERY MAN AND A TANK"

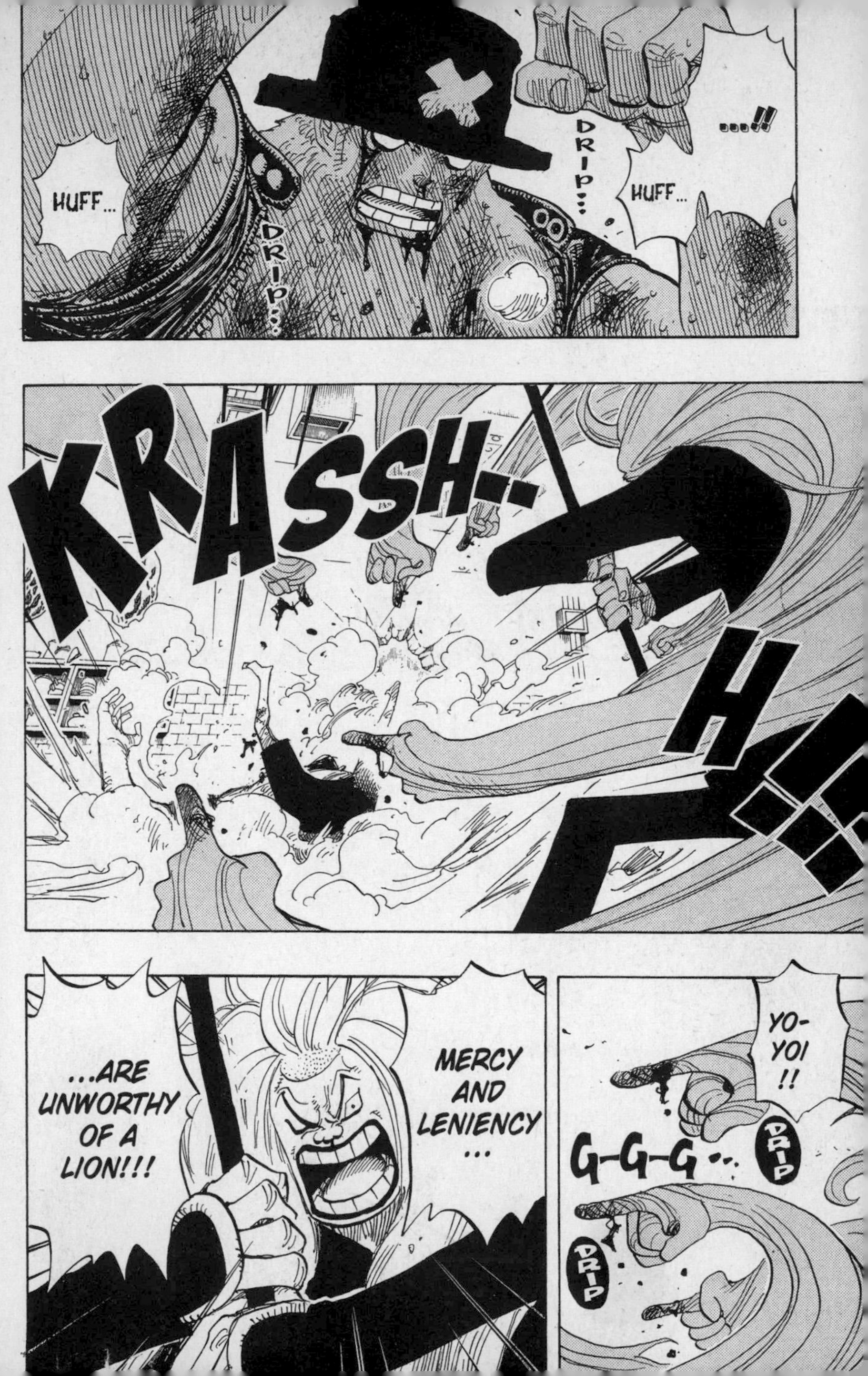

...!!
HUFF...
DRIP...
DRIP...
HUFF...
KRASSH--
H!!
YO-YOI!!
DRIP
G-G-G...
DRIP
MERCY AND LENIENCY...
...ARE UNWORTHY OF A LION!!!

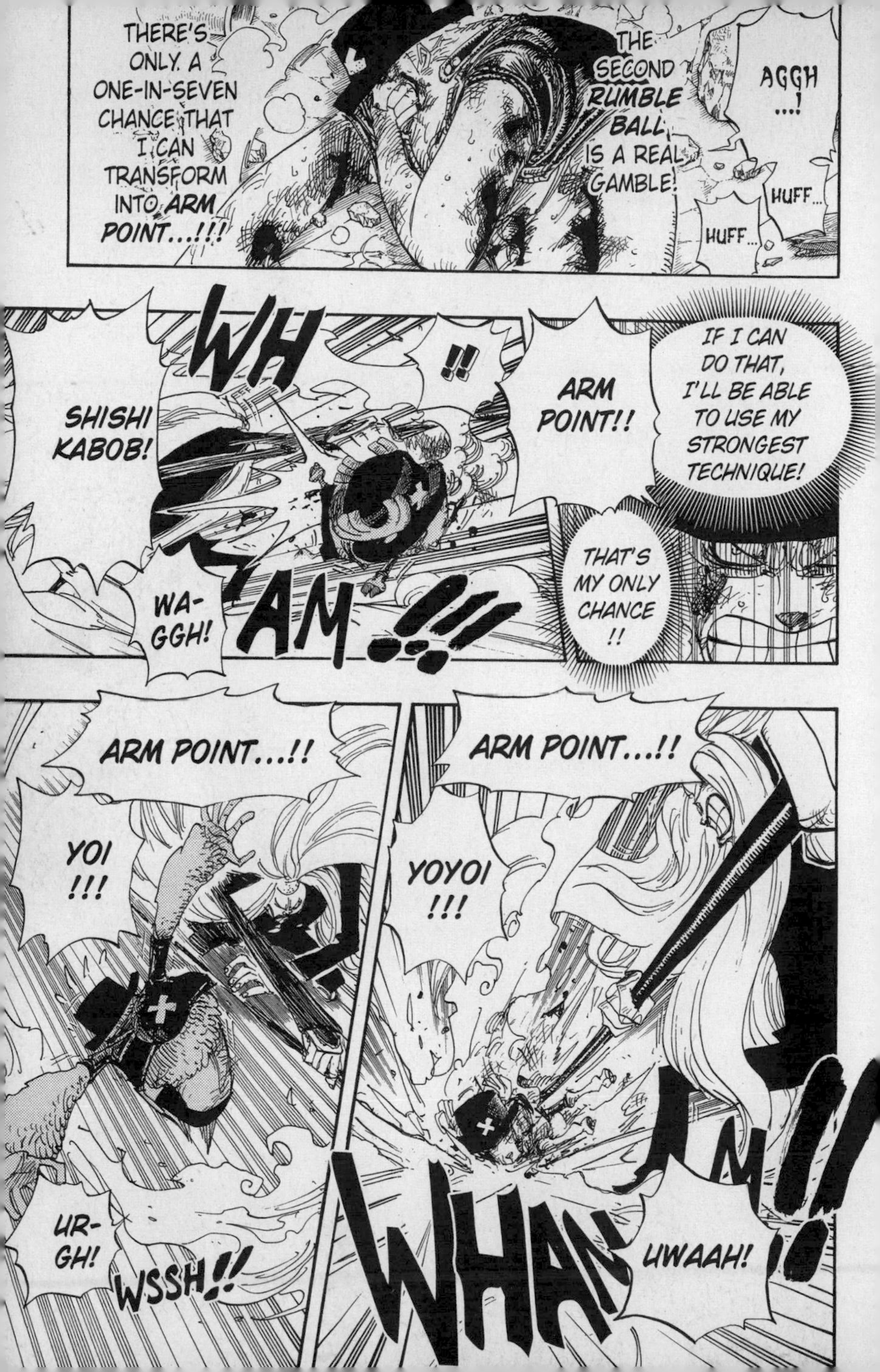
AGGH...!
THE SECOND RUMBLE BALL IS A REAL GAMBLE!
HUFF...
HUFF...
THERE'S ONLY A ONE-IN-SEVEN CHANCE THAT I CAN TRANSFORM INTO ARM POINT...!!!
IF I CAN DO THAT, I'LL BE ABLE TO USE MY STRONGEST TECHNIQUE!
THAT'S MY ONLY CHANCE!!
ARM POINT!!
!!
WHAM!!!
SHISHI KABOB!
WA-GGH!
ARM POINT...!!
YOYOI!!!
UWAAH!
WHAM!!
ARM POINT...!!
YOI!!!
UR-GH!
WSSH!!

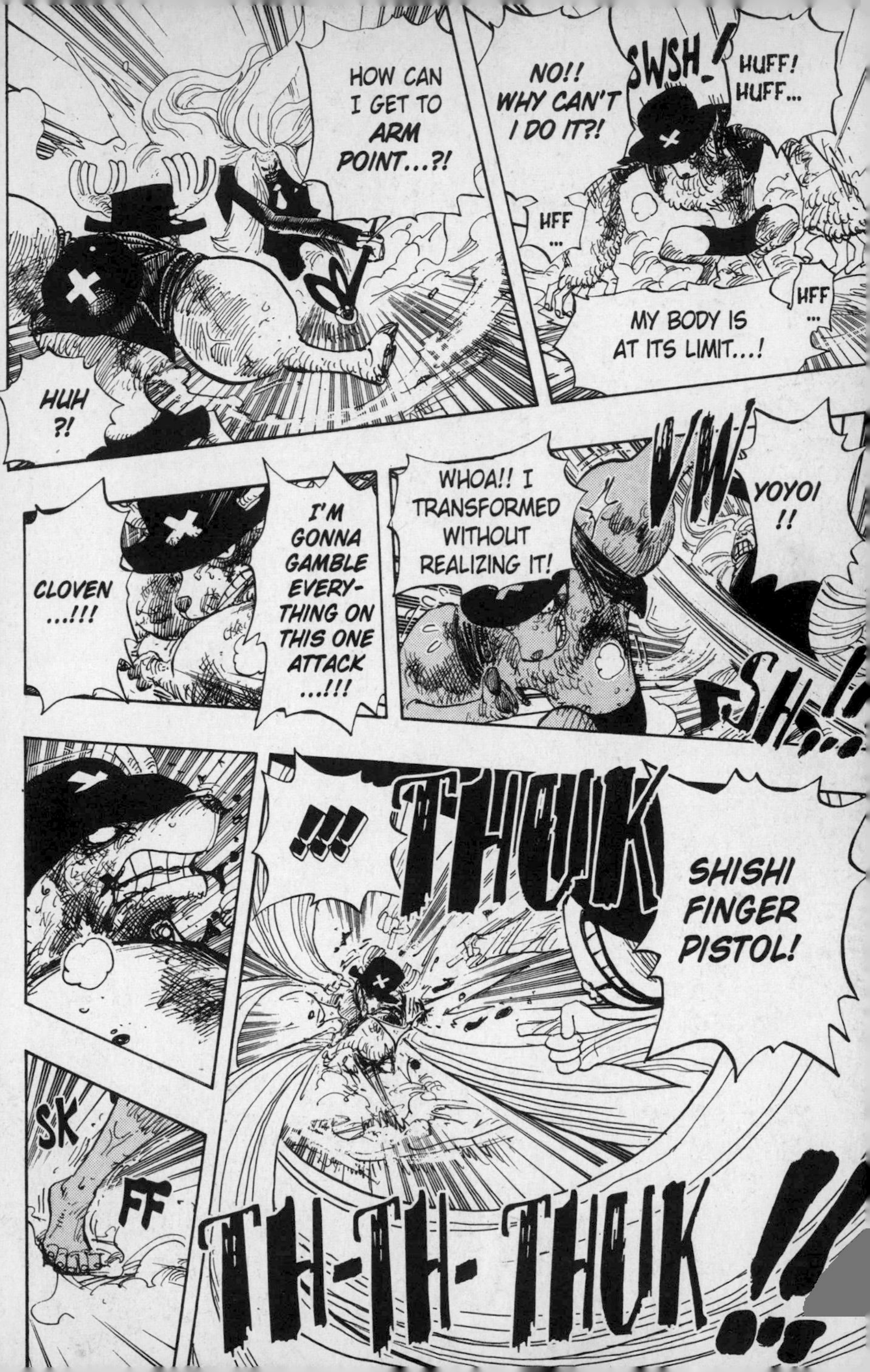
SWSH!
HUFF! HUFF...
NO!! WHY CAN'T I DO IT?!
HFF...
HFF...
MY BODY IS AT ITS LIMIT...!
HOW CAN I GET TO ARM POINT...?!
HUH?!
VW
YOYOI!!
WHOA!! I TRANSFORMED WITHOUT REALIZING IT!
SH...!!
I'M GONNA GAMBLE EVERY-THING ON THIS ONE ATTACK...!!!
CLOVEN...!!!
!!!
THUK
SHISHI FINGER PISTOL!
TH-TH-THUK!!
SK
FF

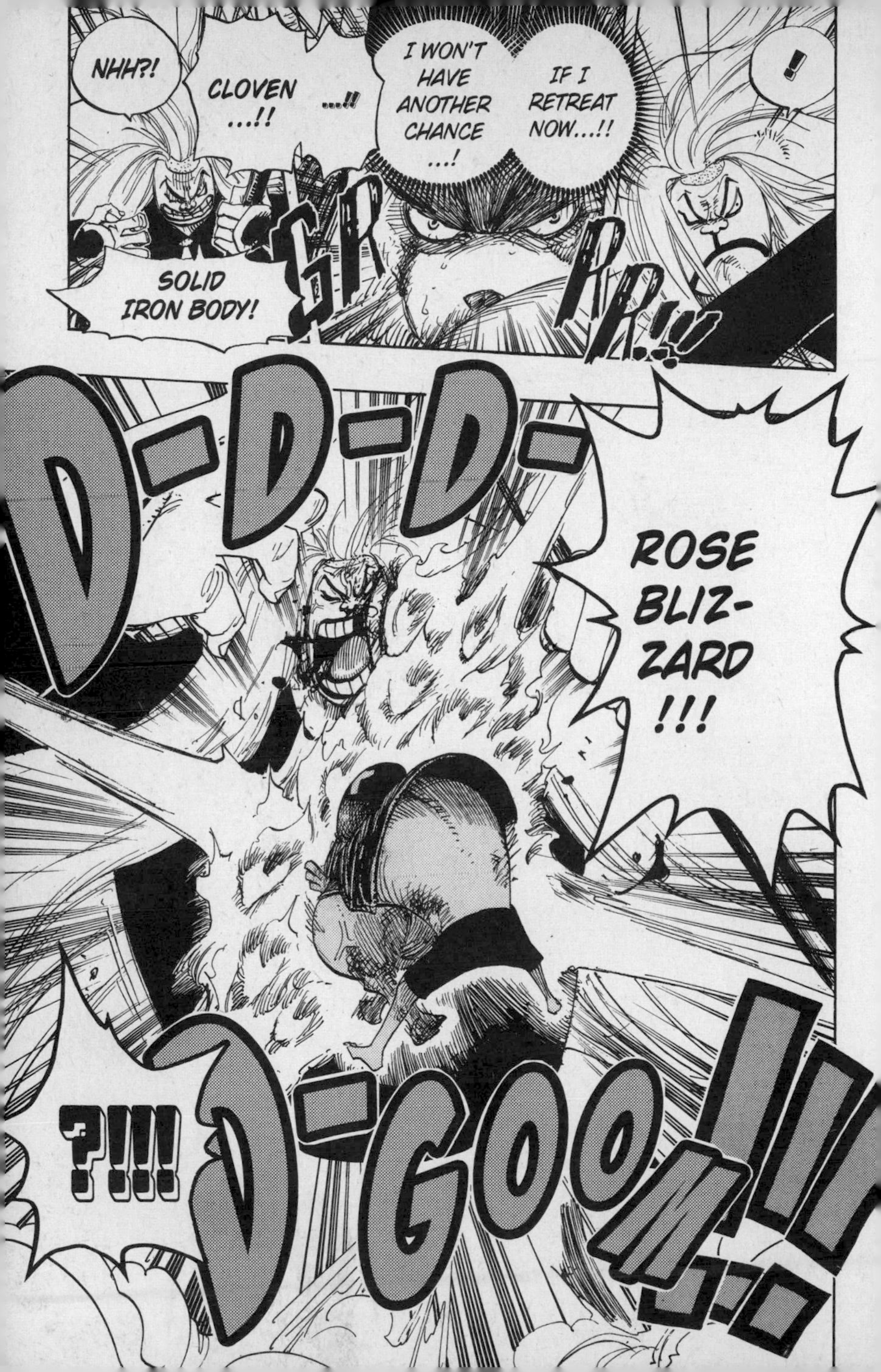
!
IF I RETREAT NOW...!!
I WON'T HAVE ANOTHER CHANCE ...!
GRRR...!!!
...!!
CLOVEN ...!!
NHH?!
SOLID IRON BODY!
ROSE BLIZ-ZARD !!!
D-D-D-
?!!!
D-GOON!!!

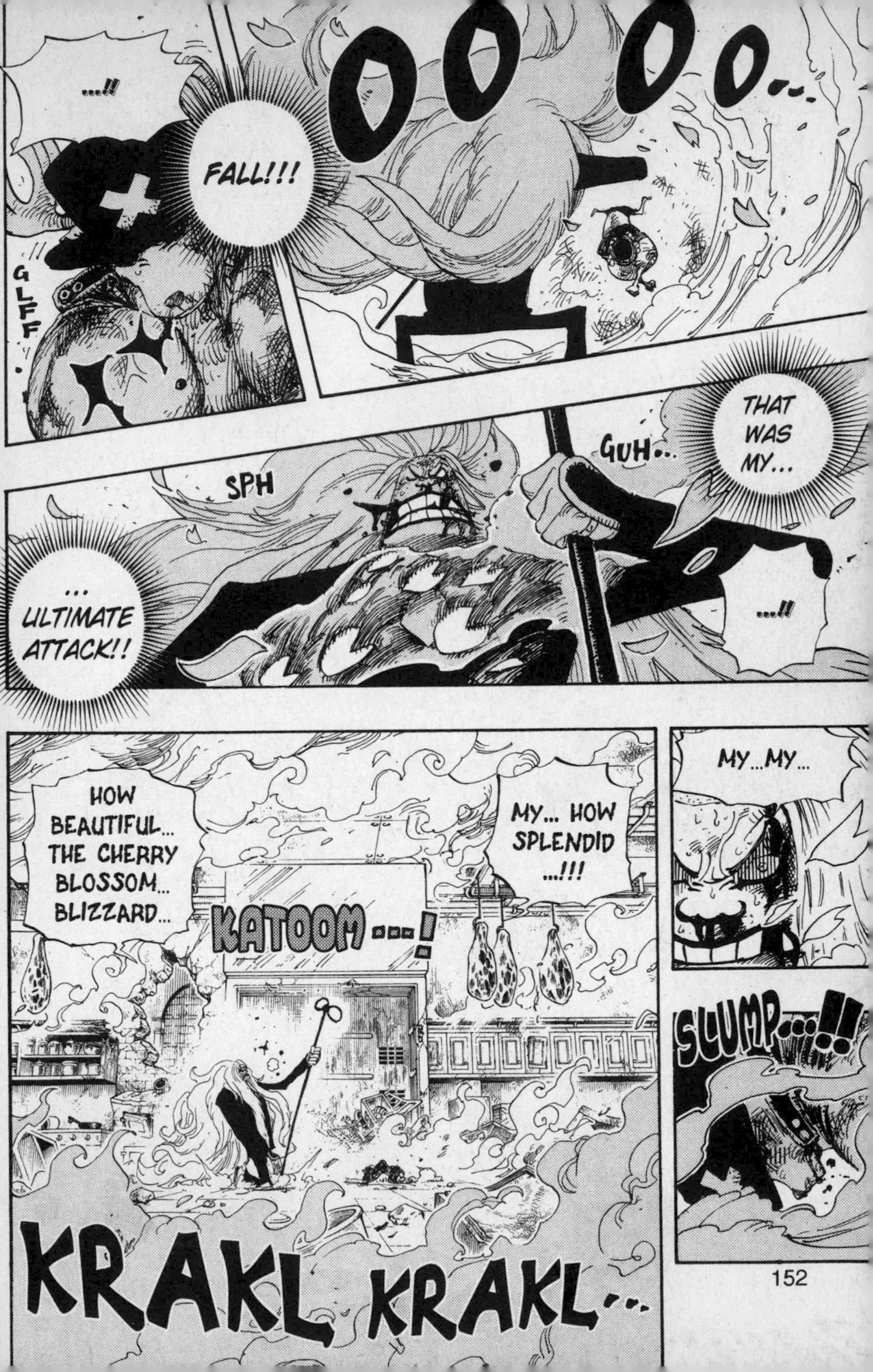
OOOO...
FALL!!!
...!!
GLFF
THAT WAS MY...
GUH...
SPH
...!!
... ULTIMATE ATTACK!!
MY...MY...
SLUMP...!!
MY... HOW SPLENDID ...!!!
HOW BEAUTIFUL... THE CHERRY BLOSSOM... BLIZZARD...
KATOOM...!
KRAKL KRAKL...

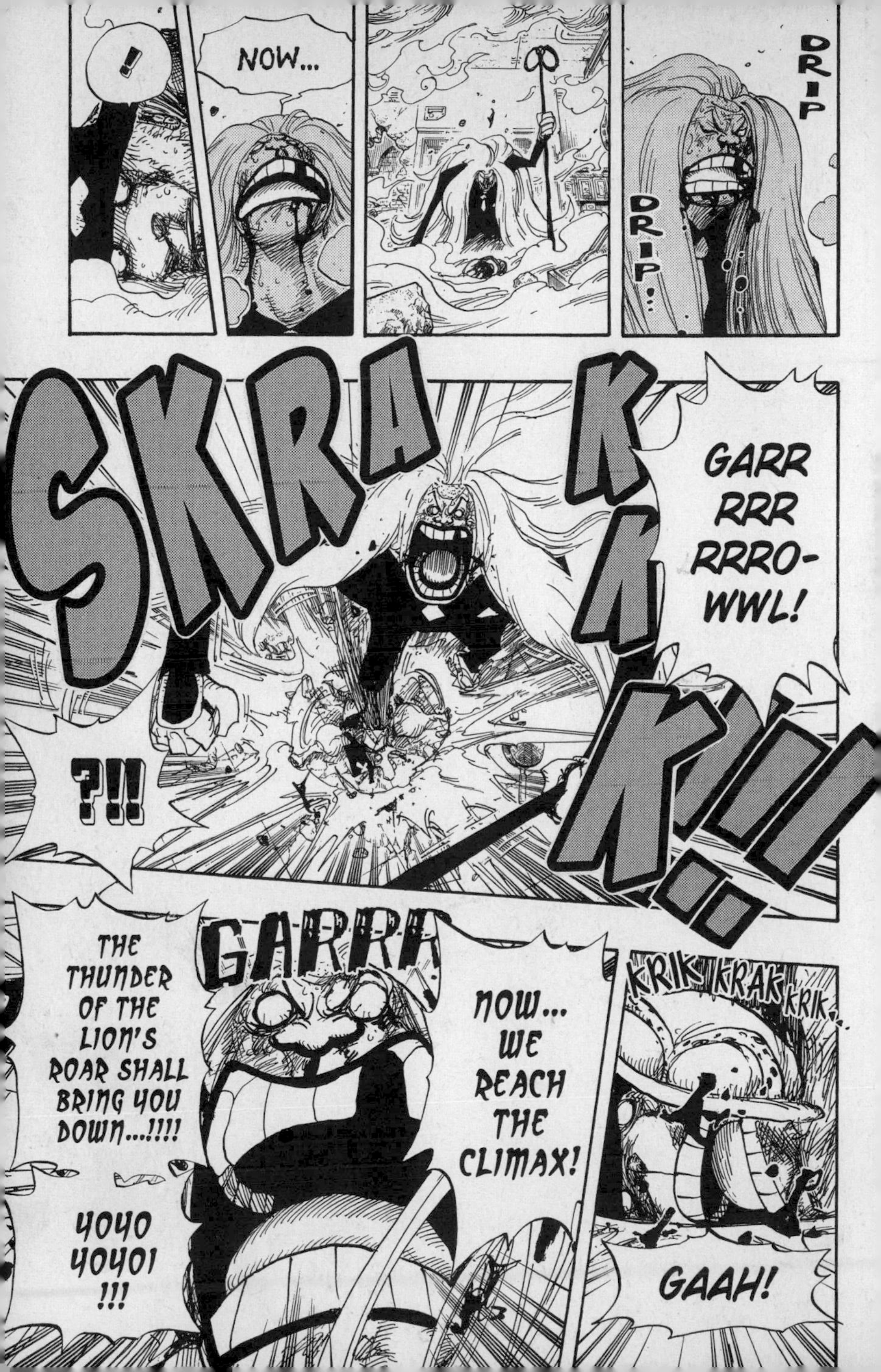
DRIP
DRIP...
NOW...
!
GARR RRR RRRO-WWL!
SKRAKKK!!!
?!!
KRIK KRAK KRIK...
GAAH!
GARRR
NOW... WE REACH THE CLIMAX!
THE THUNDER OF THE LION'S ROAR SHALL BRING YOU DOWN...!!!!
YOYO YOYOI !!!

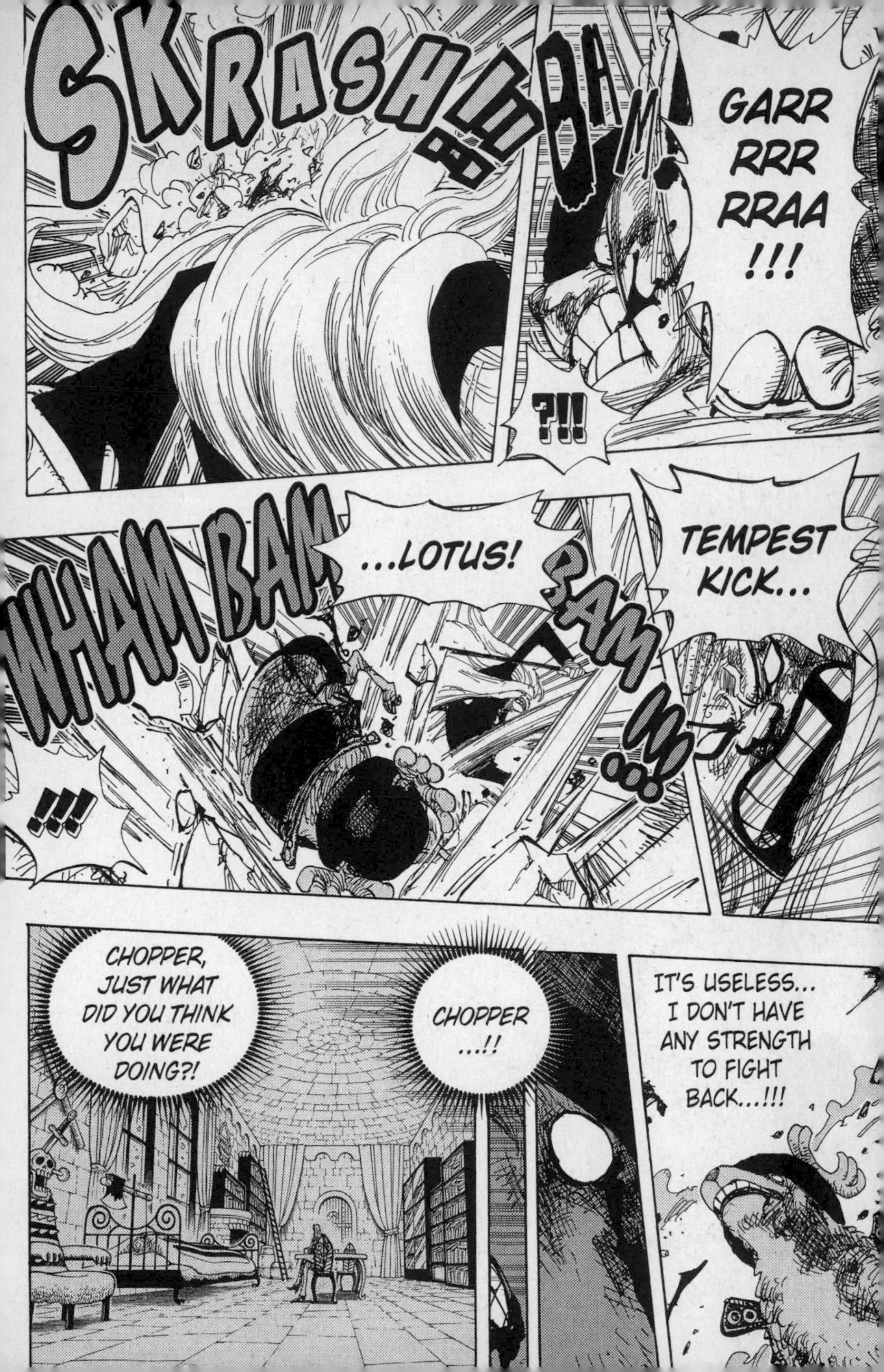
BAM
GARR RRR RRAA !!!
?!!
SKRASH!!!
TEMPEST KICK...
BAM...!!
...LOTUS!
WHAM BAM
!!!
IT'S USELESS... I DON'T HAVE ANY STRENGTH TO FIGHT BACK...!!!
CHOPPER ...!!
CHOPPER, JUST WHAT DID YOU THINK YOU WERE DOING?!

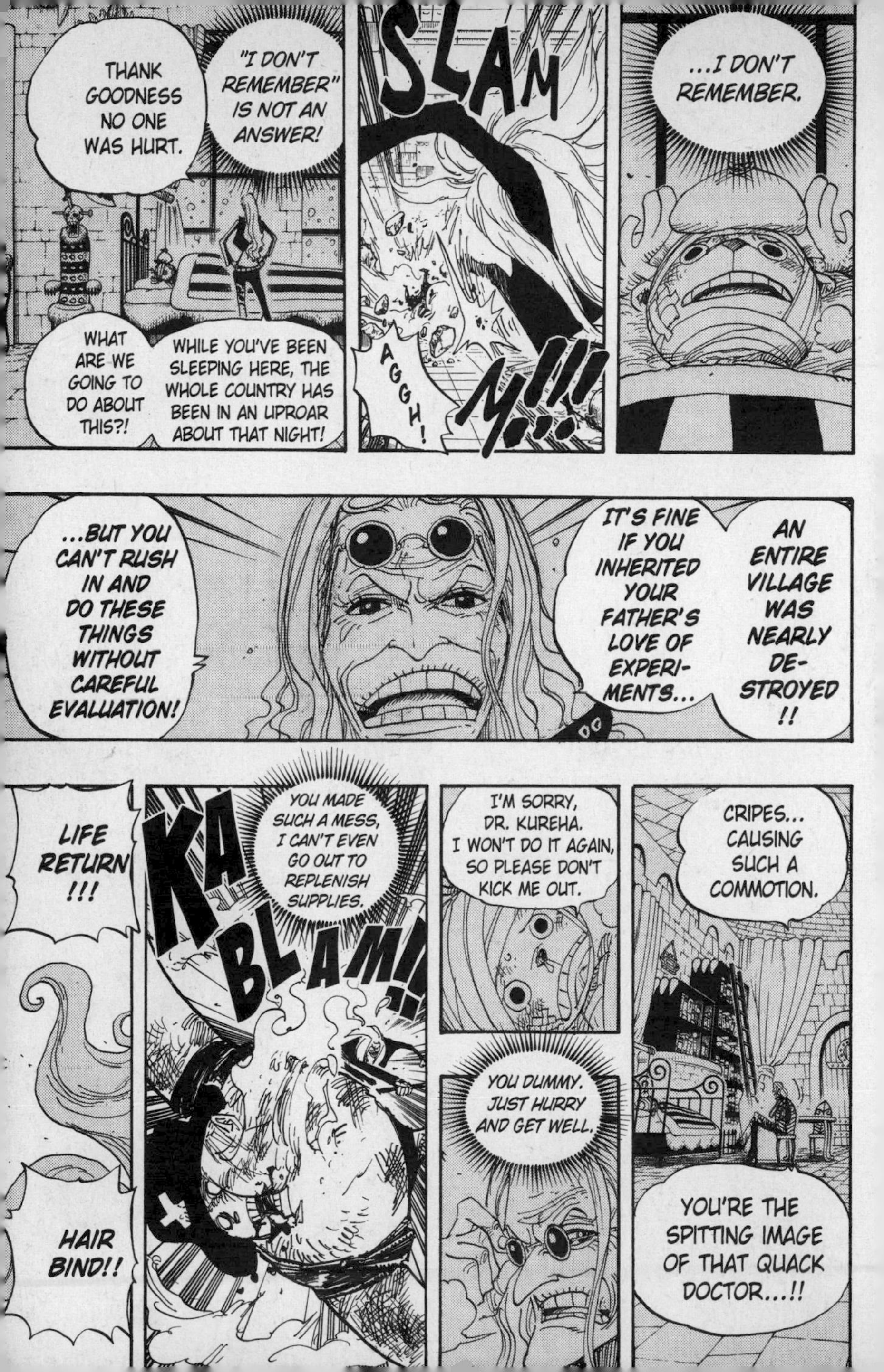
...I DON'T REMEMBER.
SLAM
AGGGH!
M!!!
"I DON'T REMEMBER" IS NOT AN ANSWER!
THANK GOODNESS NO ONE WAS HURT.
WHILE YOU'VE BEEN SLEEPING HERE, THE WHOLE COUNTRY HAS BEEN IN AN UPROAR ABOUT THAT NIGHT!
WHAT ARE WE GOING TO DO ABOUT THIS?!
AN ENTIRE VILLAGE WAS NEARLY DE-STROYED!!
IT'S FINE IF YOU INHERITED YOUR FATHER'S LOVE OF EXPERI-MENTS...
...BUT YOU CAN'T RUSH IN AND DO THESE THINGS WITHOUT CAREFUL EVALUATION!
CRIPES... CAUSING SUCH A COMMOTION.
YOU'RE THE SPITTING IMAGE OF THAT QUACK DOCTOR...!!
I'M SORRY, DR. KUREHA. I WON'T DO IT AGAIN, SO PLEASE DON'T KICK ME OUT.
YOU DUMMY. JUST HURRY AND GET WELL.
YOU MADE SUCH A MESS, I CAN'T EVEN GO OUT TO REPLENISH SUPPLIES.
KA BLAM!!
LIFE RETURN!!!
HAIR BIND!!

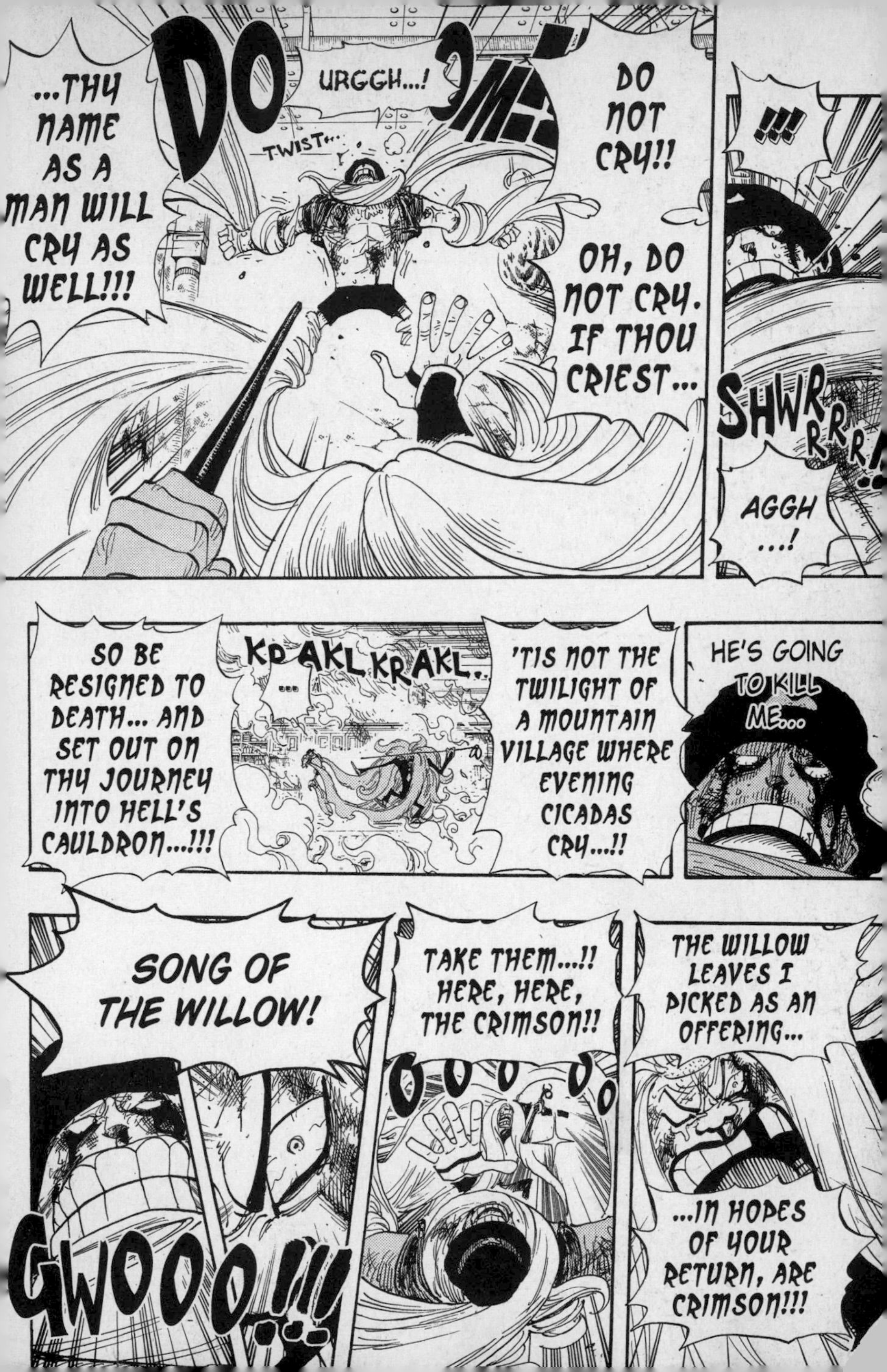
!!!
SHWRRRR!!
AGGH...!
DO NOT CRY!!
OH, DO NOT CRY. IF THOU CRIEST...
DO
URGGH...!
TWIST...
...THY NAME AS A MAN WILL CRY AS WELL!!!
HE'S GOING TO KILL ME...
'TIS NOT THE TWILIGHT OF A MOUNTAIN VILLAGE WHERE EVENING CICADAS CRY...!!
KRAKL KRAKL...
...
SO BE RESIGNED TO DEATH... AND SET OUT ON THY JOURNEY INTO HELL'S CAULDRON...!!!
THE WILLOW LEAVES I PICKED AS AN OFFERING...
...IN HOPES OF YOUR RETURN, ARE CRIMSON!!!
TAKE THEM...!! HERE, HERE, THE CRIMSON!!
OOOOO
SONG OF THE WILLOW!
GWOOO!!!

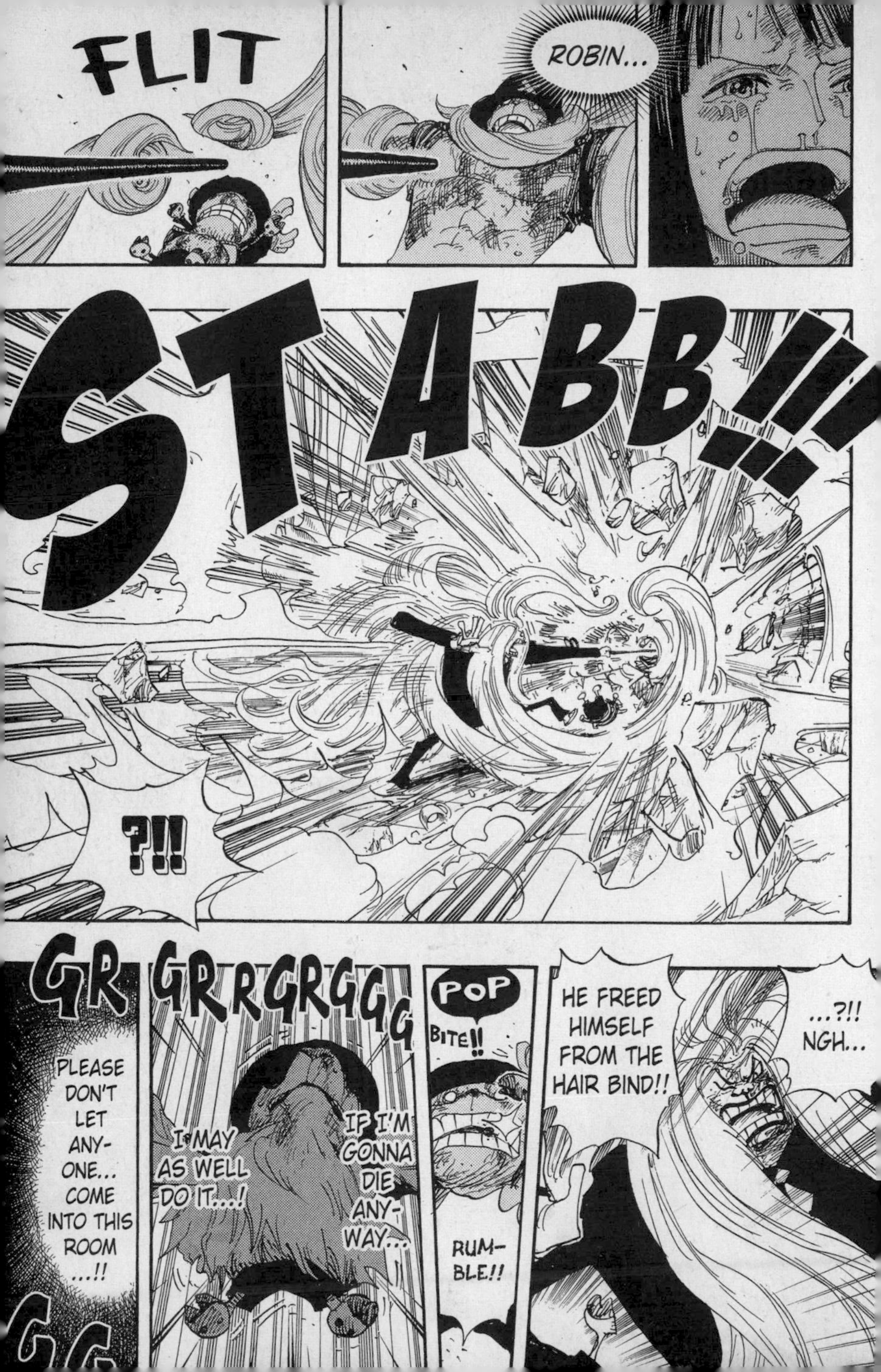
ROBIN...
FLIT
STABB!!!
?!!
...?!! NGH...
HE FREED HIMSELF FROM THE HAIR BIND!!
POP
BITE!!
RUMBLE!!
IF I'M GONNA DIE ANY-WAY...
I MAY AS WELL DO IT...!
GRRGRGGG
GR
PLEASE DON'T LET ANY-ONE... COME INTO THIS ROOM ...!!
GG

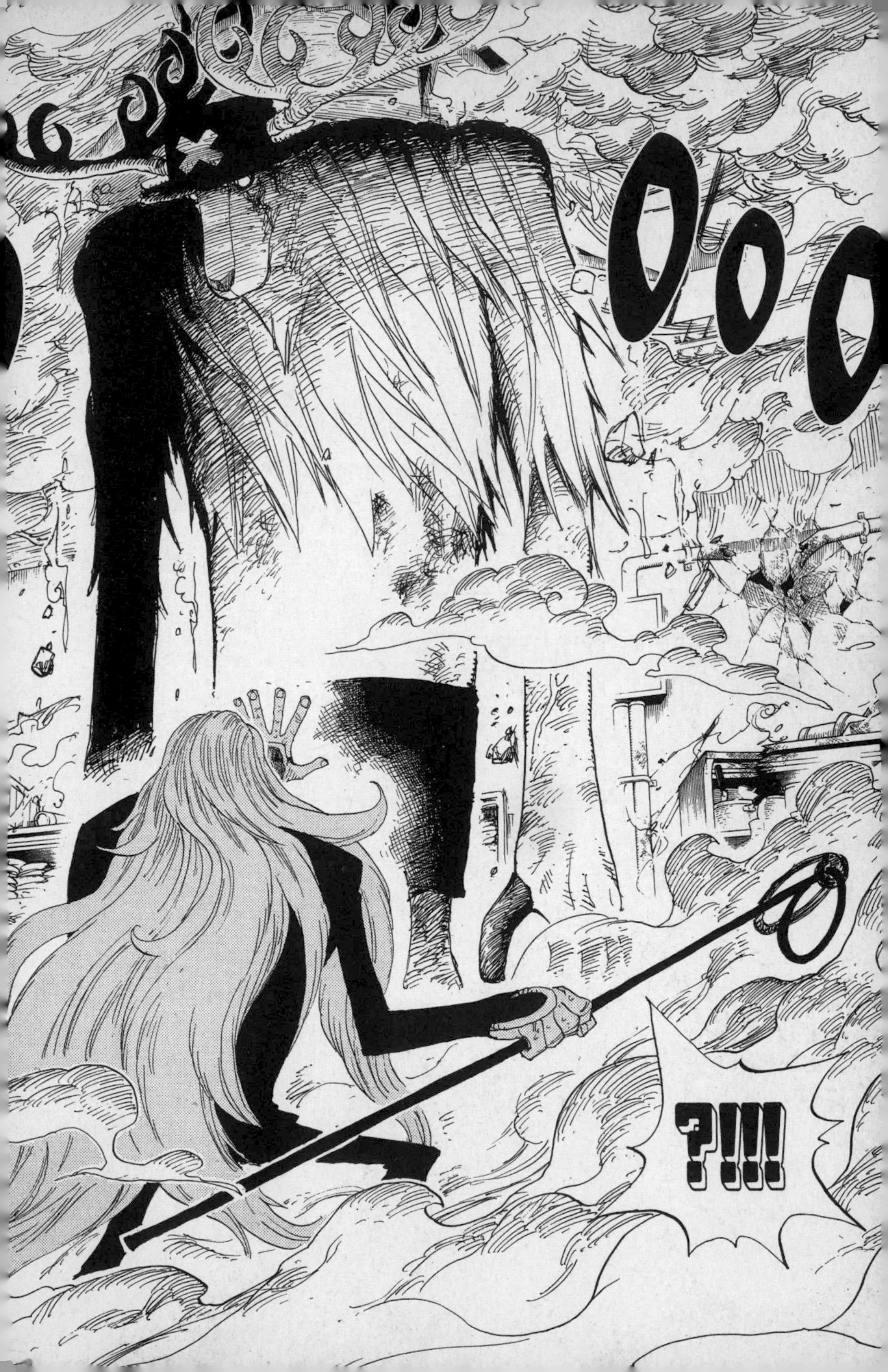
OOOO
?!!!

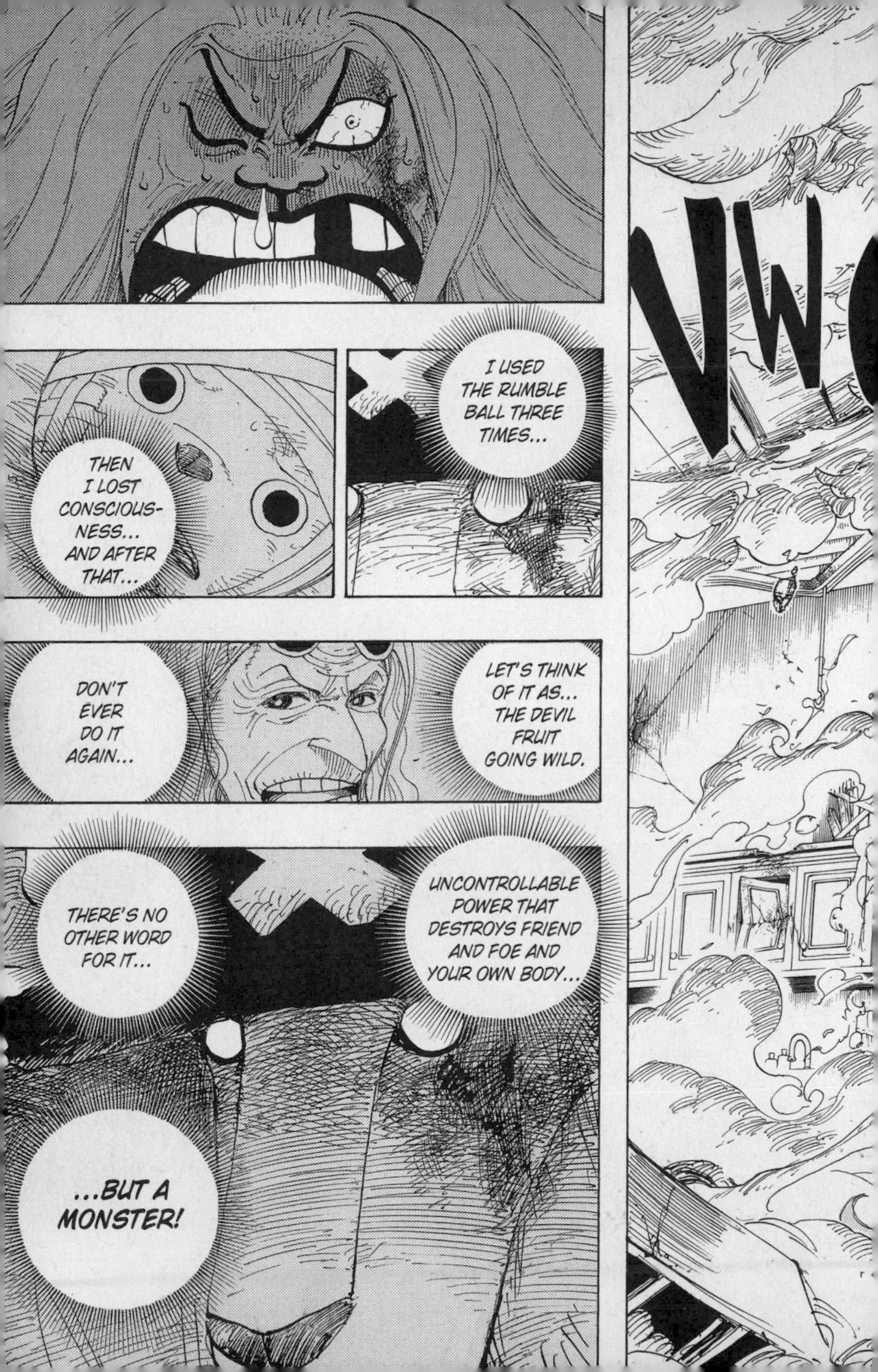
I USED THE RUMBLE BALL THREE TIMES...
THEN I LOST CONSCIOUS-NESS... AND AFTER THAT...
LET'S THINK OF IT AS... THE DEVIL FRUIT GOING WILD.
DON'T EVER DO IT AGAIN...
UNCONTROLLABLE POWER THAT DESTROYS FRIEND AND FOE AND YOUR OWN BODY...
THERE'S NO OTHER WORD FOR IT...
...BUT A MONSTER!

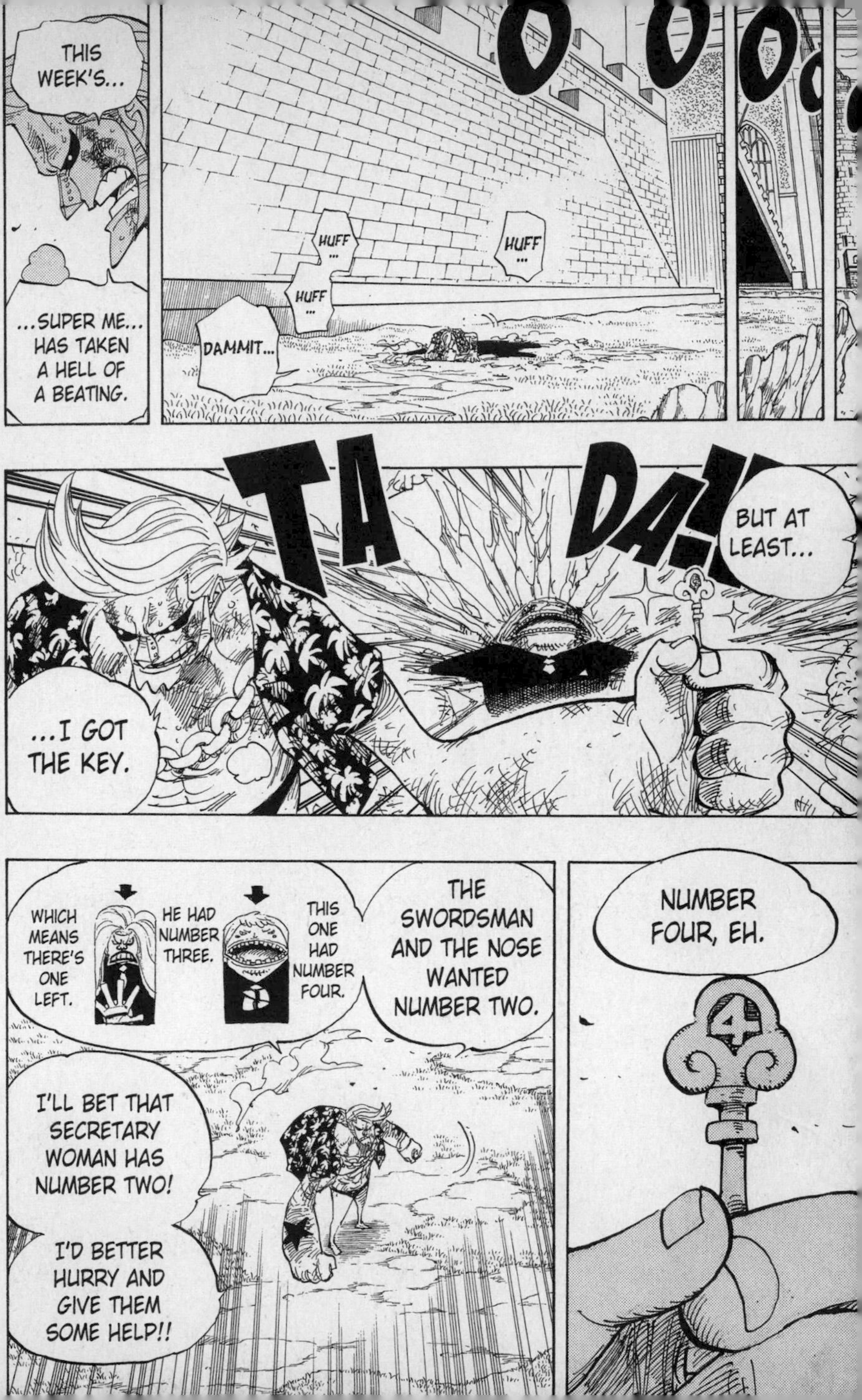
HUFF...
HUFF...
HUFF...
DAMMIT...
THIS WEEK'S...
...SUPER ME... HAS TAKEN A HELL OF A BEATING.
TA DA!
BUT AT LEAST...
...I GOT THE KEY.
NUMBER FOUR, EH.
THE SWORDSMAN AND THE NOSE WANTED NUMBER TWO.
THIS ONE HAD NUMBER FOUR.
HE HAD NUMBER THREE.
WHICH MEANS THERE'S ONE LEFT.
I'LL BET THAT SECRETARY WOMAN HAS NUMBER TWO!
I'D BETTER HURRY AND GIVE THEM SOME HELP!!

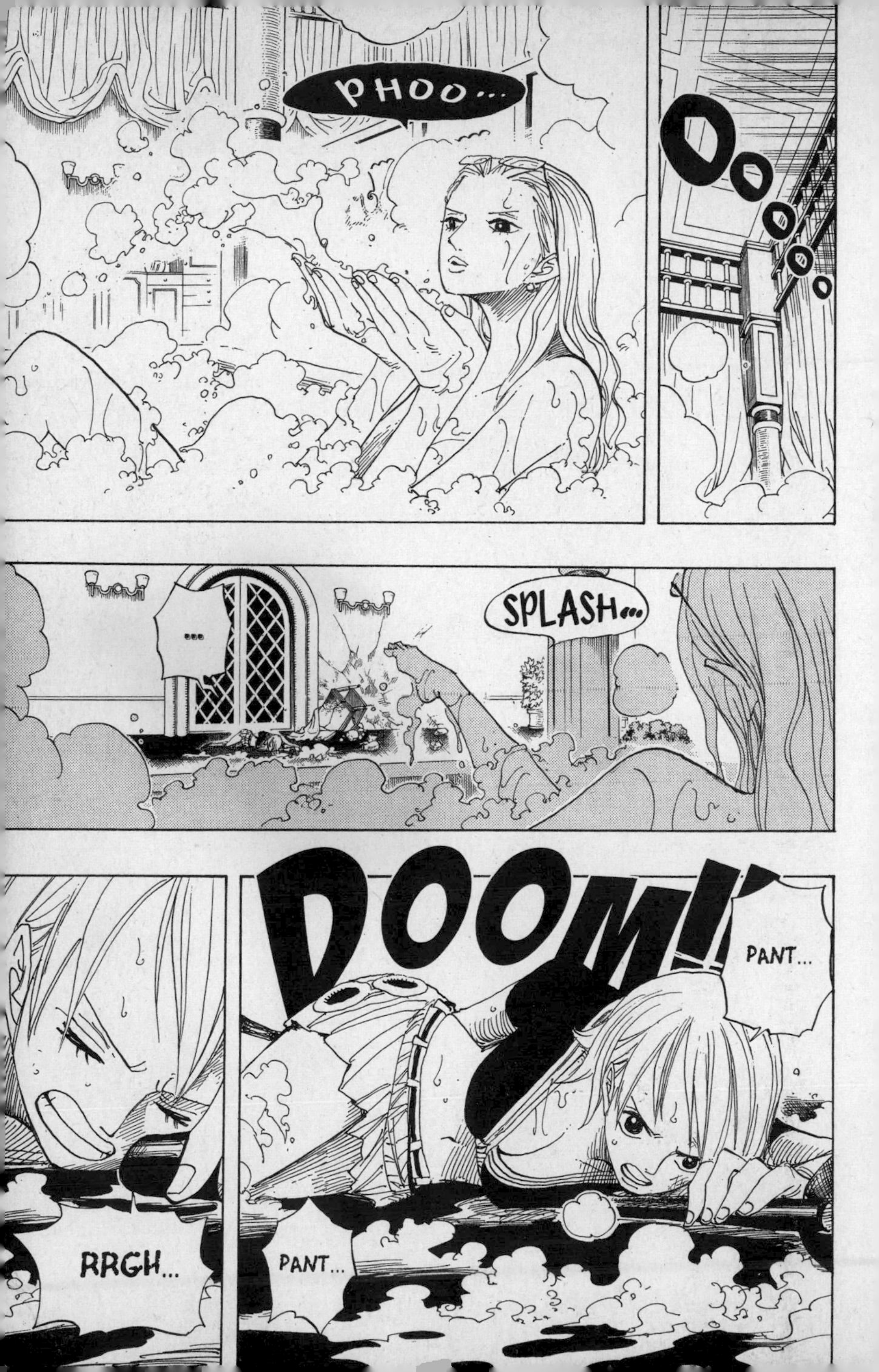
OOOOO
PHOO...
SPLASH...
...
DOOM!
PANT...
PANT...
RRGH...

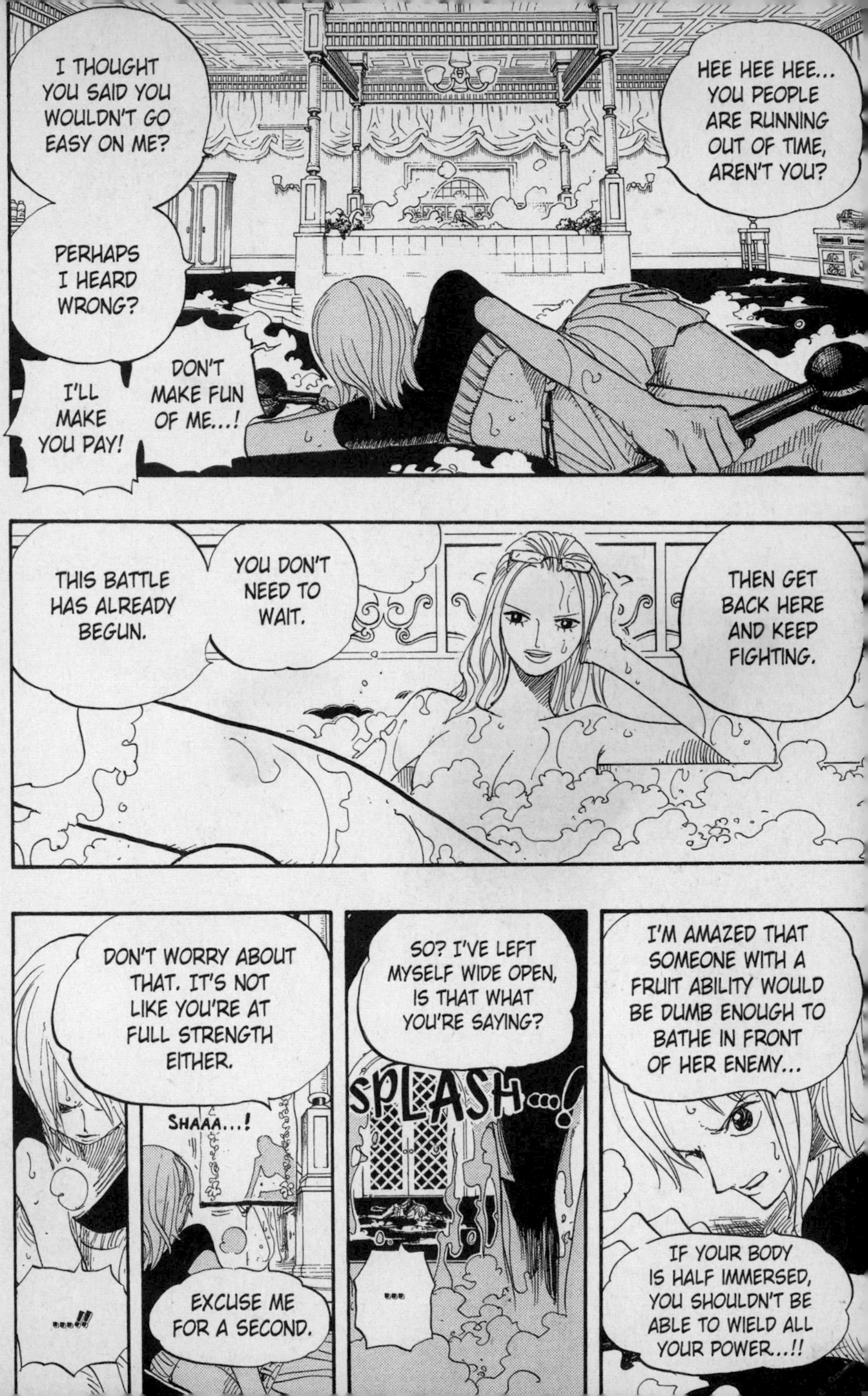
HEE HEE HEE... YOU PEOPLE ARE RUNNING OUT OF TIME, AREN'T YOU?
I THOUGHT YOU SAID YOU WOULDN'T GO EASY ON ME?
PERHAPS I HEARD WRONG?
DON'T MAKE FUN OF ME...!
I'LL MAKE YOU PAY!
THEN GET BACK HERE AND KEEP FIGHTING.
YOU DON'T NEED TO WAIT.
THIS BATTLE HAS ALREADY BEGUN.
I'M AMAZED THAT SOMEONE WITH A FRUIT ABILITY WOULD BE DUMB ENOUGH TO BATHE IN FRONT OF HER ENEMY...
IF YOUR BODY IS HALF IMMERSED, YOU SHOULDN'T BE ABLE TO WIELD ALL YOUR POWER...!!
SO? I'VE LEFT MYSELF WIDE OPEN, IS THAT WHAT YOU'RE SAYING?
SPLASH...!
...
DON'T WORRY ABOUT THAT. IT'S NOT LIKE YOU'RE AT FULL STRENGTH EITHER.
SHAAA...!
EXCUSE ME FOR A SECOND.
...!!

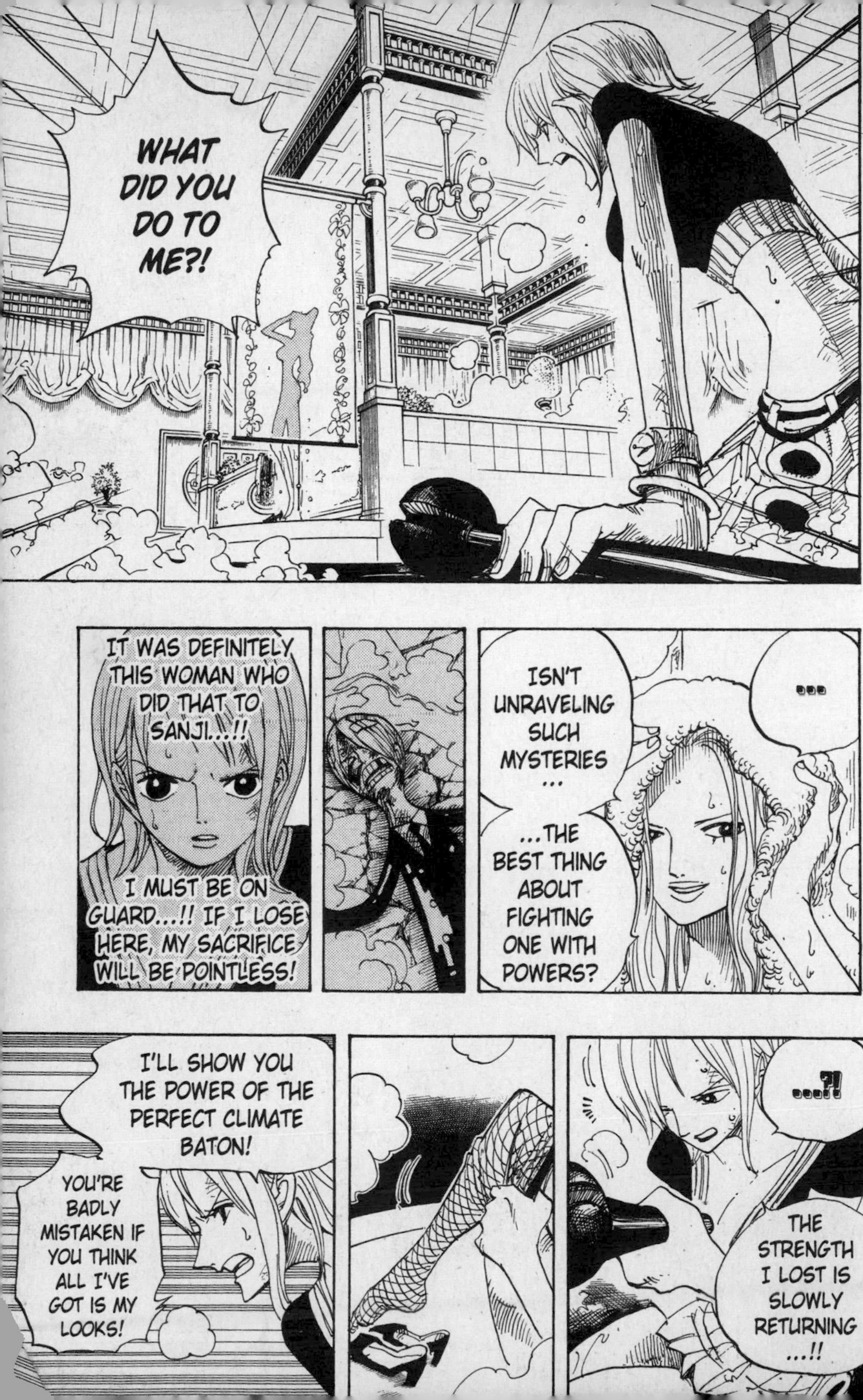
WHAT DID YOU DO TO ME?!
...
ISN'T UNRAVELING SUCH MYSTERIES...
...THE BEST THING ABOUT FIGHTING ONE WITH POWERS?
IT WAS DEFINITELY THIS WOMAN WHO DID THAT TO SANJI...!!
I MUST BE ON GUARD...!! IF I LOSE HERE, MY SACRIFICE WILL BE POINTLESS!
...?!
THE STRENGTH I LOST IS SLOWLY RETURNING...!!
I'LL SHOW YOU THE POWER OF THE PERFECT CLIMATE BATON!
YOU'RE BADLY MISTAKEN IF YOU THINK ALL I'VE GOT IS MY LOOKS!

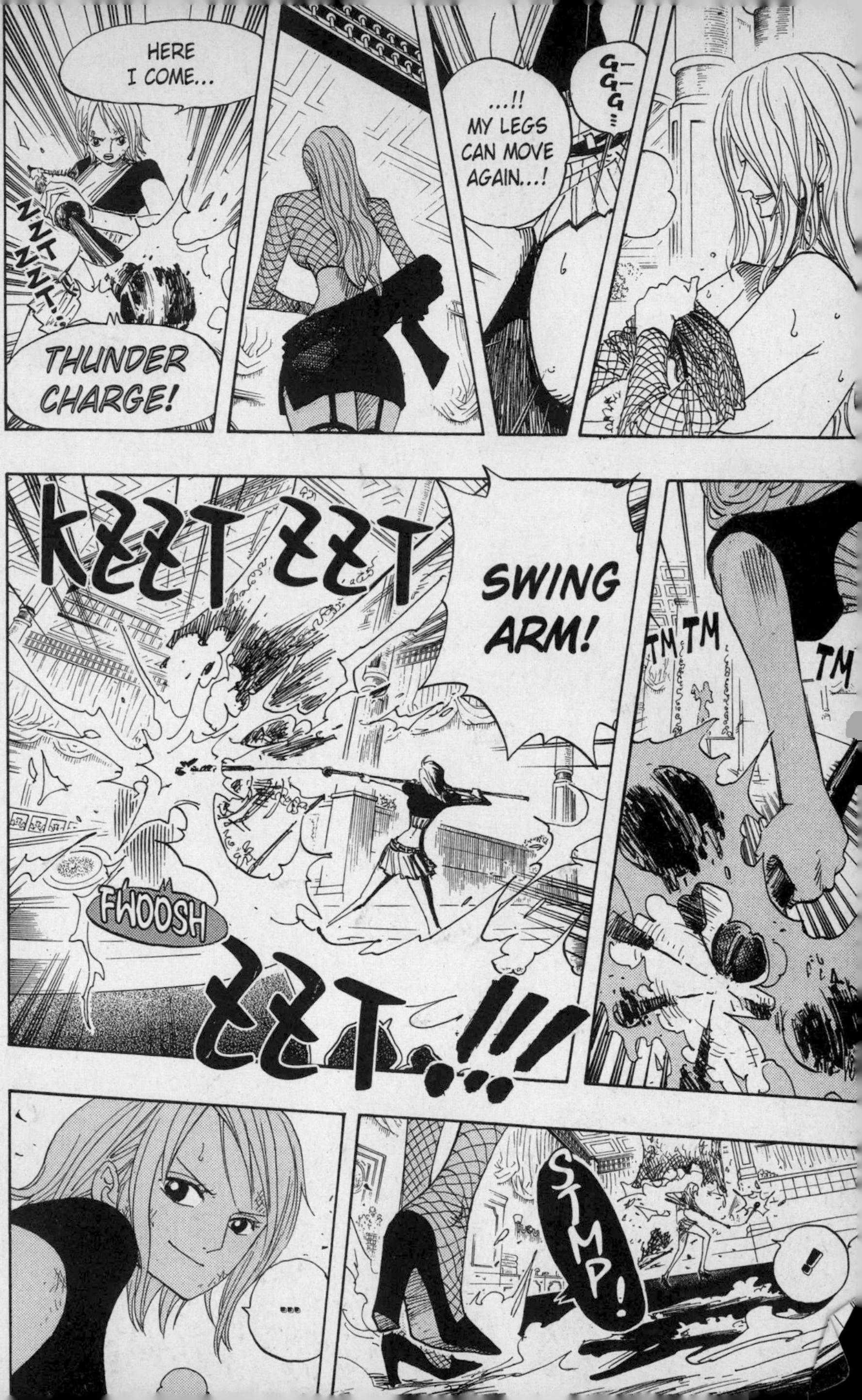
G-G-G...
...!! MY LEGS CAN MOVE AGAIN...!
HERE I COME...
ZZZT ZZZT!
THUNDER CHARGE!
TM TM
TM
SWING ARM!
KZZZT ZZZT
FWOOSH
ZZZT...!!!
!
STMP!
...

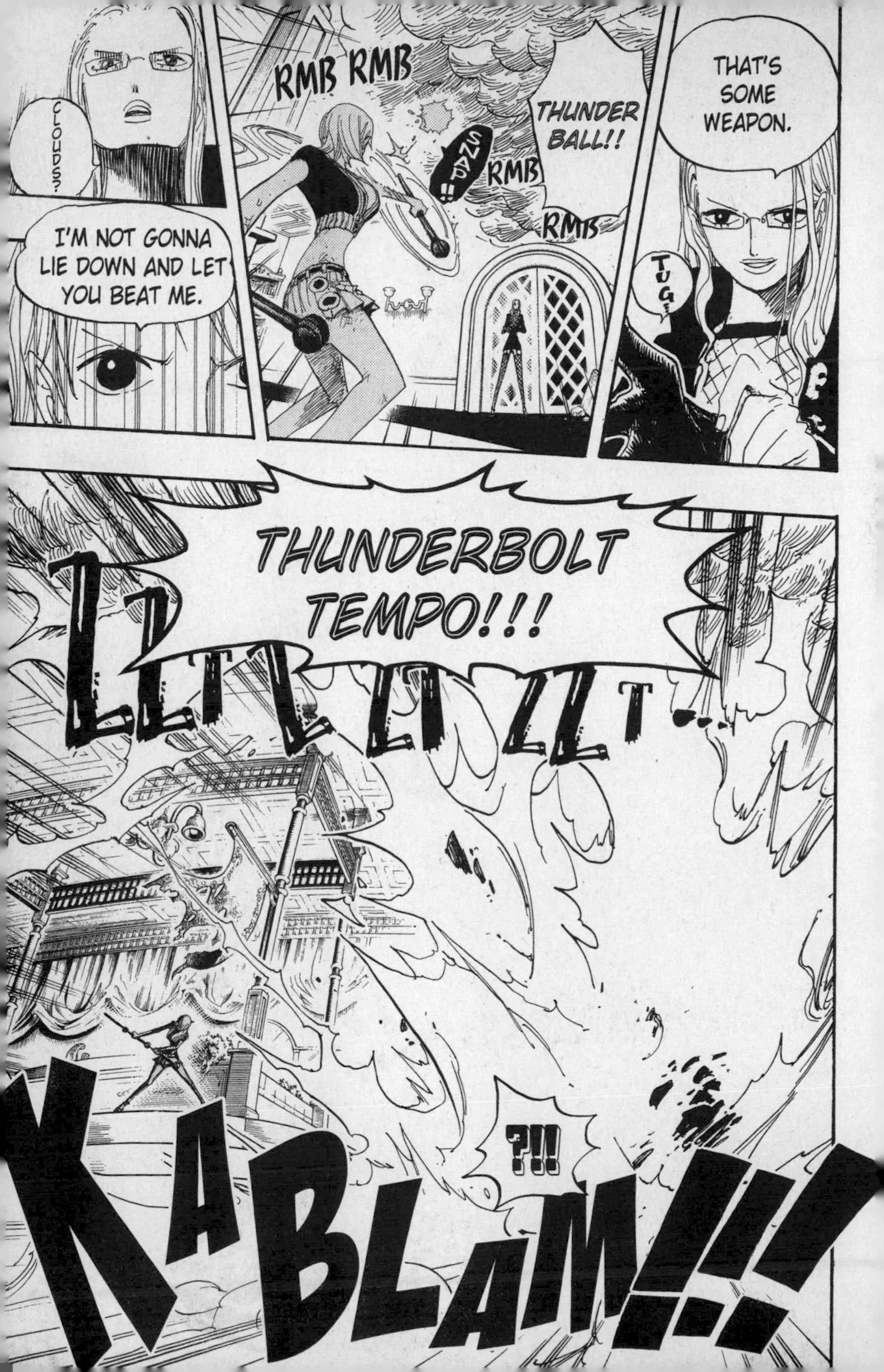
THAT'S SOME WEAPON.
TUG
RMB RMB
THUNDER BALL!!
SNAP!!
RMB
RMB
CLOUDS?
I'M NOT GONNA LIE DOWN AND LET YOU BEAT ME.
THUNDERBOLT TEMPO!!!
?!!
KABLAM!!

Chapter 408:

MONSTER VS. KUMADORI

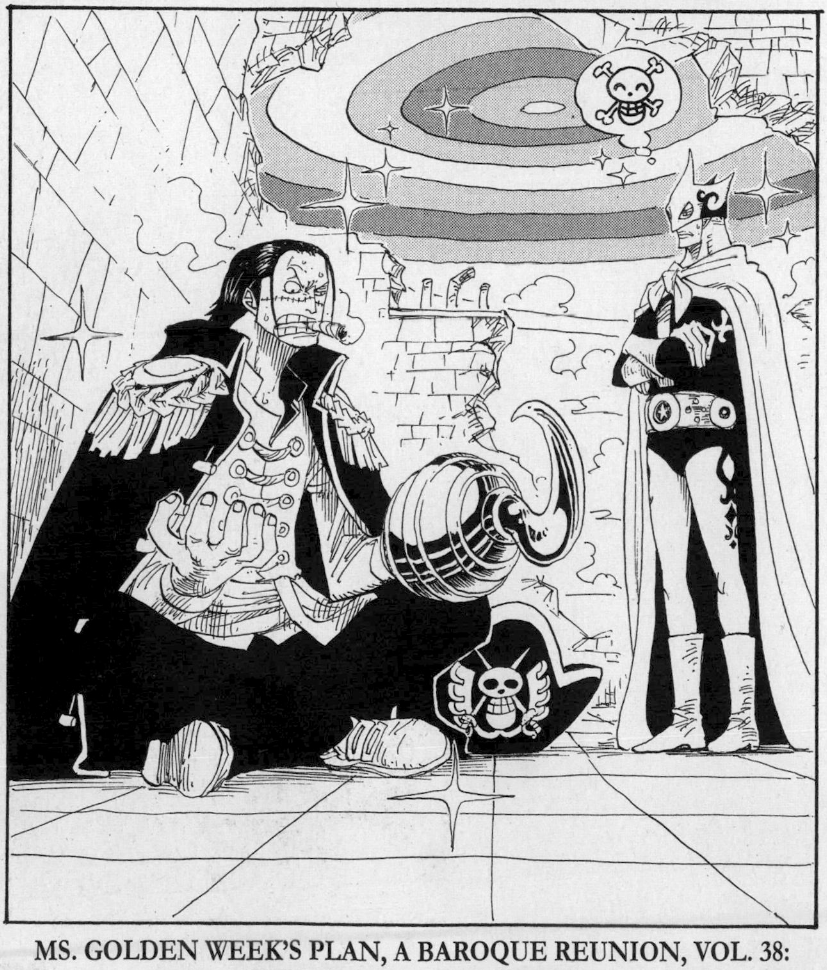

MS. GOLDEN WEEK'S PLAN, A BAROQUE REUNION, VOL. 38:
"PIRATE KING AND HERO"

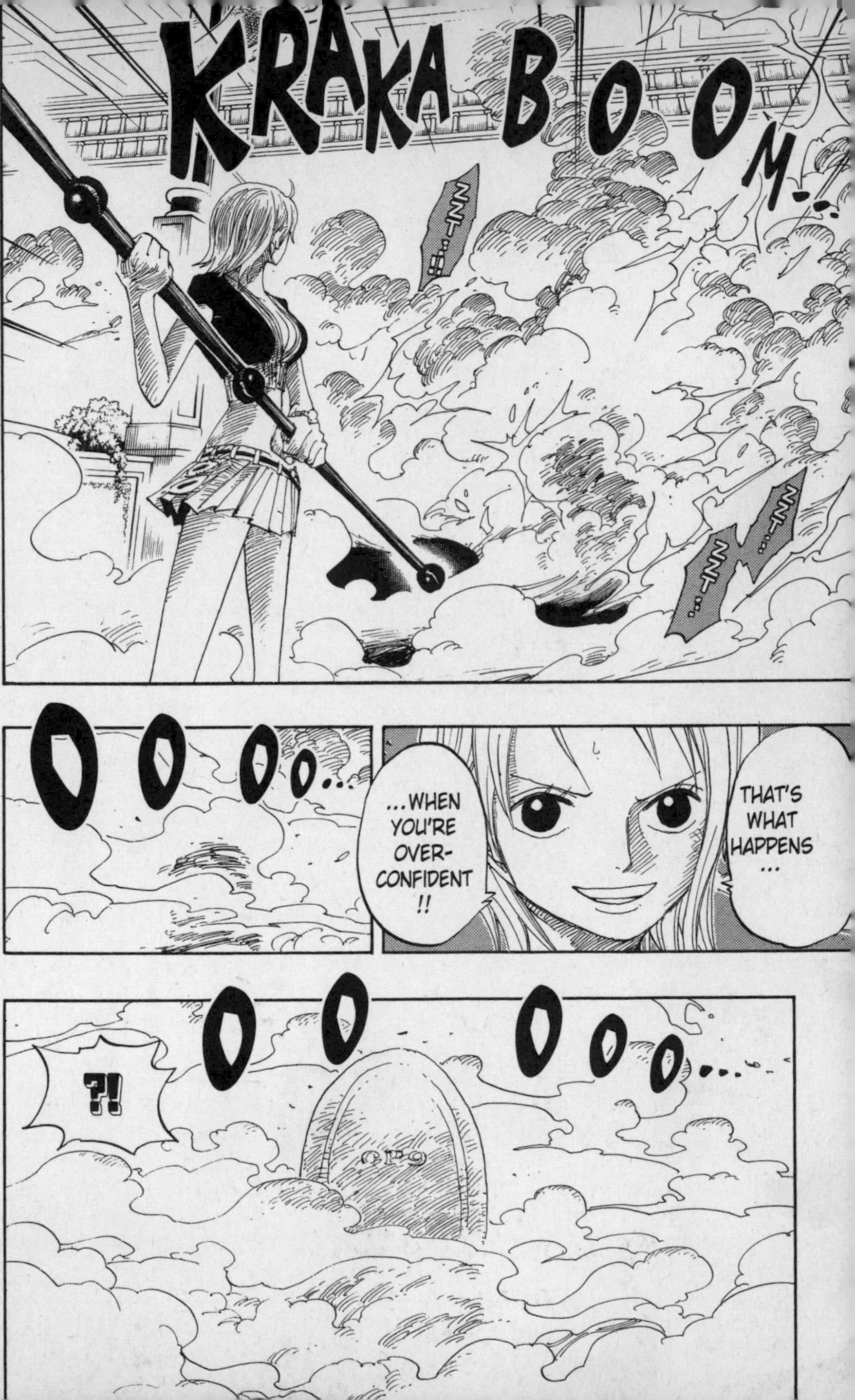
KRAKA BOOOM
ZZZT...
ZZZT...
ZZZT...
THAT'S WHAT HAPPENS ...
...WHEN YOU'RE OVER-CONFIDENT !!
OOOO...
OOOOOO...
?!
CP9

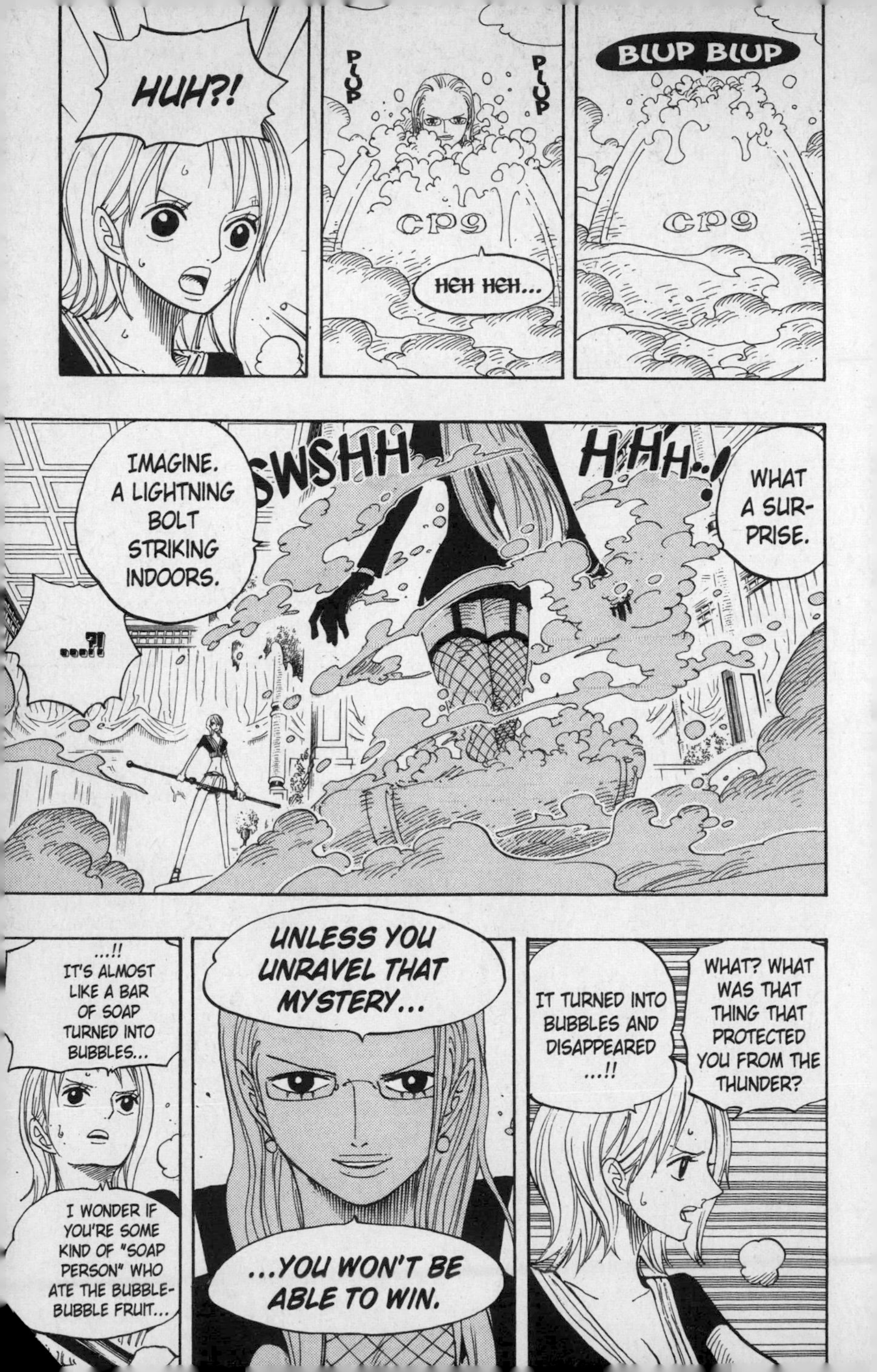
BLUP BLUP
PLUP
PLUP
HEH HEH...
HUH?!
H H H..!
WHAT A SURPRISE.
SWSHH
IMAGINE. A LIGHTNING BOLT STRIKING INDOORS.
...?!
WHAT? WHAT WAS THAT THING THAT PROTECTED YOU FROM THE THUNDER?
IT TURNED INTO BUBBLES AND DISAPPEARED ...!!
UNLESS YOU UNRAVEL THAT MYSTERY...
...YOU WON'T BE ABLE TO WIN.
...!! IT'S ALMOST LIKE A BAR OF SOAP TURNED INTO BUBBLES...
I WONDER IF YOU'RE SOME KIND OF "SOAP PERSON" WHO ATE THE BUBBLE-BUBBLE FRUIT...

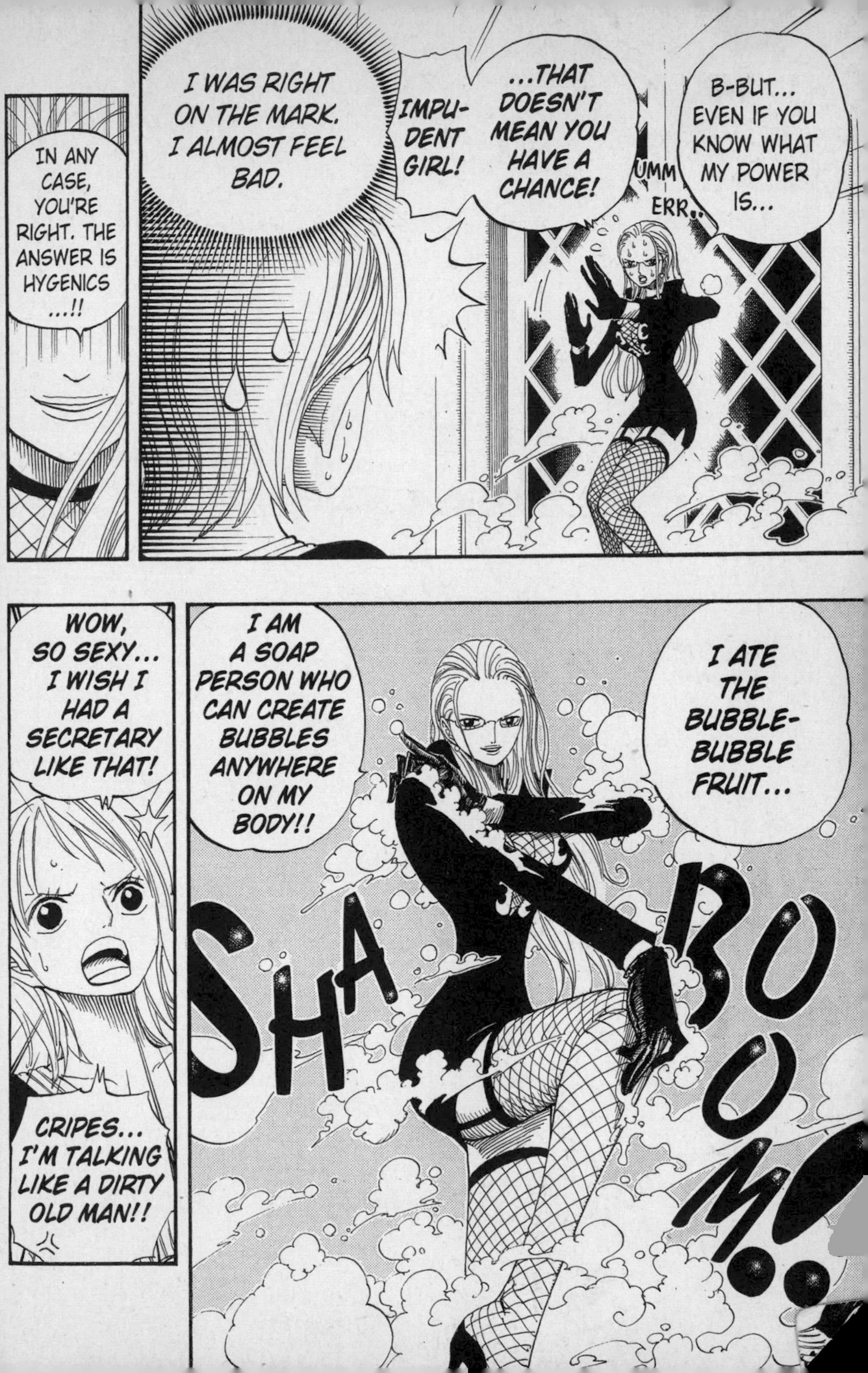

B-BUT... EVEN IF YOU KNOW WHAT MY POWER IS...
UMM ERR..
...THAT DOESN'T MEAN YOU HAVE A CHANCE!
IMPU-DENT GIRL!
I WAS RIGHT ON THE MARK. I ALMOST FEEL BAD.
IN ANY CASE, YOU'RE RIGHT. THE ANSWER IS HYGENICS ...!!
I ATE THE BUBBLE-BUBBLE FRUIT...
I AM A SOAP PERSON WHO CAN CREATE BUBBLES ANYWHERE ON MY BODY!!
SHABOOM!!
WOW, SO SEXY... I WISH I HAD A SECRETARY LIKE THAT!
CRIPES... I'M TALKING LIKE A DIRTY OLD MAN!!

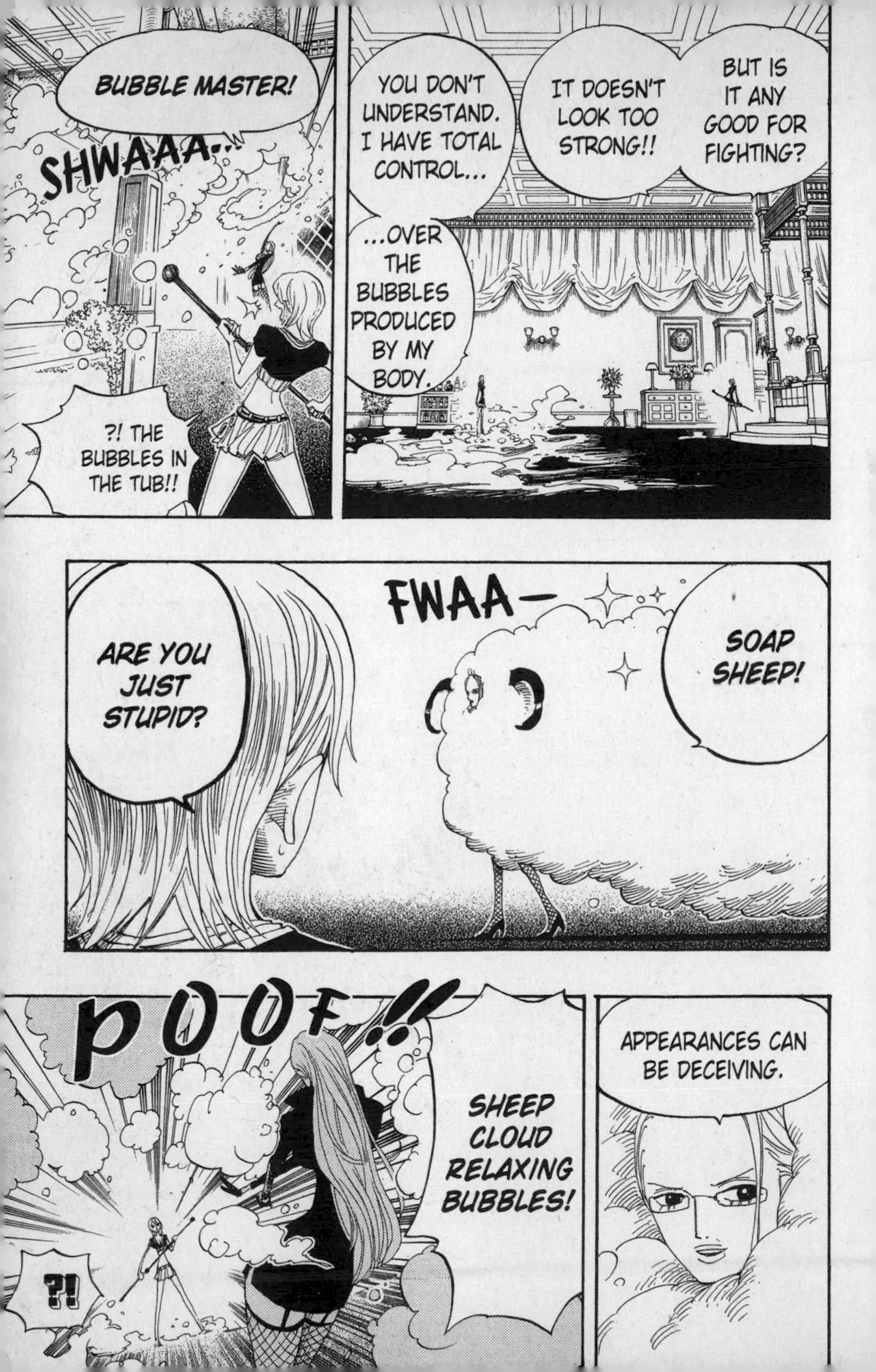
BUT IS IT ANY GOOD FOR FIGHTING?
IT DOESN'T LOOK TOO STRONG!!
YOU DON'T UNDERSTAND. I HAVE TOTAL CONTROL...
...OVER THE BUBBLES PRODUCED BY MY BODY.
BUBBLE MASTER!
SHWAAA...
?! THE BUBBLES IN THE TUB!!
SOAP SHEEP!
FWAA—
ARE YOU JUST STUPID?
APPEARANCES CAN BE DECEIVING.
SHEEP CLOUD RELAXING BUBBLES!
POOF!!
?!

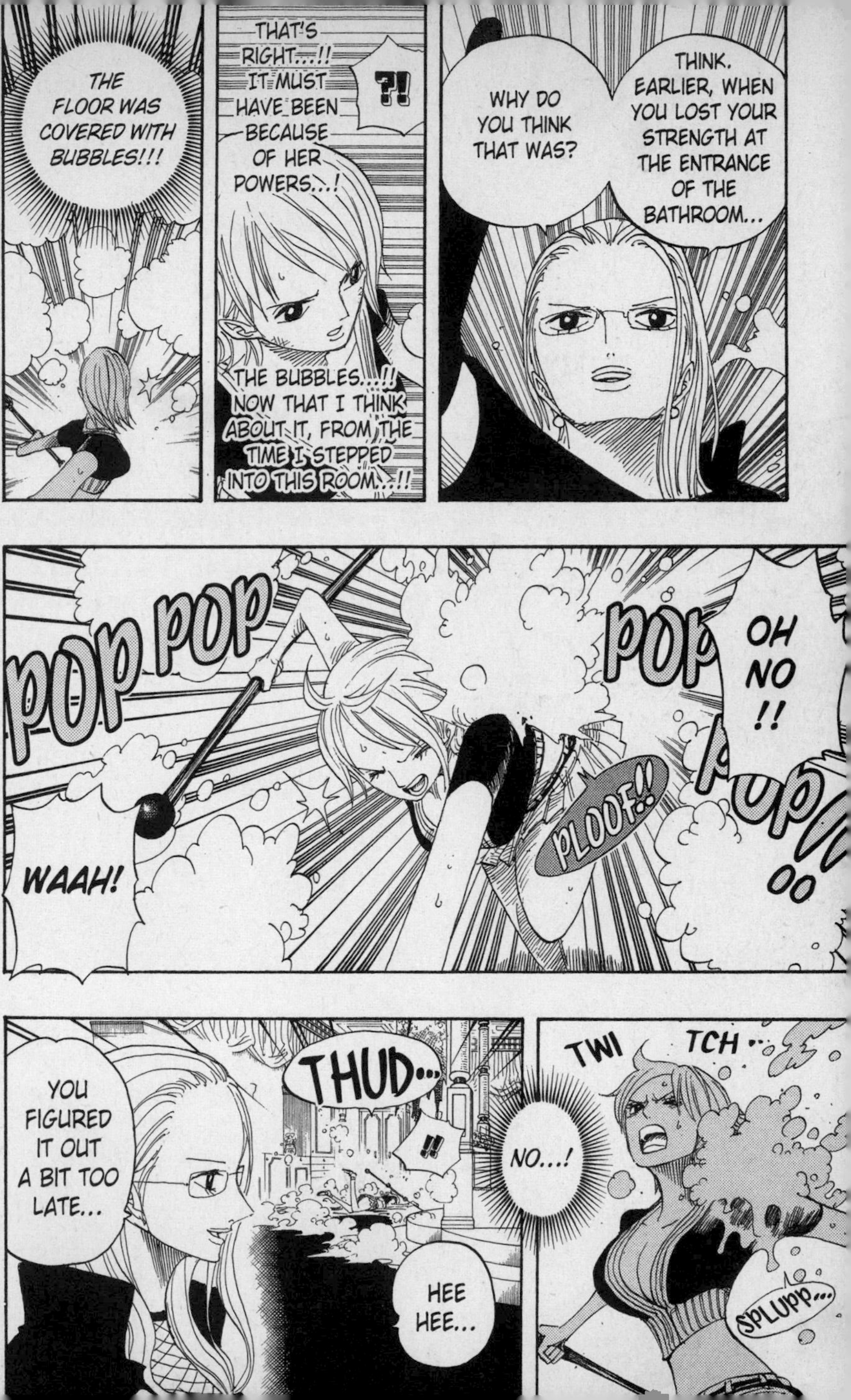
THINK. EARLIER, WHEN YOU LOST YOUR STRENGTH AT THE ENTRANCE OF THE BATHROOM...
WHY DO YOU THINK THAT WAS?
?!
THAT'S RIGHT...!! IT MUST HAVE BEEN BECAUSE OF HER POWERS...!
THE BUBBLES...!! NOW THAT I THINK ABOUT IT, FROM THE TIME I STEPPED INTO THIS ROOM...!!
THE FLOOR WAS COVERED WITH BUBBLES!!!
OH NO !!
POP
PLOOF!!
POP POP
WAAH!
TWI TCH...
NO...!
SPLUPP...
THUD...
!!
YOU FIGURED IT OUT A BIT TOO LATE...
HEE HEE...

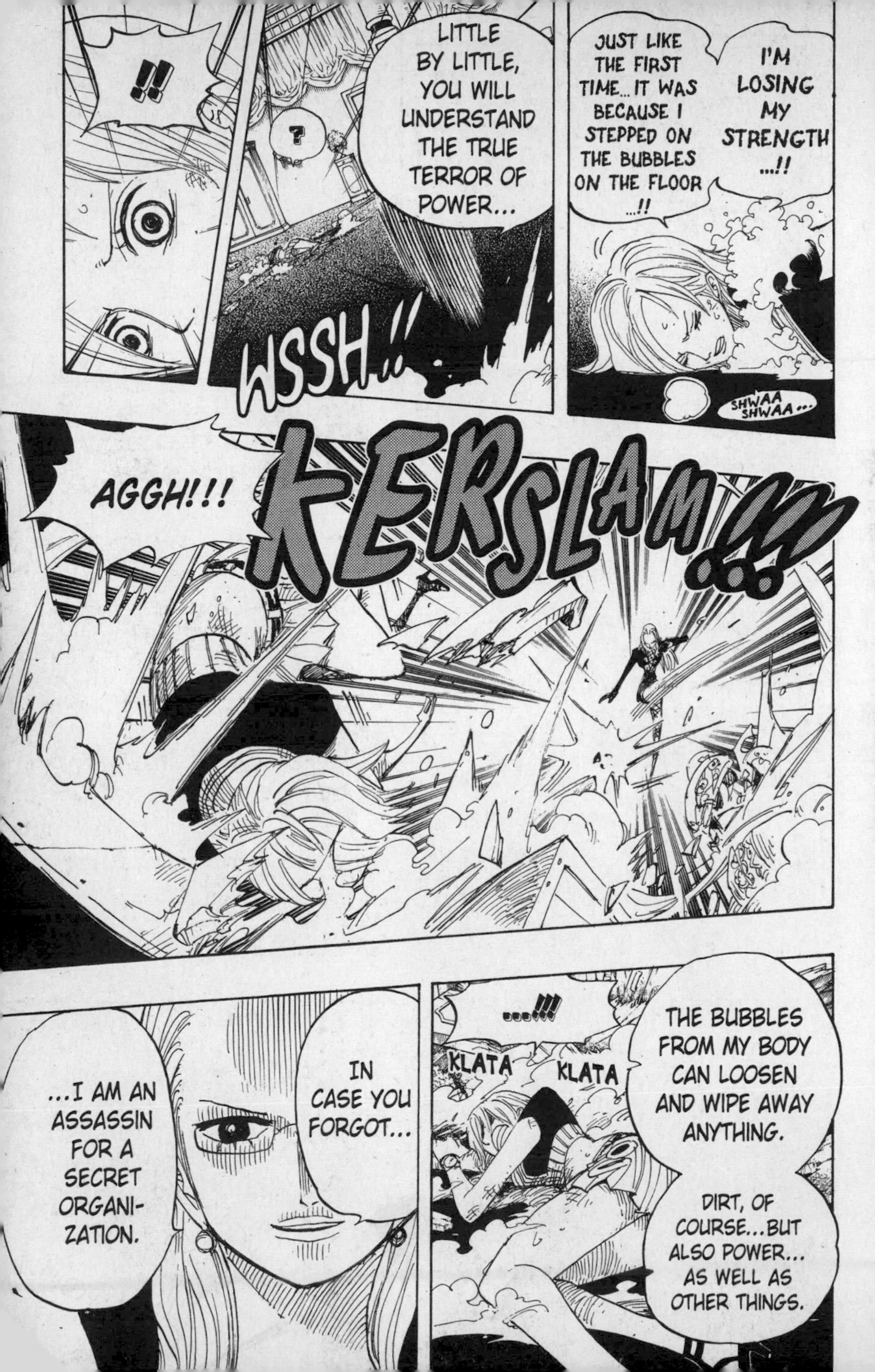
I'M LOSING MY STRENGTH...!!
JUST LIKE THE FIRST TIME... IT WAS BECAUSE I STEPPED ON THE BUBBLES ON THE FLOOR...!!
SHWAA SHWAA...
LITTLE BY LITTLE, YOU WILL UNDERSTAND THE TRUE TERROR OF POWER...
?
WSSH..!!
!!
KERSLAM...!!
AGGH!!!
...!!!
KLATA KLATA
THE BUBBLES FROM MY BODY CAN LOOSEN AND WIPE AWAY ANYTHING.
DIRT, OF COURSE...BUT ALSO POWER... AS WELL AS OTHER THINGS.
IN CASE YOU FORGOT...
...I AM AN ASSASSIN FOR A SECRET ORGANI-ZATION.

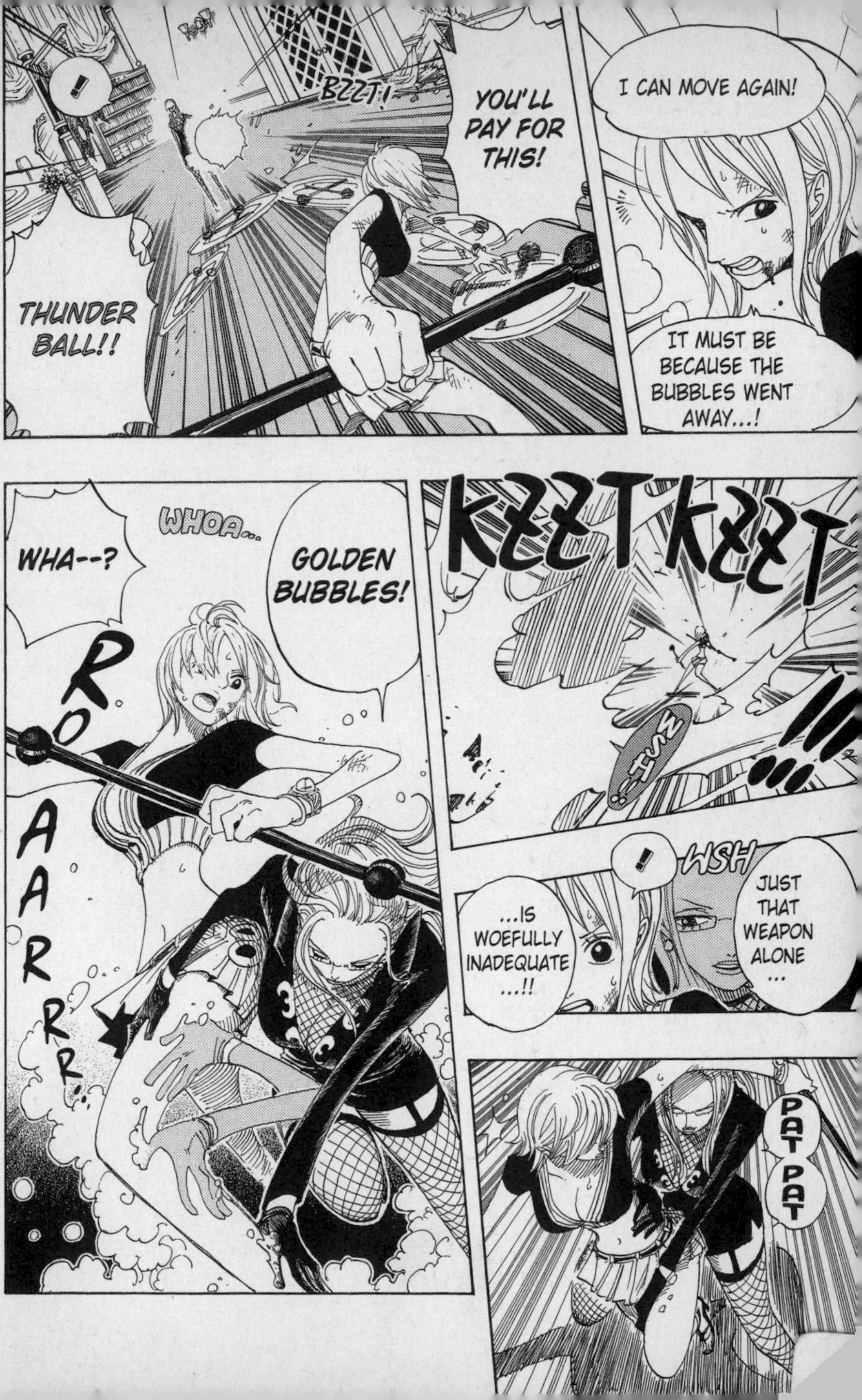
I CAN MOVE AGAIN!
IT MUST BE BECAUSE THE BUBBLES WENT AWAY...!
YOU'LL PAY FOR THIS!
BZZT!
!
THUNDER BALL!!
KZZT KZZT
WSH!!
JUST THAT WEAPON ALONE ...
WSH
!
...IS WOEFULLY INADEQUATE ...!!
PAT PAT
GOLDEN BUBBLES!
WHOA...
WHA--?
ROAARRRR

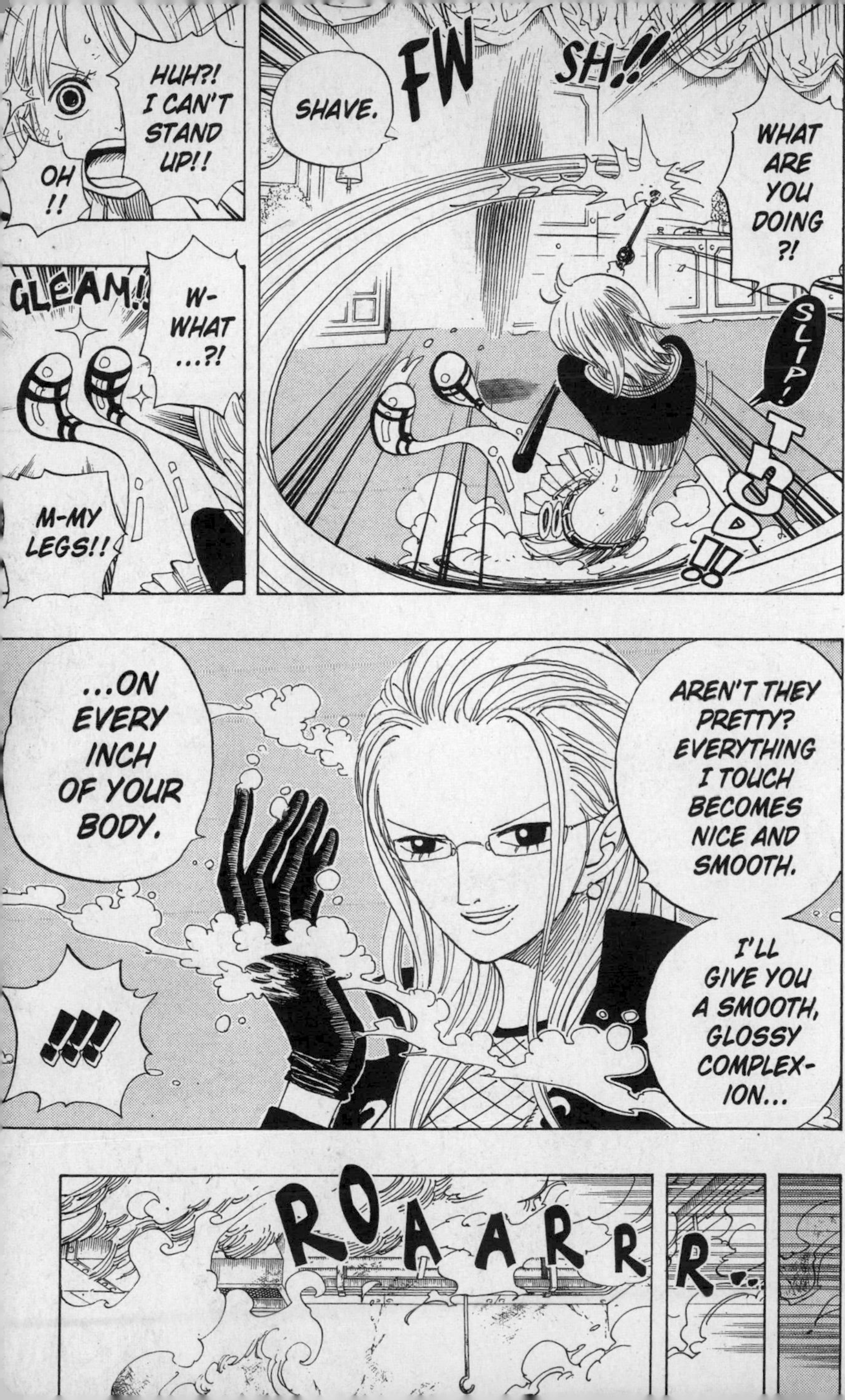
FWSH!!
WHAT ARE YOU DOING?!
SHAVE.
SLIP!
THUD!!
HUH?! I CAN'T STAND UP!!
OH!!
W-WHAT...?!
GLEAM!!
M-MY LEGS!!
AREN'T THEY PRETTY? EVERYTHING I TOUCH BECOMES NICE AND SMOOTH.
I'LL GIVE YOU A SMOOTH, GLOSSY COMPLEX-ION...
...ON EVERY INCH OF YOUR BODY.
!!!
ROAARRR...

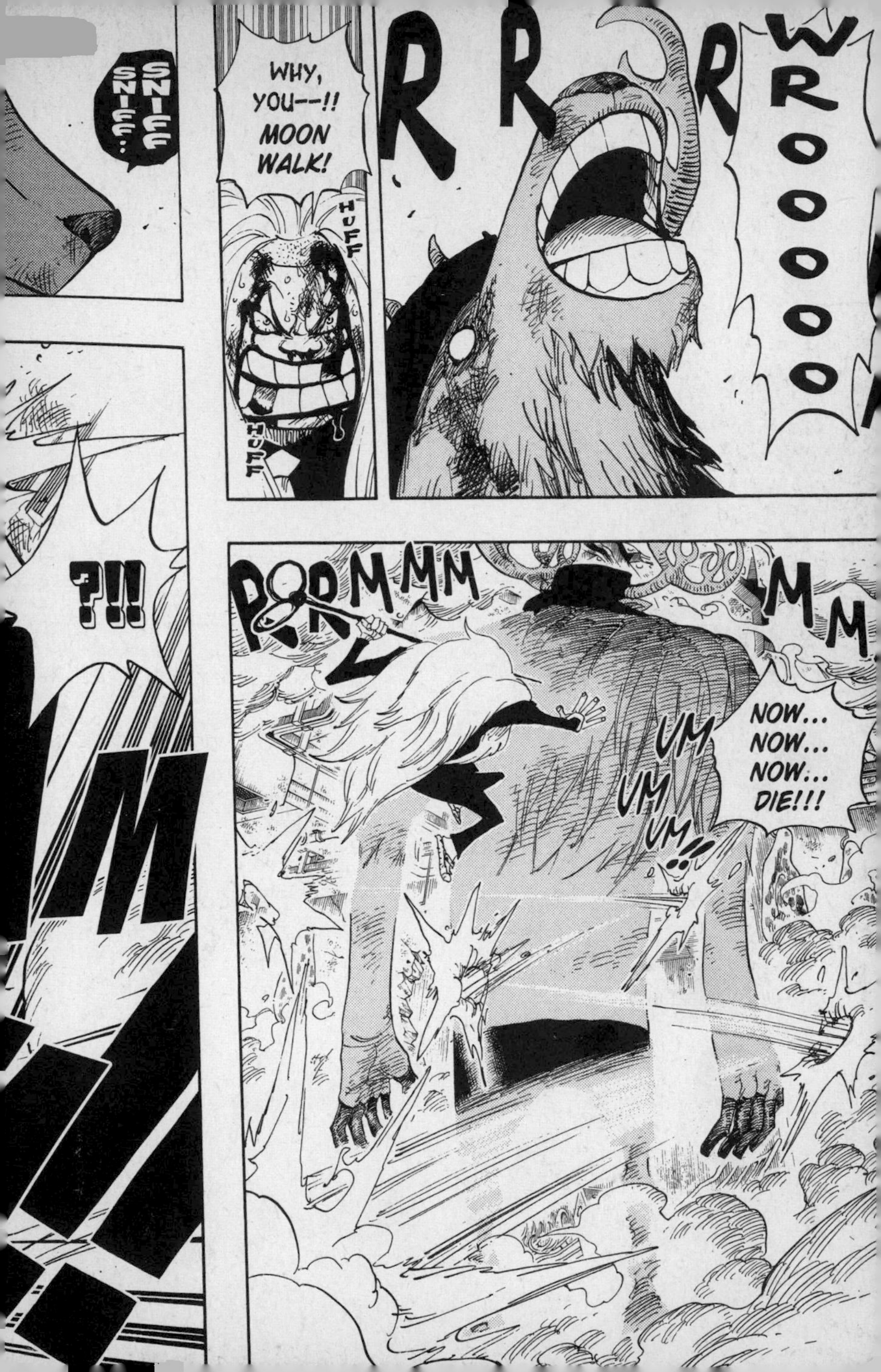
RRRWROOOOOO
WHY, YOU--!! MOON WALK!
HUFF HUFF
SNIFF SNIFF..
BORMMMM
MM
NOW... NOW... NOW... DIE!!!
UM UM UM!!
?!!
M

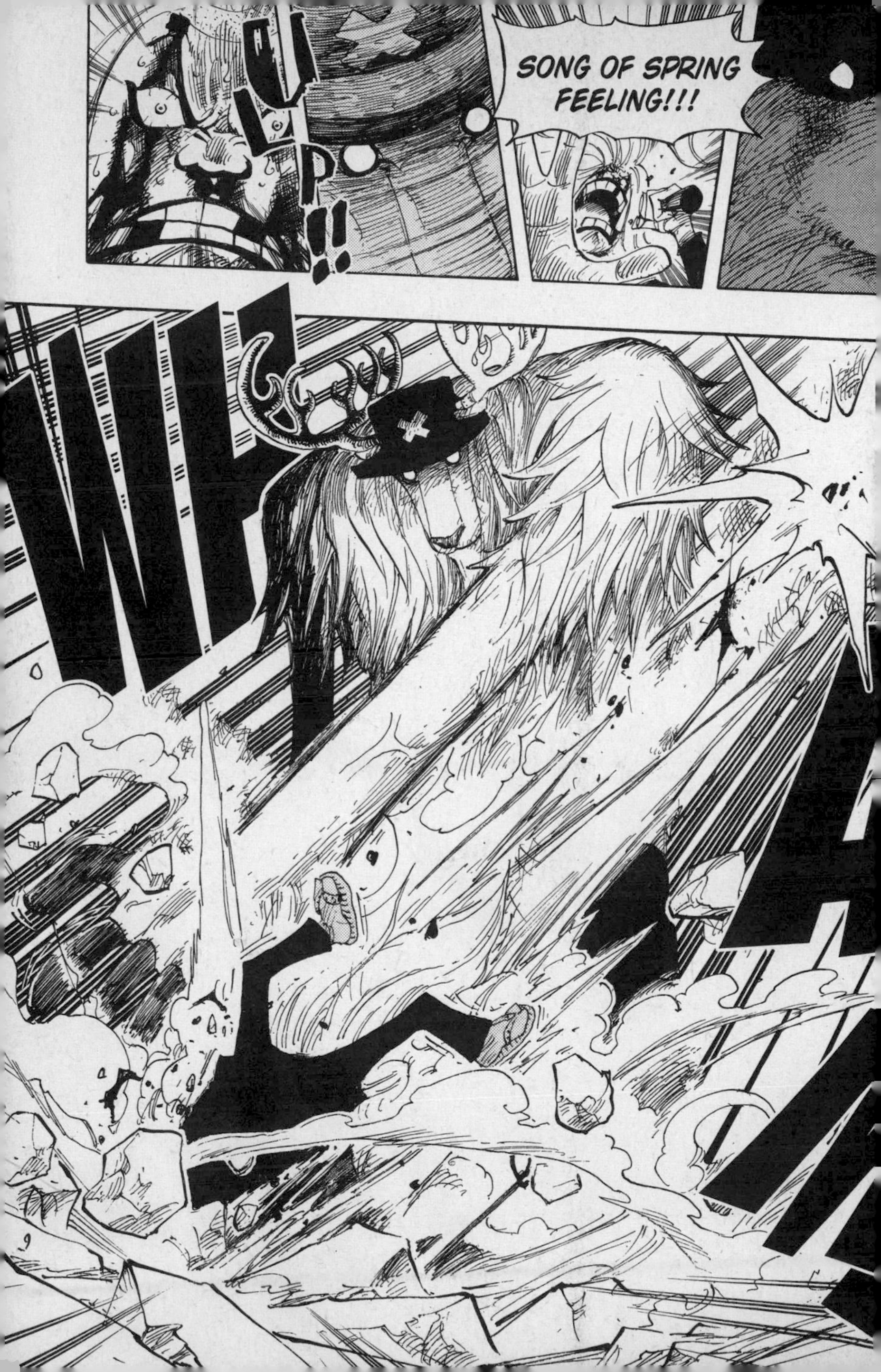
SONG OF SPRING FEELING!!!
ULP!!

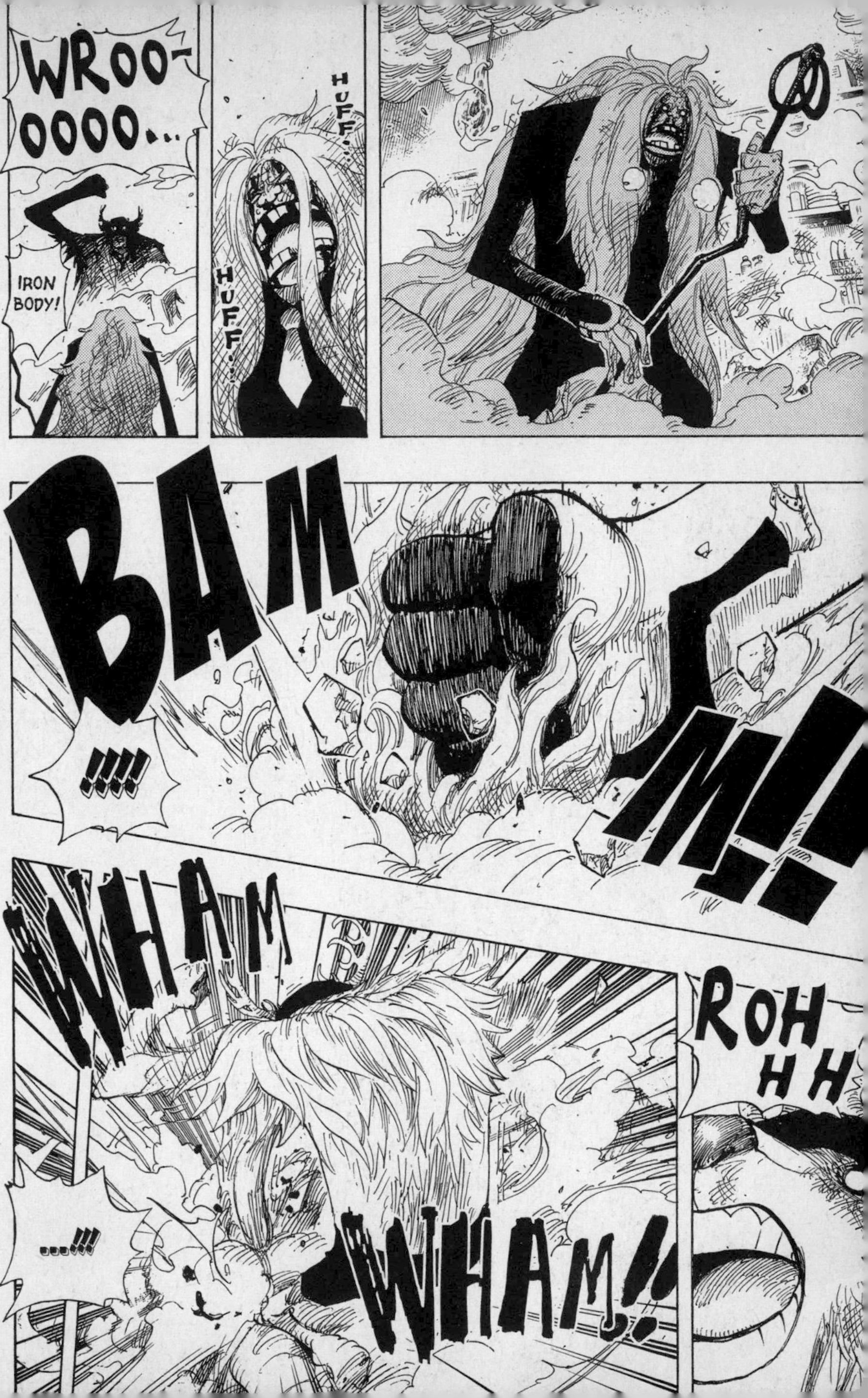
HUFF...
HUFF...
WROO-OOOO...
IRON BODY!
BAM
M!!
!!!!
ROH HH
WHAM
WHAM!!
...!!!

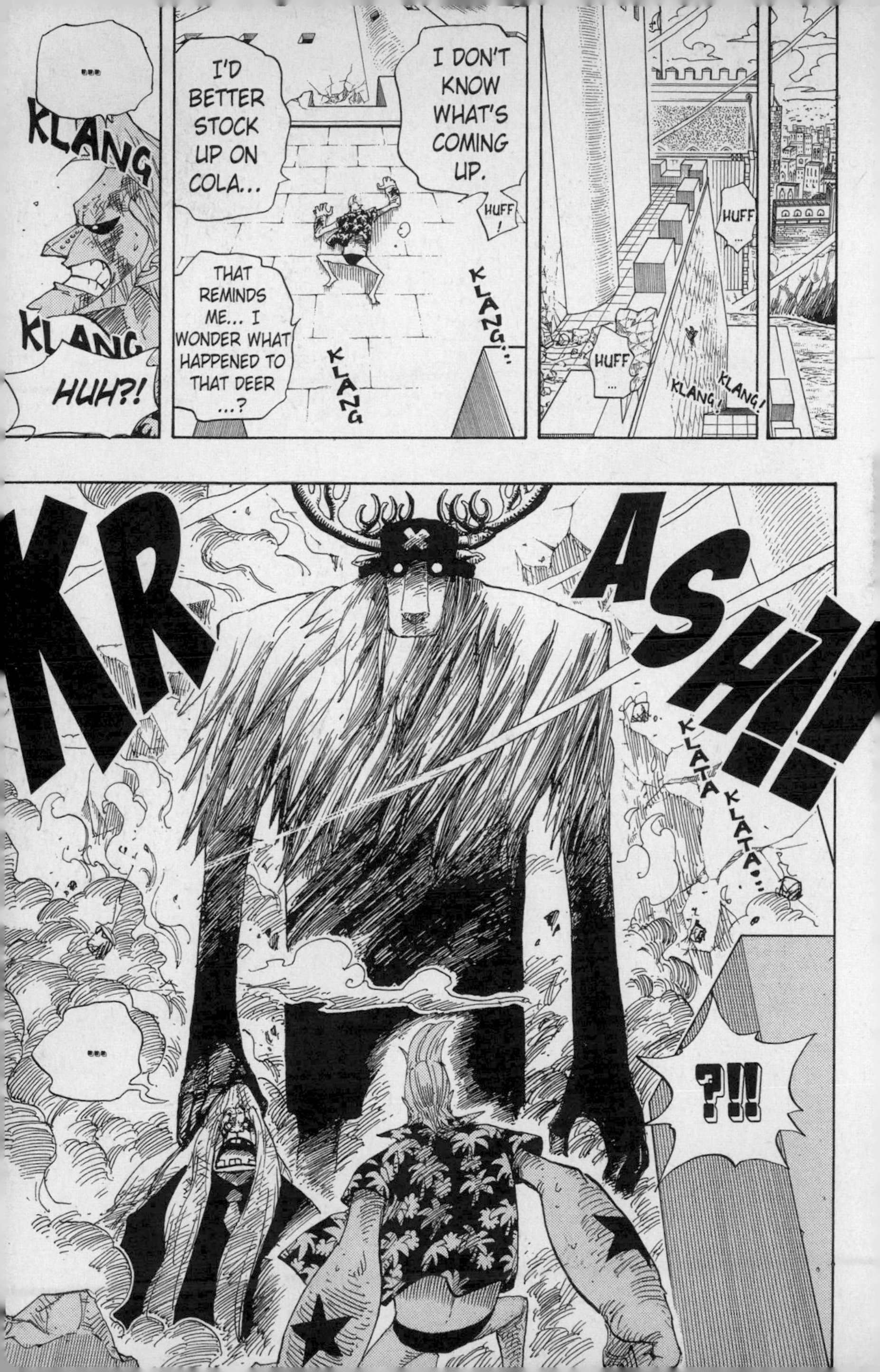
HUFF ...
KLANG!
KLANG!
HUFF ...
I DON'T KNOW WHAT'S COMING UP.
I'D BETTER STOCK UP ON COLA...
HUFF!
KLANG...
THAT REMINDS ME... I WONDER WHAT HAPPENED TO THAT DEER ...?
KLANG
...
KLANG
KLANG
HUH?!
KRASH!!
KLATA
KLATA...
?!!
...

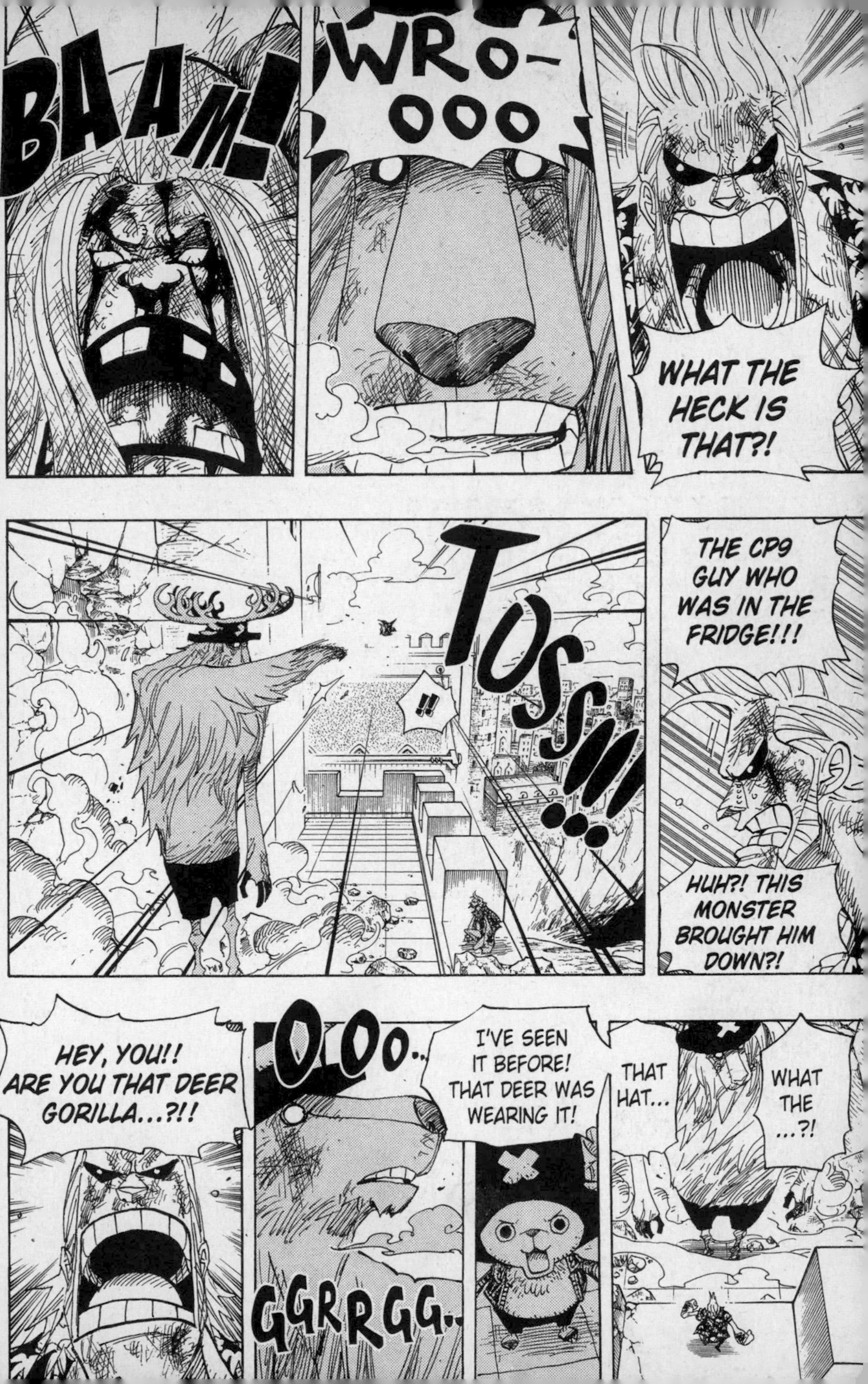
WHAT THE HECK IS THAT?!
WRO-OOO
BAAM!!
THE CP9 GUY WHO WAS IN THE FRIDGE!!!
HUH?! THIS MONSTER BROUGHT HIM DOWN?!
!!
TOSS!!...
WHAT THE ...?!
THAT HAT...
I'VE SEEN IT BEFORE! THAT DEER WAS WEARING IT!
OOO..
GGRRGG..
HEY, YOU!! ARE YOU THAT DEER GORILLA...?!!

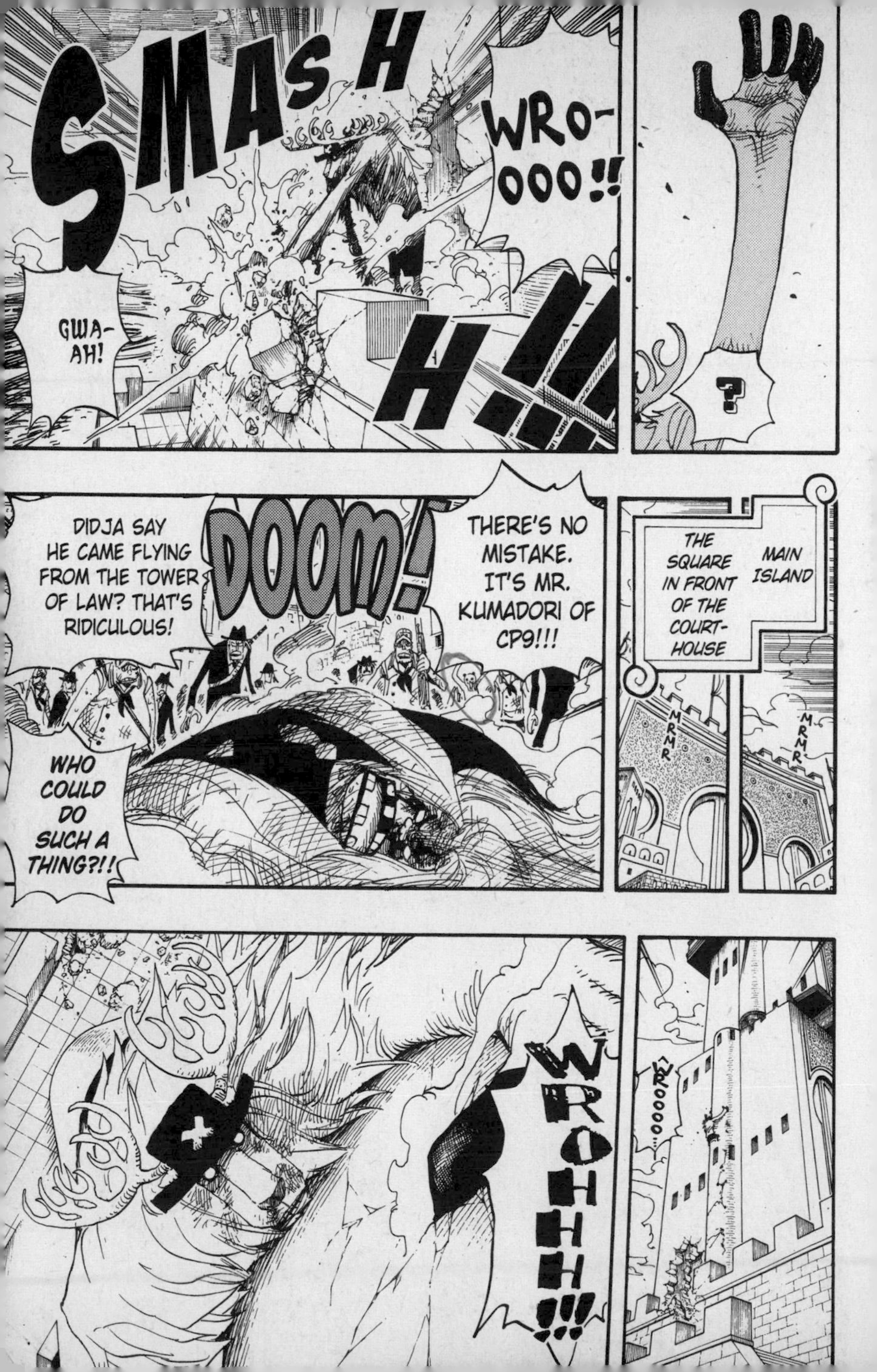
?
WRO-OOO!!
SMASH
H!!!
GWA-AH!
MAIN ISLAND
THE SQUARE IN FRONT OF THE COURTHOUSE
MRMR
MRMR
THERE'S NO MISTAKE. IT'S MR. KUMADORI OF CP9!!!
DOOM!
DIDJA SAY HE CAME FLYING FROM THE TOWER OF LAW? THAT'S RIDICULOUS!
WHO COULD DO SUCH A THING?!!
WROOOO...
WROHHHH!!!

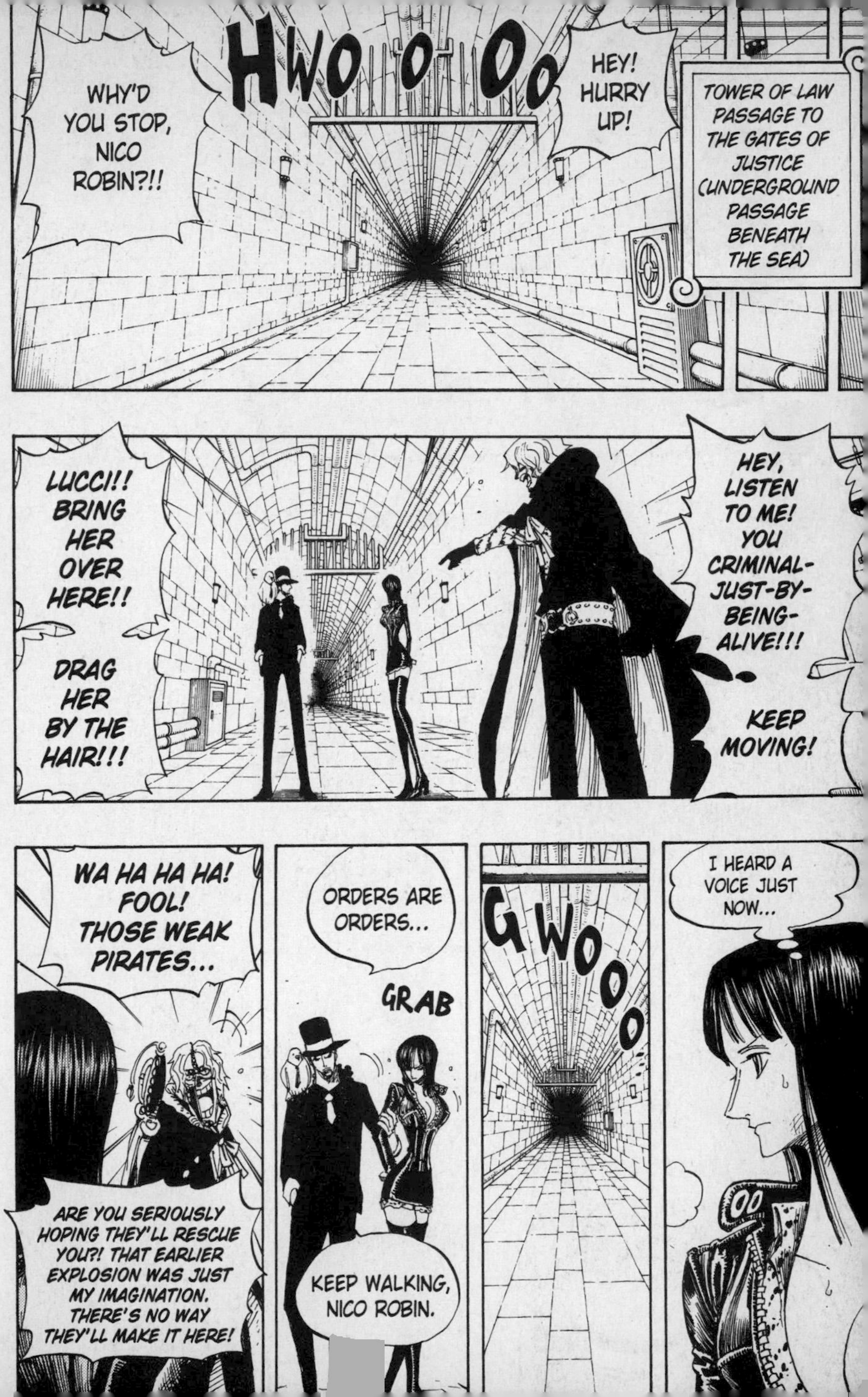
TOWER OF LAW PASSAGE TO THE GATES OF JUSTICE (UNDERGROUND PASSAGE BENEATH THE SEA)
HEY! HURRY UP!
HWO O O O
WHY'D YOU STOP, NICO ROBIN?!!
HEY, LISTEN TO ME! YOU CRIMINAL-JUST-BY-BEING-ALIVE!!!
KEEP MOVING!
LUCCI!! BRING HER OVER HERE!!
DRAG HER BY THE HAIR!!!
I HEARD A VOICE JUST NOW...
GWOOOO
ORDERS ARE ORDERS...
GRAB
KEEP WALKING, NICO ROBIN.
WA HA HA HA! FOOL! THOSE WEAK PIRATES...
ARE YOU SERIOUSLY HOPING THEY'LL RESCUE YOU?! THAT EARLIER EXPLOSION WAS JUST MY IMAGINATION. THERE'S NO WAY THEY'LL MAKE IT HERE!

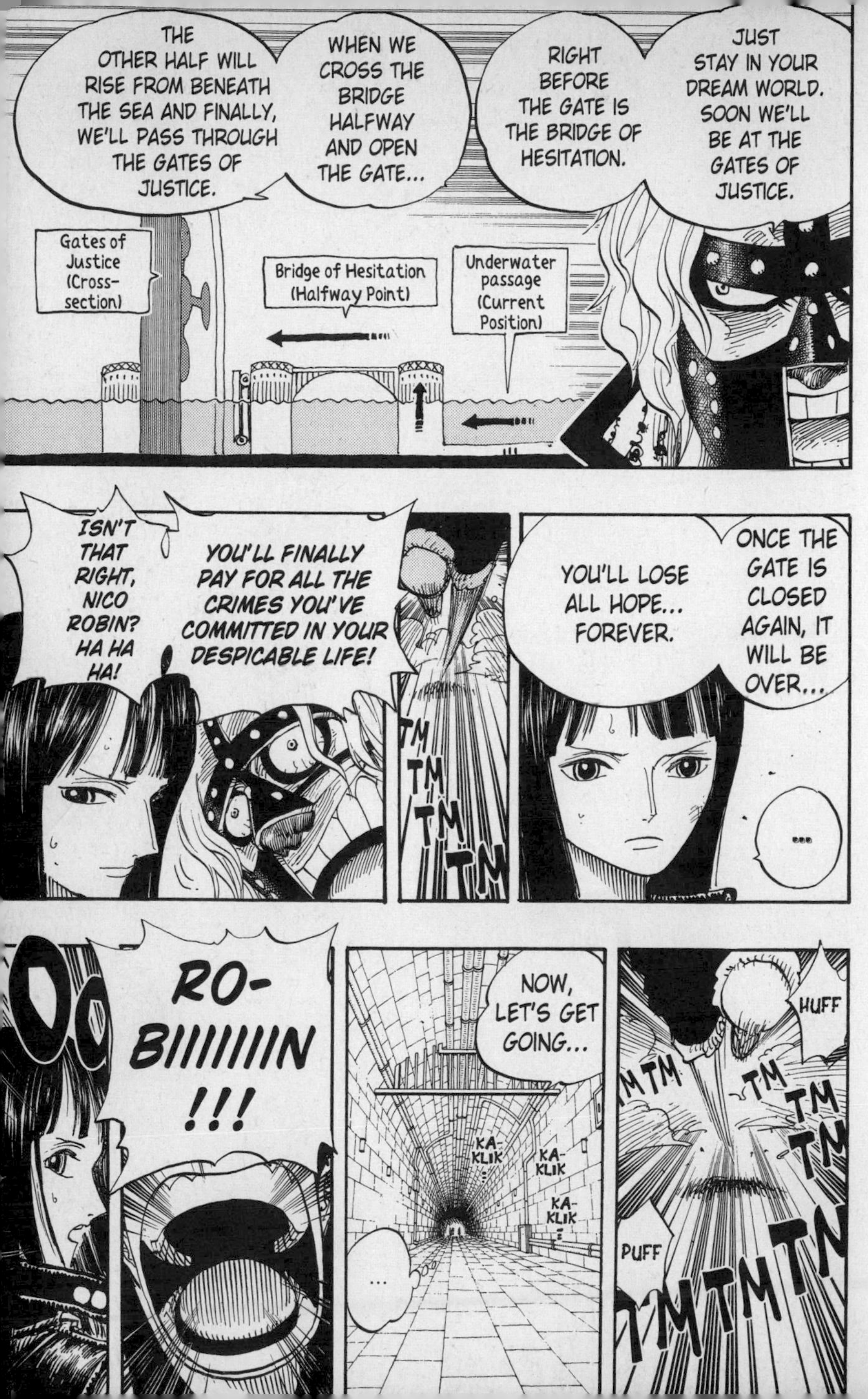
JUST STAY IN YOUR DREAM WORLD. SOON WE'LL BE AT THE GATES OF JUSTICE.
RIGHT BEFORE THE GATE IS THE BRIDGE OF HESITATION.
WHEN WE CROSS THE BRIDGE HALFWAY AND OPEN THE GATE...
THE OTHER HALF WILL RISE FROM BENEATH THE SEA AND FINALLY, WE'LL PASS THROUGH THE GATES OF JUSTICE.
Underwater passage (Current Position)
Bridge of Hesitation (Halfway Point)
Gates of Justice (Cross-section)
ONCE THE GATE IS CLOSED AGAIN, IT WILL BE OVER...
YOU'LL LOSE ALL HOPE... FOREVER.
...
TM TM TM TM TM
YOU'LL FINALLY PAY FOR ALL THE CRIMES YOU'VE COMMITTED IN YOUR DESPICABLE LIFE!
ISN'T THAT RIGHT, NICO ROBIN? HA HA HA!
HUFF
TM TM TM TM TM TN
PUFF
TMTMTMTM
NOW, LET'S GET GOING...
KA-KLIK
KA-KLIK
KA-KLIK
...
RO-BIIIIIIIN !!!

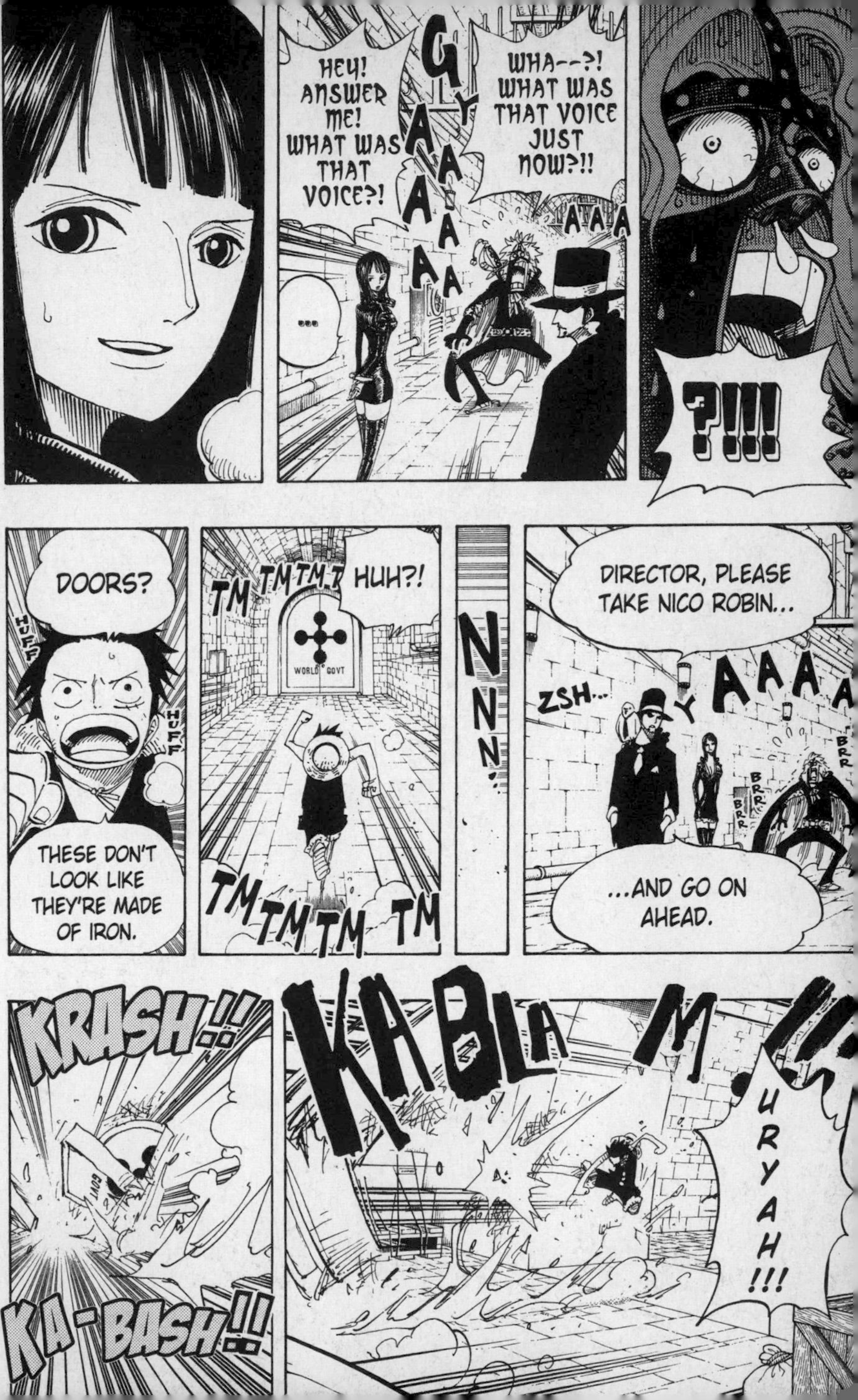
?!!!
WHA--?! WHAT WAS THAT VOICE JUST NOW?!!
GYAAAAAAAA
HEY! ANSWER ME! WHAT WAS THAT VOICE?!
AAA
...
DIRECTOR, PLEASE TAKE NICO ROBIN...
YAAAA
ZSH...
BRR
BRR
BRR
...AND GO ON AHEAD.
NNN!
HUH?!
TM TMTM
WORLD GOVT
TM TM TM TM
DOORS?
HUFF
HUFF
THESE DON'T LOOK LIKE THEY'RE MADE OF IRON.
KABLAM!!
URYAH!!!
KRASH!!
KA-BASH!!

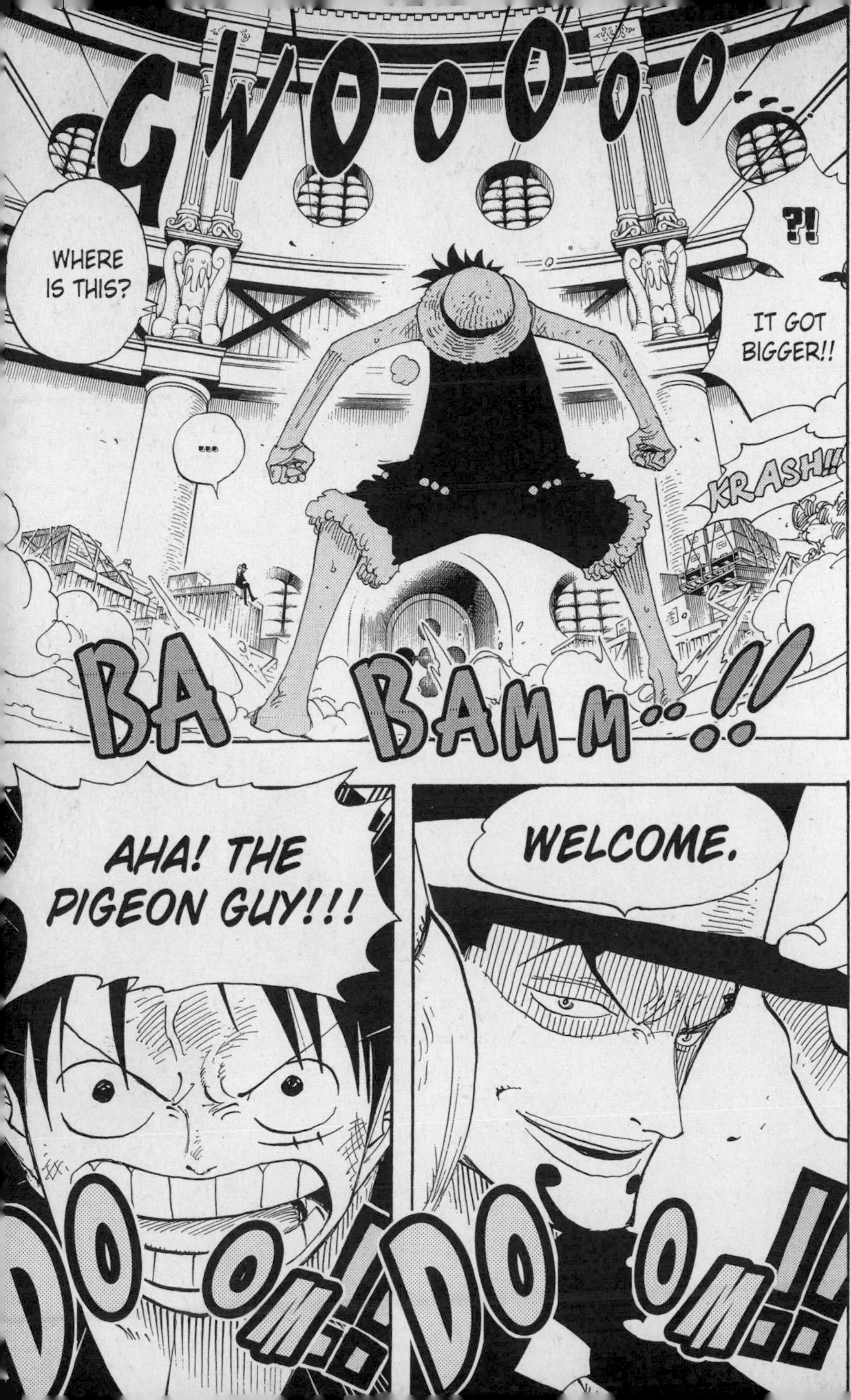
GWOOOOOO
?!
IT GOT BIGGER!!
KRASH!!
WHERE IS THIS?
...
BA BAMM..!!
WELCOME.
AHA! THE PIGEON GUY!!!
DOOM..!! DOOM..!!

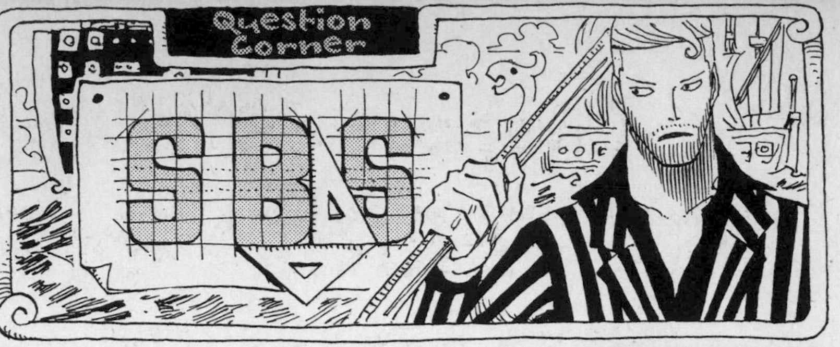
Question Corner
SBS

Q: Okay, here's a question. In volume 41, page 170, panel 5, Olvia and the others are throwing out books, and one of the books is called *Brag Men*! Isn't that the book that Nami was looking for on volume 13, page 142?! Isn't it?! Isn't it?! …All right, I asked three times. If I'm wrong, I'll "ding dong ditch" one hundred houses as punishment.

--Soge Queen ☆★

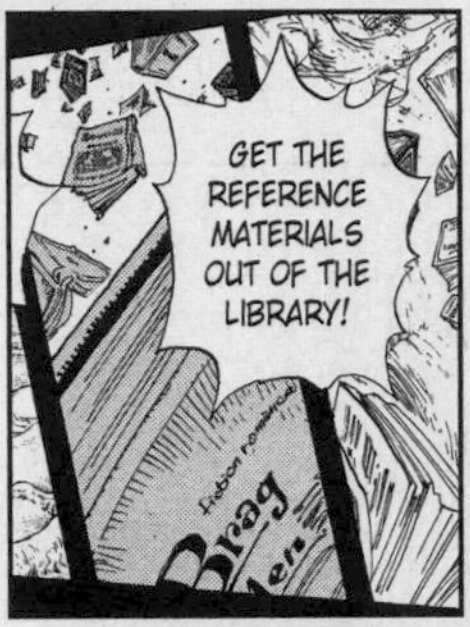
GET THE REFERENCE MATERIALS OUT OF THE LIBRARY!
Brag

↑ Volume 41

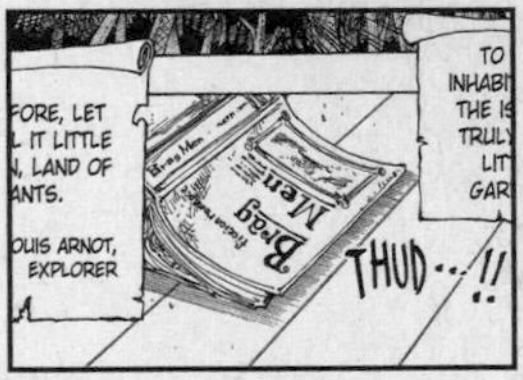
Brag Men
THUD…!!

↑ Volume 13

A: Oh. I'm surprised. Thank you for reading so deeply into the story. That's amazing. You're right. It's that book which had information about Little Garden, the "island of giants". Brag Men (as in "liars," "men who brag") is the title of this world-famous book, a book about "Adventures on the Grand Line." It records what the seafarers saw... all the unbelievable islands, mysterious people and occurrences of the sea, and things which most people around the world don't believe for an instant; they just laugh at them. When one thinks that this book was among those which the scholars in Ohara sacrificed their lives to protect, a warm feeling wells up inside me. And are these "brag men" really liars? Please answer this question yourselves by reading about the adventures of Luffy and his gang. All right then, see you in next volume's Question Corner!

Q: Oda Sensei!! Hello!! I have a question…Oh no…

The Question Corner is over…!! (DOH!)--244♪

Chapter 409:
THE TERRIFYING BROADCAST

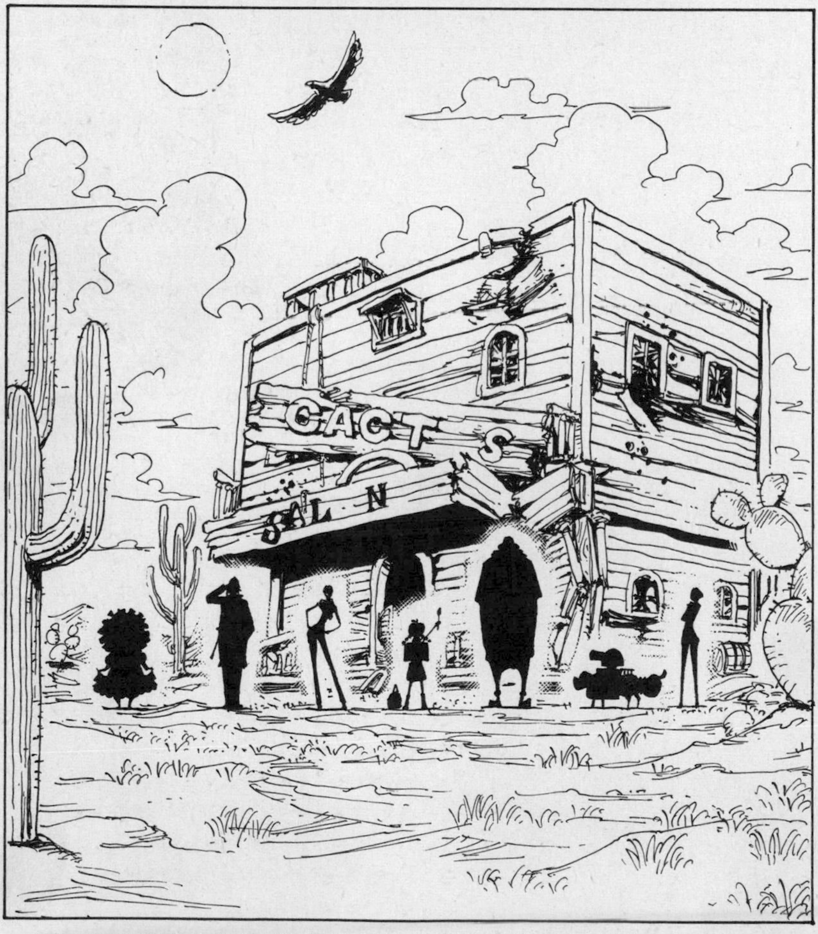

CACT S
SAL N

MS. GOLDEN WEEK'S PLAN, A BAROQUE REUNION, VOL. 39:
"A DESERTED HOUSE FOUND IN A CERTAIN WASTELAND"

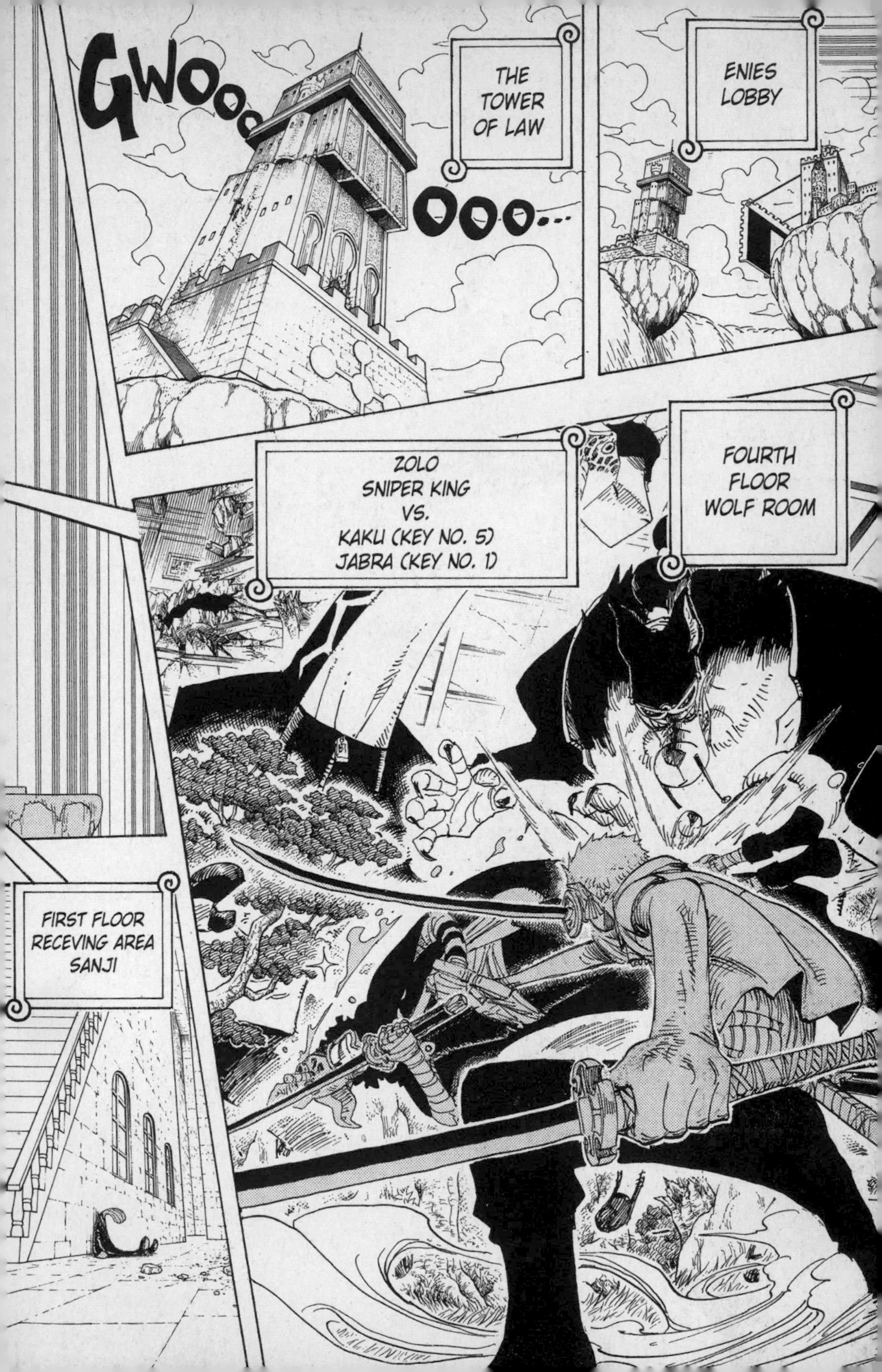

ENIES LOBBY
THE TOWER OF LAW
GWOOOOOOO...
FOURTH FLOOR WOLF ROOM
ZOLO SNIPER KING VS. KAKU (KEY NO. 5) JABRA (KEY NO. 1)
FIRST FLOOR RECEVING AREA SANJI

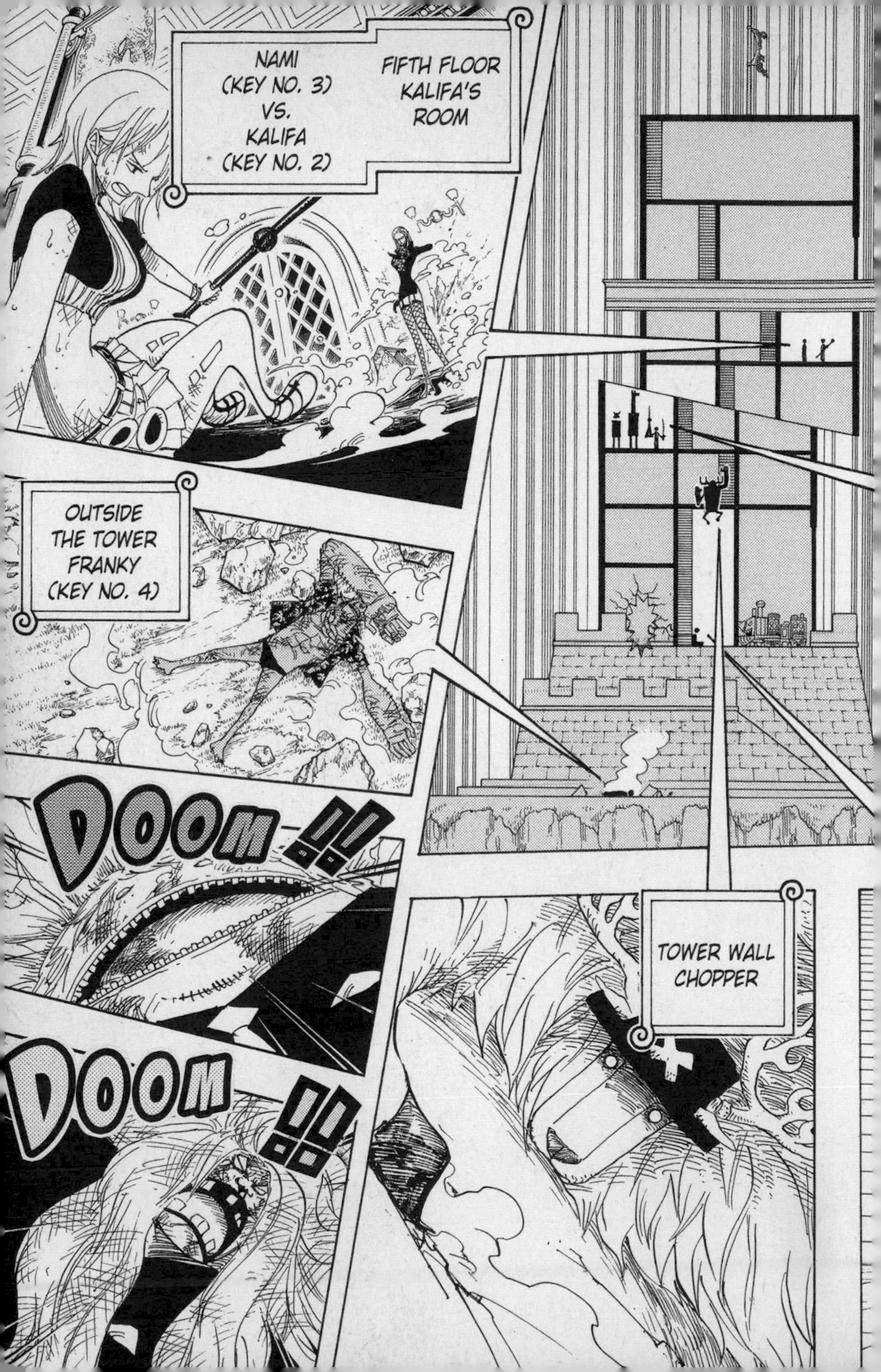
FIFTH FLOOR KALIFA'S ROOM
NAMI (KEY NO. 3) VS. KALIFA (KEY NO. 2)
OUTSIDE THE TOWER FRANKY (KEY NO. 4)
DOOM!!
TOWER WALL CHOPPER
DOOM!!

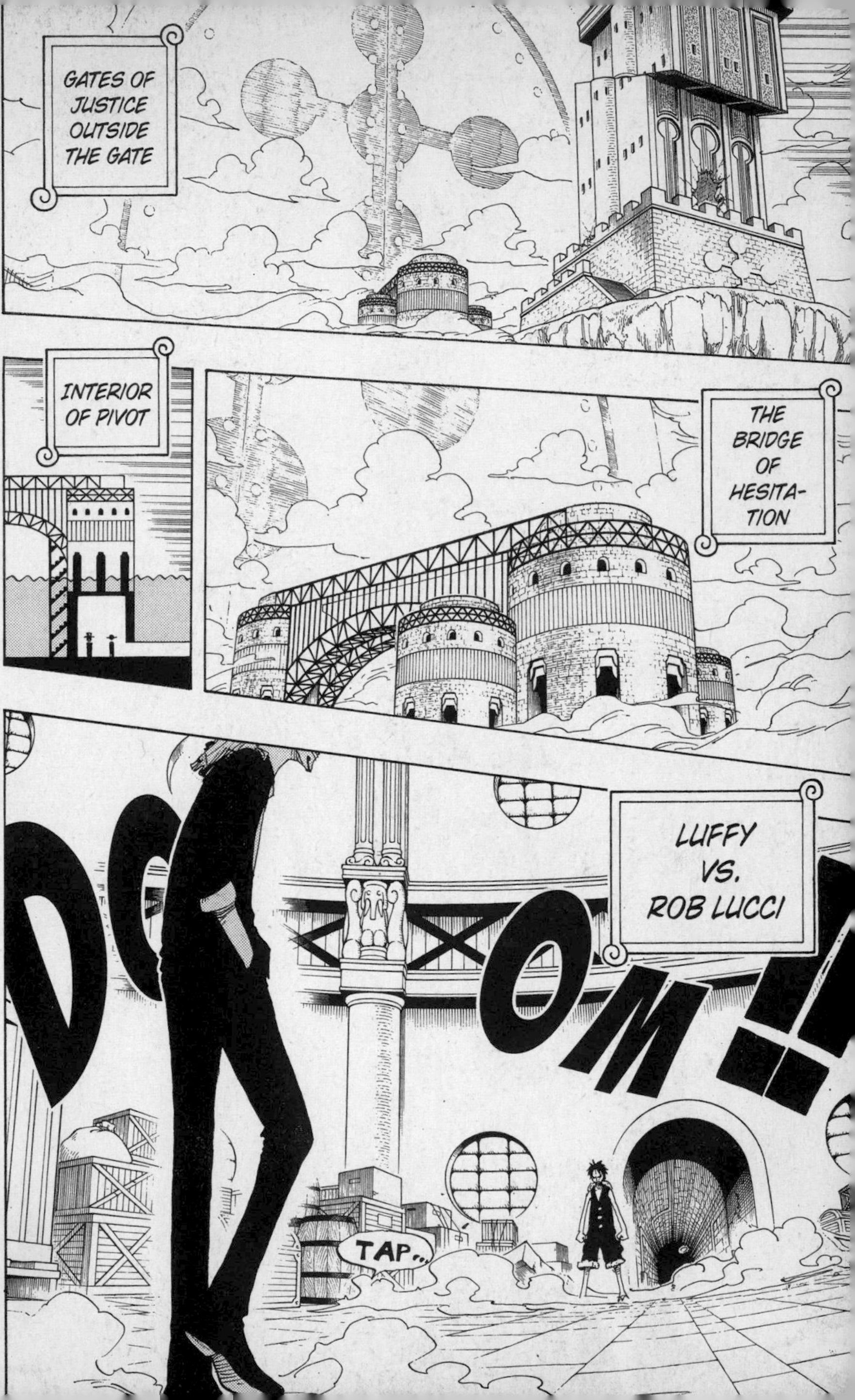
GATES OF JUSTICE OUTSIDE THE GATE
THE BRIDGE OF HESITA-TION
INTERIOR OF PIVOT
LUFFY VS. ROB LUCCI
DOOM!!
TAP...

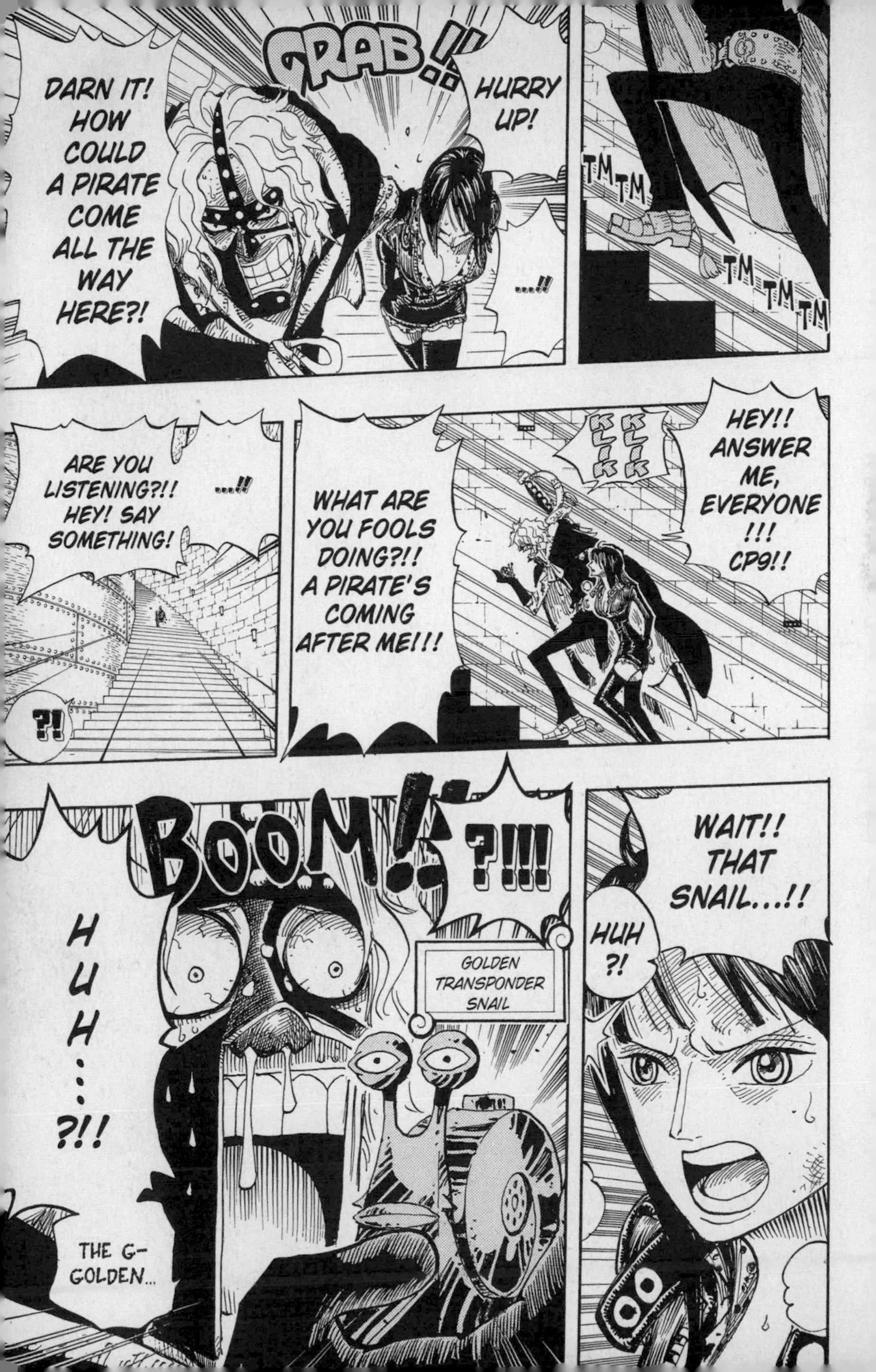
TM TM
TM TM TM
GRAB!!
HURRY UP!
...!!
DARN IT! HOW COULD A PIRATE COME ALL THE WAY HERE?!
HEY!! ANSWER ME, EVERYONE!!! CP9!!
KLIK KLIK
WHAT ARE YOU FOOLS DOING?!! A PIRATE'S COMING AFTER ME!!!
ARE YOU LISTENING?!! HEY! SAY SOMETHING!
...!!
?!
WAIT!! THAT SNAIL...!!
HUH?!
BOOM!!
?!!!
GOLDEN TRANSPONDER SNAIL
HUH...?!!
THE G-GOLDEN...

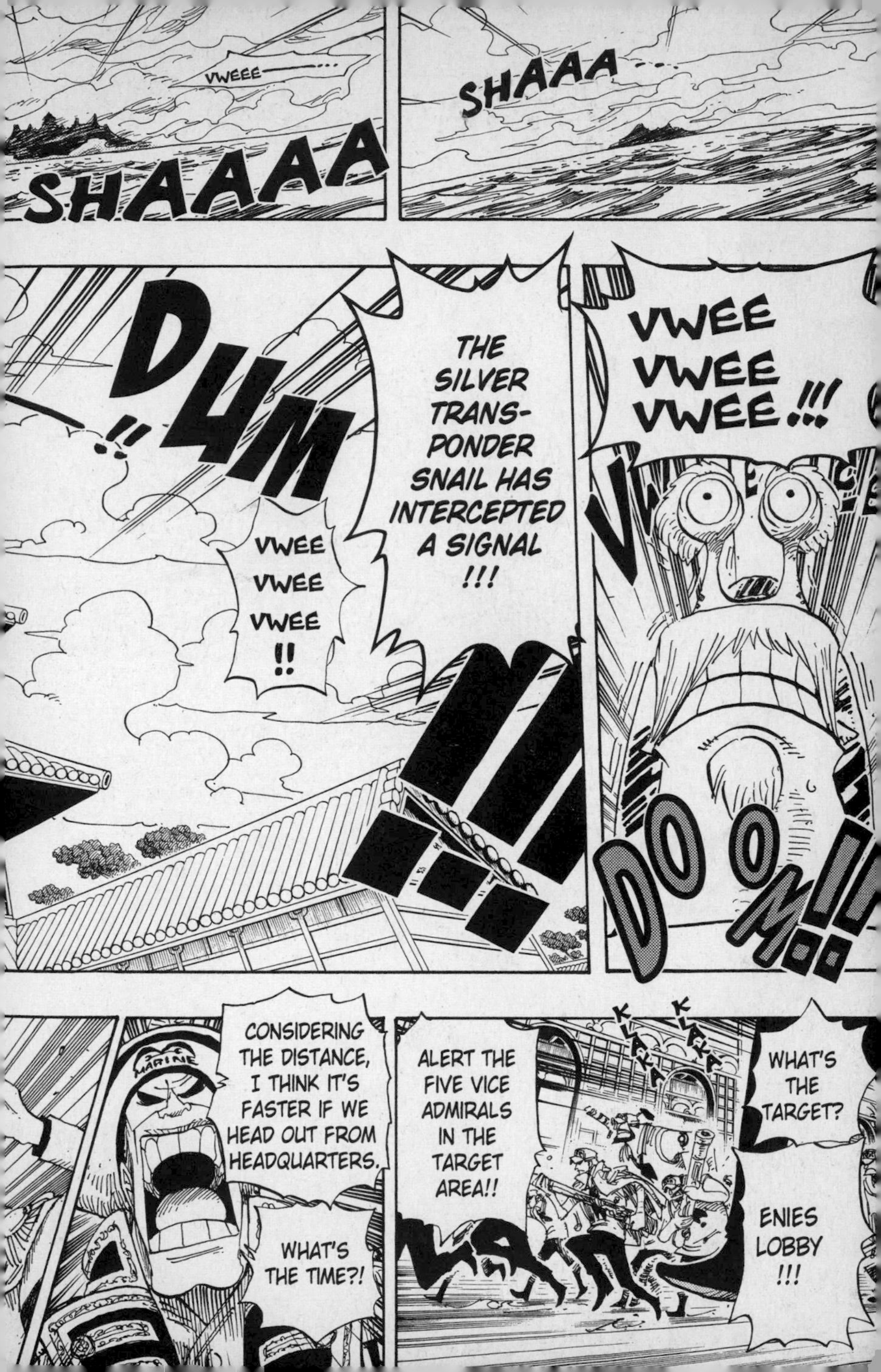
SHAAA
VWEEE
SHAAAAA
VWEE VWEE VWEE!!!
DOOM!!
THE SILVER TRANS-PONDER SNAIL HAS INTERCEPTED A SIGNAL!!!
VWEE VWEE VWEE!!
DUM!!
WHAT'S THE TARGET?
ENIES LOBBY!!!
KLAKA KLAKA
ALERT THE FIVE VICE ADMIRALS IN THE TARGET AREA!!
CONSIDERING THE DISTANCE, I THINK IT'S FASTER IF WE HEAD OUT FROM HEADQUARTERS.
WHAT'S THE TIME?!
MARINE

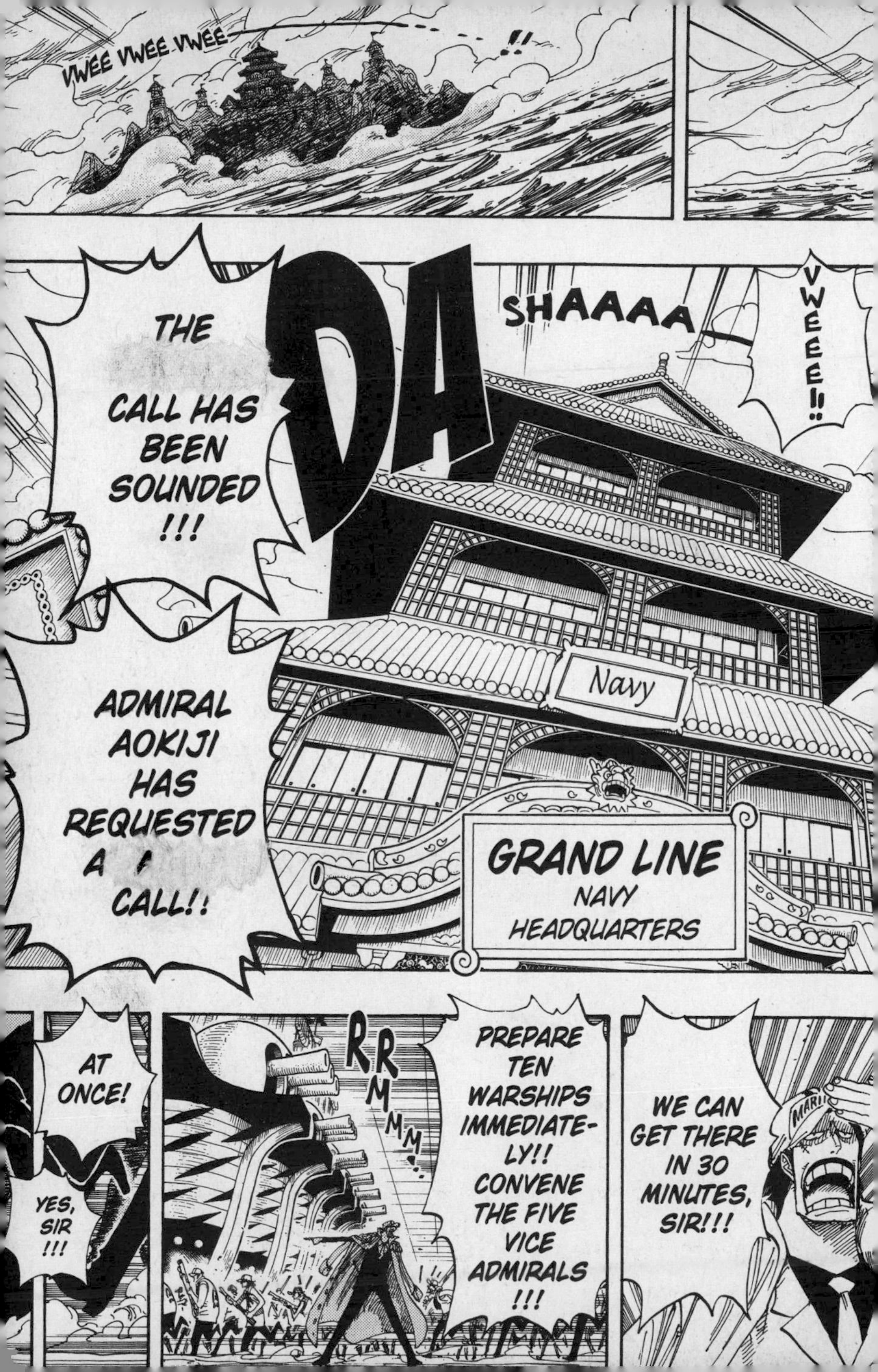
VWEE VWEE VWEE
!!
VWEEEE!!
SHAAAA
DA
Navy
GRAND LINE
NAVY
HEADQUARTERS
THE CALL HAS BEEN SOUNDED!!!
ADMIRAL AOKIJI HAS REQUESTED A CALL!!
WE CAN GET THERE IN 30 MINUTES, SIR!!!
PREPARE TEN WARSHIPS IMMEDIATE-LY!! CONVENE THE FIVE VICE ADMIRALS!!!
RRMMM
AT ONCE!
YES, SIR!!!

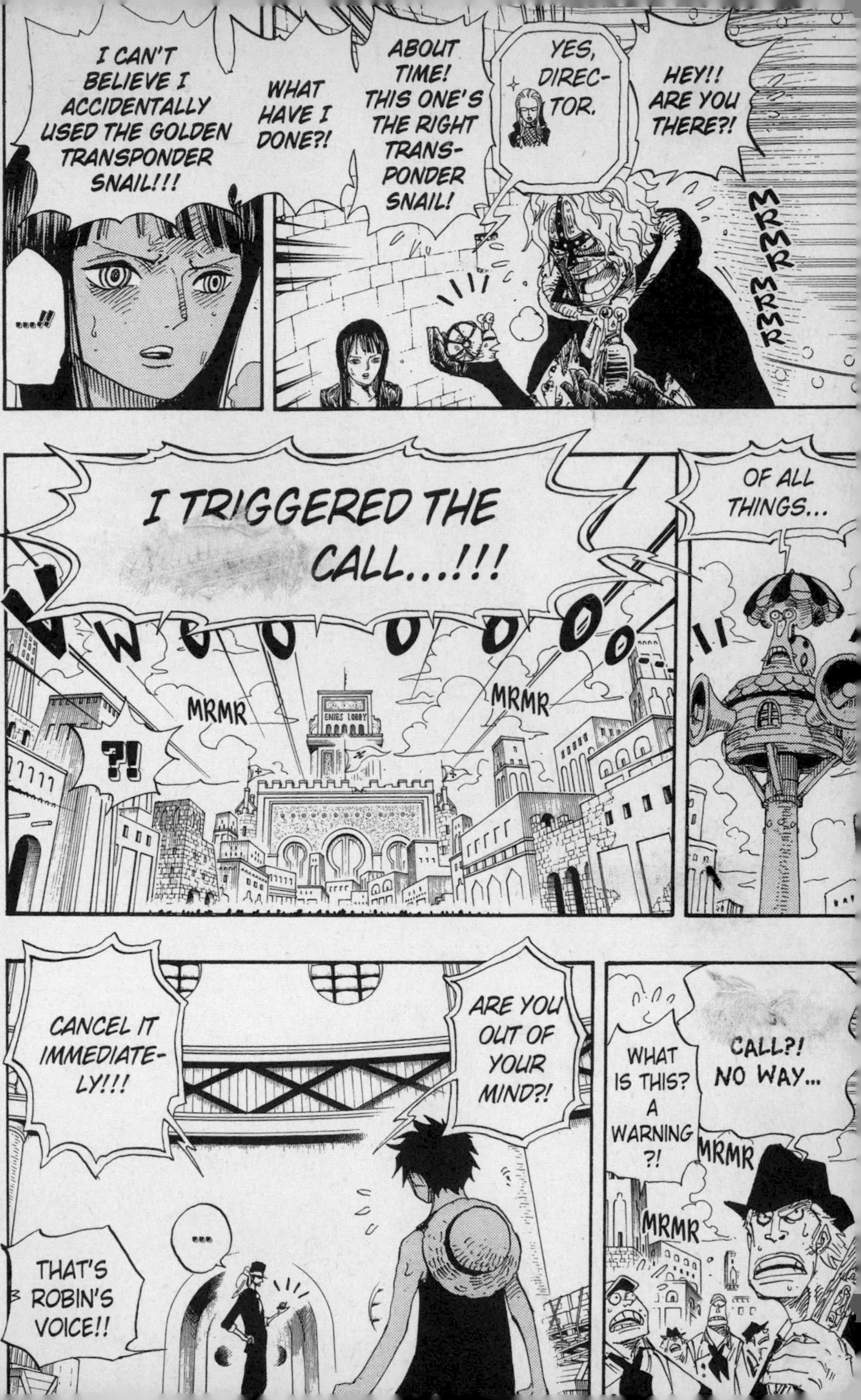
HEY!! ARE YOU THERE?!
MRMR MRMR
YES, DIRECTOR.
ABOUT TIME! THIS ONE'S THE RIGHT TRANSPONDER SNAIL!
WHAT HAVE I DONE?!
I CAN'T BELIEVE I ACCIDENTALLY USED THE GOLDEN TRANSPONDER SNAIL!!!
...!!
OF ALL THINGS...
I TRIGGERED THE CALL...!!!
WOOOOOOO!!
MRMR
ENIES LOBBY
MRMR
?!
CALL?! NO WAY...
WHAT IS THIS? A WARNING?!
MRMR
MRMR
ARE YOU OUT OF YOUR MIND?!
CANCEL IT IMMEDIATE-LY!!!
...
THAT'S ROBIN'S VOICE!!

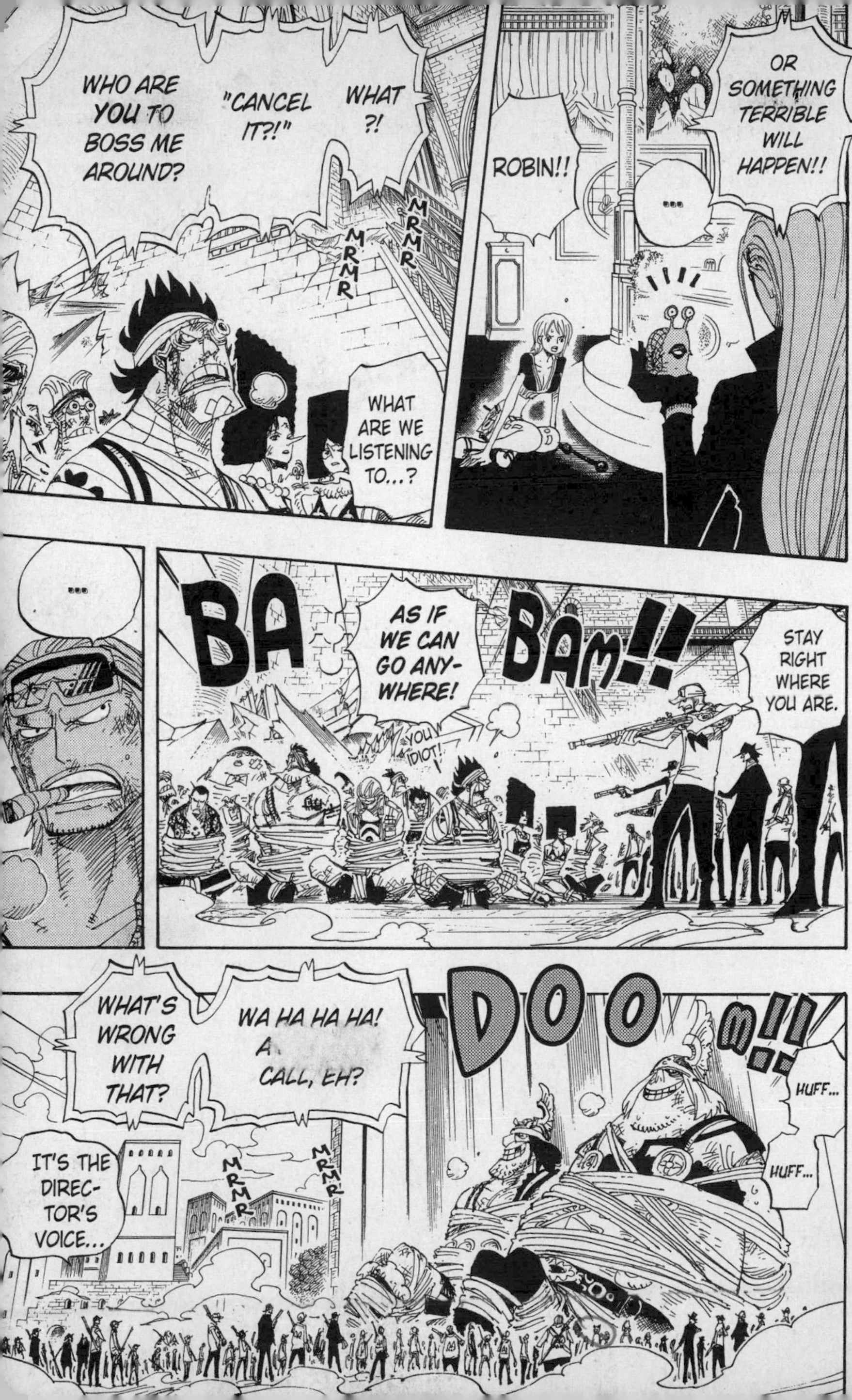
OR SOMETHING TERRIBLE WILL HAPPEN!!
...
ROBIN!!
WHAT?!
"CANCEL IT?!"
WHO ARE YOU TO BOSS ME AROUND?
MRMR
MRMR
WHAT ARE WE LISTENING TO...?
STAY RIGHT WHERE YOU ARE.
BAM!!
AS IF WE CAN GO ANY-WHERE!
YOU IDIOT!
BA
...
DOOM!!
HUFF...
HUFF...
WA HA HA HA! A
CALL, EH?
WHAT'S WRONG WITH THAT?
MRMR
MRMR
IT'S THE DIREC-TOR'S VOICE...

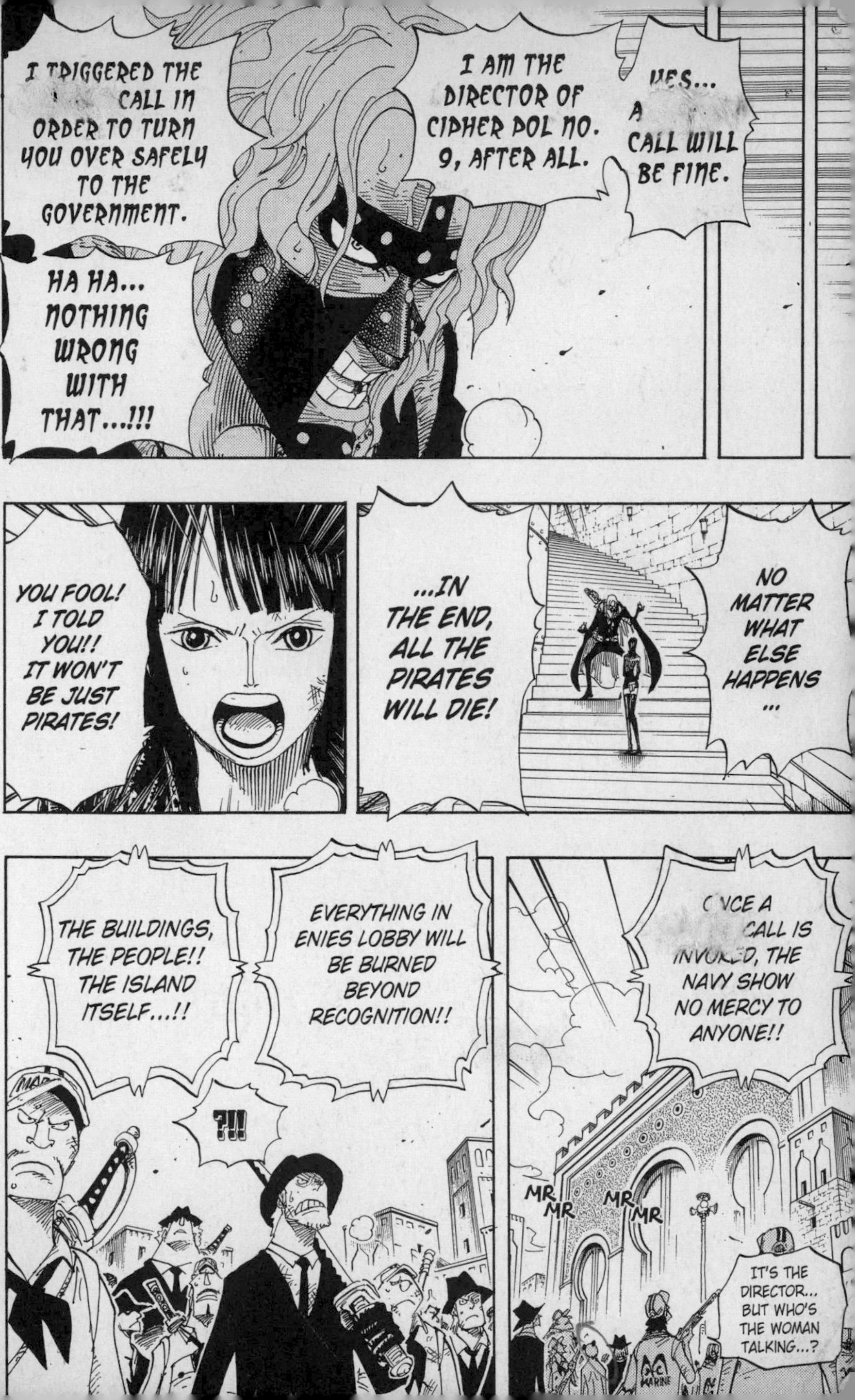
YES... A CALL WILL BE FINE.
I AM THE DIRECTOR OF CIPHER POL NO. 9, AFTER ALL.
I TRIGGERED THE CALL IN ORDER TO TURN YOU OVER SAFELY TO THE GOVERNMENT.
HA HA... NOTHING WRONG WITH THAT...!!!
NO MATTER WHAT ELSE HAPPENS ...
...IN THE END, ALL THE PIRATES WILL DIE!
YOU FOOL! I TOLD YOU!! IT WON'T BE JUST PIRATES!
CALL IS INVOKED, THE NAVY SHOW NO MERCY TO ANYONE!!
MR MR MR MR
IT'S THE DIRECTOR... BUT WHO'S THE WOMAN TALKING...?
EVERYTHING IN ENIES LOBBY WILL BE BURNED BEYOND RECOGNITION!!
THE BUILDINGS, THE PEOPLE!! THE ISLAND ITSELF...!!
?!!

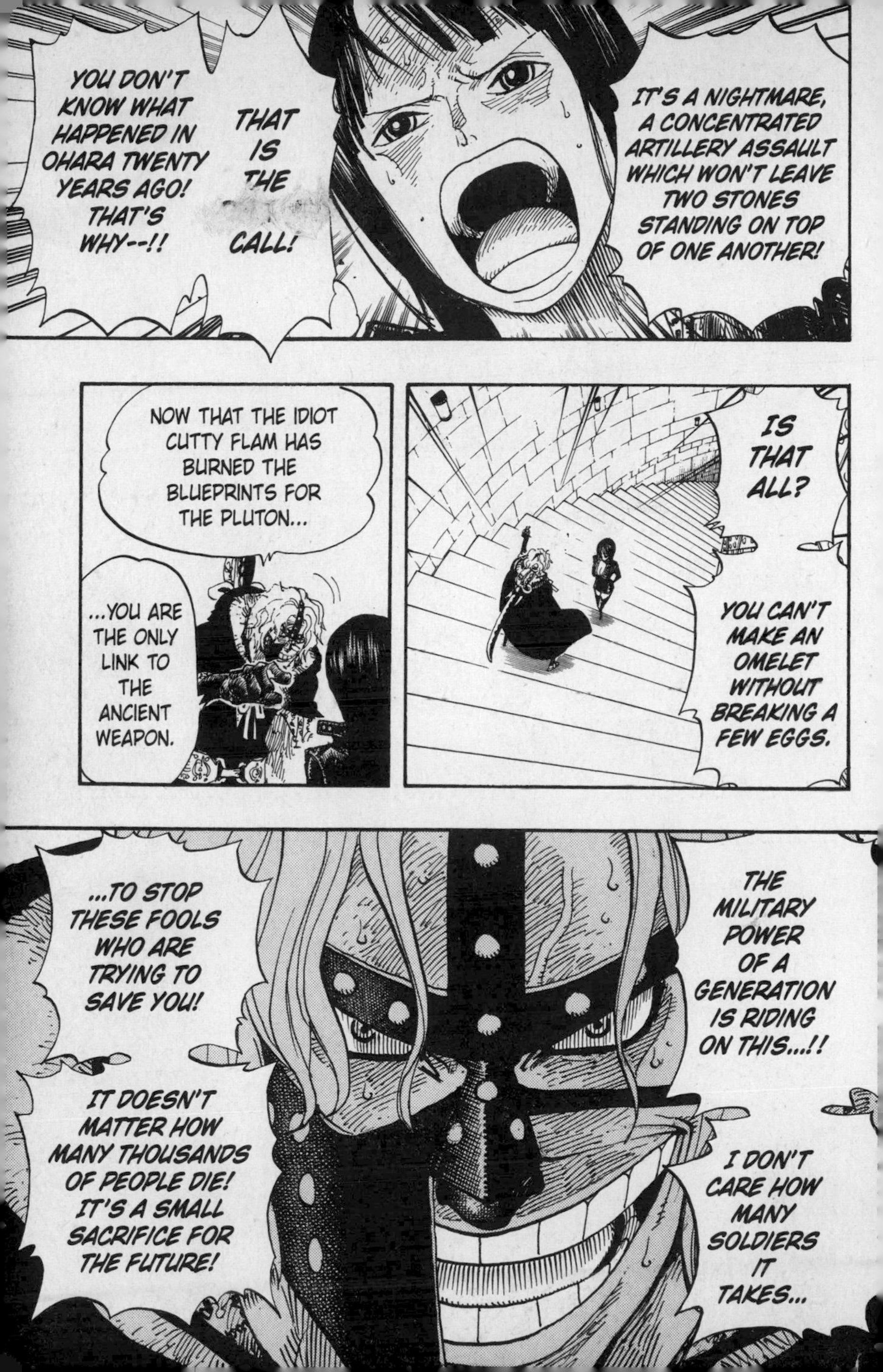
IT'S A NIGHTMARE, A CONCENTRATED ARTILLERY ASSAULT WHICH WON'T LEAVE TWO STONES STANDING ON TOP OF ONE ANOTHER!
THAT IS THE CALL!
YOU DON'T KNOW WHAT HAPPENED IN OHARA TWENTY YEARS AGO! THAT'S WHY--!!
IS THAT ALL?
YOU CAN'T MAKE AN OMELET WITHOUT BREAKING A FEW EGGS.
NOW THAT THE IDIOT CUTTY FLAM HAS BURNED THE BLUEPRINTS FOR THE PLUTON...
...YOU ARE THE ONLY LINK TO THE ANCIENT WEAPON.
THE MILITARY POWER OF A GENERATION IS RIDING ON THIS...!!
I DON'T CARE HOW MANY SOLDIERS IT TAKES...
...TO STOP THESE FOOLS WHO ARE TRYING TO SAVE YOU!
IT DOESN'T MATTER HOW MANY THOUSANDS OF PEOPLE DIE! IT'S A SMALL SACRIFICE FOR THE FUTURE!

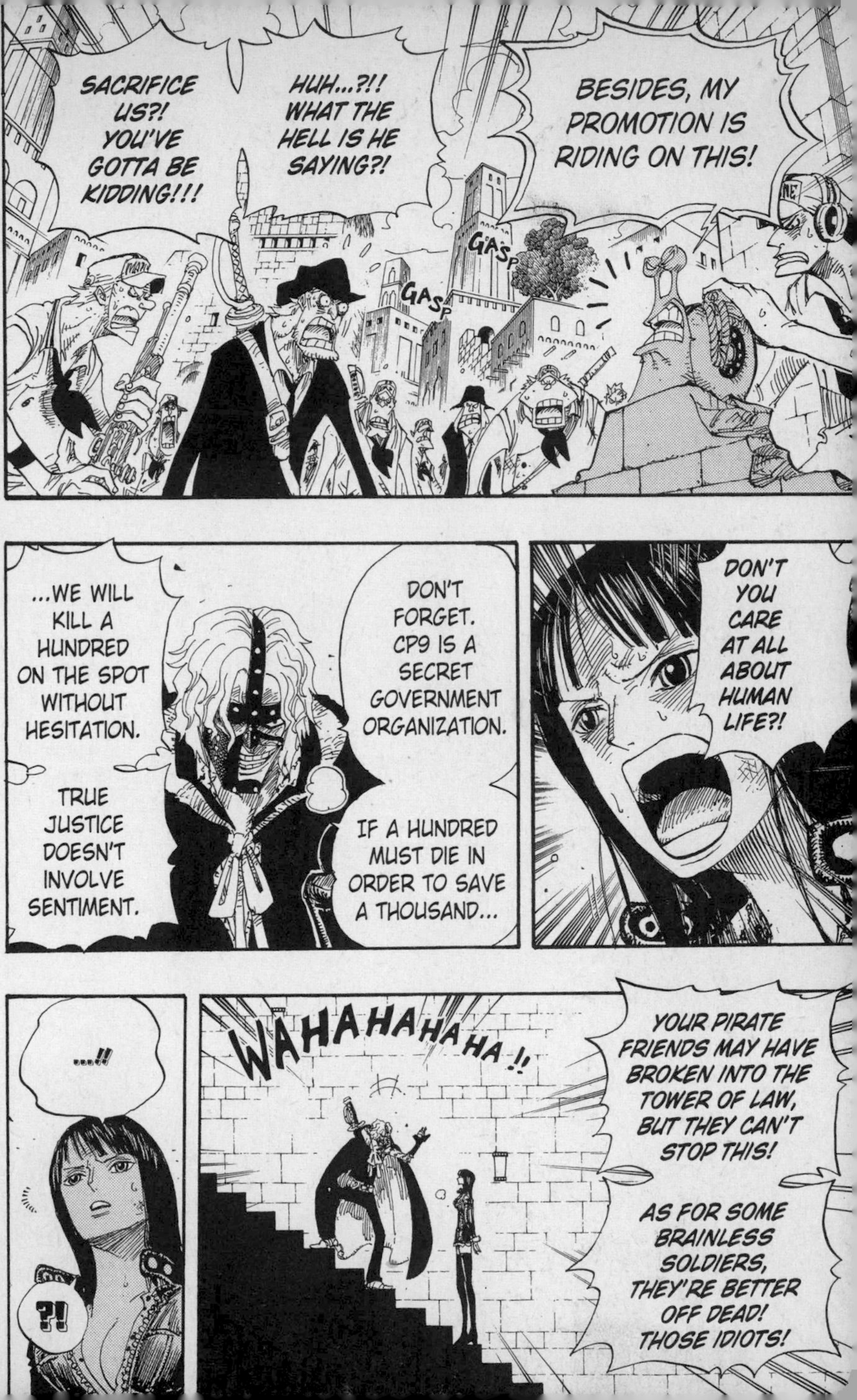
BESIDES, MY PROMOTION IS RIDING ON THIS!
HUH...?!! WHAT THE HELL IS HE SAYING?!
GASP
GASP
SACRIFICE US?! YOU'VE GOTTA BE KIDDING!!!
DON'T YOU CARE AT ALL ABOUT HUMAN LIFE?!
DON'T FORGET. CP9 IS A SECRET GOVERNMENT ORGANIZATION.
IF A HUNDRED MUST DIE IN ORDER TO SAVE A THOUSAND...
...WE WILL KILL A HUNDRED ON THE SPOT WITHOUT HESITATION.
TRUE JUSTICE DOESN'T INVOLVE SENTIMENT.
YOUR PIRATE FRIENDS MAY HAVE BROKEN INTO THE TOWER OF LAW, BUT THEY CAN'T STOP THIS!
AS FOR SOME BRAINLESS SOLDIERS, THEY'RE BETTER OFF DEAD! THOSE IDIOTS!
WAHAHAHAHAHA!!
...!!
?!

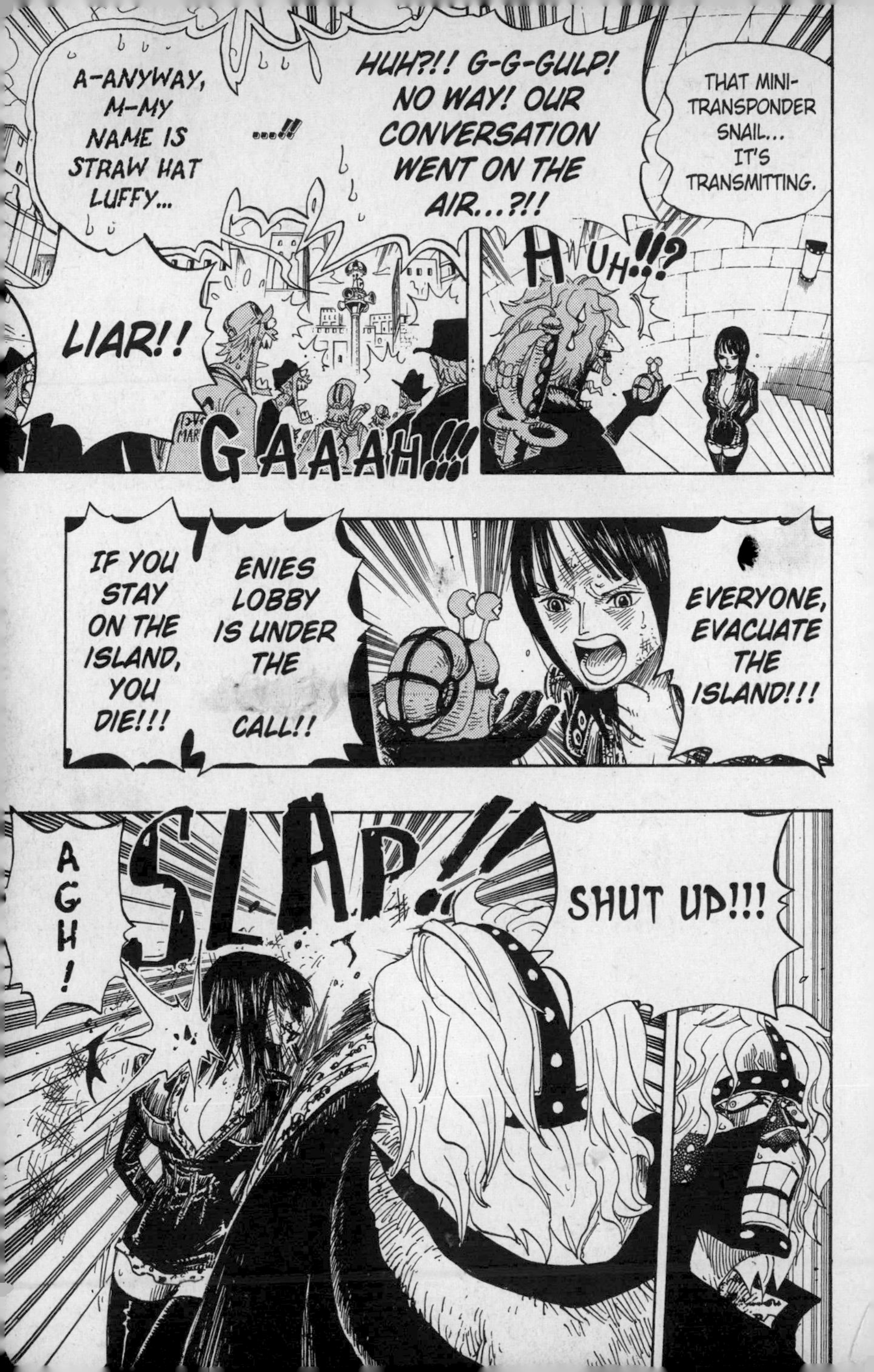
THAT MINI-TRANSPONDER SNAIL... IT'S TRANSMITTING.
HUH!!?
HUH?!! G-G-GULP! NO WAY! OUR CONVERSATION WENT ON THE AIR...?!!
...!!
A-ANYWAY, M-MY NAME IS STRAW HAT LUFFY...
LIAR!!
GAAAH!!!
EVERYONE, EVACUATE THE ISLAND!!!
ENIES LOBBY IS UNDER THE CALL!!
IF YOU STAY ON THE ISLAND, YOU DIE!!!
SHUT UP!!!
SLAP!!
AGH!

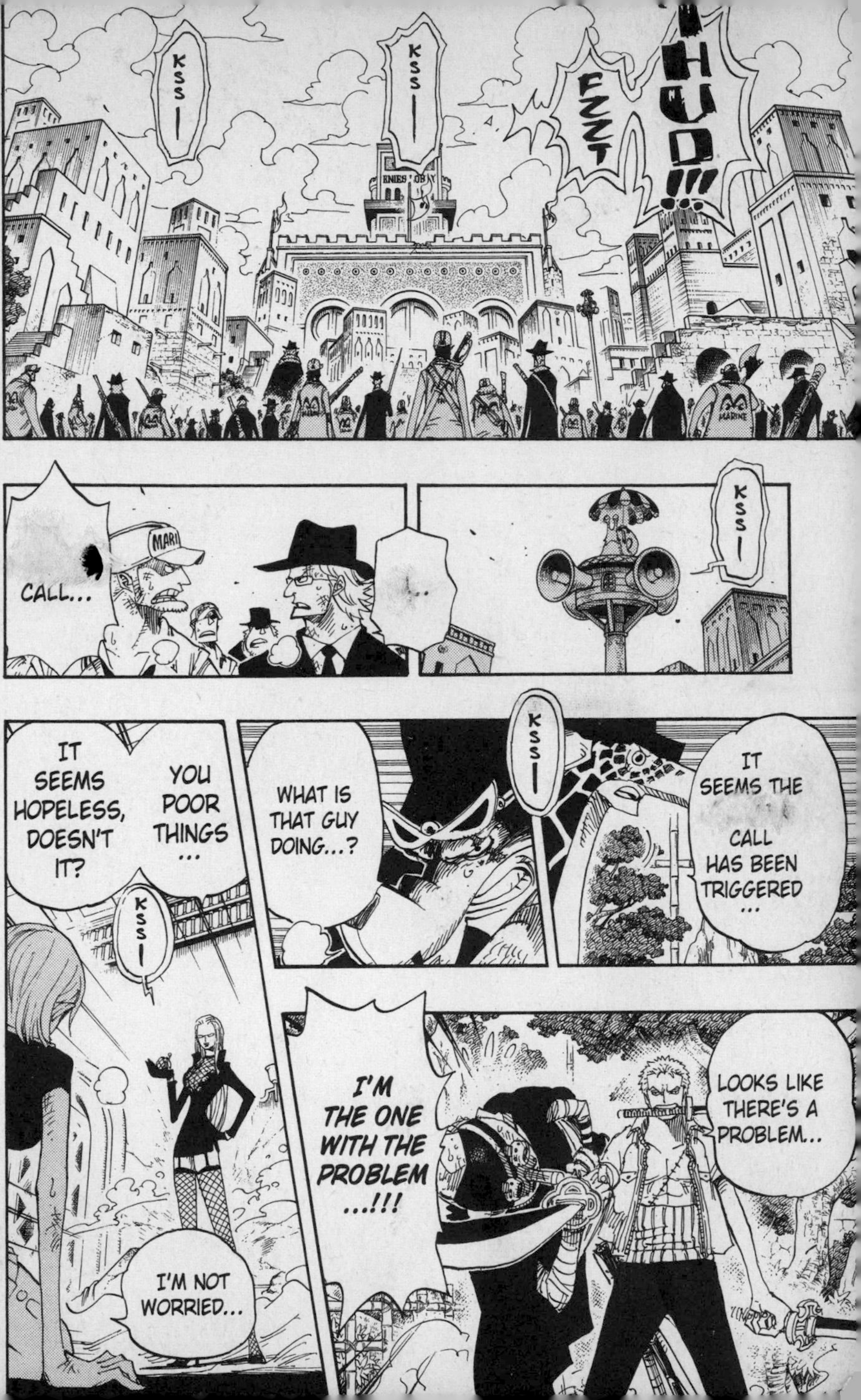
THUD!!!
FZZT
KSS—
KSS—
KSS—
CALL...
IT SEEMS THE CALL HAS BEEN TRIGGERED...
KSS—
WHAT IS THAT GUY DOING...?
YOU POOR THINGS...
IT SEEMS HOPELESS, DOESN'T IT?
KSS—
LOOKS LIKE THERE'S A PROBLEM...
I'M THE ONE WITH THE PROBLEM...!!!
I'M NOT WORRIED...

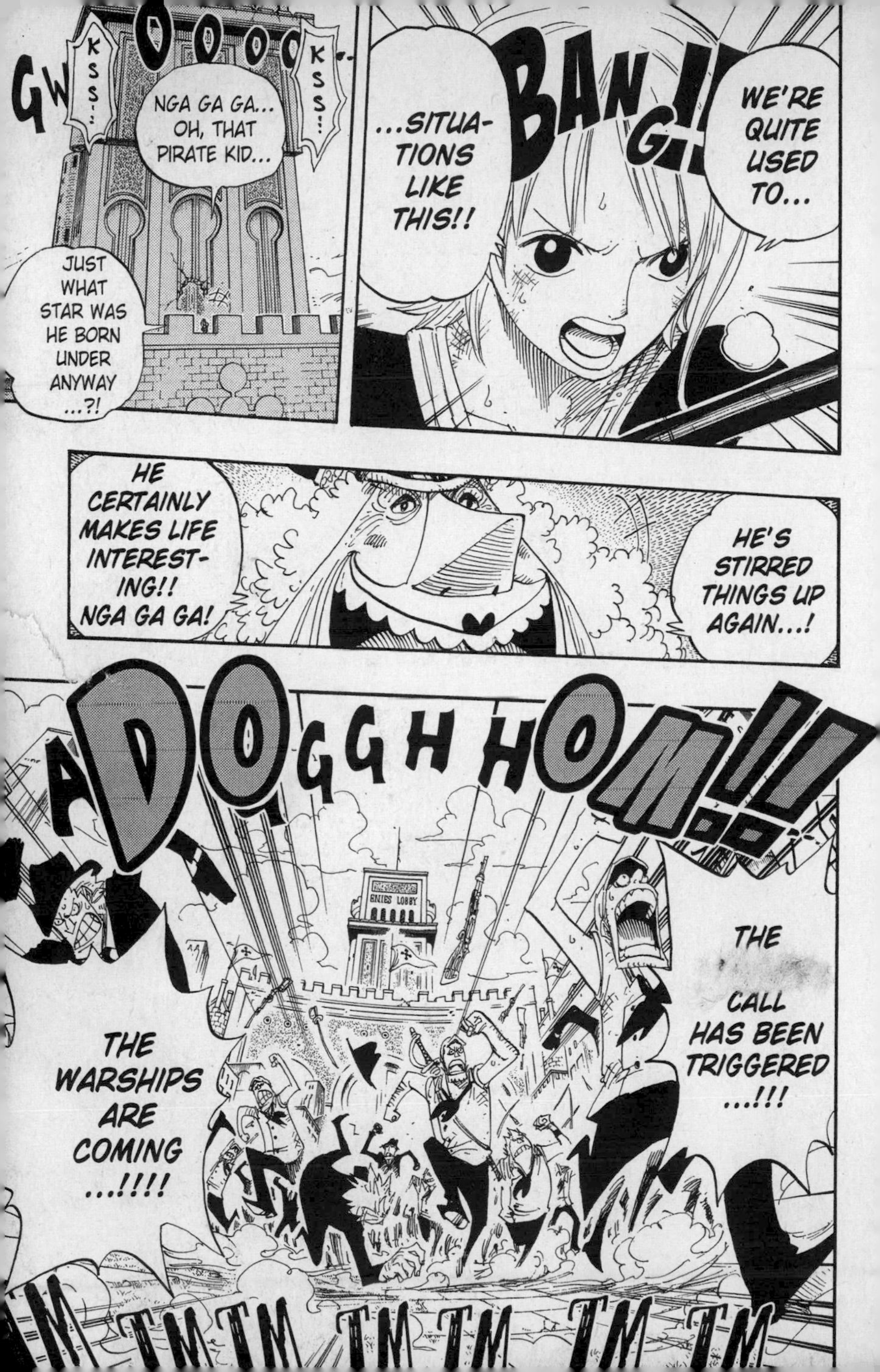
WE'RE QUITE USED TO...
BANG!!
...SITUATIONS LIKE THIS!!
GWOOOOO...
KSS!!
NGA GA GA... OH, THAT PIRATE KID...
KSS!!
JUST WHAT STAR WAS HE BORN UNDER ANYWAY ...?!
HE'S STIRRED THINGS UP AGAIN...!
HE CERTAINLY MAKES LIFE INTEREST-ING!! NGA GA GA!
ADOGGH HOM!!
ENIES LOBBY
THE
CALL HAS BEEN TRIGGERED ...!!!
THE WARSHIPS ARE COMING ...!!!!
TMTMTMTMTMTMTM

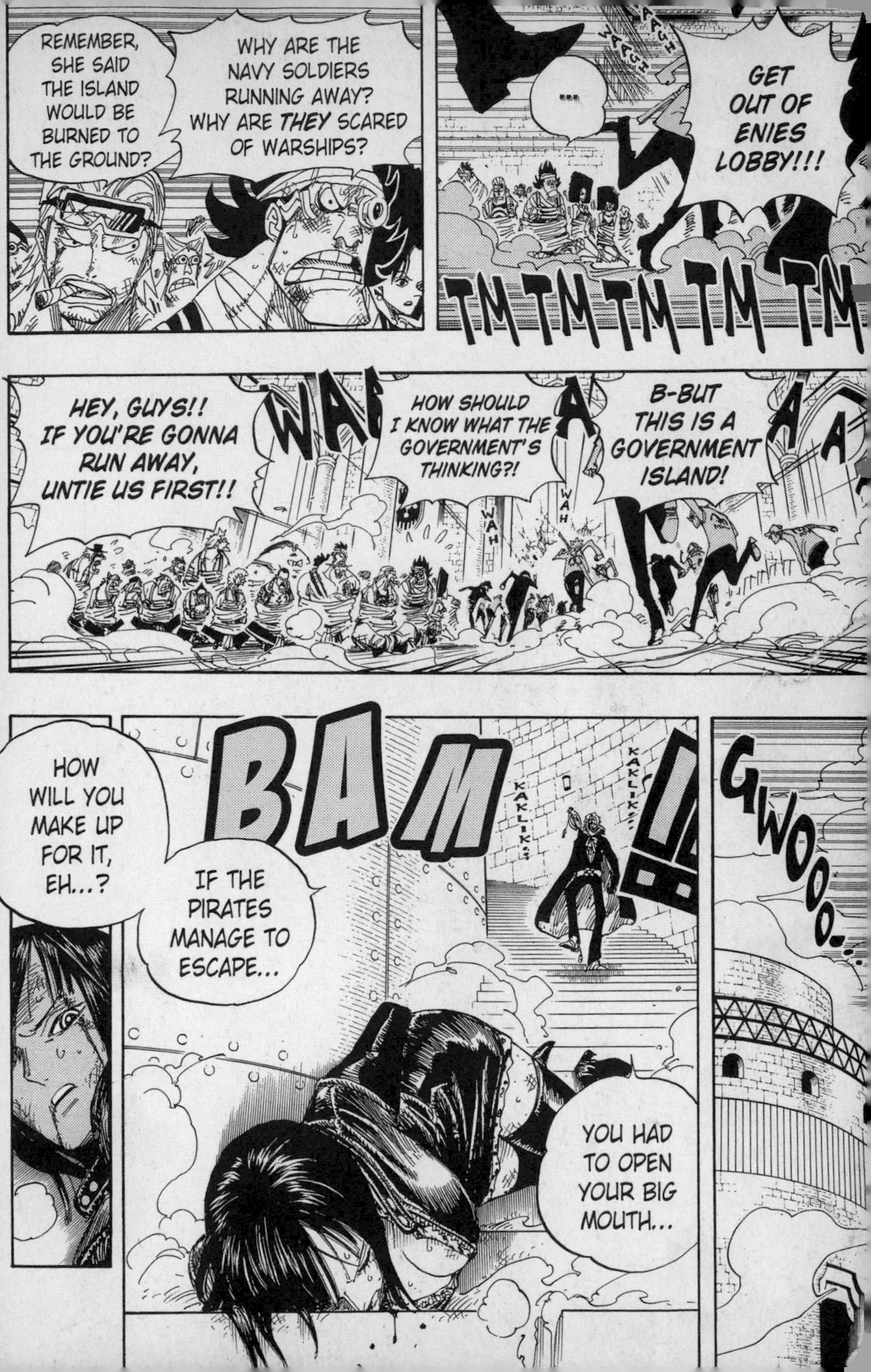
AAGH
WAAGH
GET OUT OF ENIES LOBBY!!!
...
TM TM TM TM TM TM
WHY ARE THE NAVY SOLDIERS RUNNING AWAY? WHY ARE THEY SCARED OF WARSHIPS?
REMEMBER, SHE SAID THE ISLAND WOULD BE BURNED TO THE GROUND?
A A
B-BUT THIS IS A GOVERNMENT ISLAND!
A
WAH
HOW SHOULD I KNOW WHAT THE GOVERNMENT'S THINKING?!
WAH
WA
HEY, GUYS!! IF YOU'RE GONNA RUN AWAY, UNTIE US FIRST!!
GWOOO...
BAM!!
KAKLIK
KAKLIK
HOW WILL YOU MAKE UP FOR IT, EH...?
IF THE PIRATES MANAGE TO ESCAPE...
YOU HAD TO OPEN YOUR BIG MOUTH...

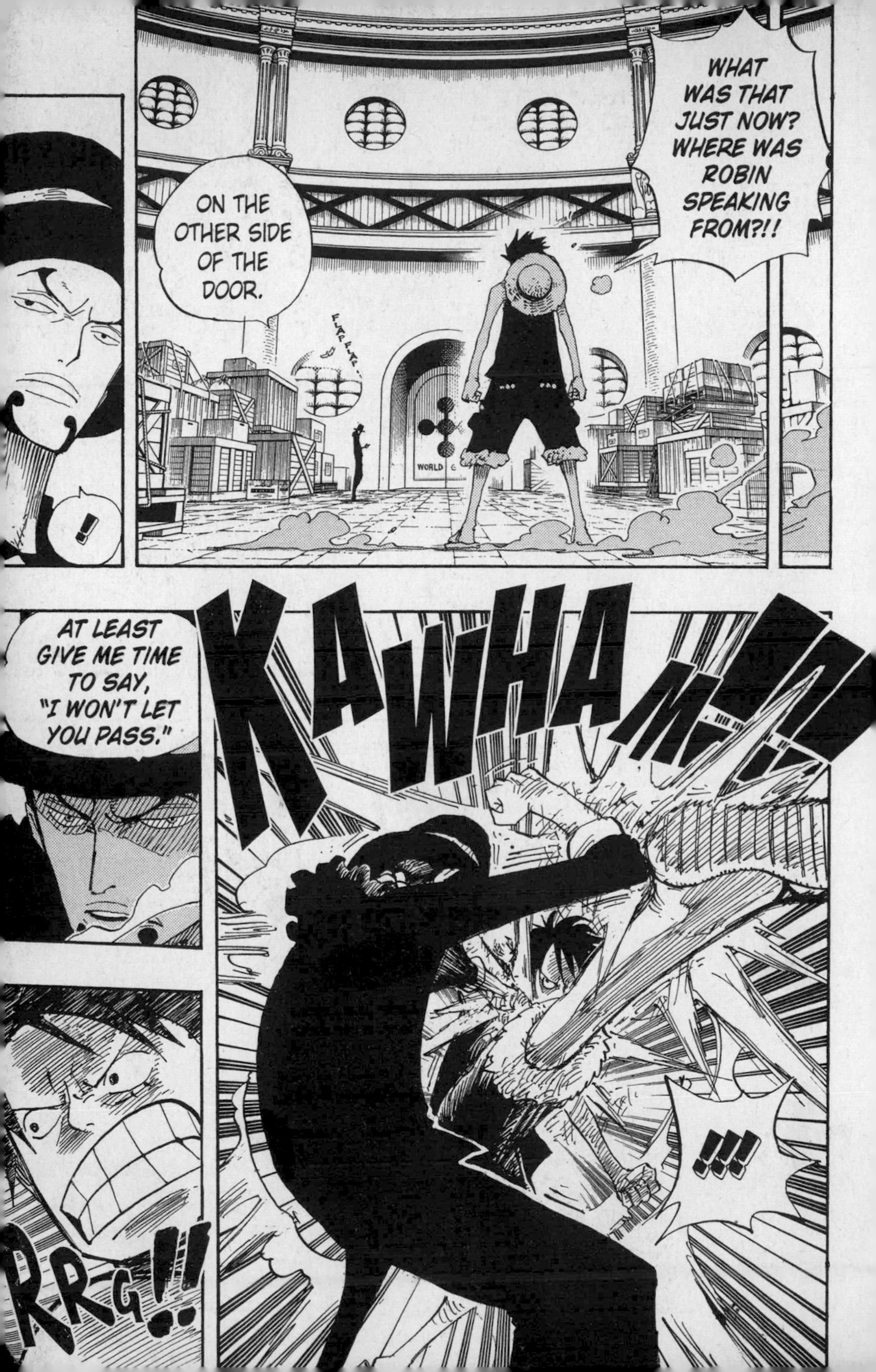

WHAT WAS THAT JUST NOW? WHERE WAS ROBIN SPEAKING FROM?!!
ON THE OTHER SIDE OF THE DOOR.
FLAP FLAP
WORLD G
!
KAWHAMM!!
!!!
AT LEAST GIVE ME TIME TO SAY, "I WON'T LET YOU PASS."
R-R-G!!

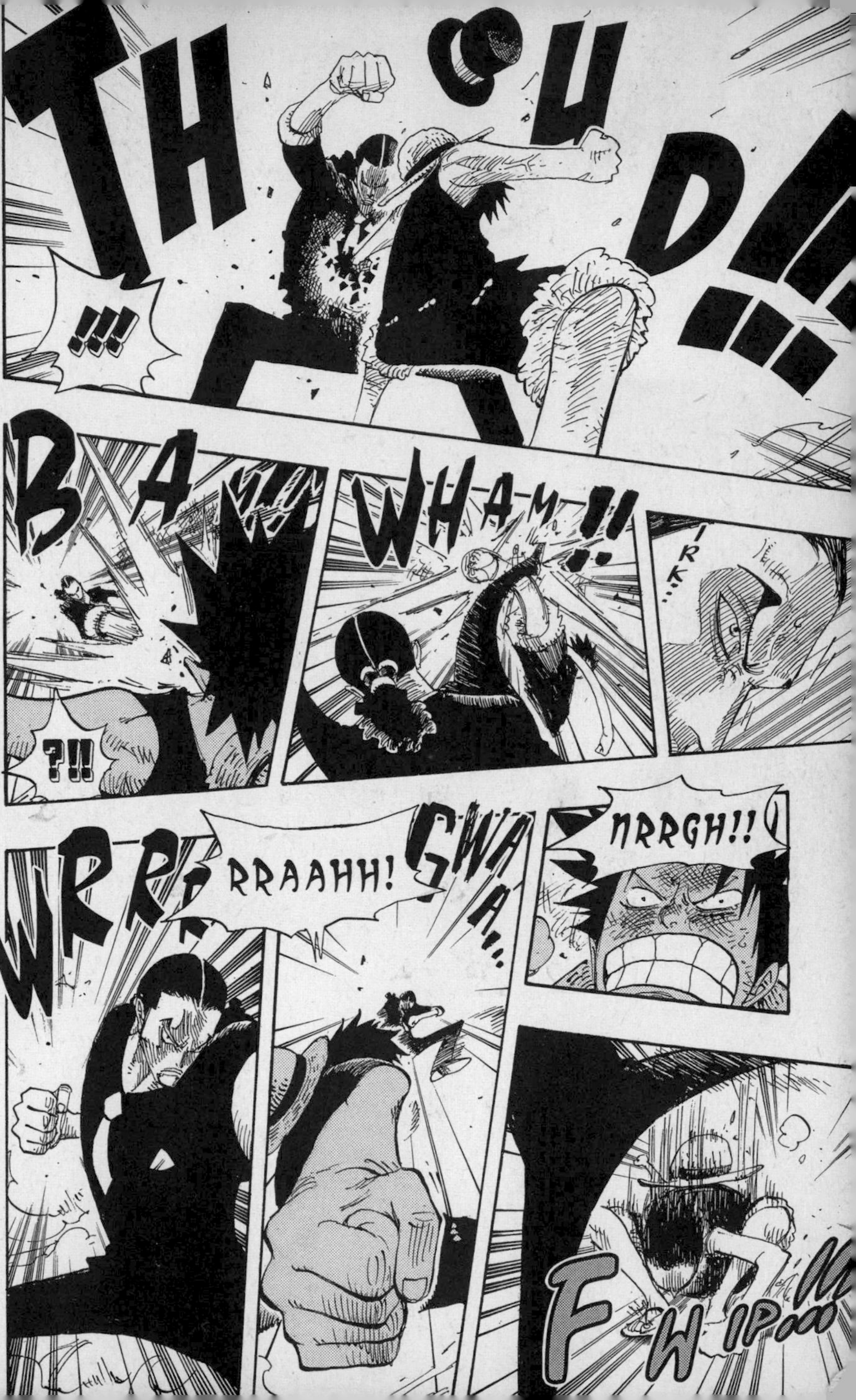
THUD!!
!!!
IRK...
WHAM!!
BAM
?!!
NRRGH!!
GWAA...
RRAAHH!
WRR
FWIP...

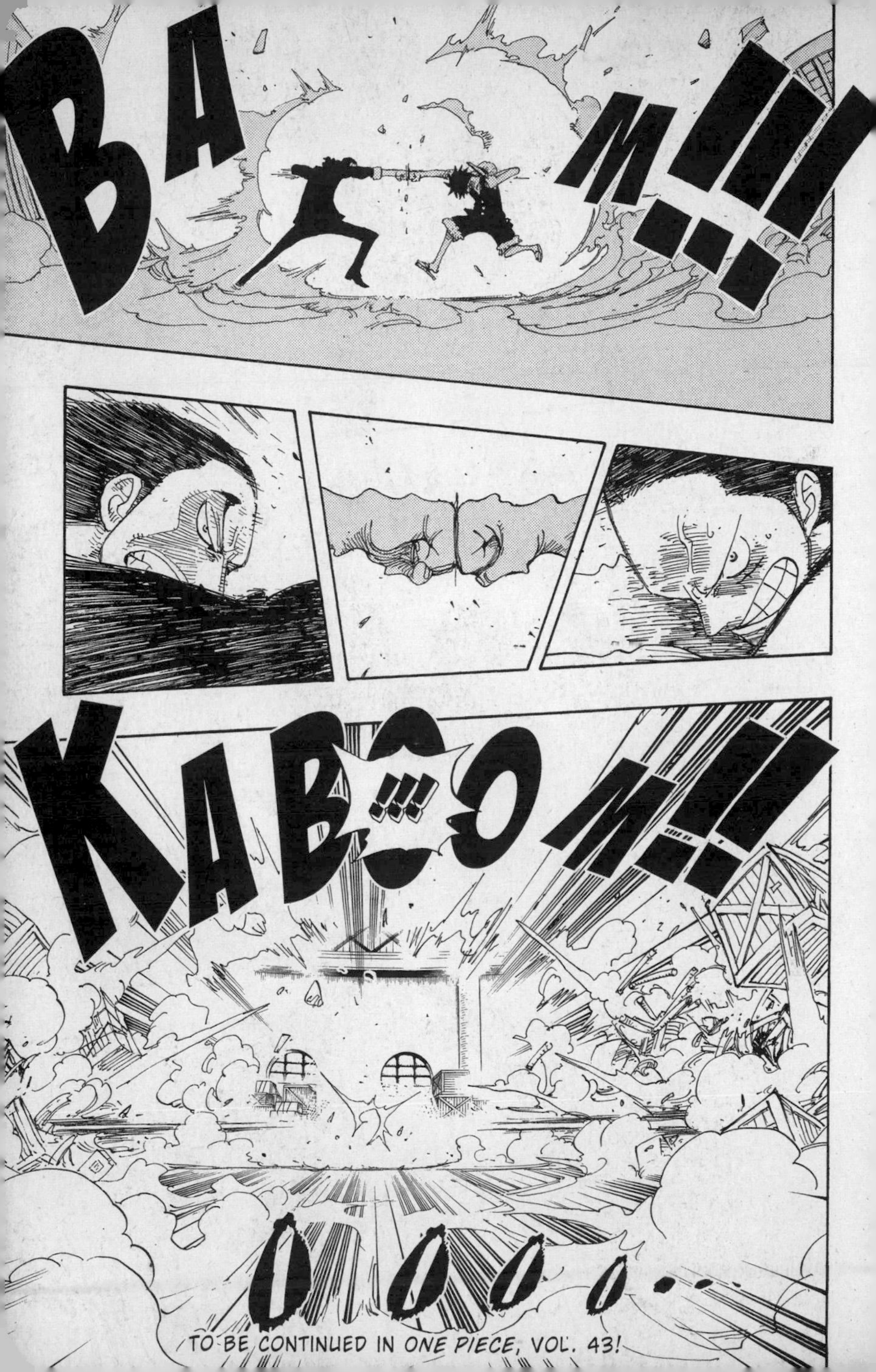
BAM!!
KABOOM!!
OOOO...
TO BE CONTINUED IN ONE PIECE, VOL. 43!

COMING NEXT VOLUME:

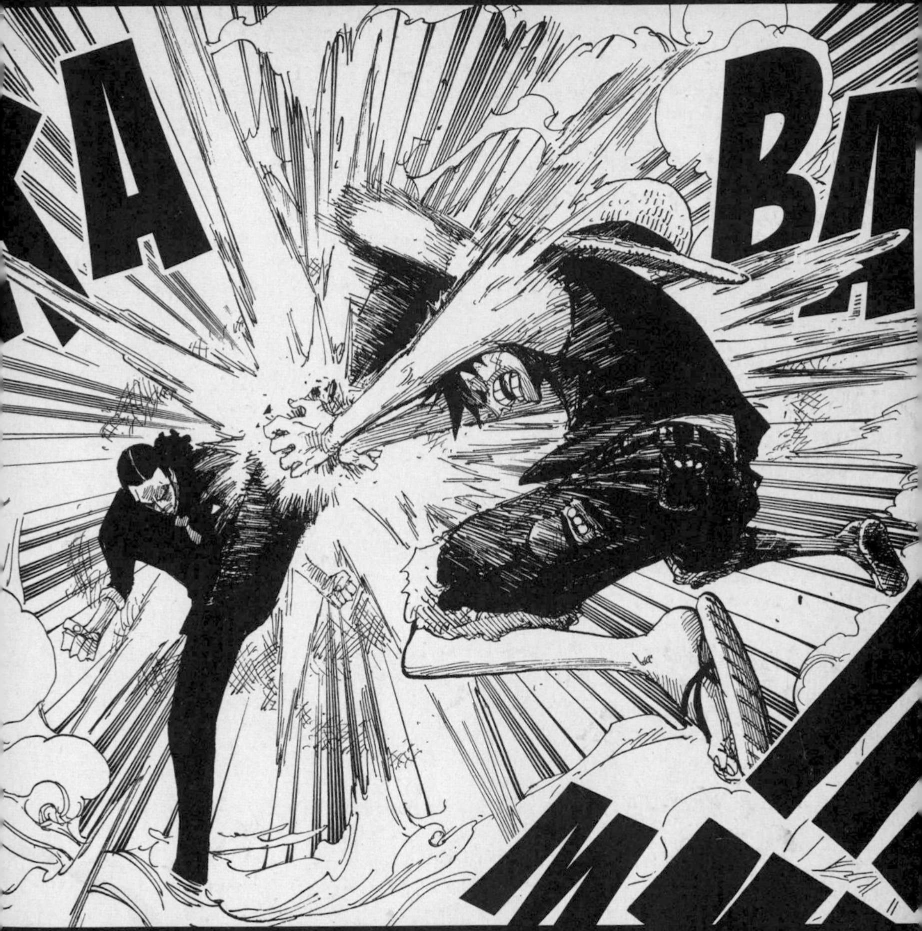
BA
A
M

Luffy has made it to the tower where Franky and Robin are being held, but in order to save his friends he must get past Spandam's most deadly assassin, Rob Lucci. The rest of the Straw Hats are busy fighting their own battles, trying to find the key that will free Robin. Can the crew find the right key in time?

ON SALE NOW!